APPROACHING DIALOGUE

IMPACT: STUDIES IN LANGUAGE AND SOCIETY

IMPACT publishes monographs, collective volumes, and text books on topics in sociolinguistics and language pedagogy. The scope of the series is broad, with special emphasis on areas such as language planning and language policies; language teaching and language learning; language conflict and language death; language standards and language change; dialectology; diglossia; discourse studies; language and social identity (gender, ethnicity, class, ideology); and history and methods of sociolinguistics

Volume 3

Per Linell

Approaching Dialogue
Talk, interaction and contexts in dialogical perspectives

APPROACHING DIALOGUE

Talk, interaction and contexts in dialogical perspectives

PER LINELL

Linköping University

JOHN BENJAMINS PUBLISHING COMPANY

AMSTERDAM / PHILADELPHIA

The paper used in this publication meets the minimum requirements of American National Standard for Information Sciences — Permanence of Paper for Printed Library Materials, ANSI Z39.48–1984.

Library of Congress Cataloging-in-Publication Data

Linell, Per, 1944-
    Approaching dialogue : talk, interaction and contexts in dialogical perspectives / Per Linell.
        p.   cm. -- (Impact : studies in language and society, ISSN 1385-7908 ; v. 3)
    Includes bibliographical references and index.
        1. Dialogue analysis. 2. Discourse analysis. 3. Semantics. 4. Communication. I. Title. II. Series: Impact, studies in language and society ; 3.
P95.455.L56   1998
401'.41--dc21   98-39787
ISBN 90 272 1833 1 (Eur.) / 1 55619 852 3 (US) (alk. paper)   CIP

John Benjamins Publishing Co. • P.O.Box 75577 • 1070 AN Amsterdam • The Netherlands
John Benjamins North America • P.O.Box 27519 • Philadelphia PA 19118-0519 • USA

Table of Contents

Preface

This book is about dialogue. It addresses two different issues at rather different levels. The primary focus is on the theoretical understanding and empirical analysis of talk-in-interaction. A second interest is more far-reaching; I begin to explore the possibilities and limitations in dialogism as a general epistemology for cognition and communication. *Approaching Dialogue* is therefore primarily an account of a particular theoretical approach, which has proved to be particularly fruitful and for which I have adopted the term 'dialogism' (from e.g. Bakhtin 1986; Holquist 1990; Marková & Foppa 1990, and others). Stressing aspects of interaction, contexts and joint construction, and drawing upon extensive theoretical and empirical research carried out in different traditions, this book aims at an integrating synthesis. It is largely interdisciplinary in nature, and has been written in such a way that it can be used at advanced undergraduate courses in linguistics, sociopragmatics of language, communication studies, sociology, social psychology and cognitive science.

Before going into the contents in more detail, it is perhaps apt to point out what this book is *not*. For example, it is not a general introduction to the whole field of discourse analysis. I do not aim at covering all major linguistically-oriented approaches — whether competing or mutually supplementary — to discourse (for such an attempt, see Schiffrin 1994). Furthermore, more macro-oriented or socio-historical aspects of discourse, such as those which are the foci of the work by e.g. Foucault and Bourdieu, will not be dealt with, and the "dialogical turn" within anthropology and ethnography is largely omitted. Finally, this work is not an application of pure Bakhtinian thinking, even if the work of Mikhail Bakhtin necessarily remains central. Bakhtin's major contributions to literary and cultural criticism will not be referenced (see Holquist 1990; Pearce 1994).

The focus of *Approaching Dialogue* is on *authentic spoken interaction*, i.e. on dyadic or polyadic dialogue in face-to-face encounters (or other verbal interactions in real time). Some conclusions concerning texts, thought, and communication in general are also spelled out. I would argue that it is all the detailed *empirical* studies of actual talk-in-interaction, based on systematic analyses of tape-recorded data, which provide the most important and convincing evidence in support of dialogism, for they have shown discourse to be social in nature: socially constructed, sequentially organized, and richly structured. Monologistic theories may have prevented many scholars from seeing this, as, for example, when Chomsky (1986) still maintains that discourse is structurally 'impoverished' and so cannot be used in the study of language and of linguistic competence. But the absence of the necessary technology, such as tape-recorders, was another reason why scholars of earlier times were handicapped in their attempts to understand spoken discourse. Thus, e.g., it was possible for Saussure (1964 [1916]: 38) to claim that "... there is nothing collective about speech ('parole'). Its manifestations are individual and ephemeral. It is no more than an aggregate of particular cases." (translation from French original/PL) We have now massive evidence to the contrary.

In this book, I shall discuss talk and spoken interaction against a backdrop of dialogism, phenomenology, pragmatism, social constructionism, and contextual structuralism. But it is not the philosophy of dialogism that will be my major concern. Rather, I am interested in a substantive theory of dialogue, and an empirically valid form of dialogism. A recurrent feature in the texts to follow is the wish to strike a balance between, on the one hand, intersubjectivity and joint accomplishment, coordination and cooperation, reciprocity and mutuality as conceptually basic to the analysis of interaction and communication, and, on the other hand, the presence of complementarity and asymmetries, partial sharedness, fragmentation, individual agency and competitive goals in communication. There is, in my view, an idealistic current in dialogistic thinking which tends to overstate and misunderstand the impact of the first-mentioned strand of this polarity.

The outline of the book is the following (here the reader may wish to consult the table of contents in parallel). Part I (Chapters 1–4: Monologism and dialogism contrasted) provides some background for the dialogistic accounts to be presented later on. Most theoretical stances presuppose some potential (implicit or explicit) rival positions with which they are supposed to compete and either to refute or to complement. Thus, the paradigm of dialogism must be understood in contrast to something else, namely 'monologism'. The latter is the dominant theoretical framework in the language sciences. The term alludes to the tendency to identify the speaker alone as the origin of the utterance. Basically, such a framework adopts some version or other of the following theories;

cognition as individually-based information processing, communication as information transfer, and language as a code. This is coupled with a long-standing tradition in the language sciences in general, and in linguistics in particular, to give priority to theories and methods that suit written language and text better than they do spoken interaction. The first two chapters are designed to sketch this general ideological context to which the subsequent dialogical explications must be related. Another relevant background is of course the historical development of dialogism. On this point I have decided to be very brief, restricting the story to a few important ideas and traditions (Chapter 3).

A theory of dialogue naturally deals with language use in discourse and interaction. This raises the issue of how to deal with language structure (and, more generally, social structure and culture). Chapter 4, which concludes Part I, sketches three positions on the issue of structure versus practice/process, selecting a sociocultural and contextual version of social constructionism, rather than a radical interactionism, as being compatible with dialogism.

After this general background, the book takes a different turn and moves into its main subject matter, the description of dialogue and talk-in-interaction (Part II: Interacting and making sense in contexts). This part is opened with Chapter 5, which aims at providing a general overview of some dialogical principles, in particular 'sequentiality', 'joint construction' and 'act-activity interdependence'. This chapter anticipates discussions in several of the following chapters, in which I try to deal with some important and more specific elements of a theory of spoken interaction.

This account of a few basic concepts for the analysis of spoken discourse is followed up in the next two chapters by a discussion of the activities of speaking and sense-making in interaction. What light does a dialogistic theory shed on such practices? Chapter 6, on speaking, stresses that the speaker is not alone in authoring his or her contributions,[1] but is always "in dialogue" with interlocutors and contexts. Chapter 7 is concerned particularly with the potentials for multiple sense-making in discourse, and how this relates to a theory of word meaning.

In accounts of discourse, it is often remarked that discursive actions are essentially situated or context-related, without any systematic attempt on the part

---

1. Instead of always using the clumsy expressions "he/she", "him/her" or "his/her" every time there is an anaphoric reference to a prior occurrence of a *generic* characterization such as, e.g., "a/the speaker", "a/the listener" or "an/the individual", I will, in this book, use *either* "he (him, his)" *or* "she (her)", alternatingly over the different chapters.

of researchers to disentangle which contexts are relevant. Chapter 8 provides some aspects of such a theory. In particular, it tries to show how the sequentially organized contributions to a dialogue continuously shape, and are shaped by, features of contexts pertaining to co-text, concrete situation and background knowledge.

Chapter 9 deals with the elementary constituents of dialogue, i.e. relatively small contributions such as 'idea units', turns and turn-constructional units. In particular, I focus on the sequential aspects of these elements and on how they are socially constructed, showing how they systematically both depend upon the prior context and, simultaneously, provide the conditions for possible next actions. The dialogistic analysis focuses on responsive and initiatory aspects of these elementary units of interaction.

Elementary contributions eventually build up into larger stretches of discourse. The flow of discourse varies in terms of local and global coherence, and in terms of topics (what it "is about"). I adopt the term 'episode' to refer to relatively bounded sequences of actions, which are somehow or other coherent internally. Chapter 10 discusses the relations between such sequences, on the one hand, and activity types and topics, on the other. I conclude this chapter by suggesting a provisional list of dialogical units of discourse. These units are ultimately based on segments of discourse of different extensions and with varying functions. It is argued that unit structure is genre-specific and to some extent interactionally negotiated.

The unit structures of Chapter 10 represent an attempt to divide the stream of discourse into sequences. If, instead, discourse is seen as embodying actors' attempts to accomplish different communicative actions and activities, we can identify a multi-dimensional stream of interlocking communicative projects, some of which are clearly entertained by individuals and others of which are observably shared among interactants, but all of which depend on collective action for their accomplishment. The theory of communicative projects, therefore, is opposed to speech act theory, as developed by Searle and others. This is discussed more fully in Chapter 11.

While Chapter 8 went more into the details of local and situational contexts, Chapter 12 revolves around the socio-culturally defined communicative genres. Communicative activities are dependent, for their production and interpretation, on the existence of norms and routines that define the genres in question. At the same time, the concrete discursive actions make these activity types, or genres, manifest, thus reconstituting them in the continuity of praxis.

Towards the end of the book (Part III: Monologism and dialogism reconciled?), I return to more abstract epistemological issues in the theory of cognition and communication. My purpose is to propose a partial reconciliation of monologistic and dialogistic perspectives. I first present a chapter (13), in which I express some reservations with regard to dialogism, e.g. that the explanatory power of dialogism is, in some respects, limited and must be seen in the context of other complementary theories. For example, I would advocate a dialogism that leaves some space for approaches that get some methodological inspiration from the natural and behavioural sciences.

Finally, in Chapter 14, I want to highlight two major points. The first is to argue that monologism, as the dominant approach to language and communication, is at least partially dependent on a "written language bias". The second is to reconcile monologism with dialogism, basically by de- (or re-)constructing monologism in terms of various activity-specific decontextualizing practices. It is true that monologism and dialogism are partially incommensurable. Monologism, being more akin to the approaches of the natural sciences, would basically focus on individual speakers as complex biological organisms, processing information and "producing" speech, actions and meaning. Dialogism has its roots primarily in the realm of the humanities and social sciences, looking primarily at dialogue itself, the meaningful discourse and interaction in its divergent social and cultural contexts, and portraying actors as participants in the various social activities. Nevertheless, monologism and dialogism must necessarily overlap in their implications and explanations, making partially different but sometimes mutually complementary claims. Dialogism points to the contextuality of cognition and communication, and this applies to the monologistic approaches to these phenomena too. They are not universally applicable but contextually bound. They make their contributions (whether useful or misguided) within contexts that are subject to activity-specific assumptions and concerns.

Several chapters in this book center around attempts to develop some concepts for the analysis of spoken interaction on its own terms, rather than on terms which are defined by structural perspectives on written language and written texts. I believe a lot remains to be done on this task, despite all the impressive empirical work carried out in different traditions (such as Conversation Analysis). One can still hear colleagues within linguistics who claim that discourse (and conversation) analysis is little more than a host of interesting observations in search of a theory. While I would contend that many linguists have a peculiar and narrow conception of 'theory', it must be admitted that discourse analysts need to achieve more on the level of a general comprehensive theory. Yet, I hasten to add that I do not think that it is reasonable to expect one single theory (or model), comparable to what some theoretical linguists still believe is possible as regards language structure. After all, a basic point in dialogue theory is that discursive practices are always subject to culture-specific norms pertaining to different activity types and communicative genres. Therefore, a theory of discourse must be socio-culturally based rather than couched entirely in universalistic terms.

Another point is that actual linguistic practices tend to be characterized, to some extent, by dynamic interplays with contexts, openness, ambiguities and potentialities. It is not an easy task to try to be exact and clear about what is arguably multi-functional, ambiguous or vague. There is a risk that readers of other theoretical persuasions will take dialogistic explorations to be exercises in unclear or woolly thinking. Moreover, since monologism is clearly the mainstream epistemology in the language sciences, proposals founded on different background assumptions will easily get "misunderstood, falsely categorized, and ultimately dismissed as a confused variant of other schools of thought" (Wertsch 1995: 59).

Despite the difficulties, my hope is that the dialogical theory, as set out in this piece of work, does not amount to confusion. If, indeed, there is some order in it, it is in no small measure due to the work and influence of many colleagues. Any piece of scholarly work is, at some level, collective and 'dialogical', and this one is no exception. In acknowledging my scholarly debts, I would like, first and foremost, to thank the members of the Bad Homburg Study Group on "The Dynamics of Dialogue": Jörg Bergmann, Rob Farr, Klaus Foppa, Carl Graumann, Thomas Luckmann, Ivana Marková, and Ragnar Rommetveit. I have learnt a tremendous lot from them. In writing this book, I have drawn on notes from meetings of the Study Group, and on published work by its members. I am also grateful to the Werner Reimer Stiftung in Bad Homburg for having hosted no less than twelve inspiring seminars from 1988 through 1993.

I also wish to thank colleagues and students at my home base in Linköping. In particular I want to thank Karin Aronsson for thoughtful comments on an earlier version of this manuscript. I have also profited from many discussions in other academic milieus. I began writing this book when I was on sabbatical leave, visiting the Department of Linguistic Science, University of Reading, and the Department of Sociology, University of Surrey, Guildford. I have also been influenced by discussions with colleagues and students at the University of Helsinki, where I have been fortunate enough to be engaged as a NorFA guest professor. I am very grateful to Paul Drew, The University of York, who read the manuscript and provided many useful comments. The same applies to Kirsten Malmkjaer, general editor of the series IMPACT. While I am profoundly influenced by many colleagues, none of them is responsible for the particulars of my version of dialogue theory. I have not always been able to follow their good advice.

Finally, I thank Lotta Strand, Christina Brage and Tomas Linell for editorial help, and my wife, Ulrika Nettelbladt, for her support at all levels, intellectual as well as emotional.

Linköping, February 1998

Per Linell

PART I

Monologism and Dialogism Contrasted

CHAPTER 1

Perspectives on language and discourse

1.1 Language as system vs. language in practice

Language can be conceptualized in basically two ways, as *system* or *structure*, or as *discourse*, *practice* (praxis) or *communication*. If one gives priority to the former, we can talk about a *formalist(ic)* framework; here, linguistic expressions can be treated in abstracto. Priorities to the latter yield a more *functionalist(ic)* paradigm;[1] its focus on communicative meanings and functions makes it necessary to take contexts into account. When the first perspective is applied, we are basically concerned with what can be said within a particular language system. By contrast, within the second perspective, we focus on, in Rommetveit's (1974) terms, "what is made known" and reciprocally made understood by "what is said" by actors in specific contexts.

Although now and then, concepts and terms have to be borrowed from one paradigm to the other, each of the two has its own characteristic vocabulary. The former formalist framework employs terms like 'sentence', 'noun', 'noun phrase', 'grammatical subject', 'phoneme', 'lexical meaning', 'proposition' and terms for countless other units of structure (S-units).[2] Terms which belong primarily to a functionalist framework include such notions of discourse (D-aspects) as 'utterance', 'interpretation', 'implication', 'message', 'context', 'understanding', 'relevance', 'coherence', 'topic', 'act', 'communicative project', 'genre', 'answer', 'response', 'perspective', 'position' etc.

According to the formalist perspective, a language is a stock of linguistic resources, i.e. expressions with associated semantic representations (abstract or

---

1. See Hymes (1974: 79). For lists of characteristics of the two perspectives, see Hymes (1974: 90), Schiffrin (1994: ch. 2), and Dik (1978: 4) (also in Figueroa 1994: 22–3).

2. These would then of course include various grammatical structural patterns (e.g. in the form of slot-and-filler structures or tree structures) and 'rules' (e.g. transformations).

decontextualized meanings) which are integrated within systems. On this view, discourse is seen as secondary, as the use of the pre-existing system, and can therefore aptly be called 'language use'. A piece of authentic discourse or text is seen as the product of processes in which S-units are put to use.[3] In other words, most phenomena listed above as D-aspects are explained in terms of the underlying S-units. These units are then thought of as becoming 'contextualized' in various situations, whereby context-bound (non-literal, derived, metaphorical etc.) interpretations are also generated. Languages are seen as representational, i.e. as forms for representing the world, and usually as neutral transparent media for describing a reality that is in principle language-independent. Linguistics, and similarly some other language sciences, have predominantly chosen a formalist perspective; examples of basic notions are Saussure's *langue* and Chomsky's *competence*.[4]

In this book, however, I will look at language as discourse, i.e. in the second-mentioned, more 'functionalistic', perspective. I shall be concerned with language as part of the communicative or cognitive practices of actors' discourses-in-contexts. Languages are constructive and constitutive of the ways we act and think in the world, and how we perceive and conceive of the world. Therefore, I propose to deal with phenomena like discourse, communication, thought, interaction, language use, linguistic practices, etc., as primary, rather than as parasitic on language structure. That is, D-aspects are primary, and S-units must be seen as decontextualized abstractions, generalizations sometimes (implicitly) made by language-users but in many cases virtually "made",[5] or at least further developed, by specialists, especially linguists, for particular purposes, such as forming a basis for language standardization, language teaching, translation between languages, construction of formal languages, etc., or simply for building abstract models of language.

There is also an alternative interpretation of the dialogistic or functionalistic stance, which would give the issue a slightly different twist; we then try to escape from positions assigning a clear once-and-for-all priority to either set of

---

3. In Clark's (1996: 29) terms, this is a 'product approach', as opposed to the 'action approach' that can be associated with dialogism.

4. For discourse and language use, Saussure (1964) and Chomsky (1965) propose their concepts of *parole* and *performance*. Whilst both authors virtually ignore the phenomena involved, their fundamental epistemologies are unequivocally monologistic.

5. Cf. Harris (1980) who looks upon linguists as 'language makers'.

entities. Instead, we claim that, for the competent language user, language and discursive practices are interdependent, and that a comprehensive study of both language and discourse should redress the bias of any polar view and call for systematic shifts between perspectives. Language structure is (more or less) abstract ("more or less" because considerable parts of language structure are genre- or activity-specific), whereas discourse is bound to specific situations (times, places, persons, activities). Language structure too is dynamic and subject to change, but *relative* to the specific discursive interactions and their microgeneses, the socioculturally established resources of language appear as stable. Structure and discourse can also be construed as 'potential' vs. 'actual'; linguistic items are associated with meaning potentials, whereas in situated discourse we encounter the actual meanings made by people who communicate in real life.

Discourse and discursive practices are themselves highly structured. It is possible to generalize across singular situations to define patterns, sequential structures, routines, recurrent strategies and situation definitions (framings), activity types and communicative genres, as well as more traditional linguistic units and rules. But this is largely *structure within discursive practices*, rather than structure apart from, above and before discourse. Moreover, it is first and foremost an organization of social actions, and not a structure pertaining exclusively to language and linguistic form. This is of course not to deny that there is a formal structure of e.g. the syntax of spoken language as it appears in actual discourse.

Within a comprehensive dialogism, structuralist and functionalist perspectives could penetrate and complement each other. That it is possible to transcend the single discourse situation and generalize in terms of discursive patterns and genres is a major assumption governing this book on dialogue. More work has to be done on the linguistic and communicative structures of discourse (cf. Hymes 1986). In this particular study, however, language as a system will not be dealt with systematically, although I will revert to aspects of it occasionally, to see how they might fit into our general framework. In the end, I want to argue that monologistic practices, in science or elsewhere, can be accommodated within a general dialogistic framework.

1.2 Discourse: Individuals' use of language or interactions-in-contexts

I shall use the term 'discourse' in a rather substantive sense: a (piece of) discourse is a stretch of concrete, situated and connected verbal, esp. spoken, actions.[6] Such a view will also assume that discourse includes accompanying paralinguistic signals and embedding contexts. However, before I elaborate on this, I need to take one step back, and delineate the two competing views on discourse, related to the dichotomy between formalism and functionalism (ch. 1.1). Formalist and functionalist views on language imply two fundamentally different approaches to discourse and communication. These approaches I will term *monologism* and *dialogism*, respectively. Marková (1982, 1990a) character-izes them as Cartesian vs. Hegelian philosophical-cultural frameworks. They can be taken as different epistemologies,[7] or, with a less pretentious term, different analytical perspectives.

Monologism, which is clearly the dominant paradigm in the language sciences, looks upon communication basically as actions exchanged between *individuals*. On this view, the whole theory of discourse is clearly secondary in relation to theories of *language structure* and *individual linguistic competence*. The theory of language structure defines various linguistic units, basically as expression types with various abstract syntactic and associated (similarly abstract) 'semantic' representations, which are assumed to be "used" in discourse by "competent" speakers. When within monologism, actual discourse and linguistic behaviour are explicated, individuals are portrayed as thinking and acting in ways which are subject to individual intentions and to conditions defined by social factors (gender, age, socio-economic status, education, power structures etc.), which, for the purpose of analysis, are taken to be stable properties of context.

---

6. Some scholars, e.g. in Foucault's tradition, take the term 'discourse' to mean something rather abstract, such as *discourse type*, a mode of speaking, or the like. "A discourse is a way of talking about and acting upon the world which both constructs and is constructed by a set of social practices" (Candlin & Maley 1997: 202). Such discourse types, 'orders of discourse' (Fairclough 1992: 43), are related to what I prefer to call communicative genres (ch. 12); they are often associated with particular professional (or other) practices or social situations.

7. By epistemology I mean a set of general (often implicit and unquestioned) assumptions, i.e. a general 'knowledge system' or *episteme,* through which we perceive and understand things in the world.

Boden (1994: 2–3) says about sociology:

"At its best, sociology exposes and illuminates the fine, delicate, and largely hidden membrane that supports, connects, and binds social actors in a flexible web of patterned relations. It is an irony of language, in my view, and a consequential one at that, that we have come to call this complex phenomenon "structure"; words carry a freight of meaning and, for social scientists, few terms are more quickly concretized and reified into a nearly immovable and insuperable object. The very semantic weight of solidness and separateness attributed to structure has had, it seems, extraordinary consequences in twentieth-century sociology, effectively driving a wedge between action and both its causes and consequences. [...] The result has been highly problematic in at least two general senses: (1) much social theory is currently driven by methodological conventions rather than genuinely empirical insights; and (2) the emphasis of structure "over" action has resulted in the invisibility of the latter in the shadow of the former."

Very much the same holds for linguistics; we could just substitute "linguistics", "language users" and "linguistic theory" for Boden's "sociology", "social actors" and "social theory" in the quotes.

In this book I shall use monologism as a background for laying out the fundamental principles of an alternative approach, that of dialogism. Whilst monologism assumes individuals and societies (cultures) to be analytical primes, dialogism takes *actions and interactions*, e.g. the discursive practices,[8] *in their contexts* as basic units. These are basic analytic units that cannot be reduced to elements of other kinds in any simple manner.[9] Discourse is then understood not as processes involving individuals and social structures (or mental functioning and sociocultural settings) as autonomous and mutually independent entities, but instead in terms of dynamic and mutual interdependencies between individuals

---

8. The word 'discursive' is commonly used in a sense like "running about, rambling, passing from one topic to another in an unmethodical way". I wish to use it, of course, in a perfectly neutral way, as the adjective of 'discourse'. This appears to square with common use in various fields of research dealing with discourse. (The wish to avoid the mundane associations of the word was the reason for Linell & Marková 1993, to prefer the variant 'discursive'. Another alternative might be 'discoursal'.)

9. The units of the language-as-a-system approach are abstract linguistic expression types, not tokens (exemplars) occurring in actual time and space. By contrast, the analysis of discourse takes its point of departure in concrete interactions (concrete meaning embodied and temporally specified) and focuses crucially on relations between discourse and contexts (ch. 8), and *then* generalizes from these, viewing language structure as patterns of verbal conduct routinely exhibited and reconstructed across large numbers of communicative events.

as actors-in-specific-interactions and contexts, the latter seen as invoked by and emergent with (inter)actions.[10] The monologist would contend that ultimately, communication is a process between individuals. The dialogist would reply that although we cannot assume any other neurophysiological substrates for the cognitive, emotive, and conative processes involved in communication than those of individual human beings, we ought, in the analysis of action and meaning, talk about individuals-in-dialogue-with-partners-and-contexts rather than individuals *tout court*.

Since monologism is the accepted mainstream epistemology of major traditions in the language sciences, the adoption of a dialogistic perspective will amount to a major perceptual shift (Wittgenstein 1958: 193ff.) on the part of many readers, who might not be familiar with the perspectives of dialogism; it involves seeing phenomena of language "under different aspects", making sense of them within another context. I shall argue that dialogism must be the overall framework for analyzing discourse and communication, and social life in general. At the same time, however, I shall argue that (what is in some respects) a monologistic stance must be taken in certain situated activities, e.g. in some scientific endeavours. Thus, I will try to reconstruct monologism as a special context-bound approach, embedded within a general dialogistic epistemology (ch. 14).

1.3 Dialogism, dialogicality and dialogue

'Monologism' and 'dialogism' as epistemologies or analytical frameworks should be kept distinct from, on the one hand, 'dialogicality' and, on the other hand, 'monologue' and 'dialogue'. Dialogicality (or, as some prefer it, 'dialogicity') is the noun used to refer to certain properties that are, at least according to dialogism, characteristic of and *essential* in, in the first place, dialogue and, more generally, all human cognition and communication. These properties, which will be extensively explored in this book, include *sequential organization, joint*

---

10. Nevertheless, I will use both 'process' and 'practice' as essential terms within dialogism. A 'process' is basically a train of causally determined events in which something is being transformed or changed. A 'practice' is a process in which an actor does (or makes) something, transforming some input material to a product (outcome). 'Practice', but not 'process', emphasizes meaningful or purposeful action, activities carried out according to some kind of routines (activity types). Processes, Clark (1996: 59) argues, are "the physical and mental systems [people] recruit in carrying out [actions]".

communicative & cognitive activities
discourse - cognition

(social-interactional) construction, and *interdependence between acts* (local units) and *activities* (global units and abstract types). These principles (cf. ch. 5.9) can be seen as elaborations of what Mikhail Bakhtin would term 'the dialogical principle' (in the singular) (Todorov 1984). They all deal with the reflexive relations between discourse (and cognition) and contexts of various kinds (ch. 8: co-texts, social participation frameworks, activity types). Scholars from other traditions, e.g. within ethnomethodology and Conversation Analysis, might prefer the concept of *'reflexivity'* to *'dialogicality'* (Woolgar 1988; Wilson 1991).

With regard to the terms 'monologue' and 'dialogue', I shall use the latter basically about any dyadic or polyadic interaction between individuals who are mutually co-present to each other and who interact through language (or some other symbolic means), whereas 'monologue' is a discourse type where only one person is, at least at face value, active as speaker or author. It should be made clear that monologism, as an epistemology, claims to be valid for all communicative and cognitive practices, whether involving monological speech, texts, and thought, or dialogical interaction (dialogue). The same holds, *mutatis mutandis*, for dialogism. In other words, apart from the obvious cases (monologistic accounts of monologues, and dialogistic accounts of dialogues), there can be a monologistic theory of dialogue, and a dialogistic theory of monologue. However, it can be said that dialogism in general uses dialogue and face-to-face interaction as its primary source of prototypical examples for explanation and illustration, and tends to depict monological activities in analogy with dialogue. The reverse would of course be true of monologism.

'Dialogical' and 'monological' properties are empirically present to varying extents in different kinds of communicative and cognitive activities. Since the matter is complicated by the fact that concepts like 'dialogue' and 'dialogism' are not always properly kept distinct, I shall begin by sorting out a few terminological difficulties.

1.4 The traditional conflation of 'dialogism' and 'dialogue'

There has been an upsurge of interest in 'dialogue' and 'dialogism' in recent years. This movement has taken place in several disciplines, including philosophy, literary studies, anthropology, linguistics, social psychology and communication studies. Though there are clearly several things in common between the various traditions and trends in question, there are also many differences in concepts, terminologies and attitudes to empirical realities. In this book I shall mainly lean towards empirical studies of dialogue, i.e. talk-in-interaction, but it seems appropriate to start out with a few remarks on some terminological practices which can be found elsewhere.

Swearingen (1990: 48) observes that dialogue is "both a kind of discourse and a way of viewing discourse". Accordingly, many scholars in philosophy and literary theory (e.g. the contributors to Maranhão 1990) consider that 'dialogue' is both a very specific type of discourse, which can provisionally be named Socratic argumentation, and also a general theoretical framework, proposed for the analysis of all discourse. I shall presently return to the first point. Let me just note in passing that the general epistemology, Swearingen's "way of viewing discourse", is what I propose to call 'dialogism', following e.g. Holquist (1990), Marková (1990a), Marková & Foppa (1990), and others. It is somewhat confusing that both 'dialogue' and 'dialogism' (as well as 'dialogicality') are related to the same adjective, i.e. 'dialogical'. If we want to be somewhat pedantic, we had better use 'dialogistic' in the sense of 'pertaining to the epistemology of dialogism'; this would leave us with 'dialogical' in the sense of 'present in, or typical of, the discourse types which are dialogues in the sense of talk-in-interaction'. (More often than not, however, people use 'dialogical' when referring to dialogism, as I have indeed done in the subtitle of this book.)

Let us now turn to the question of which discourse types should be referred to as 'dialogues'. Contrary to the traditional philosophical and literary usage, I shall adopt a broad definition of 'dialogue' as roughly *interaction through symbolic means by mutually co-present individuals* (thus tying up with the etymology of *dialogos*: "through words"). This definition (see ch. 1.5), which seems to be gaining increased acceptance in empirical studies of communication, is *not* identical to what might be called the 'classical' and normative understanding of 'dialogue'. That is concerned with a rather special language game, a kind of argumentative interaction, the model of which goes back to some of Plato's Dialogues (i.e. Socratic argumentation).[11] This has also engendered "a culturally and historically specific way of conceiving certain verbal transactions" (Crapanzano 1990: 270), and as such it has exerted considerable rhetorical force. The classical concept of 'dialogue' is basically an open interaction characterized

---

11. Associated with this is another meaning of 'dialogue', namely as a literary genre, whose texts are (supposed to be) representing (factually or mimetically) utterances by different speakers in oral discourse.

by cooperation and symmetry (with equal opportunities for participants to take turns and develop topics) and aiming exclusively at truth-finding by penetrating argumentation, *dialegesthai*, without any coercion from any party and without this process being impeded by personal preferences, emotions, power, utility considerations etc., and with a deliberate avoidance of closure and finality, i.e. the dialogue is always an ongoing process with participants open for continuous reconsiderations (e.g. Swearingen 1990: 47). Such discourses, exemplified in at least some of Plato's Socratic dialogues, involving the sifting of arguments and counter-arguments, letting good arguments win over bad ones, possibly resulting in interlocutors' reaching across understandings and "coming together" (Crapanzano 1990: 277), seem to have remained an ideal, defining a set of norms for "true dialogue" in quite wide, though perhaps mainly "academic", circles of Western civilization. (In addition to the truth-finding argumentation, later epoques may have allowed for some other kinds of maximally other-oriented interactions, e.g. mutually empathetic encounters where parties "understand each other as persons".)

The classical notion of 'dialogue' is quite viable in contemporary philosophy (see e.g. Maranhão 1990). For example, Habermas (1981) clearly presupposes it in his characterization of the 'ideal speech situation', and Gadamer's (1975) discussion of dialogue insists on the importance of symmetry of interaction. In a rather different guise, it seems to underlie the Cooperative Principle of Grice (1975); Grice's theory is (at least implicitly) normative, and it is not descriptive of actual discourse. Far from being dialogistic, Grice (and similarly Searle and, to some extent, Habermas) pictures the speaker as an entirely rational agent who speaks his mind "with clarity, economy, and planned execution, whose foreknowledge of intents, means, and effects of words conjures ready recognition of these intents, means and effects in the minds of complicitous hearers." (Tyler 1990: 296). As Tyler goes on to argue (pp. 296–7), Searle and Grice have crossed over the *dia* and instead stressed the rationality, efficiency and *logos* of the single idealized communicator. Accordingly, they stand for a monologism, which sustains the authority and domination of the speaker, at the cost of his partners, the listeners. At the same time, their theories invoke, at least implicitly, a classical notion of 'dialogue', stressing clarity, symmetry, egalitarianism, mutuality, harmony, openness, consensus, and agreement, at the same time suppressing negotiations of meaning, hedges, vagueness, ambiguity, polyvocality, misunderstanding, conflicting interests, concealment, opposition, power, domination, and fragmentation of participation and knowledge. For example, Habermas

Habermas

(1981) is consistent with his normative approach to dialogue and communication, when he calls only the former features of discourse 'communicative', while dubbing the latter 'strategic discourse'. In empirical reality, features of both kinds co-occur and are intrinsically related; we would prefer to use terms like 'communicative', 'communication', and 'dialogue' without any predefined normative conditions (see ch. 1.5).

The time-honoured ideal dialogue is also part of a fairly wide-spread everyday-culture ("lay") conception of what makes something into "a true dialogue" or "real communication". Likewise, it is interesting that the (pre-theoretical) concept of "conversation" is understood, in mundane usage, as referring to a particular genre. This genre, which has been codified in books of conversational etiquette and has a long cultural history,[12] is sometimes characterized in terms that are partly similar to those of the normative notion of "true dialogue". Burke (1993) mentions four genre characteristics in particular; the 'cooperative principle' (*pace* Grice), the equal distribution of speaker rights and opportunities, the spontaneity and informality of the exchanges, and the 'non-business-likeness' (absence of particular pre-determined tasks). Indeed, similar assumptions of interaction symmetry and absence of constraints on turn taking and topic development recur in the concept of 'ordinary conversation' as commonly used in modern Conversation Analysis (Atkinson & Heritage 1984).[13]

1.5 Dialogue: Interaction between co-present individuals through symbolic means

standard / established form

The classical tradition defines 'dialogue' in a basically normative way; we are concerned with "the good dialogue", which also implies ethical demands on a

---

12. Cf. treatises on conversation "as an art". For an interesting account, see Burke (1993).

13. In addition, in Initiative-Response (IR) analysis (Linell et al. 1988), we recognize the notion of the 'balanced' discourse contribution (symbolized as ⟨^⟩ as involving both a focal, other-oriented response and a substantial though non-imposing initiative (cf. ch. 9.6). A 'classical dialogue' would consist of only such contributions, obviously an unattainable ideal. Such contributions can hardly make up the majority of contributions in many kinds of activities, let alone be the goal for all types of activities. Many types of communicative activities, e.g. professional-lay communication of adult-child discourse, must arguably, at least from time to time, involve interactional asymmetries (in addition to the obvious asymmetries of knowledge involved). For some critical discussion of the concept of 'ordinary conversation', see ch. 12.3.

"morally charged, authentic relationship" (Crapanzano 1990: 271) between I and thou (cf. Buber 1958: *ich-und-du*). As an empirically grounded model of communication, such a view of dialogue based entirely on symmetry and equality would be unfruitful and counterfactual. In a modern empirical, yet dialogistic approach to discourse, another kind of definition of 'dialogue' seems more appropriate; 'any interaction through language (or other symbolic means) between two or several individuals who are mutually co-present' (cf. Luckmann 1990).[14] The canonical type would be talk in face-to-face interaction, but one may also include interactions which are sufficiently similar, notably telephone conversations (Hopper 1992), electronic real-time interactions (Severinson Eklundh 1986) etc. (Representations of dialogues in writing, e.g. dialogues in drama plays or novels, or transcripts of spoken interaction, are obviously also related but will need special considerations.).

The broad definition based on 'symbol-based interaction' removes the conditions of cooperation and symmetry from the essence of 'dialogue'. Our claim is that *co-ordination*, which is a weaker form of cooperation, is basic to social activities. Couch (1986) proposes a taxonomy and a partial hierarchy of 'elementary forms' of social activity, including (in his terms:) autocratic activity, chase, conflict, competition, social panic, accommodation, mutuality, and cooperation. These forms of social activity are characterized by different combinations of 'elements of sociation', whose nature need not concern us here (but cf. ch. 9.3), but it seems clear that verbal interaction falls within the category type of 'cooperation',[15] characterized by, among other things, mutual attention and responsiveness, shared focus, congruent plans, and social (communicative) objectives. From our point of view, Couch's use of 'cooperation' is too exclusive and too broad at the same time. On the one hand, virtually all types of social activity involve some kind of coordination of behaviours; thus, for example, individuals respond to and project the others' moves, even if this is often done in an asymmetrical, partial, and only partly mutual manner. On the other hand, even if dialogues, symbol-based communicative interactions, involve

---

14. Note that Greek *dia* means "through, between, across", not "two", though some etymologists have argued for a relation between *dia* and *dyo-*, *di-*."two" (Crapanzano 1990: 276). Tyler (1990: 295) points out that the "catachrestic" and "etymologically incorrect" understanding of *dia* as meaning "two" has the merit of capturing the tendency of the face-to-face encounter to develop into the mutual attending of two interlocutors to each other, thus assigning others to the margin as "third parties". Cf. ch. 6.5.2.

15. Note that Couch (op.cit.) is, on the whole, concerned primarily with non-verbal interaction.

more of (and other forms of) coordination and cooperation, many of these dialogues also involve strong interactional asymmetries and competitive positionings. Yet, the notions of cooperation (or better: coordination) and mutual other-orientation remain central to dialogue and communication, though not as absolute ideals but as basic and abstract conditions; for communication to take place, there must be *some* degree of coordination, reciprocities and mutualities (e.g. Graumann 1995). Indeed, such assumptions are logically presupposed when we identify deviations from them; for example, failures of reciprocity would not be detected unless we expected some norm of reciprocity to be honoured, and deception would not be possible if we did not routinely rely on shared background knowledge and mutual trust (Allwood 1976).

Another basic claim must be that *communication presupposes asymmetries* of knowledge and participation of various kinds (Linell & Luckmann 1991). Indeed, if there were no asymmetries of knowledge between people, i.e. if everybody possessed the same information, there would be little point in communicating. In addition, many dialogues are built upon complementary, rather than symmetrical, roles of participation. *Complementarity* is in fact characteristic of dialogue and communication in general; parties communicate from different positions and yet achieve some degree of shared understanding in and through their interaction. These aspects have not been sufficiently appreciated in normative communication theory. Other properties not generally acknowledged by the idealized dialogue model are the ubiquitous tensions between cooperation and competition, intersubjectivity and individual agency, sharedness and isolation, coherence and fragmentation. In this book, I shall begin, in ch. 5, by stressing the collective aspects, and only then, in subsequent chapters, gradually complicate the issues by paying more attention to nonsharedness.

Summing up, we can say that, at an abstract level, dialogue and communication involve, by definition, some kind of coordination (or cooperation), coherence, reciprocity and mutuality (e.g. with regard to moral commitments), but *empirically* these properties are *never* present in their entirety. Therefore, if we adopt a descriptive notion of 'dialogue', rather than an idealistic, Habermasian one, we are free to explore the empirical differences among discursive activities in terms of (a)symmetries, reciprocities, mutualities, moral dimensions etc...[16] We recognize that human dialogue is subject to temporal, spatial, sequential and

---

16. Cf. Marková & Foppa 1991; Marková et al. (1995); Bergmann (1998); Linell & Rommetveit (1998).

interactional contingencies. This position, of course, in no way denies the fact that interlocutors, in specific situations, are aware of and may indeed orient to more specific norms with regard to e.g. equality and moral considerations; one such situation type would be the special genre we may call moral (Socratic) argumentation (cf. Ferrara 1990).[17]

---

17. Yet, many situations clearly involve interlocutors orienting to other kinds of norms, e.g. norms of politeness. Foppa (1990) proposes a "principle of neutral local coherence" for small talk, basically implying that a conversationalist should not say anything that could possibly be at odds with the interlocutor's opinions, values, or wishes. There is, in other words, a trend towards mutual agreement (cf. also Foppa 1995). This points to another source of everyday conceptions of 'proper' conversations (and dialogue), i.e. books on conversational etiquette. This normative tradition lies behind the very first attempts at analytical, (semi-)descriptive approaches to conversation (cf. Lazarus 1879).

CHAPTER 2

Monologism: Its basic assumptions

In this book, I outline dialogism as an approach to discourse, cognition and communication, and above all to conversation and other kinds of talk-in-interaction. Dialogism can be seen as an alternative, or an antidote, to monologism, which is clearly the mainstream epistemology in most contemporary approaches to language, notably in linguistics, cognitive psychology, computer sciences and largely within communication studies (Marková & Foppa 1990, 1991; Heen Wold 1992). Monologism has a long intellectual history in Western philosophy and theories of the mind, and I will not attempt to review all of this here.[1] However, in order to make the dialogistic viewpoints more salient and more intelligible, it will be necessary to define the contrasting paradigm of monologism in a reasonably concise and appropriate manner. Some points will be stated in this chapter, and in later chapters the picture will become more elaborated.

2.1 Cognition and communication as empirically distinct phenomena

Dialogism is an epistemology for both cognition and communication, and regards them as simultaneously present aspects of both intrapersonal and interpersonal processes and practices. This is possible, if we define cognition, roughly, as *intelligent (non-random) behaviour and action,* often involving some aspect of problem-solving, whether in silent thinking (intramental processes) or overtly as mindful action publicly observable in the external world, and communication as *interaction between different individuals, minds, organisms or systems,* including subsystems of the individual mind. With this definition, we find that cognition

---

1. For some discussion, see Marková (1982, 1990a).

involves internal and interpersonal communication, and conversely, that any kind of communication has cognitive aspects. Monologism, on the other hand, posits a Cartesian dichotomy, and typically construes cognition and communication as distinct processes, occurring within and between (from-to) individuals, respectively.

Separating cognition and communication as distinct processes, rather than as different aspects or properties of the same (or overlapping) phenomena, may be taken as a basic and characteristic monologistic assumption. Beyond this, present-day monologism in the language sciences can be seen as involving three different, but logically interlocking, theories, i.e. *the information processing theory of cognition and the mind, the transfer theory of communication, and the code model of language structure.* Of these, the information processing model is clearly the most successful at present; indeed, it tends to supersede the others, being the grand model of linguistic processing. It is closely related to 'cognitivism', which has dominated most fields of academic psychology since the seventies. The transfer model of communication (the conduit model, according to Reddy 1979; there are many other names) and the code model of language structure, on the other hand, have more often been criticized for being overly simplified, and modern variants would allow for a more substantial share of interaction and dynamic processing. Yet, the characteristics to be described in the next sections would no doubt hold true of most mainstream theories of today.

2.2 Cognition as information processing by individuals

The cognitive sciences are heavily influenced by a computational metaphor.[2] Cognition, or thinking, is, on this view, a matter of representing various kinds of contents (usually termed 'information') and processing such representations. Note that it is the definition of cognition as information processing, rather than, say, mindful action in the world (cf. ch. 2.1), that makes the idea of cognition as an individual-psychological phenomenon almost inescapable. The processing of information takes place within the minds programmed into the brains of individuals. (Other cases of information processing involve computers.). It is hard to claim that information processing can occur in the interaction between the individual and his physical or social environments, because there is no hardware

---

2. E.g. Pylyshyn (1989); for critical comments, see e.g. Costall (1991).

supporting the processes out there. Of course, the individual receives information from his environment, but this information serves only as input to the various internal, 'mental' processes within the individual agent. The mind is thus a complex system, a "machine", for processing information from 'input' to 'output'. The dynamics of the input, what is being 'internalized', and the intricacies in the process of acquiring input are seldom problematized. Cognition is seen basically as processing different (kinds or stages of) internal re-presentations of the environment. If the partner in interaction is taken into account in a cognitivist model, he or she must somehow be *represented* as one (or several) subsystem(s) in the individual actor's information-processing system.

The theories referenced here are often dubbed 'cognitivist'. The basic assumption is, as was just noted, that some sort of information processing takes place within the individual's mind or brain. But 'cognitivism' is somewhat more specific than this. Characteristically, it assumes the existence of a level of 'cognitive' symbolic representation, which is a kind of "third" level, reducible neither to neurophysiological states and processes nor to phenomenological characterization (Pateman 1987). Cognition is, according to this paradigm, typically construed as symbol-based activities inside the individual mind. In many ways, natural language in man corresponds to some kind of programming (software) system in a computer, and it is at this level that the cognitive processing takes place. Cognition is computation in a language-like system of representation, a "language of thought" (Fodor 1976).

If 'cognitivism' is a *particular*, monologistic approach to cognition, it follows that being 'non-cognitivist' does not amount to denying that people indulge in cognition (thinking, remembering, etc), only that 'cognition' must be accounted for in other terms, partly non-individual and partly non-representational (e.g. analogical), terms. I cannot argue here for a particular stance on the issue whether 'dialogism' should be combined with some kind of cognitivist approach to individual information processing, or whether one should rather adopt some type of non-cognitivist, e.g. connectionist, approach. However, we note that A. Clark (1997: 47) argues that

"the brain should not be seen as primarily a locus of inner descriptions of
external states of affairs; rather, it should be seen as a locus of inner structures
that act as operators upon the world via their role in determining actions."
And, "[t]he internal representations the mind uses to guide actions may thus
best be understood as action-and-context-specific control structures rather than
as passive recapitulations of external reality" (ibid.: 50).[3]

Let us go back to monologism. Language is arguably a means for humans to
relate to the world. However, how this is done is a problem that is *not* seriously
probed by 'cognitivists'. Rather, information processing theories within cognitive
science or theoretical linguistics postulate information structures, or symbolic
representations (allegedly of the world), and these representations are simply
claimed to be processed by self-contained human minds. In actual practice,
monologism usually starts by assuming that the representations *are already there*
in the minds. Similarly, its account of the communicative act starts with (the
assumption of) more or less fully developed communicative intentions (see
ch. 2.3). There are no serious attempts to explain exactly how these representations of the world, or the communicative intentions, get there in the first place.
This is a point, where dialogism tries to present a coherent account, although this
is seldom formalized but couched "only" in a phenomenological type of language
of description.

Perception and thinking are not the only aspects of mental processing
characteristically treated by monologism in terms of inputs, outputs, and various
intermediate representations. Learning and memory are other examples of mental
abilities. Learning is then typically treated only as the individuals' more or less
successful internalizations of input, rather than as, say, an increasing ability to
cope with problems in interaction with the physical and social environment. A
monologistic psychology of memory is basically about storage and retrieval of
information. The lion's share of the research has been on capacities to recall
pieces of information, and retention of memorized information is then defined in
terms of the difference between input and output. A dialogistic theory would put
more emphasis on remembering as an interactive process (Middleton & Edwards

---

3. See also Still & Costall (1991) and Zlatev (1997) for some discussion.

1990),[4] and would deal primarily with memory of situated, coherently organized material. It thus seems clear that the monologistic theory has comparatively more to say about the recall of more autonomous items, such as names, but very little to say about the memory of events in everyday-life contexts.

By contrast, dialogism would stress the interaction of the mind with the physical and social environment in all the activities of perception (intake), cognition and understanding (processing), remembering, and of course, a fortiori, overt interpersonal communication. These cannot be seen and understood in terms of information processing within autonomous minds. The information-processing aspect must instead be integrated within a comprehensive model of cognition and action in the world. At the same time, interpersonal communication also involves cognition, but this is seen not exclusively in terms of individuals' thinking, but also in "interactional models of people "thinking out loud" *together*" (Boden 1994: 85, italics hers). Similarly, Leudar & Antaki (1988: 144–5) refer to G. H. Mead's conception of "conversations in terms of a *socially distributed cognitive system*" (my italics/PL).[5] Accordingly, this view on cognition implies a particular view on interpersonal communication too; rather than looking upon utterances and texts only in terms of transmission of senders' messages (the monologistic view to be expounded in ch. 2.3), dialogists take them to be "thinking devices" (Wertsch & Penuel 1996), i.e. mediational means for accomplishing understanding (see also ch. 3.4.2).

---

4. The claim is here that memory should be seen in terms of discursive activities. For critical comments on this view of remembering, see the peer commentaries to Edwards et al. (1992). On 'discursive psychology', see ch. 3.5.

5. The dialogistic approach to cognition has been formulated in terms like 'everyday cognition' (Rogoff & Lave 1984), 'cognition in practice' (Lave 1988), 'socially shared cognition' (Resnick 1991), 'situated cognition', and 'distributed cognition' (Hutchins 1991). The notion of 'distributed cognition' has in recent years been developed in cultural psychology and anthropology (e.g. Cole & Engeström 1993; Hutchins 1991; Engeström & Middleton 1996), and has been used e.g. about teamwork in technologically advanced environments (e.g. Hutchins 1991; Heath & Luff 1992; Hutchins & Klausen 1996; Resnick et al. 1997). See also Wertsch (1991) on the social distribution of mental activities. By being partly opposed to monologistic 'cognitivism', these perspectives are sometimes dubbed 'non-cognitivist'. I shall return to the perspective on dialogue as 'distributed cognition' later (ch. 11.6).

2.3 The transfer-and-exchange model of communication

When it comes to discourse in social interaction, i.e. in communication, mono-logism analyzes this quite simply in terms of utterances by speakers, who act as individuals. The utterances and their meanings are explained by recourse to the speaker's communicative intentions, and the listener's task is described as that of recovering these intentions (e.g. Clark & Clark 1977).[6] The speaker, as an individual agent, is thus seen as the absolute source of, and authority of, his contributions to discourse; hence the term 'monologism'.

Utterances are the *products* of individual speakers (or their minds).[7] This sounds reasonable enough, even perhaps to a dialogist, as long as we consider them as plain behaviours or vocalizations. But when it comes to their meanings, i.e. their communicative values, it becomes necessary, for the dialogist, to appreciate their social antecedents and social consequences. Meanings are simply not the products of autonomous individuals *alone*. As I already pointed out, monologistic accounts leave us in the dark as to *from whereabouts* speakers get their intentions and meanings, and I shall return several times to the theme of the social nature of meaning and cognition.

The function of the 'communicative chain' from speaker to listener is, according to monologistic accounts, one of transferring meanings via various kinds of representations, and processes relating such representations. John Locke (in *An Essay Concerning Human Understanding*, 1690) was an important proponent of this view on communication (Harris 1981; Taylor 1992; Shepherd 1993). In more recent times, the 'chain' model has been explicated in terms of various transportation metaphors (like a conduit, a conveyor belt etc.), and as such it appears in nearly any modern textbook of psycholinguistics or cognitive psychology (e.g. Clark & Clark 1977; etc). In its 20th century variants, this kind of model ("the speech chain", cf. Denes & Pinson 1963) received inspiration from Shannon & Weaver's (1949) theory of communication by physically represented symbols (technical information transfer). Successful communication, according to this model, takes place, if the message arrives at the destination, in

---

6. One should note, however, a certain ambivalence on the part of Clark & Clark (1977) with regard to (what is usually characterized as) the transfer model of communication. They both endorse it (in the main bulk of the text) and point to some of its inadequacies.

7. Hence Clark's (1996) term 'product approach' (ch.1, n. 3).

The speaker of a Monologic account.
↳ intentions & meanings.

The speaker of a Monologic account.
↳ intentions & meanings.

the listener's mind, in the same form as the intended message had in the speaker's mind, i.e. it has not, on its way from source to destination, been distorted by any kind of 'noise' (such as sloppy expression on the speaker's part, actual noise in the channel, listener's inattention, lack of knowledge or inability to decode the speaker's speech, etc.).

As was pointed out above, the information processing paradigm lays claims to account for interaction, speaking and listening. Willem Levelt, in his influential and comprehensive monograph on *Speaking* (1989), sees the speaker as "a highly complex information processor who can, in some still rather mysterious way, transform intentions, thoughts, feelings into fluently articulated speech" (p.1). And Jerry Fodor, perhaps one of the most extreme present-day monologists, sees the listener's understanding as a "mapping of wave forms onto messages" (1976: 108). Dialogism would regard such formulations as at most *partial* descriptions of some aspects of the necessary processing of the physical substrate ("the signals") of communication, and therefore as strongly misleading if presented as a full theory of communication through spoken interaction.

The social-interactional aspects of discourse will, according to the mainstream transfer model, be seen in terms of individual speakers taking turns in producing their respective utterances.[8] In essence, monologism portrays the exchanges involved in conversation in the following way. First, the speaker A has understood something specific which he wants to communicate to person B (how this understanding comes about is, however, typically disregarded in monologistic accounts of "utterance production"). Speaker A forms a communicative intention with a well-defined content, which reflects his understanding and which then determines the form of his utterance produced in speech. The listener B's task is to receive the utterance and understand it in accordance with A's intentions, i.e. so that it matches A's understanding underlying his speech act. B will then develop additional understandings, possibly in response to A's previous utterance; these new understandings will underlie communicative intentions and a corresponding utterance on the part of B. A now has to receive this, etc. And so it goes on: A speaks and B understands, B speaks and A understands, A speaks and B understands, B speaks and A understands etc., in a sequence of mental and behavioural acts. In the individualistic approach of monologism, the

---

8. See Levelt's (1989) ch. 2 on "The speaker as interlocutor"

interaction itself becomes largely an epiphenomenon, reduceable to sequences of individual actions. Suchman (1987: 70) expresses this in the following passage:

> "The most common view of conversation (e.g. within Artificial Intelligence and Cognitive Science/PL) is that speakers and listeners, pursuing some common topic according to individual predispositions and agendas, engage in an alternating sequence of action and response. For students of human cognition and of language, conversation generally has been treated as epiphenomenal with respect to the central concerns of their fields. Cognitively, conversation is just the meeting ground of individual psychologies, while linguistically it is the noisy, real-world occasion for the exercise of basic language abilities. On either view, the additional constraints imposed by situated language are a complication that obscures the underlying structure of cognitive and linguistic competence."

Rommetveit (1992: 19) says about "representational-computational models within mainstream individual cognitive psychology and cognitive science" that they "converge in an image of Man as an essentially asocial, but highly complex information-processing device". By contrast, dialogism portrays conversation as an intrinsically social and collective process, where the speaker is dependent on the listener as a "co-author" (as well as in other capacities) and, more generally, on the various relevant contexts, and where he, the speaker, is also a listener (to his own utterance) and is engaged in sense-making activities in the course of the verbalization process itself. (These issues will be further discussed in chs. 6 and 7.)

Monologism tends to treat communication as a *"from-to" process*; communication is therefore considered to have taken place as soon as a sender A has expressed a message and a recipient B has understood it (in accordance with A's intentions). Dialogism takes the prototypical case of communication to be a *"between" process*,[9] the requirement is not only that something becomes *shared* knowledge through the communicative process, but also that the parties somehow *mutually provide evidence* that they have established an intersubjectively valid, "shared" understanding of the things talked about. This speaks for the three-

---

9. Alternatively, instead of a "between" process, dialogists may talk about a "within" process (Marková 1995); A's and B's contributions to sense-making in dialogue can only be understood as complementary to each other, as being "within" a joint construction (ch. 5).

part exchange as (an unmarked type of) minimal communicative interaction (ch. 3.4.3).[10]

2.4 The code model of language structure

I will now turn to the role of language within a monologistic epistemology. According to this, a natural language is a highly structured phenomenon, forming systems with subsystems of a basically supra-individual nature (*la langue*). Such a language can be regarded as a stock of units and rules. Alternatively, it is seen as a structured set of linguistic signs, some of which are lexicalized, i.e. stored as ready-made units (which are modifiable in syntactic configurations), and others are syntactically produced, i.e. formed from lexicalized units which are combined according to rules. The former, lexical, expressions have fixed linguistic meanings, while the meanings of the syntactically produced, complex expressions, e.g. sentences, can be determined, computed, from lexical meanings and syntactic structures (by a principle of 'compositionality', often referred to as Frege's principle). In other words, according to this view, a language is an infinite (but enumerable) set of, basic (i.e. lexical) or derived, linguistic signs, each with a fixed expression and a fixed meaning. Sign systems consisting of such expression-meaning couplings are usually called *codes*. The degree of structural organization and integration of the language system, whichever its elements are assumed to be, is usually taken to be extremely high.

Even if linguistic signs are sometimes taken to be two-sided entities, that is, pairings between expressions and meanings (according to theorists like Saussure and Hjelmslev), for most linguists it is clearly the existence of a linguistic expression, typically that of a word, which makes something into a linguistic item; a concept without a linguistic expression would not be considered part of a (natural) language, whereas, at the same time, a phonotactically correct word without a semantic interpretation would be a potential linguistic item ('neologism', 'nonsense-word'). Thus, linguistic units (or signs) are *expression-based*, and semantic representations are defined as associated with, or tied to, expressions.

---

10. Hence, unidirectional processes of communication, e.g. from the TV reporters appearing in their programs on the screen to their spectators, would not be seen as cases of full-fledged communication. On the other hand, such processes too could of course be analyzed in dialogistic terms (e.g. ch. 13.3). (Note, in addition, that no communication can ever be complete in an absolute sense.)

Indeed, within linguistic (formal) semantics, the semantic representations themselves are treated as some kind of abstract expressions. Alternatively, one may look upon these meanings (semantic representations) as 'semantic interpretations' of linguistic expressions, a term which even more clearly indicates the priority of expression.

Talking about languages as codes and linguistics as expression-based may bring structuralist and Saussurean ideas into mind, rather than generativist and Chomskyan (or neo-Chomskyan) ones. It is entirely beyond the scope of this chapter (and this book) to characterize the differences between classical structuralist and (various versions of) Chomskyan linguistics. However, it is justified to claim that generative linguistics is a peculiar (and extreme) variant of structuralism, which is still expression-based (cf. Chomsky's priority of syntax over semantics) and quite compatible with the computational metaphor of cognition.[11] For example, talk about "principles and parameters" (Chomsky 1986; Cook & Newson 1996) fits the paradigm nicely; just as variables in a computer program can be bound by users for particular purposes, the universal parameters of the underlying language faculty have, according to Chomskyan theories, their values set by specific languages or, rather, by speakers belonging to particular language communities.

Monologism is based on a code model of language. All essential parts of the whole language system are assumed to be internalized by the individual speakers, thus constituting their 'linguistic competence'. Language provides the individual speaker with the words and constructions, and as a consequence, he can deploy these linguistic units and rules in cognition and communication. Language, conceptualized as structure (rather than practice), necessarily comes "before" the linguistic practices. Indeed, communication is seen as the "use of language"; the logic is that the code, that which is being used, must exist before it can be used. Anybody will notice that this view fits the dominant discourse about language also in everyday culture (at least in Western civilizations).

The monologistic epistemology is characterized by a number of 'Cartesian' dichotomies (e.g. Marková 1982, 1990a); sharp distinctions are set up between, e.g. cognition and communication, discourse and context, meaning and expression etc. With regard to the communicative process, utterance meaning, understood as the speaker's communicative intentions, exists prior to form; language

---

11. For some relevant and recent discussion, see Zlatev (1997).

provides the expressions for, or representations of, a message, or content, already conceived. Yet, as we just saw, linguistics in general is, and has always been, form- or expression-based rather than meaning-oriented.[12] Linguistic expressions have their associated semantic representations, or interpretations, and these are assumed to be context-free, being tied to abstract types rather than utterance tokens.[13] At the same time, these linguistic meanings, e.g. 'sentence meanings', are taken to be actualized or activated in every cognitive or communicative act, in which their corresponding expressions are being used. Expressions "carry with them" their coded meanings. Accordingly, the associated transfer model of communication is sometimes called (slightly misleadingly, in my view) 'code model of communication' (e.g. Schiffrin 1994). Of course, most monologistic theories admit that situated utterances have pragmatic 'utterance meanings', but these are assumed to be derivable given the linguistic meanings (semantic representations) and various contextual conditions and communicative maxims (cf. Grice's 1975, maxims), which would account for e.g. referential meaning (deixis), implicatures, indirect speech acts, metaphorical meanings etc. This, in a nutshell, is the 'inferential model' of Sperber & Wilson (1986).[14]

Many proponents of present-day linguistics and psycholinguistics may object to having their model of language (*la langue, competence*) presented as a "code model", on the grounds that a language is characterized not by a fixed set of signs, but by its 'creativity', i.e. the property of allowing for infinitely many expressions to be generated. However, the point I am making in this context is simply that each linguistic expression (unless it is structurally or lexically ambiguous) is assumed to have one single semantic representation (just like codes are based on expressions with singular meanings), and this semantic

---

12. Swearingen (1990) traces this trend back to Aristotle (see ch. 3.2). Clearly, monologism is very dependent on writing and literate attitudes to language and communication (Linell 1982). Crapanzano (1990) contrasts dialogue, being "agonistic, live, dramatic", not with monologue but with monograph (which "stands alone and is fated or embodies fate", being "pictorial, static, authoritative", op.cit.: 276). Accordingly, one may suggest that dialogism should be contrasted with *'monographism'* rather than 'monologism'.

13. I am referring here to the distinction between 'type' and 'token' as it is commonly used in linguistics. For example, the dictionary entry *cat* is an abstract 'type' belonging to the English language, whereas each specific occurrence of *cat* in situated utterances or texts are 'tokens' of this item. The same distinction applies to sentences, e.g. *The cat is on the mat.*

14. Inference is a central feature in a dialogistic theory of communication too. But actual situated inferencing is not predictable by rule, as in Sperber & Wilson's (1986) theory. On 'conversational inferencing', see e.g. Gumperz (1995).

representation is always activated, used and made relevant whenever its expression occurs in discourse, even if additional interpretations ("indirect" meanings, utterance meanings) are often computed in situ.

2.5 The indirect dependence on written language in monologism

Linguistics and language sciences in general (philosophy of language, logic, theory of literature, cognitive science, psycholinguistics etc), build upon a specific view on language which has been developed over centuries within Western cultures, since antiquity and onwards, both among the more specialized sciences (and arts), such as linguistics, and within civilization at large. Some characteristics of this view have been sketched in the preceding sections. A major reason why the perspectives on language such as these have become so firmly established is the role of writing and written language in our cultures. Scholars, as well as lay people, take written language, or rather certain forms of written language, as the norm for language, for its structure, use, and description. Written language is both a model for what language is like, or should be like, and it is the medium within which we work with and describe language (in texts, dictionaries, grammar books, transcriptions etc). It is therefore motivated to speak of a 'written language bias' in the language sciences (Linell 1982, 1988).

Historically, linguists worked on the standardization, preservation and teaching of (certain forms of) written languages, and as a result of these activities they developed epistemologies, methodologies and technologies, which are still dominant in theoretical linguistics as well as in other branches of the language sciences, e.g. logic, theory of literature, and cognitive science.

This 'written language bias' is seldom admitted by modern linguists. Instead, it is, ironically enough, combined with a totally unquestioned assumption of the primacy of speech over writing.[15] This is typical of the most influential

---

15. There are some good arguments why primacy (in some senses of the term) must be attributed to speech. This holds for phylogenesis, ontogenesis, sociocultural history, and perhaps also in terms of structural relations. However, Harris (1995) has shown that the issue is quite complex, and that writing cannot simply be considered to be derivative *tout court*. Writing has many different forms, functions and origins that are largely independent of speech. This becomes particularly obvious, when we include (as we should) forms of writing that are not 'glottic' (in Harris's terminology). Glottic scripts are basically logographic and/or phonographic, i.e. they have direct spoken counterparts and have been designed to be integrated with (silent or loud) speech in reading activities.

linguists of the 20th century, such as Saussure, Bloomfield, and Chomsky. For example, Bloomfield (1933) declared that "[w]riting is not language, but merely a way of recording language by means of visible marks" (p. 21), and that "[f]or the linguist, writing is, except for certain matters of detail, merely an external device, like the use of the phonograph, which happens to preserve for our observation some features of the speech of past times." (p. 282).

The 'written language bias' (WLB) involves the definition of language as structure or system, rather than as text, discourse or praxis (ch. 1.1). It is also systematically connected to the three approaches to cognition, communication and language structure outlined in the preceding sections. In addition, it comprises a large number of more specific, but quite fundamental and consequential, and yet often unquestioned, assumptions about language. When I now turn to listing some of these, sometimes referring to them as "overemphases", "preoccupations", etc., the reader should keep in mind that my concern is their application to spoken language and interaction (rather than to written language and literacy) (cf. Linell 1982, 1988):

1. Regarding language in general:

- the view that language is the full medium for representing knowledge about the world; in principle, anything can be expressed and communicated in and through language. This reflects the view that a written text can be made indefinitely explicit and precise (and that it, allegedly, liberates the reader from memory constraints that apply to the on-line processing of speech),[16] while it tends to deny that media like pictures, film, music etc. may have potentials that cannot be matched by spoken or written language.[17]

- defining language itself; in the analysis of spoken interaction, the boundaries between language (and verbal communication), on the one hand, and paralanguage and "body language" (non-verbal communication),[18] on the other, are drawn so that the verbal is that part which has a conventional notation in writing.

---

16. Cf. Searle's (1969: 19f) 'principle of expressibility'. For discussion, see Rommetveit (1988: 19f).

17. In cognitive psychology (and, to some extent, also cognitive science), there has been a general 'language bias' also in the sense that cognition is supposed to consist in computations in a language-like system of representation, a "language of thought" (Fodor's (1976) "mentalese") (ch. 2.2).

18. Prosody and paralanguage should be considered part of spoken language (as argued by e.g. Bavelas & Chovil 1994, and Scollon & Scollon 1995). Unfortunately, both dimensions are still strongly under-investigated by discourse analysts (something which applies to this work as well). See, however, Couper-Kuhlen & Selting (1996).

2. In phonetics and phonology:

- the overemphasis on phonemic segments (which are bits and pieces with fairly regular counterparts in alphabetic writing) at the expense of prosody and paralanguage;
- the study of phonetic properties of written decontextualized words, phrases and sentences read aloud (so-called laboratory speech), neglecting the properties of authentic situated talk-in-interaction;
- the concept of 'pronunciation', which presupposes the existence of a linguistic norm sustained by writing (when, alternatively, we could think of speech at the phonological level as consisting in "direct" phonetic acts that are not parasitic on written-language-dependent mental representations); the 'pronunciation' of words is the correct way of representing them in speech (some of the words being encountered first in writing, only then in speech)

3. In grammar:

- the view of mundane conversational language as grammatically incorrect or impoverished;
- the overemphasis on sentences (cf. norms for punctuation in writing expository prose) at the expense of other structures; shorter non-sentential utterances are analyzed as 'fragments', derived by 'ellipsis' from full sentences;[19]
- the idea that grammatical structures are necessarily defined in relation to sentences (cf. the preceding point), i.e. forms that correspond to (what is/was sometimes believed to be) "complete thoughts" (cf. units recommended as units of expository prose);[20]
- a particular perspective on grammatical ambiguities in written language; the grammatical system of the language is understood as generating certain kinds of ambiguous sentences (e.g. *Visiting aunts can be a nuisance*), and such sentences are then 'disambiguated' (by prosody) in speech (i.e. one does not contemplate the opposite theory that writing sometimes "ambiguates" what may be unambiguous in situated talk);

---

19. Cf. what Harris (1981) calls the "doctrine of ellipsis".

20. It is outside the task set up for this book to suggest a grammatical model of spoken language. However, it seems reasonable to argue that basic grammatical constructions are fitted to such chunks of talk that are routinely created as talk and thought are incrementally laid out in real, partly unplanned discourse. For such an approach, see the theory of 'grammar in interaction' (Ochs et al. 1996).

4. In lexicology:

– the preoccupation with fixed literal meanings (cf. definitions in terms of necessary and sufficient conditions in dictionaries)[21] rather than with flexible and open meaning potentials;

5. In semantics and pragmatics;

– the preoccupation with truth conditions at the expense of situational sense-making and interactional meaning, considerations of politeness and tact etc;

– the concentration on representational meaning and the expression of beliefs about the world, at the expense of e.g. practical, instrumental and interpersonal uses of language;

– the overemphasis on individual acts at the expense of social interaction, and an excessive reliance on individual intentions in the explanation of utterances;

– a perspective on the semantics of texts and discourses in terms of signification rather than significance (the latter dealing with how texts and discourses relate to human concerns and interests);

– the view that discourses are consciously planned in advance (rather than being interactionally occasioned and locally produced in an incremental fashion).[22]

– a view of 'direct reported speech' (i.e. the alleged reporting of other people's discourse) as one of verbatim reproduction (as in direct written quotes from other('s) written texts), when we know that such 'reported' discourses are typically constructed by the reporting speaker in his context (by the use of a technique which assigns responsibility for the utterance to somebody else).[23]

Even if many of these points, in radical interpretations of them, may not accurately describe writing and written language either, and even if I have not laid out the full arguments behind the points listed here, it is easily recognised, I think, that all the claims mentioned are much more easily accommodated to facts or assumptions about written language than about spoken language.

---

21. The assumption of literal meanings is what Harris (1981) calls 'the fixed code fallacy'.

22. Classical rhetoric, though dealing with (norms for eloquent) speaking, was, or soon became, heavily based on literate attitudes. Cf. ch. 3.2.

23. See, on this point, Tannen (1989) and Clark & Gerrig (1990). Cf. also Vološinov (1973) and several of Bakhtin's works. Outside of discourse analysis, a related point was made much earlier by Bartlett (1932/1961: 204): "In a world of constantly changing environment, literal recall is extraordinarily unimportant."

Models of verbal language carry over to other semiotic systems and practices. There is a tendency, within the sciences of cognition and communication, to work more or less exclusively with language-like semiotic systems. As we observed earlier, cognition is assumed to be computation in a "language of thought". As a more specific example, consider the case for 'sign language'; even if targetted shapes and configurations are important in this dynamic behaviour, signing is (like speech) more characterized by motion and movement than by postures and positions. Yet, the phenomenon is called "sign language" rather than "signing language".

Once again, the point of my claims about the WLB in linguistics is not that linguists deal exclusively with written language. They clearly don't. Instead, the WLB means that the same theories of language have been, and still are, applied *also to spoken language and interaction*. In Olson's (1994) terms, writing and written texts provide people, including linguists, with "a model for speech". As such a model, it is largely misleading. For these reasons (and others as well), an alternative framework is necessary, an approach to dialogue on its own terms. That alternative account must take seriously such basic properties of spoken language and interaction as *embodiment*, *temporality* and *embeddedness in social action* (cf. Schegloff et al. 1996: 19ff); it must be an account which does not treat language exclusively in terms of abstract, atemporal structures or timeless mental competences.

Finally, it must be pointed out that linguists, especially within certain influential and prestigious branches (e.g. generative grammar), actually do not deal with naturally occurring (authentic) written texts at all, but rather with invented, i.e. normatively redressed and cleaned-up, language, often in the form of contrived isolated sentences, which are both decontextualized and detextualized (Linell 1988). As Harris (1980) has put it, linguists are "language-makers". Yet, this language, described and analyzed by linguists and partly made up by them, is heavily (though sometimes indirectly) dependent on conceptions of written language, and it is of course represented (in papers and books) as written sentences.

2.6 The ontological assumptions of monologism

The monologistic theory of discourse is based on an ontology which acknowledges two kinds of basic entities, *the abstract language system* (and other social structures) and *the individual language users*. The language system is internalized by individuals and is intentionally used by them in cognition and communication. The individual should then be seen as a 'highly complex information processor'. The theory is monologistic, since it assigns authority to two basic systems, the language and the individual speaker. The former 'determines' the linguistic meanings of (well-formed) expressions belonging to the language, and the speaker is responsible for the communicative intentions behind the specific discursive act. At one level, the individual speaker is sovereign in relation to his interlocutors and contexts, and at another, the supraindividual language system is sovereign with respect to the patterns in situated practices. One may talk about a 'double monologicality'.

Accordingly, the monologistic account of language use is secondary to, and parasitic on, a theory of language structure; in the fundamental choice between structure and praxis, priority is given to structure. No primary importance is given to interaction in context; rather, the communicative exchanges are portrayed as 'epiphenomena' (Suchman 1987). By contrast, the dialogistic theory of discourse, which I am going to propound here, assigns primary importance to linguistic praxis. The basic units of analysis are *the communicative interactions* themselves, rather than individuals, intentions, or abstract language systems. In the following chapters I shall lay out some of the properties and consequences of this theory.

CHAPTER 3

Dialogism: Some historical roots and present-day trends

3.1 Interactions, contexts and social (re)construction

Having briefly sketched the fundamentals of what might be taken as the episte-mology of some mainstream theories in the language sciences, I will now proceed to outlining the other major epistemology of discourse and cognition, that of dialogism.

Dialogism will stress *interactional* and *contextual* features of human discourse, action and thinking. Putting it in somewhat loose and metaphorical terms, we look upon the the individual who indulges in communication and cognition as being "in dialogue" with (various kinds of) interlocutors and contexts. The description and explanation of language and language use must be based on a theory of human actions and activities in cognitive and interactional contexts. More specifically, we deal with communicative actions which are other-oriented (and *mutually other-oriented*) in character, i.e. they must be couched in social-interactional, rather than intramental and individual, terms. The other-orientation is there even if the other is not actually co-present.[1] Dialogism stresses the contextual nature of interaction, and the relevant contexts are not only situational but also sociocultural, i.e. historically constituted.

Since we can never ignore the interactional and contextual aspects, it is possible to argue that dialogism regards every cognitive and/or communicative act as an "answer", as *responsive* to something (often only implicit) in the

---

1. I will use the term 'virtual other' about the (intended or imagined) partner in (seemingly) monological activities, e.g. in many cognitive activities performed by individuals when *not* interacting with an actual, co-present person.

contexts.[2] A contribution to dialogue, whether a single utterance or a lengthy spate of talk, is made coherent by being related to some (often implicit) issue ('quaestio') of current relevance; the contribution must be rendered accountable (by the actor or the analyst) in relation to the ubiquitous meta-question "why that now (to me, etc.)". In opposition to this, monologism may be said to put an undue and onesided emphasis on speakers' and actors' initiatives. However, the action attributes of being *'responsive'* and *'initiatory'* are not mutually exclusive. On the contrary, both aspects are always present (in different combinations) and co-determine each other.[3]

In a dialogistic framework, language use cannot be isolated from language structure. The structural (and structuring) resources of language are put to use in cognitive and communicative activities, and are also reconstituted in and through these activities. It is in fact possible to analyse a language (dialect, sociolect, etc.) as part of the abstract contexts of situated communicative actions (see ch. 8). But it is important to realise that, with the dialogistic epistemology, language structure cannot be given priority over communicative practices.[4] These two notions co-determine one another.

In general, one might propose that dialogism, at an abstract level, insists on the *conceptual intertwinement*, the interdependent or dialectical relations, between concepts like discourse and context, content and expression, cognition and communication, tradition and (re)construction, structure and process, individual and society, self and other, speaker and partner, knower and known, initiative and response, background and focus etc. Such notions are only analytically separable. That is, neither of the terms in any such pair can be thought of as explaining (causally or otherwise) the other, or as existing prior to or as definable independently of the other; one cannot analyze one of them without at the same time presupposing something specific about the other. Dialogists sometimes talk about these conceptually intrinsic relationships in terms of *reflexivity* or

---

2. Rommetveit (1990: 97f) attributes to Bakhtin the idea that the "answer" is the canonical utterance type.

3. See esp. ch. 9.6 and ch. 13.4.1.

4. Even the simple term 'language use' is slightly misleading in this context, since it suggests that language is primary, something that is only secondarily put to use in communicative practices. Some researchers (e.g. Liberg 1990) have proposed that we should create a verb which suggests that language is primarily a matter of processes and practices ("to language"; "languaging" instead of "language use"). In ch. 4 I shall briefly discuss the relation between language structure and situated discursive activities.

complementarity (Rommetveit 1992; Marková 1992:56ff., 1997). (A mono-logistic paradigm would prefer to construct each of the above-mentioned pairs as a Cartesian dichotomy of clearly distinct phenomena; it also tends to assign analytical and conceptual primacy to one member of the pair, and can end up with analyses that focus entirely on only that member.)

Dialogism is the general term chosen for the basic theoretical framework propounded in this work. I made this choice with some hesitation, since the term itself has a certain Messianic ring; after all, "dialogue" sounds more positive than "monologue" in many contexts. This is definitely not an advantage for those who want to argue for dialogism; if the term itself is heard as inherently persuasive, it may decrease readers' willingness to approach the real issues with an open mind. It would have been possible to adopt some other general term, such as interactionism, contextualism or social constructionism. However, none of these three can in isolation identify the theoretical stance endorsed here; rather, dialogism incorporates essential aspects of all three of them.[5]

3.2 Dialogism of classical times

In this chapter, I shall briefly describe some of the historical roots of present-day dialogism. However, I cannot account here for their place in an adequate historiography of ideas. Rather, I will use a few historical notes as a way of introducing some recurrent themes of present-day dialogism.

Monologism and dialogism have competed as frameworks for understanding the human mind, and language, cognition and communication, throughout the history of Western scholarship. It is entirely beyond the scope of this work, and beyond the competence of its author, to trace these trends back through history. However, a brief note on an early development in classical Greek philosophy may give a small glimpse of what is sometimes described as the first steps into the hegemony of monologism.

---

5. Other researchers use different names for related frameworks. Marková (1994, 1995) proposes the term 'mutualism'. Shotter (1990: 120) talks about a 'non-cognitive, social-constructionist approach'. Many of my arguments are definitely social-constructionist in nature. However, I do not share all the assumptions of radical social constructionism (ch. 13.4). Rather, I endorse a 'contextual' social constructionism (e.g. Miller & Holstein 1993: 11).

Swearingen (who in turn derives some arguments from Heidegger 1975 [1933]) points to an interesting development from Heraclitus to Aristotle in views on language, from an "ontology" of language as 'action' (in Heraclitus) to one of 'expression' (in Aristotle). Plato, in his dialogues, occupies a middle position, acting, as he did, in a period of transition from a more or less oral culture to a more literate one. The "texts" of the pre-Socratic philosophers were first made public in the context of oral transmission, and Heraclitus's approach to language, or to *logos*,[6] was distinctly fitted to describing oral activities and processes, arguing being seen as active knowers' doings in contexts, 'picking out', 'selecting' and 'stringing together' arguments in discourse. With Aristotle, *logos* was already much more of product and expression, arguments were seen as propositions, the logic of argumentation in syllogisms was begun.

As is well-known, Aristotle contributed greatly to establishing a literate attitude towards the world. With regard to language, there evolved the three language-related arts of grammar, logic and rhetoric, all of which took language to inhere in expressions. Within grammar, the task of categorizing expressions in terms of 'parts of speech' was taken on, and in logic the properties of statements and their interrelations were studied. Rhetoric too, though concerned with the art of speaking, was heavily dependent on a literate attitude, with the speaker first planning and laying out his arguments in a "text", and only then memorizing and delivering this text. In other words, some of the characteristic ingredients of the conception of language within linguistics (and also within other language sciences and in Western literate cultures at large) were firmly on their way to being established as the received view already in Aristotle. If Heidegger and Swearingen are right, an earlier more dialogistic outlook, more salient perhaps in Heraclitus, became overridden and then retrospectively misinterpreted; Swearingen (op. cit.: 59) points out that "[l]ike modern analytic philosophers, Aristotle tends to view earlier philosophers as incipient predicationalists". Thus, we can see "the written language bias" (Linell 1982; cf. ch. 2.5) in operation, and a monologistic perspective inaugurated in classical times. Heraclitus's 'language as action' and Aristotle's 'language as expression' correspond closely to the perspectives on language (and logos) as discourse (practice) and structure (form), respectively.

---

6. *Logos* is a notoriously ambiguous Greek word which is etymologically derived from the root of *legein* 'to speak', cf. Swearingen (1990: 60).

3.3 Before the 20th century

Monologistic approaches, supported by the attitudes of literate societies, have clearly dominated the scene in Western philosophy of mind and language, at least since the Renaissance. The influence of Descartes' thinking seems to have cemented a number of ("Cartesian") dichotomies, taken by monologism to involve contradictory rather than complementary notions: cognition and communication, self and other, expression and content, etc. (see ch. 3.1). These approaches and conceptions have also penetrated deeply into everyday language, and as a result, it is often quite difficult to say anything coherent about discourse without, at least some of the time, slipping into monologistic language (cf. e.g. Reddy 1979). As Giddens says (1984: 32), having once retreated into the code, it proves difficult to reemerge into the world of activity and event.

This does not mean that dialogistic voices have been totally absent in intellectual history. For example, the Italian early 18th-century philosopher Giambattista Vico is sometimes mentioned as an important dialogist (Shotter 1993; Hermans & Kempen 1993; Marková 1997). The French encyclopedist Denis Diderot is another name. One of the forerunners of modern language sciences, Wilhelm von Humboldt, proposed that language should be seen as *energeia*, 'activity', rather than *ergon*, 'product'. In today's terms, this implies an emphasis on praxis and discourse rather than on structure (ch. 1).[7]

A short introduction to the 19th and early 20th century developments in dialogism can be found in Marková (1990a), and Marková (1982) gives a more general treatment of Cartesian vs. Hegelian philosophies.[8] The history of constructivist epistemologies during the last two centuries is largely connected with the philosophy of Immanuel Kant and the various 19th century neo-Kantian approaches, which, in some form or another, stressed the ("dialogical") *interaction between mind and world*. For example, this was the intellectual background of Mikhail Bakhtin (e.g. Holquist 1990).

---

7. For a forceful critique of modern (Saussurean) linguistics for its preoccupation with 'dead objects' (*ergon*, products, texts) rather than living linguistic practices (*energeia*), see Vološinov (1973).

8. Still (1991) provides some relevant historical background to a related ideological contrast, between the mutually opposed metaphysics of cognitivism and social constructionism. Yet another version of the history of the contrasts between monologism and dialogism is provided by Shotter (1993).

Another theme in dialogistic thinking during the past centuries is the *evolutionary perspective*, the interplay of continuity, stability and change. We shall be concerned mainly with the microgenesis of utterances and the socio-historical genesis of communicative genres here, but the arguments pertain to phylogeny and ontogeny as well.[9] Concerning evolutionary perspectives, there are historical links from W. v. Humboldt, Herder and Hegel (Marková 1990a) through Darwin and Wundt to Mead in America (ch. 3.4.3; cf. Farr 1991) and Vygotsky in Soviet Russia (ch. 3.4.4).

I shall not attempt to account for all these historical trajectories of dialogistic ideas. Instead, I will, in the next sections, quite briefly trace a few constituent features of modern dialogism from four different, though mutually dependent, scholarly sources within (mainly) the 20th century.

3.4 Some 20th century traditions

Four intellectual traditions in the 20th century philosophy of the social and human sciences that seem to have exerted decisive influence on modern dialogism are phenomenology, pragmatism, social psychology (social behaviourism), and socio-cultural semiotics. The last-mentioned tradition is largely Russian and Czech, and includes the contribution of, among others, Bakhtin. I shall here simplify my account of these traditions as far as to identify only one or two major ideas deriving from each tradition.

3.4.1 *Phenomenology: Perspectives and multiple realities*

While many of its ideas derive from the philosophy of Kant, phenomenology was largely developed by Edmund Husserl. After him, it was taken further, in somewhat different directions, by Heidegger, Merleau-Ponty and others.

Perhaps the most fundamental insight of phenomenology is that the world appears to us, in our experience, as 'seen' from some *perspective* (Husserl 1973); it is perceived and conceived from a certain point-of-view or position in terms of categories (aspects) that are 'visible' from that particular position (Graumann 1990: 109, 1995: 12). What is perceived and understood is then under the

---

9. Cf. several contributions to Marková et. al. (1995), in particular Pfloog (1995), Papousek (1995) and Farr & Rommetveit (1995).

influence of the subject and his/her point-of-view, rather than being inherent only in the objects "out there". A perspective will make certain aspects of the world stand out as salient; the objects are seen "under certain aspects" (Wittgenstein 1958: 194 et passim). The world as perceived, perspectivized, is "in the eye of the beholder". This applies to perception, cognition and understanding; the subject continuously acts as an active sense-giving force, focussing on certain aspects of the things perceived, conceived or talked about. This implies that an utterance which expresses some kind of understanding will tell its recipient something not only about that which is perceived, understood and talked about, but also about (the position of) the subject who has perceived and understood it, and tries to communicate his understanding; if somebody says, for example, "The population consists of 30% whites and 70% non-whites", the formulation reveals that the speaker finds the categorization of whites vs. non-whites, in contrast to alternative categorizations, to be contextually relevant. As Cuff (1993: 40) puts it, "in telling about the world, [the speaker] is also inescapably telling about himself; in seeing the world 'that way', he is inescapably open to possible findings that he is 'that kind of person who sees the world that way'."

Positions and perspectives, also when taken in an abstract sense, presuppose *contexts*.[10] If something is perceived in a certain perspective, then it is ipso facto viewed against a 'horizon', within the contexts of given background assumptions and with a focus on some objects and events against a background of an environment of more peripheral objects.[11] The thing perceived, which is thereby also being made focal, belongs to a 'thematic field' of relevant phenomena (Gurwitsch 1964; Luckmann 1992). Since acts, and in particular communicative acts, are co-constituted by their contexts, a speaker's utterance also reveals something about the — usually tacit and taken-for-granted — perspective of that speaker, about his "world", frames, 'thematic fields', and horizons.

We have said that perspectives are largely defined by their points of departure; they "originate", have an origo, in some particular position and background. But at the same time, they are "future-oriented" in pointing to a direction in which something, e.g. an understanding or an argument, may be developed. They are parts of specific human concerns and commitments, and

---

10. On contexts, see ch. 8.

11. Thus, notions like background and horizon refer to both 'inner' assumptions and 'outer' margins. On inner and outer horizons, cf. Graumann (1990).

hence also of 'communicative projects',[12] what people are "driving at" in dialogue.

The insight that the world is always seen from some particular point of view, naturally leads us to acknowledge that our various discourses are replete with different 'versions and visions' of the world (Goodman 1978), or in others' words, a multiplicity of perspectives (Dewey, Mead), and therefore multiple realities (James 1996 [1909]). The notion of multiple realities is associated first and foremost with the phenomenology of Alfred Schutz (1962: 207ff.). His work has subsequently been taken further by Berger & Luckmann (1967), Goffman (1974) (the analysis in terms of different 'frames' of understanding), and others. The different versions of persons, events and states of affairs are constructed and occasioned in dialogue, and "discourse analysis focusses upon how specific versions are produced and fitted to the occasions of their production" (Edwards et al. 1992: 441). For example, Rommetveit (1988) discusses how, under different situation definitions, the same activity of a certain Mr. Smith mowing his lawn outside his house in a fashionable suburb, can be discursively described and rhetorically exploited in many ways. Mr. Smith can be seen as doing many different things simultaneously: keeping up his property value, living up to his neighbours' expectations, beautifying his garden, getting some physical exercise, and avoiding the company of his wife, just to mention a few. Similarly, what we say and do in discourse can be heard as belonging to several overarching projects.

In the communicative act, the speaker tries to express some kind of perspectivized understanding. The listener, on his part, must try to understand the message, and is of course, to some extent, subject to his own perspectives. Yet, a communicative exchange is built upon some kind of *reciprocity of perspectives* (Litt 1924); the listener has to try to take the speaker's perspective, and the speaker must monitor his utterances on the premises of the listener, and some-how anticipate the latter's perspectivized reactions and attune his own perspective to that which he (implicitly or explicitly) assumes the listener to entertain (Rommetveit 1974: 55, 112). Communication presupposes some degree of coordination of perspectives, some sort of mutually assumed vantage-points; in empirical fact, however, various kinds of asymmetries exist in how parties manage to set and take each other's perspectives (Graumann 1990, 1995).

---

12. On communicative projects, see ch. 11.

The reciprocity of perspective-taking may be understood as based on an implicit 'contract' on the part of interlocutors, who, in the unmarked case, assume that the other strives for intersubjectivity in communication. Therefore, intersubjectivity is at the same time both the presupposition and the project of the communicative exchange. Rommetveit (1974: 86) formulates this in quite succinct terms: "intersubjectivity must be taken for granted in order to be achieved."

3.4.2 Pragmatism: The gradual emergence of meaning

Some ideas of American pragmatist philosophy (Ch.S. Peirce, W. James, W. Dewey, G.H. Mead) have already been introduced.[13] Here, I shall draw attention to one single feature, particularly associated with the name of William James, and in the next section, I shall point to another specific contribution by G.H. Mead.

As we have seen, monologistic accounts of utterance production assign an almost unrestricted authority, and responsibility, to the speaker, whose communicative intentions purportedly determine the contents of the utterances to be produced. Plans for content and form (cf. Clark & Clark 1977; Levelt 1989) are allegedly distinct and determinate as to the locutionary and illocutionary content of these utterances. A dialogistic account emphasizes the gradual emergence of meanings, as utterances are successively constructed, often in collaboration with the other interlocutors. Plans for utterances are often rather vague and partial (which is one reason for preferring the term 'communicative project', as in ch. 11). There is some leeway for seemingly random processes in utterance production, e.g. as regards instances of lexical access.

The American pragmatist philosopher William James has been credited with giving 'the vague' a proper place in the theory of mind (Still 1991). He argued that the human mind is like a flow of thought, a stream of consciousness, in which only some things are focussed upon and provide resources for talk. As some things are made explicit (and stand out as comparatively distinct), other things remain on the fringe of consciousness, vaguely present as possible associations and implications and potential continuations of the discourse. These

---

13. The term 'pragmatism' (or Peirce's 'pragmaticism'), as used here, refers rather narrowly to a movement largely confined to American philosophy. In modern language sciences, the term 'pragmatics' is of course much broader.

vaguely present meanings are a 'vehicle' for generating further thoughts and verbalizations, offering a horizon of what is not yet fully visible but stands a chance of emerging in the next moments. New ideas and associative linkages "dawn upon" the actors, to borrow an expression from Wittgenstein (cf. Rommetveit 1983). In this dialogical process of topic progression (ch. 10.10), meanings move from vagueness to salience, which gives rise to new vaguenesses on the "fringes". Such an account of the micro-genetic development of vague thoughts into verbalized talk is an example of the evolutionary perspective. It recurs in other traditions too, e.g. in Vygotsky (1986: 218):

> "Thought is not merely expressed in words; it comes into existence through them. Every thought tends to connect something with something else, to establish a relation between things. Every thought moves, grows and develops, fulfils a function, solves a problem."

The same idea can be found in the writings of leading phenomenologists, for example in Merleau-Ponty (1962: 183): "Thought and expression [...] are simultaneously constituted." Shotter (1993: 44) adds to this: "Unformulated in words, a thought-seed remains vague and provides only the possibility of having a meaning."

There are obvious commonalities between phenomenology and pragmatism, e.g. as regards ideas about the movements, in thought and speaking, from potentials to actualized meaning. As we just saw, new perceptions, cognitions and verbalizations occur against a 'horizon' of potentialities for further experience. Even if actors pursue discourse, and understandings, on a topic for an infinitely extended time, there is always an openness left for further exploration. Bakhtin (1984: 313) referred to this by the suggestive phrase "the loophole of consciousness and the word".

3.4.3 *Symbolic interactionism and social behaviourism: The three-step model of communicative interaction*

George Herbert Mead is an important figure for dialogism in several ways, and his work can be interpreted in several perspectives (e.g. Denzin 1992; Farr 1996). He was heavily influenced by the pragmatists (ch. 3.4.2), and can also be thought of as a (kind of) phenomenologist (ch. 3.4.1); his form of 'social behaviourism' which takes anticipation and interactive responding into account is compatible with phenomenology. Most often, Mead is mentioned as a (forerunner of) symbolic interactionism (along with e.g. James and Dewey) (Denzin 1992), although the denomination 'symbolic interactionism' is due to Blumer, not to Mead.[14] Here, I shall draw attention to him as a 'social behaviourist' (a term proposed by ch. Morris, cf. Farr 1996: 81). Mead (1973) argued that "activities are social in that the acts begun within the organism require their completion in the action of others" (p. 446); communicative projects are not individual but require the contribution by the other (interlocutor) for their completion (Leudar & Antaki 1988: 146).[15] It is important, therefore, to distinguish Mead's view on 'behaviour' (or better, interaction), i.e. his social behaviourism, from other types of behaviourism (such as Watson's or Skinner's, or various received views of mainstream behaviourism).[16]

Mead's (1934) analysis of the 'conversation of gestures' is commonly cited for its argument that there need to be minimally three steps (actions, gestures) in a communicative interaction in order for intersubjectivity to get (a chance to be) established. Suppose actor A wants a certain utterance meaning m to be made known to actor B in such a way that (i) B comes to understand m, (ii) A comes to know that B understands m, and (iii) B comes to know that his understanding of m corresponds to what A wanted to make into shared knowledge. If, accordingly, communication aims at making knowledge (meanings, messages) common or shared, then this process involves at least three steps: first A indicates his targetted understanding by an action, most typically an utterance, $a1$, then B indicates his understanding of this by some (responsive) action $b2$, e.g. another utterance, and then A has to show his reaction on B's response by yet another action (utterance, gesture) $a3$. Note that without the third step, while A has access to B's understanding as displayed, or at least partially displayed, in $b2$, B has not yet received any reaction from A and hence cannot know whether $b2$, and its presupposed understanding of $a1$, fits in with A's ideas; hence, no mutual ground and shared knowledge have been established (unless, of course, there are contextually established routines which make such checking procedures unnecessary).

The Meadian argument just reviewed thus provides the conceptual underpinning of Marková's (1987: 137–8; 1990b) three-step analysis of communication, and it also underlies the conception of the single contribution to discourse as Janus-like (ch. 9.2). Similar ideas about minimal communicative interactions

---

14. According to Farr (1996), Blumer's interpretation of Mead is partly a misinterpretation.

15. This perspective permeates the work of Clark (e.g. 1996), who, however, fails to refer to Mead.

16. Cf. Morris (1991). On Mead, see Farr (1990, 1996).

have been propounded by Clark & Schaefer (1987, 1989, who call the whole three-part sequence a "contribution to discourse"). Note that the three-step analysis presupposes that communication ideally involves the *mutual recognition* of the attaining of *shared knowledge*, not only the possible recognition by B of A's intended message. A monologistic theory, on the other hand, with its heavy emphasis on the speaker (here: the one who wants the meaning *m* made known), would rather analyze the communicative encounter as bipartite: saying *a1* (thereby meaning *m*) and then (sometimes but not obligatorily) getting a response *b2* is enough.[17]

3.4.4 *Sociocultural theory: Activity types and semiotic mediation*

While some of the above-mentioned points take care of the local contexts and the dialogical interdependencies between actor and interlocutors, they do not specifically deal with the abstract contexts provided by traditions and routines established over longer periods of time and belonging to the sociocultural environment (frames, genres, cultural definitions). In Mukařovský's terms (Marková 1992: 49), the former are concerned with the 'immediate situations' rather than the 'living traditions' of the latter phenomena. Naturally, the socio-cultural and socio-historical traditions and interdependencies have often been recognized in scholarly history, but not so often within modern psychology and communication studies.[18]

Of particular importance for us here are notions like situation types, activity types and communicative genres. They have been introduced, or perhaps reintroduced, over the last few decades largely via two East European (Russian (Soviet) and partly Czech) traditions,[19] i.e., on the one hand, the sociocultural theory of Mikhail Bakhtin (1986; Holquist 1990; Todorov 1984; Wertsch 1991) and of Prague structuralism (Mukařovský 1977; Marková 1992), and, on the other hand, the social semiotic psychology of Lev Vygotsky (e.g. 1986) and the neo-Vygotskyan 'activity theory' largely developed in the West (Wertsch 1991, 1997; Rogoff 1990). The concept of 'speech genre' (Bakhtin 1986) has later

---

17. See also the account of elements of social action in ch. 9.3.
18. But cf. Bartlett (1932) and others.
19. These traditions are related, and yet clearly distinct. Cf. Wertsch (1990).

been developed, along partly different lines, through Luckmann's (1992, 1995) concept of 'communicative genre'.[20]

Thus, an important point in (my interpretation of) activity theory is that human activities have a history that starts long before the singular encounter in situ. Knowledge, feelings, meanings and messages are not entirely constituted on the spot, but they are re-created, re-produced, re-negotiated, re-conceptualized and re-contextualized in situ.[21] A central idea in Vygotskyan theory is the insistence on finding the genesis of meaning in the combination of the socio-cultural genesis and the situational 'micro'-genesis (but also, when appropriate, its phylo- and ontogeneses), thus recapitulating the 'evolutionary perspective' identified above (ch. 3.3).

Dialogism insists on the inherently sociocultural nature of discursive activities and dialogue. The individual is always supported by, and negotiates with, his partners in talk-in-interaction and the available cultural artefacts. These latter artefacts are crucial also in solitary activities, such as when one is thinking by oneself. They comprise language itself and other symbol systems, and the knowledge borne by these semiotic systems and inscribed in history and in the physical artefacts carrying symbols (writing, computer interfaces, etc.).

What has just been said points to the importance of another idea in 'activity theory': the role of artifacts and tools in human work and human activities in general. Many 'mindful'[22] activities in the world are mediated by tools. The basic unit of analysis in this Vygotskyan theory is "mediated action", i.e. action operating through "mediational means" (Wertsch 1985). This holds for technical tools in various manual or locomotional activities (the carpenter's hammer, the potter's wheel and clay, the blind man's stick, the pole-vaulter's pole). The mediation, and the integration of the tool use in these activities, means that it is meaningless to think of the bodily and mental processes and the mediating tools as two distinct parts of the human work activities; they are integrated as whole systems in human activities. Vygotskyan theory has talked about the role of human language in similar terms; it is a case of semiotic mediation in our interaction with the world. Some researchers prefer to talk, in the case of human

---

20. See ch. 12 for a more elaborated account.

21. On the meaning of the prefix 're-' in these cases, see ch. 4. 'Recontextualization' will become a central notion in ch. 8.

22. 'Mindful', as compared to 'mental', is used as a more comprehensive and appropriate term by activity theorists (e.g. Engeström & Middleton 1996b).

language, about a social prosthesis,[23] rather than a tool; it is embodied and cannot be put aside like a material artefact. Of particular interest are all those technologies that combine properties of material artifacts ("hardware") and language or any other symbolic medium ("software"); writing, pictures, computers, tele- and videotechnology, money, and lots of other artifacts imbued with meaning.

3.4.5   *Summary: Some dialogistic ideas*

By way of summary, I have suggested, so far, a number of related ideas, all opposed to the monologistic idea of a single and sovereign authority and (only) one individual's intention behind any one communicative act. We can summarize the points as follows:

(a)   Cognition and communication are always perspectivized. Each thought or utterance views aspects of the world from some particular vantage-point, thus telling us (as recipients or analysts) something not only about the things talked about but also about the actor's background.

(b)   The meaning of a cognitive or communicative act does not exist in a ready-made form beforehand. Instead, the actor focuses upon and elaborates something (to be) talked about in a process where the vague is verbally constructed and gradually developed into something more precise.

(c)   Any communicative act is interdependent on other acts, usually but not necessarily acts by other actors. A given utterance is a response to what was done (just) before, and in turn it anticipates some sort of expected subsequent response.

(d)   Although cognitive and communicative acts are situation-specific, they make manifest aspects of culturally constituted routines and ways of seeing the world. Cultural identities "speak through" the individual actor.

(e)   Cognition and communication are mediated by language as a sociocultural semiotic 'artifact'.

Dialogistic thought has a long history; the above references give but a few glimpses of it. There has of course also been major theoretical work done in this century. Apart from names already mentioned, one may perhaps point especially

---

23. This is a term proposed by Ragnar Rommetveit (pers.comm.). Cf. Shotter's (1993: 11, 60 et passim) term 'conceptual prosthetics'.

to the philosophy of Ludwig Wittgenstein (1958),[24] who, for example, launched the concept of 'language game', another notion referring to the communicative practices within particular activity types.

On a general level, these points together show how dialogism assigns a central place to contexts and dynamic change. Acts are seen as embedded in a stream of activities, and this applies at different time scales (phylogenesis, sociocultural history, ontogenesis, microgenesis). These points will be part of the leitmotif of this book. In the course of going through additional aspects, other dialogistic points and perspectives will be introduced.

3.5   Some present-day research traditions.: Empirical studies of discourse in interaction and contexts

In recent years the *term* 'dialogism' has become closely associated, if not identified, with the work of the Russian literary scholar and philosopher Mikhail Bakhtin (1984, 1986; also Vološinov 1973).[25] For example, Holquist (1990) uses "Bakhtin and his world" as a subtitle for his book called *Dialogism*.[26] As should be clear by now, I will give the term a broader significance, drawing together threads from many different scholarly approaches that share a number of fundamental principles. Though some ideas of Bakhtin will be ventriloquated (to use his own term) throughout this book, an attempt will be made to ground the dialogistic theory more in empirical data drawn from spoken discourse. After all, Bakhtin was primarily a literary scholar (cf. Bakhtin 1984), and was not in a position to make analyses of conversation. Apart from his very different political predicament, he made his contribution long before the advent of tape-

---

24. For overviews of various theoretical sources of inspiration for dialogistic accounts of human communication, see also e.g. Goodwin & Duranti (1992) and Jacoby & Ochs (1995).

25. As is well-known, there is a scholarly controversy concerning the authorship of Vološinov (1973), and several other works by Vološinov and Medvedev, which have been attributed to Bakhtin (see Clark & Holquist 1984; Holquist 1990). Yet, some specialists, e.g. I.R. Titunik, who translated Vološinov (1973), dispute this view. Others, notably Todorov (1984), have argued that some of the disputed texts were written in collaboration between Bakhtin and the official authors. For a recent summary of some disputes around Bakhtin's work, see Steinglass (1998).

26. When it comes to the *term* 'dialogism', Holquist (1990: 15) claims that it was never used by Bakhtin himself. Marková (1994: 28), traces the term back to the German neo-Kantian philosopher Rosenzweig.

recorders and other necessary technologies.

Modern dialogism has received its main impetus, I argue, from the vast *research into authentic discourse*, especially conversation and institutional discourse, carried out during the last two decades or so. This body of research will be heavily drawn upon in the chapters to follow.

Presently, I will briefly introduce some of the relevant research traditions and sketch some of their characteristic similarities and differences. I will group them partly along lines of disciplinary origin, even though this may seem counterproductive in view of the fact that problems of human action, cognition and communication can only be understood with an interdisciplinary approach. Moreover, it is impossible to give anything like a full account here. That would have necessitated a book of its own. On the other hand, the picture will be filled out with particulars in the subsequent chapters.

It is appropriate to start with *ethnomethodology* and *Conversation Analysis* (CA). Etnomethodology (Garfinkel 1967; Heritage 1984a, 1987) "introduced the idea that familiar and unproblematic as they may appear, mundane social encounters rely on detailed indexical understandings of what might be happening now, what just happened, and what will likely happen next in some particular, located routine activity". (Jacoby & Ochs 1995: 174). Ethnomethodology has later developed into several different directions, notably CA (Sacks et al. 1974; Atkinson & Heritage 1984; Boden & Zimmerman 1991; Sacks 1992; Hutchby & Wooffitt 1998), which is probably the major present-day empirical approach to talk-in-interaction. While Garfinkel has moved more into studies of work in e.g. science labs (cf. Heritage 1987), CA has typically concentrated on 'ordinary conversation', looking at (usually) quite short sequences of actions, each consisting of rather few turns at talk, in great detail. Thus, the cotextual and situational environments of talk are explored, whereas the sociocultural contexts have, mainly for methodological reasons, been left out (Schegloff 1991).[27] However, in recent years, many CA practitioners have moved into the *study of institutional discourse* (e.g. Drew & Heritage 1992), with researchers quite often combining strict CA methods with ethnography and context studies.[28]

---

27. A strict adherence to ethnomethodological principles is not, according to some theorists (Watson 1992), compatible with other more 'contextualistic' micro- (or macro-) oriented approaches.

28. A lot of concepts in this book have been taken from CA, or have their counterparts within that framework. For some introductions to CA, see Atkinson & Heritage (1984; the introduction), Goodwin & Heritage (1990), Heritage (1995) and Pomerantz & Fehr (1997).

To the extent that CA has been concerned only with mundane conversations in Western middle-class (American or British) societies, it has not indulged in any systematic analyses of the sociocultural environments of these conversations. The analysis of activity contexts as well as more comprehensive sociocultural environments becomes more urgent, when studies go into foreign cultures, specialized institutional activities, or communication in technologically advanced environments, to mention just a few examples. While researchers within several of the traditions to be mentioned have utilized many CA insights, they have often also pursued ethnographic studies and/or focused on cognition (e.g. situated or distributed cognition) or the work activities in specialized institutions.

Among those studies that have worked with foreign cultures (or treated specific cultures in anthropological ways), some may be dubbed *ethnographic and context-based discourse analysis* (Corsaro 1982; Moerman 1988; M.H. Goodwin 1990; Goodwin & Duranti 1992; Duranti 1993b). They share many concerns with ethnomethodology and CA, but combine this with ethnographic approaches. A special focus for some sociolinguists and linguistic anthropologists is the analysis of narratives and story-telling (Gee 1991; Gülich & Quasthoff 1986; Ochs & Taylor 1992). Others have combined *linguistic and literary discourse analysis* (Tannen 1984, 1989), often with an anthropological touch (Hanks 1996). An important tradition is that of *ethnography of speaking and interactional sociolinguistics* (Hymes & Gumperz 1972; Gumperz 1982; Auer 1992), where the reflexive relationship between contexts and discourse was recognised at an early stage, partly by opposing an earlier sociolinguistic approach which assumed that discourse features could be predicted from contextual factors. Later work within interactional sociolinguistics, particularly by Gumperz (e.g. 1995), has incorporated a good deal of CA. The same could be said about several strands of *interaction analyses of verbal and non-verbal communication* (Goodwin 1981; Heath 1986, 1992; Kendon 1990).

Most of the approaches mentioned so far have their roots mainly within sociology and anthropology, with some ingredients of (socio)linguistics. There are also various contributions from *empirical or social pragmatics* (Thomas 1995), which combines linguistics with social theory and cultural studies, and should be distinguished from more formal-pragmatic approaches (largely) within mainstream linguistics. Other related traditions, originating from Britain and particularly from the Firth and Halliday traditions (cf. Halliday 1978), can be termed *semiotics of language and culture* and *Critical Discourse Analysis* (Fairclough 1992, 1995), the latter also being influenced by Foucault's discourse notions and, in its empirical analyses, so far more concerned with texts than talk-in-interaction. Being partly emancipatory in orientation, it is also geared towards uncovering partly concealed functions of utterances and texts, thus in some respects being quite different from the more neutrally descriptive concerns of e.g. CA.

Moving into social psychology, it is appropriate to mention the work of Erving Goffman first. In his own ways, he reinterpreted some aspects of the post-Meadian *symbolic interactionism*. Important here are both his earlier work on the presentation of selves and others and on the staging of different interaction types (Goffman 1959, 1961, 1963), and his later work, where he was more concerned with talk in different activity types (Goffman 1974, 1981, 1983). Notions like frames, framing and the multilayeredness of discourse are important here. There are also other forms of symbolic interactionism (Couch 1986; Couch et.al. 1986) that deserve mention. An *interactionist* type of *social psychology* incorporating many features of dialogue theory, Goffman's framing theory and CA is that of Herbert Clark (1996; cf. also Clark & Schaefer 1987, 1989).

Yet another tradition, which has become increasingly CA-oriented, is *discursive psychology* (Harré & Gillett 1994; Edwards & Potter 1992; Shotter 1993;[29] Hermans & Kempen 1993, Edwards 1997); these scholars argue for an entirely "discursive" understanding of psychological phenomena such as cognition, memory and attribution. The claims made are often quite radical, almost amounting to conceiving of the "realities out there" as completely discursively constructed (Potter 1996)[30]

Most of the theories mentioned so far, with the possible exception of semiotics of culture, have been fairly interactionist in character and distinctly social-constructionist (rather than social-realist), as far as social theory is concerned. A dialogistic theory must, in my view, embrace some form of social constructionism. However, it must also take care of the sociohistorical dimension of discourse, the construction of culture, knowledge, attitudes, ideologies, activity frames and situation definitions across situations and time periods. This will take us into sociocultural kinds of social psychology. A major line of research here is *social-constructionist versions of social representations theory* (Moscovici 1984, 1988; Wagner 1996). Social representations theory has been accused of social realism (Potter & Litton 1985), but the main line within Moscovici's theory has

---

29. Shotter (1993) adopts the term 'rhetorical-responsive version of social constructionism' for his present (rather Bakhtinian) position.

30. I find this radical social constructionism contextless. For some arguments, see ch. 13.2.

always stressed the communicative construction, circulation and stabilization of social representations (e,g. knowledge, belief and value systems, ideologies, ways of thinking, acting and talking). However, it must be admitted that few studies within this theory have been made of how these representations are actually constructed or manifestly reconstructed in concrete communicative practices.

Other contributions to the study of cultural and social practices have been made by *socio-cultural semiotics and cultural psychology*, including 'activity theory' (Vygotsky 1986; Wertsch 1985, 1991, 1997). Some of the roots of these approaches have already been introduced (ch. 3.4.4). Central notions include situated and distributed cognition (Engeström & Middleton 1996a), situated learning, apprenticeship in learning and guided participation (Rogoff 1990, Lave 1993). Many studies deal with work activities (often in technologically advanced environments) and with learning under different real-life conditions. Other studies might be termed developmental work studies (Engeström 1987), dealing, for example, with work activities as they materialize before and after technological innovations or administrative reforms.[31] Engeström (1996) argues for a comprehensive notion of 'activity system', comprising agents, objects (topics, cases), communities and their divisions of labour, rules, tools (documents, technology), and arrangements of physical environments, as the locus where work and other activities develop through "tensions and contradictions"; actors are continuously accommodating to such systems, yet at the same time moulding them while making an impact of their own.

Finally, one might mention *interdisciplinary dialogue analysis* (Marková & Foppa 1990, 1991; Marková et al. 1995) as a kind of integrative approach, in which theories of dialogue and dialogism have been particularly emphasized. Ragnar Rommetveit (1974, 1980, 1988, 1990, 1992) has been a key figure here, with his insistence on an interdisciplinary integration of research lines as ultimately the only option for the understanding of human cognition, action and communication.[32] My own approach, as well as work by Marková, Luckmann and Graumann, ties in with this fairly closely.[33]

---

31. See e.g. Haavisto (1998).

32. Besides, Rommetveit's *On Message Structure* (1974) formulates several of the basic dialogistic ideas independently of Bakhtin, i.e. before Bakhtin was known and read in the West.

33. There are developments in *other* fields of the human sciences (i.e. fields that are not primarily concerned with authentic talk-in-interaction) that are, at least in some general respects, compatible with the approach proposed here. One might think of the following traditions (which are obviously

As Jacoby & Ochs (1995: 172) remark, these lines of research have, for a long time, been carried out "in parallel with little or no awareness of one another". Only rather recently, attempts have been made to integrate insights from different traditions. This book can be seen as a contribution to this recent trend. With regard to the notion of co-construction, Jacoby & Ochs (op.cit.: 174) note:

> "Whereas child language and Soviet psychological studies focus on co-construction predominantly on an ontogenetic plane, and whereas Bakhtinian-inspired research focuses on co-construction predominantly on an historical plane, conversation analysis focuses squarely on the microgenesis of co-construction over the span of interactional time."

In other words, some of the traditions mentioned here focus on the situated interactions, sometimes (especially in CA) with an almost total concentration on details in (typically rather short) sequences of talk-in-interaction. Others, e.g. cultural psychology and social representations theory, deal with the sociocultural contexts. The stance to be taken in this book is that dialogue exhibits a *double dialogicality*; it is 'dialogical' both in the contexts of in situ interaction and within the sociocultural practices established over long traditions of indulging in such interactions. Therefore, we need an interdisciplinary and eclectic approach to dialogue.

---

mutually different, and compatible with dialogism on different grounds): various computer-science approaches to dialogue, situation semantics (Barwise & Perry 1983), cognitive linguistics and functional grammar (for an account, see Schegloff et al. 1996), 'cognitive sociology' (Cicourel 1973, 1981), Bourdieu's structuralist constructivism (1989, 1977), 'interpretive interactionism' and 'cultural studies' (Denzin 1992), Lotman's (e.g. 1990) cultural semiotics of texts, dialogism in modern ethnography (e.g. Tedlock 1979; Dwyer 1982), Harris's (1995, 1996) 'integrational semiology' (applied by him mainly to written communication), etc. Finally, there are also points of commonality between our approach and phenomenological and hermeneutic philosophy, e.g. the work of Heidegger, Gadamer, Apel, Ricoeur, and Habermas (e.g. Maranhão 1990; Kögler 1996). These traditions are certainly wildly different on many points, and yet they have some features in common with dialogism. However, it is hardly feasible to explore all these connections here.

CHAPTER 4

Language structure and linguistic practices

A dialogical approach focuses first and foremost on language use, rather than on language structure. However, one can hardly propose a theory of discourse and communication without having some theory of language as a system. The view associated with mainstream monologistic and individualistic theories of language is clearly that of the language system and the individual agents as primary and of interaction as a derived phenomenon; I shall associate this position with *social realism*, since it tends to view language as a system of abstract social objects.

Dialogism may be characterized as a kind of interactionism. But it cannot be construed as (what I will call) *radical interactionism*, which is another position which I shall sketch briefly. Rather, I would argue that dialogism is best conceived of as a kind of *social constructionism* (or even, "reconstructionism") of a kind that I find fully compatible with, for example, Giddens' (1984) theory of structuration. In the following, I shall sketch the two extreme positions first, and then focus on social constructionism.

4.1 The monologistic theory: Social realism plus individualism

The dominant ontology of language which has been underlying much of structuralist linguistics from Saussure (1916 [1964]) onwards has been social realism (objectivism, abstractionism).[1] Languages, as superindividual systems of abstract objects, exist, like other cultural and social structures, as irreducible social facts. Following Durkheim's sociology, languages are simply taken to be "there" as parts of the preexisting social and cultural environment in which language users

---

1. It should be mentioned that the allegedly social-realist position is not the only interpretation that has been made of Saussure's work. Philosophers like Maurice Merleau-Ponty and Paul Ricoeur have argued for an interpretation more in line with phenomenology.

find themselves. Linguistic units are abstract and object-like, and extrinsic to communication. These social objects force us to organize our linguistic conduct in certain rule-governed ways; as social beings and language users, we act according to the logic of society.[2]

Saussure arrived at a model of the superindividual *langue* by abstracting from, i.e. by disregarding, many features of actual linguistic practice (language use, *parole*) The assumption of the abstract objects as socially given is now, in present-day monologism, combined with the postulate that *langue* has become internalized in the minds of all fully competent language users (Chomsky's notion of linguistic competence). Thus, the linguistic structures gets transformed into mental realities.[3] Instead of (only) social realism, we get mental ('cognitive') realism; language exists as individual speakers' cognitive abilities.[4] Through the language use by these individuals, language will then be seen as deployed in actual communication and cognition.

As Rommetveit (1983) points out, the social realism plus individualism characterizing monologism is a fairly peculiar combination. First, a world of abstract entities has been derived through Saussurean abstraction, then the entities of this world are reified, and finally transformed to mental entities, i.e. they are assumed to be part of individual minds, acquired by these minds through a process of internalization. When linguistic structures are assumed to be internalized in individuals' minds, we may come close to an extreme individualism, which denies the existence of social structures as entities sui generis.[5] However, the most plausible interpretation of the monologistic ontology is a dualistic one; there are social structures, on the one hand, and individual agents with their linguistic competence (and other cognitive abilities) on the other.[6] The social

---

2. Objectivist social-realist theories are of course not limited to the case of language. Cultural phenomena in general may be construed as super-individual 'social representations'. For a critique of this version or interpretation of social representations theory, see Potter & Litton (1985).

3. See Katz (1964) for a very clear statement of this 'mentalism'.

4. On 'cognitivism', see Shotter (1991) and ch. 2.2.

5. This is also close to a nominalist position. Cf. Giddens's (1984: 218) critique of Althusser.

6. Real speakers' linguistic competences are of course not quite the same as Chomskyan 'competence', since the latter is, at least according to the classical statements (e.g. Chomsky 1965), a radical abstraction: "Linguistic theory is concerned primarily with *an ideal speaker-listener, in a completely homogeneous speech-community, who knows its language perfectly* and is unaffected by such grammatically irrelevant conditions as memory limitations, distractions, shifts of attention and interest, and errors (random or characteristic) in applying his knowledge of the language in actual

interaction is, on this view, an epiphenomenon, something which can be reduced to the competences and intentions of the individuals acting in a social environment. The Cartesian dualism, on the one hand individuals and on the other abstract social and cultural entities, has created a breeding ground for endless arguments about which of these poles should be assigned analytical (and ontological) primacy. This controversy has been academically institutionalized in terms of the competitive disciplinary interests of psychology and sociology. For example, modern cognitivism is clearly inclined to view individuals as the only basic entities, whilst sociologists like Parsons have argued for sociocultural structures (cf. Heritage 1984a). One may look at interactionism as an attempt to overcome this classical antinomy between individual and society. However, I shall first turn to radical interactionism, a variant distinct from dialogism and an approach which cannot, in my view, resolve the difficulties.

4.2 Radical interactionism

According to this position, there are virtually no other things than the actual interactions themselves, with their interactants entertaining thoughts and producing discourses. The discourses exhibit structures that can be observed *there* in situ, i.e. in the interactions. 'Macro'- phenomena are then simply aggregations over 'micro'-interactions, and macro-theorists are argued to have (misleadingly) reified social structures (social realism, ch. 4.1). The radical interactionist position, which can be said to be micro-reductionist in character,[7] is, I believe, largely a strawman, since there are few, if any, philosophers of language or other scholars who would actually endorse it wholeheartedly. However, Giddens (1984: 140–2) and Turner (1991: 229ff.) have strongly argued against the position of Randall Collins (1981), who, in his plea for a 'micro-translation' of macro-structures, has argued that time and space coordinates (plus number) are the only 'macro-variables' there are outside of the micro-interactions themselves.

There are also some radically interactionist features in behaviourism, e.g. Leontiev's variant of activity theory; according to Wertsch (1991: 120), "Leontiev

---

performance" (op.cit.: 3, italics added). Chomskyan 'competence' deals with (parts of cognition in) a disembodied thinker.

7. It would correspond to what Turner (1991), somewhat loosely and derogatorily, calls 'micro chauvinism'. Similarly, social realism (ch. 4.1) is related to 'macro chauvinism' (ibid.: 628).

lost sight of some of Vygotsky's insights about semiotic mediation", the latter being a crucial part of social constructionism (ch. 4.3). Paradoxically, such an extreme interactionism is paramount to taking a monologistic stance; individuals react causally and unidirectionally on social stimuli and get other individuals to respond in their turn. In fact, both cognitivism (ch. 4.1) and behaviourism are based on individualist psychologies and are therefore monologistic (cf. Farr & Moscovici 1984b; Costall 1991).[8] Farr (1987: 206) notes that the "behavioral basis (of Allport 1924) had a powerful individualizing effect", and Graumann (1986) has pointed out that the individualization of the social goes hand in hand with the desocialization of the individual.

Dialogistic theory stresses the importance of interactions in contexts, but it would be a mistake to equate the position of dialogism (or its variants discussed in this book) with that of radical interactionism.[9] Dialogism is best construed, I will argue, as 'social (re)constructionist' in nature (ch. 4.3); actions, meanings and contexts are situationally constructed, but they are filtered through sociocul- turally sedimented meaning potentials and social representations. These are, of course, themselves of a communicative origin. Thus, dialogism is not 'astruc- tural' in the sense of assuming the absence of a (partially) coherent set of definitions and positions underlying the situated interactions.

Some forms of symbolic interactionism can be interpreted as basically astructural (Denzin 1992; 62–3). The case of Conversational Analysis too (e.g. Atkinson & Heritage 1984; Schegloff 1991; Wilson 1991) is interesting in this context. In its orthodox methodological recommendations, it is strongly inductive, and wants to base its generalizations on properties which are "demonstrably" or "arguably" "there in the discourse itself", and has therefore sometimes been accused of radical interactionism. However, the CA stance appears to be a

---

8. "Cognitive psychologists have perhaps been too busy congratulating themselves on not being behaviourists to notice that they themselves treat people as machines (Skinner 1974: 110; Morris 1991). The mechanistic scheme, and computer metaphors in particular, lead us to regard the problem of cognition as nothing other than the internalized re-presentation of the environment." (Costall 1991: 163). Somewhat in this vein, Linell (1979) points out that Chomskyan mentalism is not incompatible with a behaviourism that builds upon internal mediating variables.

9. Nystrand (1992) dubs Bakhtin and Rommetveit as 'social interactionists', contrasting their position with 'social constructionism'. However, Nystrand appears not to use the terms in the same manner as I do. Though there are several points that need clearing up, Nystrand's 'social interactionism' is rather close to "my" 'social constructionism' (ch. 4.3), whereas his 'social constructionism' is more like "my" 'social realism' (ch. 4.1).

methodological, rather than an ontological, assumption; most CA theoreticians would not deny the cultural embeddedness of interactions. Yet, it may be fair to say that the CA reluctance to bring in ethnographic knowledge into the analysis and its insistence on the construction of social relations, networks, structures, and routines in human practices as being something happening there-and-then in a sequentially and locally organized manner (e.g. Zimmerman & Boden 1991) tend to stress the local dialogicality and contextuality, at the cost of the more global dialogicality which deals with the sociocultural embeddedness of cognition and communication.

4.3 Social constructionism

A structuralist or realist position (ch. 4.1) faces difficulties in explaining the indeterminacy of situations, the practical ingenuity of agents, and the constructive and variable elements in the situated practices of interaction. On the other hand, a radical interactionist theory (ch. 4.2) tends to ignore the impact of material, socio-economic and cultural contexts on ongoing and new interactions. An antidote to these extreme positions is the structuralist constructivism of Pierre Bourdieu (e.g. 1977). Another proposed solution to the theoretical dilemma is Anthony Giddens' (e.g. 1984) theory of 'structuration'.

Giddens (1984) has remarked, with reference to a radical interactionist position, that "social institutions (and language is among them/PL) are not explicable as aggregates of 'microsituations', not fully describable in terms that refer to such situations, if we mean by these circumstances of co-presence (i.e. interactions in space and time/PL)". We would therefore rather adopt a position of social constructionism,[10] according to which linguistic structures, cultural

---

10. I will use the term '(social) constructionism' rather than 'constructivism' in this book. Elsewhere, the terms are sometimes used interchangeably, sometimes with a slight difference in meaning; 'constructionism' (derived from the noun 'construction') might connote an association with socially accessible resources ("construct(ion)s"), whereas 'constructivism' (derived from the adjective 'constructive') has, from time to time, been associated with the individual's constructive activities. Thus, Shotter (1991) argues for the former term, suggesting that 'constructivism' conjures up too individualistic ideas: the individual constructing his or her reality without a social context, a position sometimes (unjustifiably) attributed to Piagetian constructivism. But even if Piaget clearly endorsed an interactional theory of the mind and of cognitive activities, he assigned analytic primacy to the individual (e.g. Wertsch & Penuel 1996: 418–421). Cf. also Wagner (1996: 116).

routines, norms etc. do exist prior to interactions (but only in and through the interactants' being acquainted with them). At the same time, however, these structures, routines and norms are interactionally generated, traded down and reconstructed. That is, they exist prior to individual interactions, yet would not exist without a living historical continuity of interactions. Social structures are (re)created, tried out, tested, negotiated and modified every time they are instantiated or drawn upon. Habit is modified by accommodation, while accommodation is enabled and constrained by habit. Mukařovský's theory of two contexts, the immediate situation and the living tradition (cf. ch. 8.2), should be brought to the fore here; accordingly, Marková (1992: 49) comments, with regard to the dynamic relationship between these two contextures:

> "Within each *living tradition* art is collectively perceived and evaluated in a manner specific to its time (cf. Moscovici on social representations, 1984). This collective perception, however, is not just a straightjacket in which the individual's own perception is imprisoned. Rather, collective perception is constantly shaped and changed through individual perception (immediate situation)." (italics in original). "

In other words, this form of social constructionism assigns the key role to interactions and practices, but views these interactions and practices as dialogically related to a *continuity of praxis*. This, then, is just another way of referring to what I called (ch. 3.5) the 'double dialogicality' of human activities and discourse. Giddens (1984) argues that "(h)uman societies, or social systems, would plainly not exist without human agency. But it is not the case that actors create social systems; they reproduce or transform them, remaking what is already made in the continuity of praxis." (p. 191). And,"[i]n reproducing structural properties, agents also reproduce the conditions that make such action possible. Structure has no existence independent of the knowledge that agents have about what they do in their day-to-day activity." (p. 26). Similarly, a constructionist account of social representations theory (Wagner 1996: 111) views "representation as the significant structure which is exhibited in a series of constructive events."

Peter Berger and Thomas Luckmann (1967), in their seminal book on *The Social Construction of Reality*, view "society as part of a human world, made by men, inhabited by men, and, in turn, making men, in an ongoing historical process." (p. 189). Social structures, taken by social realism to be static objects, will then instead be reanalyzed in terms of a continuously ongoing production and reproduction of social facts. They are lived, situated, practical accomplishments by actors in interaction. In Giddens's "theory of structuration", the dualism of abstractionism-cum-individualism is abolished in favour of a duality of structure (1984: 31, 371, et passim). Structure is "behind" practices, yet not external to them: "structural properties of social systems do not exist outside of action but are chronically implicated in its production and reproduction" (p. 374). It is through communication that relationships, organizations and institutions are talked into continued and renewed 'being' (cf. Boden 1994). There is an "essential reflexivity of action and structure" (Zimmerman & Boden 1991: 19), we see "structure-in-action", rather than structure and action, when "the everyday organization of experience *produces* and *reproduces* the patterned and patterning qualities we have come to call social structure" (ibid.; 19). That is, the relation of language structure to linguistic action and practice is a dialogical one, just like the relation between discourse and contexts.[11]

Social constructionism, in this form, emphasizes two dialogically related phenomena: the constructive and reconstructive practices in interactions, and the sedimented routines and cultures. The latter are global structures superimposed on interactions and embodied in traditions of relatively long-term continuities of practices (cultural traditions), these long-term practices building systems of sedimented, cultural knowledge. Such knowledge has been treated in the theory of 'social representations' (Moscovici 1984, 1988)..[12] New generations of language users can modify these practices, but by and large they have to subordinate themselves to them; we learn from others who take or are assigned privileged positions in communicative activities, these activities being character- ized by asymmetries of knowledge and participation.[13]

The position of social constructionism stresses two 'facts' about communi- cation and cognition, facts which a radical interactionism has difficulties in accounting for. On the one hand, language serves as 'tool' in social interaction; both cognitive and communicative activities are mediated by the use of symbolic means, first and foremost language. Such tools cannot be seen simply as part and parcel of individual interactions. At the same time, these semiotic 'mediational

---

11. Cf. ch. 8. In other words, praxis as actualized discourse and praxis as tradition co-constitute each other, somewhat like acts and activities do (according to the principle of act-activity co-constitution, ch. 5.9.3).

12. While Moscovici, Wagner (1996), and others acknowledge the interactional origin of social representations, such a theory easily gets interpreted as a (weaker) form of social realism.

13. These points will be further explored in chs. 11.6 and 12.8.

means' and the activities in which they are put to use, are sociocultural in nature; they cannot be separated from their contexts. Thus, Wertsch, spelling out neo-Vygotskyan theory, argues that "(t)he processes and structures of semiotic mediation provide a crucial link between historical, cultural, and institutional contexts on the one hand and the mental functioning of the individual on the other" (1991: 67).

The other crucial point is precisely that language lives in different communicative genres or activity types (ch. 12). So, even if a language should not be reified, e.g. understood as abstract, fully integrated 'grammars' or as 'codes' in a strong sense (the ways in which mainstream linguistics would have it),[14] we must of course admit that linguistic behaviour is both structured and symbolic (i.e. codified in a weak sense) and that speakers, and communities of speakers, have accumulated systematized experiences from being acquainted with linguistic practices. In addition, some linguistic structures generalize across situations and genres; this applies particularly to phonology, morphology, parts of syntax and lexicon.

Language structure lives through the continuity of practices, where it gets reconstructed continuously. Within cultures and cultural practices, the role of artifactual support becomes important. The role of writing, and nowadays computers, as infrastructures (hardware) for language (software) can hardly be underestimated. The literate cultures have also had a tremendous standardizing influence on language, thus providing an important part of the explanation why some parts of language structure can be used cross-contextually.

I have characterized the position adopted here as social-constructionist in character. It must be stressed, however, that it is a particular version of social constructionism, roughly what Holstein & Miller (1993) calls a 'contextual' social constructionism.[15] It is contextual in at least three different respects (which will be further discussed in ch. 13):

(a) It stresses the social, rather than individual-psychological, environment for constructing, and reconstructing, versions of the world. However, it must still leave space for individual agency.

---

14. Cf, Harris (1980), Linell (1982, 1997). See also ch. 2.5.

15. Variants of social constructionism have been subclassified in several other ways, e.g. by Krippendorff (1993: 37–38), and in various contributions to Holstein & Miller (1993). A strong version is 'strict social constructionism'. according to which virtually all that there is to "reality" consists of discursively constituted "social constructions".

(b) It does not deny the material environment in which people construct and live their versions of the world.[16] Dialogism does not exclude the existence of the external world.

(c) It transcends (radical) interactionism and argues for the necessity to assume continuities of sociocultural practices. However, it does not support a social-realist point-of-view either.

The construction, conceptualization, negotiation and contextualization of understandings of the world that take place in situated interactions build upon constructions, concepts, negotiated contracts and contextual frames that are in a sense taken as given, and used as resources for re-construction, re-conceptualization, re-negotiation and re-contextualization there-and-then. This aspect of 're'[17] (-conceptualization, -contextualization, etc.) is central to the approach, as it captures the sociohistorical component in human action and communication, and I have sometimes contemplated (but still refrained from) using the somewhat peculiar and awkward term 'social reconstructionism' for this variant of social constructionism. However, in ch. 8 I shall argue for the centrality of the notion of recontextualization.

---

16. There are variants of social constructionism which seem to bracket all kinds of impact from the material world on people's conceptions ('strict constructionism' in Holstein & Miller 1993). See ch. 13.4.2.

17. On the meaning of the prefix 're-'in this context, see ch. 8, n. 32.

PART II

Interacting and making sense in contexts

CHAPTER 5

The dynamics of dialogue

5.1 Conversation as the habitat of dialogical principles

Dialogism is a general framework for understanding discourse, cognition and communication. However, its basic principles are derived from observations of talk in focussed, face-to-face encounters between people; the principles are most salient in conversational interaction and they can be more clearly stated by reference to such data. An empirically adequate theory of dialogue must be based on authentic discourse. To introduce the basic notions of dialogism I will therefore use a number of examples, which are mainly drawn from conversations in informal settings.

My first items are borrowed from Tannen (1984), which is a comprehensive discourse analysis of one single, more than four-hour long dinner table conversation, which took place at Thanksgiving in Berkeley in 1978. Six persons, all around 30 years of age, were present: De(borah) (i.e. the author of Tannen 1984), P(eter), C(had), St(eve), Sa(lly) (who was Steve's former girlfriend), and Da(vid). Extract (1) occurs rather early in the four-hour recording; a couple of the participants have discussed some interesting books (by Erving Goffman, in fact) that they have read, and now De(borah) asks P(eter) about his general reading habits:

(1) READING, EATING AND BEING BUSY (Tannen 1984: 81–2)[1]

(...)
```
1.  De:    do you read?
       (1.0)
2.  P:     do I read?
       (0.5)
3.  De:    do you read things just for fun?
       (1.0)
4.  P:     yeah (1.0) right now I'm reading Norma Jean the Termite
           Queen ((laughs))
5.  De:    what's that? (1.0) Norma Jean like uh: (1.0) Marilyn Mon-
           roe?
6.  P      it's (.) no (.) it's a book about -- (2.0) a housewife
           (xxx)
7.  De:    is it a novel or what.
8.  P:     it's a novel.
9.  De:    yeah?
10. P:     before that (1.0) I read the French Lieutenant's Woman?
           have you [read that?
11. De:             [oh yeah? no. who wrote that?
12. P:     John Fowles.
13. De:    yeah I've heard that he's good.
14: P:     he's a great writer. I think he's one of the best writ-
           ers.
15. De:    =hm. (xxx)
16. P:     he's really good.
17. De:    (xxx)
       (3.0)
18. P:     but I get very busy. (1.0) [y'know?
19. De:                              [yeah I (.) hardly ever read.
       (1.0)
```

---

1. See Appendix I for a summary of the transcription conventions adopted in the examples. There are some inconsistencies in the ways excerpts are reproduced. These are mainly due to differences amongst the source transcriptions used in works cited.

In relation to CA practices (cf. Atkinson & Heritage 1984) (and also to my own interactionist credo, according to which many subtle interdependencies and details of delivery could (and should, when appropriate) be explored; on the importance of narrow transcription, see the comparative exercise in Hutchby & Wooffitt 1998: 85ff.), transcriptions are very much simplified. The reasons are mainly the following:

(a) The excerpts are used to illustrate and discuss points of general significance. The aim is not an exhaustive analysis of the individual excerpts. In general, I am more concerned with dimensions of meaning other than those which are dependent on subtle timing and prosody.

(b) The source transcripts cited are often simplified in the originals.

(c) Several excerpts have been translated from another language, i.e. Swedish, which makes the rendition of some verbal subtleties as well as the prosodic patterns very problematic.

It should also be said, however, that CA transcriptions are also selective; for example, they pay very much attention to exactly timed pauses, at the expense of stress patterns, intonation contours etc. No transcript can capture everything.

```
20. P:   what I've been doing is cutting down on my sleep.
21. De:  oy! ((sighs))
22. P:   =and I've been ((St laughs)) (1.5 ) and I [s-
23. De:                                            [I do that too
         but it's painful.
24. P:   =yeah. fi: ve, six hours a night, and
25. De:  =oh God, how can you do it. you survive?
    (1.0)
26. P:   yeah late afternoon meetings are hard (De: mmm) (1.0) but
         outside of that I can keep going [pretty well
27. De:                                   [not sleeping enough is
         terrible (1.0) I'd much rather not eat but [not sleep
                                                     [((Sa laughs))
28. P:   I probably should not eat so much, it would (.) it would
         uh (0.5) save a lot of time.
29. De:  if I'm (like really) busy I don't I don't I don't eat. I
         don't yeah I just don't eat but [I
30. P:                                   [I- (.) I tend to spend a
         lot of time eating and preparing and [(xx)
31. De:                                        [oh: I never prepare
         food. (2.0) I eat whatever I can get my hands on.
32: P:   =yeah.
```

The second extract from the same dinner-table discourse, and the talk has now focussed on hands (sic!):

(2) SHAKING HANDS WITH RUBINSTEIN (Tannen 1984: 122–3)

```
1.  Sa:  I shook hands with Rubinstein once? (1.0) [and his hand
2.  St:                                            [yeah we did
         together.
3.  Sa:  that's right. we were together. wasn't it incredible?
4.  St:  ((laughing)) oh it was like a cushion.
5.  Da:  =what's this?
6.  Sa:  [I (0.5)      we shoo]k hands with Rubinstein.
7.  St:  [Rubinstein's hands.]
    (2.0)
8.  De:  and he had --?
9.  Sa:  =his hands --
10. De:  short stubby hands?
11. Sa:  =they were like (0.5) [jelly. they were like -- (1.0)
12. St:                        [a famous concert pianist
    Sa:  they were like (0.5) putty. (0.5 )
13. De:  [really?
14. Sa:  [just (.) completely soft and [limp.
15. St:                                [mush
    (1.0) ((De chuckles))
16. Sa:  just mush. it was as though there was [no bone
17. St:                                        [and warm.
18. De:  and short stubby fingers?
```

```
19. Sa:    >short stubby fingers but just< (0.5) totally covered
           with --
    (1.0)
20. St:    fat.
21. Sa:    =fat.
```

5.2 The sequential organization of a social activity

The first point to notice about a dialogue is that it cannot be adequately characterized as a series of individual actions. Each utterance, act or turn by any
speaker is thoroughly dependent on what his or her interlocutor(s) do(es) in the
same interaction; we are confronted with a *social practice*, in which actors
interact and communicate, and in which the individual contributions cannot be
understood in isolation from each other. The utterances or turns are *sequentially
organized*, i.e. their interactional significance is intrinsically dependent on their
positioning in the sequence.

If, correspondingly, we phrase the issue in terms of utterance meaning, we
would claim that the individual utterance has no communicatively relevant
interpretation if taken in isolation. Rather, the verbal composition of the utterance
in combination with its sequential positioning (and other contextual factors) make
actors mobilize inferrable meanings.

Turning now to the excerpts, take, for example, Peter's question in 1: 2, "do
I read?, which must be understood in relation to Deborah's preceding question
in 1: 1; what Peter does in 1: 2 is apparently to ask for a repetition or clarification of a prior utterance, and it uses the same words as that prior utterance,
barring the obvious change of pronouns. Arguably, Peter did not quite understand
what Deborah meant by her somewhat unpredicted general question about
reading habits in 1: 1. At least, this seems to be how Deborah herself interpreted
Peter's counter-question; in responding to 1:2, she reformulates her own previous
question (1: 1) in 1: 3, adding a specification ("just for *fun*"), which is then
sequentially dependent on both 1: 1, the start of the speaker's (Deborah's) local
'communicative project' (ch. 11) of finding out about Peter's reading interests,
and on 1: 2, i.e. the addressee's request for additional specification of what sort
of communicative project he is supposed to contribute to.

The utterances 1: 2 and 1: 3 thus derive a good deal of their meaning from
their positioning within a particular sequence of communicative actions. This
point applies quite generally to acts in discourse. Even the very first act in the

topical episode involved, Deborah's soliciting initiative in 1: 1, is not entirely unrelated to what went before (the talk on reading Goffman not cited here), though apparently it came a bit unexpectedly.[2] Yet, the contextual relevance and sequential dependence are of course more clearly displayed, once we have moved into a topically more close-knit sequence. One cannot rip out any single utterance and understand what it means in isolation, for example by figuring out what the words mean in and by themselves. This is obvious for both minimal responses like 1: 8, 1: 12 and 2: 20 or expanded responses[3] like 1: 19, 1: 24 or 2: 4: it is just impossible to understand the meaning or appreciate the significance of, for example, "five, six hours a night" (1: 24), "John Fowles" (1: 12), "fat" (2: 20) or "it was like a cushion" (2: 4) without knowing what questions they answer or what local contexts they appear in. Many utterances are quite elliptic, and yet they make perfect sense in their particular sequential position. The relevance of the position also applies to initiatives which take up new topics or topical aspects, such as 1: 18 or 2: 1. Each and every contribution to a dialogue gets interpreted partially on the basis of the sequentially prior contributions. Conversely, these prior contributions display their 'sequential implicativeness' (Schegloff & Sacks 1973: 296) through this impact on the situated meaning of the following contributions. We can therefore say that elementary contributions to discourse are 'doubly contextual' (Heritage 1984a: 242); they are responsive to prior contexts and contribute to renewing contexts.

5.3 Coordination and synchronization of utterance segments in dialogue

The principle of sequentiality does not necessarily mean that utterances and actions literally *follow* each other in the interaction.[4] They can be simultaneous or partially overlap. The crucial aspects actually concern the *timing* and pacing of different segments with respect to each other (Clark 1996: 42). Separate actions by different speakers must be coordinated and mutually adjusted in a subtle process of dove-tailing utterance segments. The joint alignment involves

---

2. It is an example of recontextualizing an element from a prior episode, according to the taxonomy of ch. 10.7.

3. On minimal and expanded responses, see ch. 9.

4. In fact, the idea of a strict sequential ordering might be an aspect of the 'written language bias' (cf. how lines are printed in written dramas) as discussed in ch. 2.5.

pace and rhythm, stress and intonation patterns, and non-verbal accompaniment. Many interactions exhibit astonishingly perfect timing and synchrony, others involve asynchronies that may be perceived as misalignments and uncomfortable moments. To see such subtleties, one needs rather detailed transcriptions of a kind that have not been used in this book.[5]

To see some aspects of timing in a very short excerpt, consider the following strip of discourse taken from Goodwin & Goodwin (1992):

(3) THE ASPARAGUS PIE (Goodwin & Goodwin, 1992: 168–172, et passim) ((D = Dianne, C = Clacia.[6]))

```
1.  D:    Jeff made an asparagus pie

          it was <s::so[:> <goo:d>
               <--1----> <--2--->

2.  C:            [<I love> ≤it>.   <°yeah I love tha:t°
                   <--3---> <4->    <5----

((in intervening turns, Dianne describes in greater detail Jeff's
asparagus pie))

3.  D:    en then jus'(cut-up) the broc'-'r the asparagus coming

          [out in spokes.<=°it wz s<o good°>
               <6---       <---7--->

4.  C:      [°°(<oh Go:d that'd be fantastic)°°
               <8----
```

Legend: <1> = D lowers upper trunk; <2> = D: nod with eyebrow flash; <3,4> = C nods; <5> = C starts to withdraw gaze; <6> = D withdraws gaze from C; <7= D: assessment headshakes; <8> = D withdraws gaze

Goodwin & Goodwin analyze the finely attuned verbal and non-verbal aspects of this "small activity system" (op.cit.: 181) in great detail, making many observations. We see how the activities are collaboratively produced, but with different contributions by the two interlocutors due to the asymmetry of knowledge about

---

5. Cf. fn. 1.

6. The pointed brackets (<, >) inside and under the relevant parts of the verbal utterances indicate where in time the associated para-linguistic gestures occur. Note, therefore, that < > does not carry its conventional (CA) meaning (slowed-down speech) in this particular example!

things talked about; Dianne knows about the particular asparagus pie (Jeff's pie) being assessed in the talk, while Clacia joins in with general assessments. Note the differences in tense and referential expressions: Dianne uses the past tense (3: 1: "made", "was") and specific reference (3: 1: "it (was so good)"), whereas Clacia uses the present (generic) tense (3: 2: "I love") or the hypothetical conditional (3: 4: "that'd be") and a generic reference (3: 2: "that"), presumably referring to asparagus pies in general.

In the first exchange given (3: 1–2), we see Dianne projecting (what is apparently going to be) an assessment, and Clacia perceiving the initiation ("s:so:") of the assessment even before the main assessing item ("goo:d") has been pronounced: she joins in (3: 2), apparently herself adopting the assessment project cued by Dianne as her own. Clacia contributes to the assessment, overtly transforming it into a joint one, though she does it from her point-of-view, expressing a generic appreciation of asparagus pies (rather than of Jeff's specific pie).

The second exchange unfolds in a rather similar way. The assessment progresses from a preparatory stage to a peak of heightened mutual involvement, and then through a stage of withdrawal, all orchestrated both by verbal and various non-verbal means. Thus, we can discern an assessment structure approximately as follows (cf. Goodwin & Goodwin, op. cit.: 182):

A.   precursors to assessment (=B)

B.   peak of involvement (jointly produced assessments)

C.   procedures for withdrawing from (B)

The episodes analyzed embody several communicative projects at the the same time (on communicative projects, see ch. 11); we can see the multi-functionality of utterances, actions and discourse segments clearly illustrated. For example, the episodes exemplified can be heard not only as assessments.·. The discourse contributions are also resources for closing the topics involved. The assessments seem to mark the events or circumstances mentioned, or the story told, as worth mentioning or telling (as 'mentionables' or 'tellables'). At the same time, in the second exchange, the conversationalists jointly project and carry out a topic closure (op.cit.; 170). By withdrawing gaze while saying "spokes", and then lowering her speech volume, Dianne proposes a (project of) topic closure, and Clacia, in and through her *sotto voce* utterance "°°oh Go:d that'd be fantastic°°", accepts this and contributes to closure by lowering volume even more and by upgrading the assessment (from "good" to "fantastic"). Thus, the closure project, too, unfolds according to the pattern: first initiation/proposal, then acceptance and joint completion (cf. ch. 11.4).

5.4 Co-accomplishment in concerted activities

Structures in discourse take shape through the collaboration of the interactants involved. This applies to participation and interaction, to meaning and content, and also to expressions used in dialogue.

In and through their dialogue contributions, parties *guide each other's participation* in dialogue.[7] Due to various asymmetries of knowledge and interests, parties are often not equal in these endeavours. One party may sometimes, at the expense of the others, take on more of the role of the guide and perspective setter. This was, for example, true of Deborah in (1). An asymmetrical participation is typical of many institutional interactions, in which professionals tend to ask questions, and lay clients, patients and interviewees respond to these questions (ch. 12).

Another point is the joint development of topics and conversational episodes (ch. 10). Note, for example, the topic development in (1) with topics gliding from habits of reading to eating (and preparing food) via talk on sleeping habits. This is clearly a result of the collective, and collaborative, *development and negotiation of meaning*. True enough, Deborah seems to be the one who introduces eating (1: 27), but she does it because there has been talk on lack of time and on sleeping, the latter topic first mentioned by Peter (1: 20), who, however, in his turn is dependent on the common topic of reading which the two together developed into the topical aspect of "finding time for reading when you are very busy" (cf. 1: 18), which provided the bridge for proceeding to talking about other ways of saving time (1: 19ff.). Topics, then, are typically joint constructions; it takes two to establish something as a topic, and the same is true for the development and closing of topics (ch. 10). Similarly, communicative projects and speech events, e.g. miscommunication sequences, are collaboratively managed (cf. ch. 11). Conversationalists are partners in concerted activities.

The co-accomplishment of discursive activities and the resulting texts (with their topics) is a property first and foremost of the interactions and their meanings,

---

7. On 'guided participation', cf. Rogoff (1990).

but it applies to expressions, i.e. the more overt behavioural units, as well. Thus, conversationalists typically borrow words from each other, when they build up their utterances; the other's utterances provide the basis for frequent repetitions of key words. Re-use, or repetition, of others' (and one's own) words is typical of impromptu speech and conversation (Ochs 1979). (Also, the occurrence of particular words may "touch off" the use of semantically or phonologically similar words (ibid.: 74). In addition, prior words occasion anaphoric practices such as the use of pronouns and ellipsis.) Thus, (1) is replete with occurrences of the same (or lexically closely related) words over adjacent utterances; compare, e.g. "read" (and the whole construction "do I/you read") in 1: 1,2,3,4, "Norma Jean" in 1: 4,5, "book" to "novel" in 1: 6,7, "novel" in 1: 7,8, "good" in 1: 13,16 (and "good" to "great, best" in 1: 13,14) etc., all involving transitions across different speakers' turns. The same applies of course to (2), which is an episode where two speakers tell about a common experience, that of shaking hands with Rubinstein. In (2), we witness how a story can be told collaboratively, with a lot of reciprocal feedback seeking and giving, duetting (speakers saying almost the same thing at the same time)[8] and completions of other's utterances and thoughts. For example, Sally's sentence in 2: 18 is left unfinished by her, but Steve steps in and supplies a word, "fat", which completes the sentence,[9] whereupon Sally herself immediately echoes this completion. Together, in talking about Rubinstein's hands in lines 2: 11–12,14–16, they compose two different 'three-part lists', "they were like jelly, they were like...they were like putty, just mush", and "completely soft and limp and warm," both lists initiated by Sally and completed by Steve. The collaborative use of such lists is a resource for them both to demonstrate their shared experiences and to construct the telling of them.[10] As a result, the coherent, situated interpretation is assembled over two speakers' different utterances.

In other words, in dialogue speakers often "appropriate other's words" (Wertsch 1991: 59). Speakers are deeply dependent on others, not only in the

---

8. Cf. 'conversational duet' (Falk 1980).

9. This phenomenon is usually called 'collaborative completion' (Lerner 1989), 'spontaneous completion' (Wilkes-Gibbs 1986, 1995) or 'proxy completion' (Clark & Wilkes-Gibbs 1986). See also Sacks (1992: I: 321, 647ff. et passim) on 'co-producing utterances'. Lerner (op.cit.: 173) characterizes collaborative completion as follows: "In the course of one speaker's turn, a next speaker begins to speak, producing an utterance which is a syntactically fitted continuation of the current speaker's utterance-in-progress". See also Leudar & Antaki (1988) on 'other-completion'.

10. On the use of three-part lists, see Jefferson (1990).

long-term perspective of cultural competence (using words from the language traded down to them), but also in the most local contexts, from utterance to utterance, where they find each other's words reasonably relevant and felicitous for the current concerns, and hence appropriate them for their own use. Bakhtin (1981: 293–4) captured this insight in the famous wording: "the word is half someone else's" (cf. Wertsch 1991: 70).

The locally occasioned appropriation of other's words seems to be a universal dialogical phenomenon, and it is sometimes called 'tying'.[11] There are of course empirical variations in its use and occurrence. Children and adolescents, for example, seem particularly prone to take up others' words and concepts, reuse them and often elaborate on them in a mocking way. The following is an example discussed by Sacks (1992: I: 538–9):

(4) THE BIRTH CONTROL PILLS (Excerpt taken from a conversation between several teenagers attending a group therapy session. T=therapist, R=Roger, A=Al, K=Ken, L=Louise)

```
 1.  T:    'cept that it is part of the function of the group to
           begin to share uh in some of these things, so that the
           others can understand themselves (xxx)
 2.  R:    well that's why we're pumpin'...him
 3.  T:    right. right. no, I was (xxx) answering Ken.
 4.  A:    I have to adapt myself to the idea that I want --
 5.  R:    you don't feel secure with us.
 6.  T:    butchu don't... wanna --
 7.  A:    that's right.
 8.  T:    as I said... earlier you don't want to adapt...yourself out
           of existence, Al
 9.  R:    I'm gonna blackmail you.
10.  A:    fuck you ((K indicates laughter))
11.  R:    better not, I become pregnant easy heh... hehh heh hhhh
           ((laughs))
12.  L:    ((laughs)) take birth control pills.
           ((R laughs))
13.  A:    hey I saw... saw a real neat ... joke
14.  K:    the little green pills?
           ((somebody coughs))
15.  A:    I went down to the Ports O'Call Village, not to be
           changing the subject but she brought it up --
16.  R:    not to be change -- *I wouldn't change the subject*
17.  A:    but there was a birth con-- they had a joke shop with a
           birth control pill and it was made out of styrofoam. put
           it between your le- legs' n press very hard.
     ((L laughs and A joins in))
```

---

11. Sacks (1992); M.H. Goodwin (1990: 177ff.) ('format tying').

The point about this example has to do with how these adolescents develop their topics very rapidly by non-focal associations to and comments, partly meta-comments, on prior contributions.[12] Thus, when Roger challenges Al in 4: 9, the latter snubs him with the expression "fuck you" (4: 10), which makes Roger counter this expletive comment by mockingly (it seems) taking it "literally". This provides Louise with an opportunity for another, similarly "funny" comment (4: 12). This, in turn, apparently (note "hey" as a sudden recall marker) reminds Al of a topically related joke (4: 13), which he subsequently (4: 17) tells. However, in the meantime, Al has exculpated himself of "changing the subject" (4: 15) claiming that Louise is actually the one who "brought it up" (presumably through 4: 12, i.e. the contribution which made Al associate to the joke, as indicated in 4: 13). Al's side comment on "not changing the subject" (4: 15) makes Roger issue yet another mocking remark (4: 16). Sacks suggests (op.cit.: 540) that the 'tying structures', i.e. the local recontextualizations (ch. 8) of concepts in prior utterances (tying utterances together in pairs), provide conversationalists, at least in this kind of situations, with a resource for developing topics.

If conversationalists develop topics jointly in such a way that no topic is uniquely a particular individual's property, if speakers appropriate words and concepts from each other and complete each other's utterances and thoughts, then we are obviously faced with very complex cause-effect relations in discourse. No speaker is alone in authoring her utterance; to some extent she shares the responsibility for what gets said with her fellow conversationalists (ch. 6). Through the interplay of their actions, actors try to guide each other's participation and understandings in dialogue. There is a *reciprocal and mutual*, partly simultaneous, *shaping of the discourse*.

If discourse, with its constituent episodes and topics, develops as a joint construction, then it seems hard to explain it properly by recourse only to individual speaker intentions (ch. 11.2). Utterances do not realise communicative intentions that have been established prior to verbalization; rather, there is a constant interplay between the speaker, his interlocutor(s) and contexts. Verbalization and content formation are locally and jointly produced, and have *emergent* qualities.

---

12. 'Non-focal' means, in this context, that a contribution ties up with semantically and contextually so-far peripheral or tangential aspects of a prior contribution. See also ch. 9.3.

5.5   Interaction as expressing and testing mutual understanding

Communication serves to develop shared and mutual understandings. The chief mechanism for exposing one's own and testing the other's understandings is inherent in dialogue itself, in the successive steps of sequences of utterances and turns. Thus, each utterance in a dialogue, e.g. in (1), (2), (3) or (4), can be taken to expose parts of its speaker's understanding of a certain topical aspect, with the proviso, of course, that much of this understanding is taken over from others and need not always represent any remarkable depth of understanding on the part of the speaking individual. At the same time, speakers use utterances to elicit responses from their interlocutors and to test their own understandings of various topics and topical aspects. For example, one can say that Peter's 1: 2 displays his provisionally limited understanding of what Deborah's question in 1: 1 is about, and that Deborah's 1: 3 represents an attempt on her part to specify a little more clearly what she meant in 1: 1. At least, this seems to be what she *then*, after having heard Peter's 1: 2, claims her interest to have been in 1: 1. Peter's 1: 4 then is his answer to 1: 3, and indirectly to 1: 1, and provides (parts of) his understanding, or knowledge accessible at the moment, of the topic raised by Deborah's communicative project. In 1: 5, Deborah shows her interpretation of 1: 4, which evidently comprises a request for further information on some details involved in Peter's answer (1: 4). And so on, and similarly in the other dialogues.

Understanding a prior utterance and responding to it are closely related activities. Indeed, understanding an act or an utterance involves, as central elements, fitting it into some kind of context, prior knowledge etc, and reacting to it by preparing an adequate response. When Bakhtin says that all understanding is responsive, this must be taken to refer to both retrospective elements, i.e. assigning a situated interpretation to something just encountered, e.g. a prior utterance, and prospective elements, i.e. preparing for a response to that utterance which was just encountered.[13] Bakhtin thus points to the fact that the understanding of somebody's utterance ordinarily involves active treatment of that utterance, this treatment partially consisting in the formulation of an actual 'response', i.e. a new utterance. (In some cases, such a reaction may of course remain a silent, "inner" response.) In Bakhin's (1981: 282) words:

---

13. Thus, both the utterance and the understanding of it are bi-directionally related to the immediate surrounding action context. More on this "Janus-faced" nature of dialogue contributions in ch. 9.

"[...] To some extent, primacy belongs to the response, as the activating principle: it creates the ground for understanding, it prepares the ground for an active and engaged understanding. Understanding comes to fruition only in the response."

Accordingly, in authentic dialogue each speaker uses her own turn to display how she takes up the other's prior contribution. Conversely, each speaker can take the other's response as an indication of how he (the other) understands what he has just heard and responded to. Specifying or determining understandings "involves a complex back-and-forth process of negotiation both between speaker and hearer, and between what has already been said and what currently is being said." (Shotter 1993: 27).

Schegloff (1984: 38) also points out that "utterances are built to display speakers' understanding". One might propose, as a minor amendment, that they display *parts of* speakers' understanding, since there are clearly some layers of interpretation which never get expressed. Yet, one can say, following Schegloff, that by displaying parts of their understandings speakers make them publicly accessible and therefore communicatively relevant. Other parts of individuals' understandings may remain private, and therefore communicatively irrelevant, until they somehow get expressed or "leak out".

Speakers know, at some level, what they say and what they mean by their utterances. This means that they can ordinarily 'account for', i.e. explain or justify what they say and why (they think that) they do it. Ethnomethodologists refer to this as the 'accountability' of social actions. As we have seen, interlocutors use their utterances to demonstrate, or document, to each other how they interpret what is going on.[14] This aspect has a clearly moral dimension; speakers are 'held accountable' for their actions and utterances, and use the very same utterances to 'account' for what they mean (Garfinkel 1967: 1).[15]

Thus, if understandings are to be communicated, and intersubjectivity is to be achieved, "one's responsive action to them (i.e. others' utterances/PL) can be

---

14. To some extent, it is a question of demonstrating to the other how one would *want him or her to interpret* what is going on, which opens up for opportunities of redressed (indirect) expression (on politeness phenomena, see Brown & Levinson 1987) and also attempts at downright deception.

15. On 'epistemic' (and other kinds of) responsibility for discursive actions, see Rommetveit (1991a) and Linell & Marková (1993). See also Muhlhäusler & Harré (1990). On the ethnomethodological notion of 'accountability', see e.g. Garfinkel (1967), Watson & Sharrock (1991), among others.

reflected only in the expression of one's own speech" (Bakhtin 1986: 91). In other words, there is a fairly close interdependency between understanding and responding/speaking (preparing for one's own verbalizations), and not the great divide assumed by monologism, i.e. between an active speaker, who has already understood what he wants to say, and a "passive" recipient, whose task is merely to recreate the speaker's understanding. Both speaking and listening involve sense-making (ch. 6).

The foundation of communication and intersubjectivity lies in interlocutors' display of understanding, or partial understanding, and of (partially?) shared and mutual understanding, in and through their utterances. But communication does not presuppose or produce total sharedness of meaning; rather it consists in people's *attempts to expose and test their understandings*. Shotter (1993: 1) argues: "Most of the time, we realize, we do not fully understand what another person says. Indeed, in practice, shared understandings occur only occasionally, if they occur at all. And when they do, it is by people testing and checking each other's talk, by them questioning and challenging it, reformulating and elaborating it, and so on." Goodwin & Goodwin (1992) argue that "in order to achieve coordinated action participants must display to each other the intelligibility of the events they are engaged in, including what activities are in progress and what they expect to happen next." (p. 173). This is what we have seen actors doing repeatedly in the examples above.

Speakers do not, and can not, express all aspects of meaning that could be made relevant for the interpretation of their utterances, or for the situation at large. Rather, speakers give cues to the interpretation of their utterances, i.e. they give indications of their understandings of things talked about and of the social identities and interpersonal relations that are presupposed, or are being developed and achieved. In other words, understandings are *inferred* from utterances-in-contexts (ch. 8), rather than expressed in utterances. Gumperz (1982, 1995) has developed a theory of contextualization cues and conversational inferencing, which builds upon these kinds of insights.

We can sum up these points by claiming that discursive interaction is used to expose and test mutual understanding. In the textures of actions, responses, and new responses to these actions and responses, each conversationalist is "able to monitor not only what the other says but what the other understands (himself) to have said" (Bilmes 1988: 35).

5.6 The local production of meaning and coherence

Shared understandings in dialogue are supported by the interpretive work done by actors in interaction; achieving (or, as ethnomethodologists sometimes put it, "doing") understanding is a *"practical* 'problem' which is routinely 'solved' by social actors in the course of their dealings with one another" (Heritage 1984a: 54/italics in original). In this communicative process interlocutors manufacture utterances and meanings on a moment-to-moment (turn-to-turn or utterance-to-utterance) basis. Discourse, understandings and relevant contexts are subject to *local production.* In (4) we saw this illustrated in a case of rapid topic transitions, but the general principle is valid for all authentic discourse,[16] even when the various constituent utterances are held together by aspects of global coherence (see ch. 12 on different communicative genres). Utterances are building-blocks in the local production of meaning and coherence: "the initiation of an action and and the response to it (i.e. in approximately what I will call (ch. 11) a local communicative project/PL) create the immediate sequential context of these events (i.e. the events where situated understanding takes place/PL), and occasions as well as exhibits analysis and understanding of the unfolding course of interaction" (Boden & Zimmerman 1991: 10). Through this incremental process, understandings are constantly updated.

Elementary discourse contributions, whether these are taken to be sentence-sized 'idea units' or turns at talk (cf. ch. 9), contain the resources for responding, displaying one's understanding and taking the discourse further by introducing new content. This *double-sidedness* of the discourse contribution, its 'response-initiative' structure, the *movement from* what is *given* in prior context *to* something *new*, will be discussed at some length in ch. 9.2. At the level of sequences and episodes there is a similar double-sidedness (ch. 10.7). Indeed, there is a ubiquitous and inherent tension in communication and discourse, and its constituents, between exhibiting relevance and coherence with respect to what is given and proving opportunities for new initiatives and new sense-making; at a deeper level, if you will, a dialectics between stability and change.

Dialogue contributions, we have just argued, are produced in their local contexts. But this does not tell the whole truth. The products of "small" local

---

16. In some cases local production is limited to aspects of phonetic, prosodic and paralinguistic performance, such as in the recital of a written text.

actions add up to discourses and texts, which also exhibit global regularities. At the same time, local productions take place in the contexts of socio-cultural traditions, within a 'continuity of practices' that extends far beyond single situations. Meanings are of course not constantly created ab novo; rather, meaning potentials are part of actors' knowledge of language and are used in the negotiation of situated interpretations (ch. 7.2).

5.7 Dialogue as a series of opportunities for relevant continuations

In dialogical interaction, almost everything, i.e. every utterance or even sometimes the absence of an utterance, gets a meaning. There is a continuous effort, on the part of actors (and observers), for meaning, to make sense of what is happening around them. This holds especially for discourse, where behaviours are couched in a symbolic system (i.e. language). In a dialogue, even silences are sometimes social acts with meanings. Consider an episode like the following:

(5) WHAT TIME IS IT? (contrived example, after Bilmes 1988: 46–9)

```
1. A:    what time is it?
2. B:    ((no overt response))
3. A:    thank you very much
```

This simple example can be used to illustrate several fundamental properties of dialogue. It shows, first of all, how a response can be relevantly absent. This is possible because A's initiative (query) has established a sequential slot, where an answer is expected. The absence of the answer thus gets a meaning *through its position in a sequence*. B's silence is not simply an empty space, but a significant 'silence-in-context'. Secondly, it shows how people orient to rules, without being totally constrained by them. Though the sequence may be considered pragmatically odd, it is not meaningless. On the contrary, "to break the rule is no less meaningful than to obey it" (Bilmes 1988: 46); "not answering is usually meaningful *precisely* because it is a violation" (Bilmes, op.cit: 49/italics original). By "doing silence", not answering, B shows "a correct way to do a snub" (ibid.: 49). In other words, not obeying the rule, and thereby providing a certain social meaning, shows that the rule is "in effect". Similarly, by "doing thanking" (5: 3) under these circumstances, A can be heard as being sarcastic.

Some of the insights just reviewed are often discussed under the rubric of *relevance*. In principle, every contribution to a dialogue sets up conditions of relevance; some kinds of next actions are more relevant continuations than others. For example, Deborah's first question 1: 1 in (1) creates a social expectation on the addressee, Peter, to respond in a certain way; first, Deborah has posed a question, which rather strongly solicits (ch. 9.4) a response from him, and, furthermore, the formulation, or specific direction and reference, of the question requires that a relevant response should specifically concern his reading habits. As we saw, Peter did not appear to understand fully what kind of answer was required of him, and yet he had to provide some relevant response. Hence, instead of providing an answer, he produced another type of relevant response, a request for clarification. This can be considered relevant primarily because it can be regarded as a cooperative action taken to carry further the communicative project initiated by Deborah. In her turn, *she* will then, after Peter's 1: 2, be required to provide a relevant response to the new "micro-situation" which has emerged from the prior contributions. After Deborah's 1: 3 addressed to Peter, *he* is again expected to respond relevantly, given the new conditions set up locally in the sequence, etc. Providing relevant next contributions thus amounts to building coherence in the joint discourse (Hopper 1983; Allwood 1985).

Each contribution to dialogue is framed by *expectations, entitlements and obligations* with respect to possible meaning attributions and actions. This is then a moral (or 'proto-moral'; Linell & Rommetveit 1998) dimension of dialogue. By saying something, a given speaker takes on some responsibility for what she says or does. For example, an assertion normally commits the speaker to the truth of what is asserted; Sally and Steve, through their contributions to (2), have put themselves in a position where they cannot deny that they once shook hands with Rubinstein, unless of course they explicitly annul their previous statements (e,g. by claiming "no, we were just kidding").

But, as we have noted, utterances also oblige or invite the other interlocutor(s) to respond, and to do so in a relevant manner. We could say that each contribution occasions a new *micro-situation with specific conditions on relevant continuations* (and partly new expectations, entitlements and obligations). Of course, next speakers are not totally constrained by these relevance conditions. They can initiate new topics, for example, though this often forces them to do some extra work, i.e. explaining that what they say now is not immediately relevant to the preceding discourse. (Indeed, in spite of the juvenile habits of doing non-focal 'tyings', Al, in 4: 15, apparently felt some demand for him to explain how his contribution could be taken as relevant, "without changing the subject".) Another possibility is for an actor to flout the principle of relevance;

as B did in 5: 2, thereby creating a certain interactional effect. Indeed, if this was the intended effect, B may well have considered 5: 2 as a situationally relevant response, although it obviously violated social rules of etiquette.

At any given moment, an unfolding discourse is often indeterminate (from the points of view of speaker, addressee, and observer, who, in addition, may have mutually partially inconsistent interpretations); this is quite often true particularly of the illocutionary values of specific contributions; is the speaker informing or advising, asserting or requesting, being serious or non-serious, or doing several of those things at the same time (which is not uncommon)? This means that the addressee is often faced with several options of how to respond. At the same time, the existence and experience of the discourse as it actually materialized may sustain an illusion, on the part of analysts as well as actors, that there were, after all, not so many *other* opportunities for differential interpretations and discursive developments. When somebody has responded in a specific way, and the first speaker does not object to the implied interpretation of his prior utterance, both interactants are somewhat committed to this interpretation (ch. 11.3). Other opportunities for interpretation that may have been there, have simply got "lost" through this process (cf. ch. 10.10). Actors cannot pursue the consequences of all possible ambiguities, if they want to make progress in their communicative projects.[17]

5.8 The dynamics of discourse units

To describe talk-in-interaction one needs a vocabulary based on dynamic rather than static concepts (cf. Marková & Foppa 1990). The units are units of interaction, actions which bring about, or attempt to bring about, changes in cognitive and communicative states. A communicative action originates in one micro-situation and creates a new micro-situation, which in turn makes various more or less specific continuations relevant. Such are the elementary contributions to dialogue (ch. 9). Interlocutors are engaged in building situated discourse, i.e. they

---

17. Cf. some of Garfinkel's (1967) well-known experiments. A theoretical discussion of alternative routes of interpretation and continuation for a given piece of discourse may reveal the ambiguities and multiple opportunities, but the combinations soon become too numerous to be accounted for within reasonable limits of space. See Rommetveit (1980) for some theoretical calculations, and Blum-Kulka & Weizman (1988) for a partial elaboration of an authentic example.

make discourses and contexts emerge in and through their actions (ch. 8). As a result the discourse moves through topical episodes and across episode boundaries (ch. 10). Through their discursive and interactive work actors carry out various communicative projects (ch. 11). Such projects are embedded within and co-constitute activity types, in which communicative tasks are solved, often in routine-like ways (communicative genres) (ch. 12).

In other words, the pragmatics of language use is dynamic (Thomas 1995). At the same time, it is not an easy task for analysts to be consistent in applying a dynamic perspective; we often slip back into using static terms and concepts. To some extent, this is undoubtedly linked up with problems related to the 'written language bias' (ch. 2.5).[18] But it may also be partly due to a necessity for analysts to "freeze" their objects of study within particular scientific projects. This latter point will be discussed in ch. 14.

5.9 Summary: Some dialogical principles

In this introductory chapter, I have pointed to a number of characteristics of social interaction and discourse as they appear to us, if we try to apply consistently a dialogistic analytical framework. Many of these aspects will be further elaborated in subsequent chapters (see the cross-references made above). Before that, however, I shall summarize some aspects of dialogue in terms of *three fundamental dialogical principles*.[19] I shall also indicate that the choice of these principles is partly a matter of which perspective you choose as an analyst (ch. 5.10).

5.9.1 *Sequentiality*

The first principle says that all discourse, whether monological or dialogical, has a fundamental *sequential organization*. Each constituent action, contribution or sequence, gets significant parts of its meaning from the position in a sequence (which in real-time interaction is of course temporal in nature). That means that one can never fully understand an utterance or an extract, if it is taken out of the

---

18. For some additional consideration of this point, see also Linell (1997).

19. Alternatively, one may think of these as three elaborations (in different directions) of one dialogical principle, as Bakhtin (1986) and Todorov (1984) might prefer it. Cf. ch. 5.9.4.

sequence which provides its context.[20] (A more accurate formulation would be "taken out of the sequences which provide its contexts", since sequences of very different scopes constitute relevant contexts.[21] Cf. ch. 8.)

All discourse is essentially *contextualized*. When pieces of discourse are taken out of their original context, and used, maybe discussed or commented upon, they occur in a new context, that of the quoting discourse, the discussion or commentary. In other words, it has been *recontextualized*. At the micro-level, instances of recontextualization occur routinely; these aspects are indeed fundamental to human communication (ch. 8).

5.9.2   *Joint construction*

Language and discourse are fundamentally *social* phenomena. The language used in communication is of a social-interactional origin, both in its historical genesis and in the child's socialization; furthermore, it is socially traded down, distributed, negotiated, and recreated in interaction. But, above all, discourse itself, which is the main focus in this book, is deeply social and interactional in nature. A dialogue is a *joint* construction (or a co-construction, Jacoby & Ochs 1995); it is something which participants (to varying degrees) possess, experience and do together. This collective construction is made possible by the reciprocally and *mutually coordinated actions and interactions* by different actors.[22] No part is entirely one single individual's product or experience. On the other hand, the distribution of contributions to the co-constructed dialogue is usually asymmetrical (ch. 11.6).

In several respects, there are of course important differences between monologue and dialogue (as defined in ch. 1.3). The examples brought up so far

---

20. The use of extracts from dialogues, which is a practical necessity in analysis and exposition (such as in papers or books on authentic discourse), must therefore be done with caution. Some of the 'dialogicality' of the authentic piece of discourse will get bracketed by this kind of operation.

21. The principle of sequentiality, and even more so the notion of 'sequence', are given a broader interpretation in this work than in C(onversation) A(nalysis) (e.g. Atkinson & Heritage 1984), where 'sequence' refers to a local, close-knit sequence, such as an adjacency pair or a repair sequence.

22. It is possible to talk about the mutual coordination necessarily involved in communication in terms of cooperation (cf. Grice 1975; Allwood 1976) or collaboration. However, it should be noted that the basic coordination still leaves a lot of room for competitive attitudes and strategies on the part of mutually opposed actors (e.g. Linell 1990). For an analysis of concepts like 'commonality', 'reciprocity', and 'mutuality' with regard to dialogue, see Graumann (1995).

were taken from dialogues, in which actions and meanings were *actually* jointly constructed (e.g. through collaborative completion). In some cases, even sentence-sized (or smaller) constituent expressions were jointly produced. But also lengthy monological speech events (or written texts, for that matter) are dialogically built up, even if the construction of the overt construction is not always obviously a joint venture. Yet, there is a social character, in that this discourse too is *other-oriented*; it is designed for some (particular or anonymized) recipients (ch. 6.5). We may therefore talk about a *virtual* (rather than actual) *joint construction* in these cases; the sender (speaker or writer) interacts with a 'virtual other',[23] when he makes his message other-oriented.

5.9.3   *Act-activity interdependence*

Acts, utterances and sequences in discourse are always essentially situated within an embedding activity (dialogue, encounter) which the interactants jointly produce. This activity can most often be seen as representing some general type or as belonging to a particular genre. Some meaning aspects of the elementary acts derive from the fact that they are embedded within, and contribute to realising, this overall activity. At the same time, the activity type or genre is shown, in a Wittgensteinian sense, i.e. implicitly shown rather than explicitly formulated ("said"), in the ways actors express themselves in discourse. Constituent acts and embedding activities mutually define, or co-constitute, each other in a part-whole relationship.

The property of act-activity interdependence (or co-constitution) is most easily demonstrated in those communicative genres which are task-oriented, and perhaps also institutionally congealed (see e.g. examples (1, 2) of ch. 12). However, the point can be demonstrated with respect to mundane examples, such as the extracts above, as well. For example, Louise's casual remark about birth control pills (3: 12) contributes to the enacting of the entire mocking activity, rather than to the overarching frame of group therapy, from which the adolescents seem to have moved out temporarily. Peter's remark that he should not eat so much in order to save time (1: 28) is characteristically part of the conversational activity in which the parties are involved; it is not part of, say, a counselling session on issues of diet. Conversely, the same utterances get some of their

---

23. This concept is elaborated upon in Bråten (1992).

meaning from being interpreted as part of the activities just mentioned. Their interactional significances would have been different, if they had been part of, say, a medical interaction such as a doctor consultation.

The act-activity interdependence is another feature of the essential situatedness of all discourse contributions. It will be further explored in the chapters on contexts (ch. 8), and activity types and communicative genres (ch. 12). Many aspects of discourse, such as patterns of topic progression, coherence and participation structures, are activity- or genre-specific, rather than subjected to universal rules.[24]

5.9.4   A superordinate principle: Reflexivity between discourse and contexts

The three dialogical principles deal with the fact that the speaker "is in dialogue with" his interlocutor(s) and a matrix of contexts. As I will argue in ch. 8, there is a multi-way *reflexive* relation between discourses and their contexts. In fact, the term 'reflexivity' is often used roughly in the sense of 'dialogicality' (as that term is used here).[25] Reflexivity means that two orders of phenomena are intrinsically related, so that one of them is conceptually implicated by the other, and vice versa.[26] In other words, the two mutually constitute each other (or at least they do so partially). For example, the positioning in the sequence is built into (the interactional status of) the single contribution (turn) in dialogue, and conversely, the sequence is constituted by the contributions embedded within it. The contributions by the different interlocutors reflect each other, and jointly produce meaning. Finally, of course, the activity and the elementary acts are mutually constitutive; they are reflexively related too.[27]

---

24. The arguments for activity-specificity generalize to cognitive operations. Whereas Piaget tried to set up a universally valid theory of cognitive operations, later research has reduced the power of this theory by demonstrating the domain- or task-specificity of many cognitive practices (e.g. Rogoff 1990).

25. Duranti (1991, cf. ch. 5.10) takes 'reflexivity' to mean roughly act-activity co-constitution.

26. Marková (1995) discusses *'complementarity'* as the fundamental dialogical principle, in a way which roughly corresponds to how the reflexivity between discourse and contexts is treated here.

27. Dialogism insists on reflexive relation between many concepts, cf. ch. 13.1. A primary and general case concerns the relationship between 'figure' and 'ground', which must be defined in terms of each other. With regard to this, the paired concepts of 'discourse' and its 'contexts' are a special case (ch. 8).

Note that this notion of reflexivity is different from another one which is common in analyses of

5.10 Differing perspectives on dialogicality

Principles similar to the three sketched here have been proposed in the literature, though sometimes under somewhat different names. Duranti (1991) deals roughly with these aspects of dialogue under the headings of sequentiality, interactivity, and reflexivity, respectively. In addition, he gives 'multi-functionality' as a fourth principle of dialogue (see ch. 11.2). Other specific examples could be added. However, it seems important to acknowledge the general point that the particular analytical perspective adopted will have repercussions on which properties stand out as the most central dialogical features of discourse.

Accordingly, in this chapter (and to some extent throughout this book) I have taken as a point of departure that there is one common discourse jointly attended to in dialogue, rather than a number of unconnected utterances by different individual speakers. (However, in some multi-party settings, there are quite often several parallel floors of discourse.) The relative coherence and unity of the discourse, rather than the predicaments of the different actors involved, are thus constitutive of this particular perspective. If, alternatively, we look upon a discursive interaction as a struggle on the part of the interlocutors to achieve (some sufficient degree of) intersubjectivity or to obtain discursive power over others, then the weighting of the above-mentioned and other 'dialogical principles' may change. Within this latter perspective, we would stress features like multi-functionality (of utterances and contributions) (ch. 11.2), polyvocality (ch. 6.5), discrepant relevances and competing communicative projects (chs. 8.9, 11.6–7), dominance and power (ch. 12.8), asymmetries of knowledge and participation (Marková & Foppa 1991), and complementarity of dialogue roles (ch. 11.6). Put in other words, which dialogical principles get foregrounded may have to do with which activity types and communicative genres we want to analyze (ch. 12).

I shall devote separate chapters to contexts, elementary contributions to dialogue, topics and episodes, communicative projects, and activity types later on. Before proceeding to them, however, I shall deal with the dialogistic account of speaker-listener relations and linguistic meaning.

---

language and cognition. This is the notion of reflexivity referring to, on the one hand, the ability of speakers to reflect upon and comment on their own thinking and, on the other hand, the capacity of natural languages to express propositions about language itself. A similar notion of reflexivity can be applied to culture (Fornäs 1995; Giddens 1991).

CHAPTER 6

Speakers and listeners

6.1 Monological speakers or dialogical interlocutors

The monologistic framework portrays the communicative interaction as a sequence of individual actions by speakers who take turns. The listener's role becomes basically that of trying to recover the current speaker's intentions. Thus, the speaker and listener roles are clearly separated — one of the Cartesian dichotomies of monologism -, and the listener's role is very much subordinated to that of the speaking agent's; the speaker alone is the active interlocutor and the only authority, when it comes to determine what the words in discourse mean. Utterances are meant to make known all and only what the speaker has meant; hence the term 'monologism'.

Monologism looks upon the utterance as the speaker's own product and the speech act as monological, i.e. as having one single authoritative source in the speaker and his intentions. Accordingly, the speaker or sender is assigned a self-evident identity and individuality. Dialogism, by contrast, regards the utterance as socially, i.e. collaboratively, constituted and generated, and looks upon communicative actions as contextual and dialogical in several senses; they are (doubly) contextualized, socially generated and culturally embedded. Accordingly, the concept of speaker/sender becomes problematized and differentiated. Dialogism locates the primary habitat of language in conversation and social interaction, thus far from regarding the latter as an epiphenomenon. I shall return to these points in due order.

The monologistic view that utterances and their meanings are due to speakers' intentions are part of dominant Western philosophy.[1] It has received

---

1. The ethnocentrism of this idea has been argued by anthropologists studying other cultures. See e.g. Duranti (1993b).

additional force in the 20th century through some of the most influential theories in philosophy, linguistics and psychology, to which speech act theory (ch. 11.2) firmly belongs.

6.2 Speaking: The production of utterances?

Linguistics has a long-standing tradition of dealing primarily with linguistic expressions. This also applies to the classical language-related disciplines, such as logic and rhetoric, at least from the time of Aristotle and onwards (Swearingen 1990). Linguistics and other language sciences have been more concerned with language in writing than language in spoken discourse (Linell 1982). The privileged status of expression over content gets enhanced, as you go from spoken interaction to writing and written representations. When spoken interaction gets transcribed, you will most often be faced with only (counterparts of portions of) the behavioural aspects, whereas meanings, projects and their contexts will be at best fragmentarily and incompletely notified.

Psycholinguists appear to have been more concerned with how speakers produce utterances, than with how they produce utterance meaning. One explanation for this can be found in the above-mentioned traditions within language sciences. But there are of course additional reasons. Utterances are units of linguistic behaviour, and behavioural units are always much easier to observe, identify and describe in an intersubjectively satisfactory manner than are meanings and interpretations. Communicative projects (see ch. 11) may appear to be too ambiguous, multifaceted and fugitive. Naturally, it is much easier, partly even seemingly mandatory, to stick to monologistic individualism, when you deal with the behavioural form, rather than with the social meaning, of spoken utterances. And yet, we have seen in the previous chapter that even expression units like sentences or information units are sometimes overtly produced collectively.

Within psychology, behaviourism implied a strong emphasis on behaviour, and later, the now dominant information processing paradigm within cognitive psychology is focussed on formal representations and their processing. Only recently, there has been a growing interest in meaning and culture within cognitive and social psychology (Bruner 1990; Billig 1987). All in all, there are strong historical reasons why monologism is still dominant, and why it tends to deal with form (expression) rather than meaning.

The monologistic theory describes the production of an utterance as a highly complex series of information processing (or, as is increasingly being assumed, parallel, as well as serial, processing of plans and representations) (Levelt 1989; Clark & Clark 1977, Cooper 1980).[2] The starting point for the processing is to be found in the speaker's communicative intentions. However, there is, in the typical monologistic account, very little said about how these intentions got there in the first place. Communicative intentions are largely treated as given, even though most, or even all, scholars would pay lip service to the contention that they usually come about as a function of the speaker's interaction with his physical and social environment.

A dialogistic account would not deny the contribution of individual agency, i.e. that some aspects of action and utterance meaning are due to active and conscious mental planning. However, such "intentions" are generated in a dialogical process with contexts and interlocutors. In addition, there are significant aspects of talk which do not seem to originate in individual, active intentions. A great deal of coherence in discourse results from, or is supported by, syntactic processes that are highly automatized, and other cultural routines for sequentially ordered actions (e.g. 'scripts'; Schank & Abelson 1977; Brown & Yule 1983: 241ff). Furthermore, many aspects of meaning result from the juxtaposition of local contributions; parts of global coherence emerge from locally coherent moves, and need not be specifically planned (ch. 10.10). The dialogistic theory does not reduce discourse entirely to cognition, let alone individual cognition (ch. 2.1). Rather cognition and social interaction are assumed to penetrate each other.

In order to explain cognition in practice, we must assign prime importance to the interactional aspects. Not only are messages and communicative projects socially constructed and constituted, but this interactional process between the talking individual and his environment usually goes on more or less continuously, also while the speaker is actually in the process of talking, i.e. producing his utterance. The production of meaningful action does not start with (only) individual intentions. As Hobbs & Evans (1980: 350) observed:

---

2. The term "utterance production" itself has a certain monologistic ring. It seems to imply that what speakers do in discourse is "producing utterances", when in fact they are arguably involved in more comprehensive communicative projects (ch. 11). In addition, the received view has it that the utterances are "products" of the individual speakers, a view which will be discussed further in the ensuing text.

"A number of researchers (e.g., Dore & McDermott 1980 [i.e. 1982/PL]; Wynn 1980) investigating conversation from an "interactional" point of view have emphasized the "emergent" quality of conversation, i.e. the fact that participants' purposes and their sense of what is going on may only emerge during the course of conversation."

Speakers do not speak out of their heads, on the basis of preplanned cognitive structures that exist prior to verbalization. The meaning of an utterance cannot be identified with the speaker's intentions as "fully defined in the speaker's mind before the act of speaking" (Duranti 1993b: 25). As phenomenologists and pragmatists have underscored (ch. 3.4.2), the process of verbalization involves the simultaneous shaping of expression and content; "speech does not translate thought but accomplishes it" (Spurling 1977: 56). This process in the speaker starts from more or less vague communicative goals (or projects), being subject to external stimuli, feedback from interlocutors, self-generated impressions and associations, etc. In the course of these complex processes, goals and meanings get more precise, detailed, enriched, and conscious. There is no meaning, at least no utterance meaning of the kind we associate with linguistic expressions in context, before the verbal form; interpretations are made possible and accessible through verbalization. This, of course, applies most typically to impromptu speech, not to preplanned discourse which may have been more or less carefully rehearsed before it is made "public" by the speaker when he confronts his audience. Thus, utterance production cannot be construed as a translation of semantic representations into an acoustic output (or a mapping of underlying structures into utterances), as Levelt (1989) would have it.

Speakers talk not only in order to be understood by their interlocutors, but also in order to understand what they themselves say and think. The speaker is also a recipient of his own utterance. He will often only gradually realise new meanings, make new associations, and see novel aspects or additional problems connected to his topics, and this often happens in and through the very process of verbalization, in the very moment of saying something or having just said something. Therefore, there are some similarities in the speaker's and his interlocutor's predicaments: they both go from pre-understanding to a more advanced or enriched understanding, or from one contextualization of the things talked about to a recontextualized version of them.

The fundamentals of this dialogistic stance, with its background in phenomenological philosophy (cf. Spurling 1977), are laid out by Dore & McDermott (1982), for example in the following quotations from their paper:

"[...] talk [...] is fundamentally indeterminate; and [...] in the course of organizing sensible moments with each other, people use talk as a social tool, relying on the social work they are doing together to specify the meaning of utterances" (p. 395)

[...] participants are never exactly certain of 'what is going on' at any moment of interaction, and must do communicative work to inform themselves of what they are doing together. [...] What is at issue for conversationalists is always an *emergent* phenomenon, explicitly specifiable only in retrospect. [...] What people operate with from moment to moment are "working consensuses" of what they might be doing together on several levels." (p. 386) The working consensuses are "the momentary and often fragmentary understandings which people must share in order to organize their concerted behavior." (p. 386; fn.)

To take a somewhat more extreme, but still quite common, case: if a speaker A regards himself (or is regarded by others) as (at least partly) incompetent, inconclusive or insecure, sensing that he cannot express himself clearly, he has to look at his addressee B and her responses to see how his utterances are taken up and what his own words mean, or at least: (seem to) mean to his partner. Hence it is not only B, the listener, who has to find out what A, the speaker, means; A must do so himself. We are faced with a coordinated management of speaker's meaning.

In interactions with speech-impaired persons, e.g. individuals with aphasia or cerebral palsy, the impaired speaker might know a good deal of what he or she wants to say but may be unable to realise these communicative projects. Such a person must rely heavily on the interlocutor to have his or her intended meanings expressed. Goodwin (1995) analyzes a case with an aphasic man, who could only say the three words "yes", "no" and "but"; his intentions was largely brought into language by his partners in interaction. In ch. 11, I shall analyze how another aphasic man is helped by his partner in a story-telling project ((6): THE TRIP TO SÄLEN). Collins & Marková (1995) similarly demonstrate how speech-impaired persons with cerebral palsy are assisted by partners in having their meanings formulated in discourse.

The emergent form and content of a dialogue is a product of social interaction, as a collaborative accomplishment. Interlocutors complete each other's actions and mutually influence each other. The "appropriate" interpretation of a given utterance is not entirely the speaker's own privilege (Duranti 1986). A given speaker often produces reinterpretations of his own prior utterances, by treating the other's utterances as being competent remarks which presuppose a certain reconstrual of his own prior utterances. On the general level, however, one might say that the speaker has more of an absolute authority as regards referential meaning (he knows which referents he is talking about), whereas relatively more is often negotiable as regards descriptive meaning and the utterance's action status.

6.3 Embodied minds and persons in interaction

Even if many accounts of verbal behaviour are, in effect, focussed on expression aspects, there is hardly any disagreement that communication and cognition concern the conception, manipulation and exchange of meanings and messages. The monologist deals with this in terms of information processing within individual minds, as internal, cognitive processes. (As we have observed, terms like 'mental' and 'cognitive' have come to denote, almost by definition, intrapsychic, rather than interpsychic (intersubjective), processes). Cognitive psychology, which is under heavy influence of a computer metaphor (Graumann 1988; Bruner 1990), will then try to 'represent' meanings and, to some extent, presuppositions and contexts within 'mental models' (e.g. Johnson-Laird 1983), i.e. meanings appear in the form of abstract expressions (called 'semantic representations', 'information structures', or the like), thus further strengthening the priority of form over meaning (cf. ch. 2.3).

Dialogism would rather argue that information processing takes place in a complex interaction between the individual and his or her social (and physical) environment, i.e. interlocutors, situational aspects, abstract frames (communicative premisses, background knowledge, cultural routines etc; cf. ch. 8 on contexts), i.e. entities which require, for their description and explanation, reference to social, cultural and situational circumstances, objects and other agents.

But if we consider information processing, where else could it take place except within individuals' minds? Few, if any, modern dialogists would posit collective souls. When we propose that "speakers do not speak out of their heads", this cannot be understood as a denial that information processing takes place in individual minds, and only there. We would not deny that information processing needs a neurological substrate, i.e. basically brains, to be executed, nor would we contest that individual speakers, i.e. individual bodies, produce the peculiar, and richly structured, sounds that we call speech, or verbal behaviour. The dialogist's point is simply that we cannot understand what these behaviours mean, unless we have recourse to social and cultural phenomena outside of, or in the interactions of, the individuals. Meaning, according to Harré & Gillett (1994: 23), is found "in structuring the interaction between a person and a context". This applies to intentions, projects and, indeed, 'information' as well (unless 'information' is taken to mean only uninterpreted physical states of the symbolizing hardware).

Accordingly, the need for a dialogistic account would, at least at face value, seem most obvious with regard to *meanings* (functions, significances etc.) of utterances and actions, perhaps less so when it comes to expressive behaviours with their phonetic and grammatical aspects. But even there, at the level of linguistic expression, we find interactional influences and effects, e.g. as regards intonation (Local & Kelly 1986; Couper-Kuhlen & Selting 1996), and the collaborative construction of syntactic units (ch. 5.4). Therefore, dialogism applies just as much to the outer form of interaction; we can hardly account for the finely grained attunings and accommodations of one person's behaviours without describing what the interlocutors are doing in the same interaction (e.g. Erickson 1982; Goodwin 1981; Goodwin & Goodwin 1992).

The theory that tries to derive utterances as produced from prior speaker intentions is deficient in other respects as well. It cannot deal with unforeseen utterance meanings, i.e. the fact that speakers sometimes detect or are made aware of interpretations of their own utterances that they never intended. In addition, not everything in utterance production can be explained in terms of specific influences, whether intentions or detectable causal factors. There seems to be some space for non-predictable and perhaps random moments in utterance production. We cannot entirely govern and monitor lexical access and actively decide which particular words will become available to us as speakers in any given moment. Slips of the tongue testify to this, as do various difficulties to access words, such as in the tip-of-the-tongue phenomenon (when words searched for are "nearly" at hand but become available only later, often without any particular and evident reason why they should appear just at that later moment).[3]

---

3. For an analysis of so-called speech errors within a dialogistic framework, see Dufva (1992).

6.4 The production of utterance meaning

That the meaning of utterances in contexts is not inherent in the (linguistic) meanings of the constituent linguistic items, is a theme to which I will return in several chapters of this book. Nonetheless, I shall substantiate some points in the sections to follow immediately.

As a point of departure it would be possible to use the monologistic assumption that the basic (and literal) meaning of an utterance follows from its lexical and semantic composition. However, this view is, if unamended, somewhat outdated, and I shall therefore instead take the view of many of the proponents of linguistic pragmatics that *some* (but not all) phenomena do in fact necessitate explanations in terms of contexts. Many text-books of pragmatics and psycholinguistics, as different as Levinson (1983) and Levelt (1989), list some of the "problems" for a purely linguistic-semantic approach under four different headings: deixis, presuppositions, implicatures, and indirect speech acts. One implicit background assumption seems to be that only these phenomena will need an anchorage outside the individual and his/her utterances (with their semantic representations). This theory is, however, also untenable. The dialogistic stance, is that *all* utterances, and many of their properties, are *indexical*; large parts of their meanings are unstated and must be supplied by actors in communicative contexts. Accordingly, all utterances are *essentially* contextualized, and are *always* understood by our going beyond language; the dependences on contexts are not a question of just *some* utterances which are semantically and/or pragmatically complex.

6.4.1 *Reference and situated description*

The classical case, where semanticists have admitted the necessity of a contextual anchorage of utterances, is deictics. Pronouns, pronominal adverbs and pro-verbs, such as "I, you, he, here, there, now, yesterday, do so", etc., derive their interpretations, by definition, from the time, space and person specifications of the individual utterance event (cf. e.g. the example from the rowing lession (THAT'S PUSH) in ch. 12). Similar considerations pertain to verb tenses etc. But the problem is much wider than this; it is a question of finding the referential meaning of all referring expressions, not only of those which involve only deictic words in the limited sense. Referring expressions abound in utterances. The most obvious category is the (majority of) nominal expressions (noun phrases). But a moment's reflection reveals that most descriptive terms, i.e. also verbs and adjectives, refer to (or are constructed as if they referred to) processes, properties etc in the world outside the discourse, and therefore they too need a referential anchorage. Accordingly, we are not only concerned with the binding of expressions to particular referents, or properties of referents; it comprises also the specification or precisization of descriptive content, of properties predicated of the referents. Thus, the situated interpretation of, say, *His brother is sick.* normally involves some precisization of "sick" ("sick in what way?"). If somebody says *France is hexagonal.* (an example used by Austin 1962: 142), the appropriateness of this formulation depends on some implicit standard of comparison (accuracy), etc. And then there is the issue of *why* particular utterances are issued (ch. 6.4.4). We have also argued (ch. 3.4.1) that referential and descriptive meanings in discourse are dependent on speakers' *perspectives*; from which point-of-view do speakers view things talked about, and what are their *positionings* (Muhlhäusler & Harré 1990; Hermans & Kempen 1993) with respect to the utterances and their addressees. Reference is not always a matter of identifying an unequivocally defined referent in a monistic world, but referring (and understanding the reference) may pertain to something under a certain aspect in a world of multiple versions.[4] All these phenomena are of course properties of situated acts, not of linguistic expressions per se.

Words do not contain or reflect their meaning and reference. "Words serve mainly as cues" in the task of finding "things-meant" (Gardiner 1932: 65), and in finding out speakers' positionings. We can take almost any stretch of discourse and make sure that most of the utterances exhibit this kind of context-sensitivity.

6.4.2   *Responsive properties*

The next point pertains to (what I will term) responsive aspects of utterances (ch. 9.2). Utterances are often linked to previous utterances, and thus to their prior co-text. Moreover, we can, following Bakhtin, argue that all utterances are somehow 'responding' to additional aspects of the contexts. Of course, so-called 'minimal responses' are most dependent on their positioning for being interpreted, but, as argued in chs. 5.2 and 9, the argument applies to any dialogue

---

4. For discussion of many (hypothetical but realistic) examples, see Rommetveit (1974: ch. 4).

contribution, although some utterances are intended as (co-textually independent) 'free initiatives'. A contribution to dialogue is, at any particular point of interaction, evidence of (some attempt at) understanding, and at the same time, it represents a continuation of the social interaction. The meaning of the dialogue contribution is social; it never stands by itself, as it were 'containing' its own meaning. Instead, it is (inter)relational in nature, interdependent with and co-constitutive of local and global contexts. Sense-making activities in producing an utterance includes an interpretation of prior contribution and a prospective interpretation, or anticipation, of what is going to follow, what would be a relevant continuation.

6.4.3   Obligational aspects

An important point of Austin's and Searle's work on the meanings of utterances (or speech acts) was that referential and descriptive aspects will not make up the whole story. Utterances also have performative values or illocutionary meanings. Yet, the major monologistic theory of linguistic action is precisely Searle's speech act theory, which, as I will argue later on (ch. 11.2), cannot deal with this properly. The subject matter of illocutions are obligational aspects of utterances; responsibilities, rights and commitments that speakers, and listeners, assume and assign, or are assigned, in and through their communicative acts (cf. also Muhlhäusler & Harré 1990). These aspects, again universal rather than exceptional features of discourse, concern interlocutors and their social relations, not the linguistic properties of the expressions used in communication. Again, we must go beyond language itself to explicate the functions of discourse.

Similarly, to explain why, in a given situation, a speaker may, or may not, utter something specific with a particular formulation, it is not enough to invoke Grice's (1975) maxims of cooperative, rational communication. (It is reasonable to argue that these maxims basically reflect the view of communication as just an efficient transfer of information.) One must also consider rules of social propriety (Goffman 1983), tact (Leech 1983), or politeness (Brown & Levinson 1987); "the moral norms of considerateness which bind individuals qua inter-actants. Delicacy, courtesy, modesty, politeness — these are the sort of attributes that are involved." (Goffman 1983: 28).

6.4.4   The 'why' of communication

This concept is due to Ducrot (1972) and concerns yet another universal aspect of discourse contributions. Human communicative actions are meaningful, i.e. speakers know (at some level, except perhaps in some quite exceptional cases) why they say what they say, and can be held 'accountable' for their communicative acts;[5] at least in principle, one must be able to explain why one has put a specific question, why one can assert something, etc. The listener can always ask "why that to me now?" (Sacks 1992: I: 452; Schegloff & Sacks 1973: 209; Bilmes 1985). The point is close to the preceding one; both belong to the fundamental moral dimensions of dialogue.

6.4.5   Social languages

All language use has cultural and social dimensions of an even more far-reaching kind than has been alluded to under the previous headings. Since language is socially constructed and socially distributed, it means that it is also unevenly distributed; not all parts of language (e.g. lexical categories) or communicative genres are equally available or familiar to everybody (e.g. Luckmann 1992). Therefore, when somebody uses a particular kind of language, he or she says something, usually unintentionally, about his or her social world(s) (traditions, classes, gender, age, profession etc). Even 'descriptive words' are usually not neutral in this respect; e.g. the differential use of quasi-synonymous terms within a semantic field points at particular sets of referents, alludes to other situations of use, positionings, lects and categories of speakers, i.e. different 'social languages' (Wertsch 1991). Here, again, we can refer to Bakhtin's work on the appropriation, whether intended or not, of others' words and their meanings.

6.5   The role of the speaker's partners in authoring utterances

According to monologism, the utterance is, to put it bluntly, a monological speaker's utterance. As we have seen, this also holds for the monologistic account of an interactively embedded conversational contribution. The speaker

---

5. Ethnomethodologists refer to this in terms of the 'accountability' of social actions (e.g. Garfinkel 1967; Heritage 1984a; Watson & Sharrock 1991; cf. also Sacks 1992).

hosts the information processing which enables and results in the utterance, and he alone is responsible for what it means (meaning goes back to his individual communicative intentions). Dialogism would of course admit that the verbal behaviours, the physical movements, are the speaker's. But we recall, once again, that some syntactically coherent expressions are in fact jointly produced (cf. ch. 5.4). And more importantly, we would emphatically insist on the social nature of functions, meanings and understandings (Jacoby & Ochs 1995; Goodwin 1995). An action is social, because it is an action with regard to others ('other-orientation'); the speaker "talks with an active expectation of a response" (Shotter 1993: 52). Another matter is that the nature and degree of other-orientation ('speech' or 'communicative' 'accommodation' in the terminology of Giles et al. 1992) vary empirically between situations. But negative accommodation, i.e. distancing from the other through the accentuation of interpersonal differences in perspective or language, is of course also a form of other-orientation.

In interaction parties reciprocally adjust their actions with respect to, and in respect of, one another.[6] Of course, the speaker will still play a major role here; one cannot reduce away his individual agency, i.e. Goffman's notion of 'author' (on agency, see ch. 13.4). At the same time, the listener is not just a recipient, but a co-producer of thought and meaning. Audience co-participation is crucial; communicative acts and their interpretations are partly constructed by the audience's responses. As Duranti (1993a: 226) explains:

> "This is related to the retrospective, typically post hoc, nature of any act of interpretation (cf. Wittgenstein 1953). Without others to carry on our messages, to complete them, expand them, revise them, we would not be able to communicate. Ultimately, we would not be able to know what we are talking about."

In other words, the speaker may be said to have different partners in his endeavours (cf. Graumann 1990: 107–8). I shall now briefly discuss these under three different headings.

6.5.1   The addressee

Utterances display what Bakhtin calls 'addressivity'; they are always addressed to somebody. Sometimes, the primary addressee is absent, or the audience is

---

6. This goes back at least to Max Weber's definition of social action. For some discussion of notions of reciprocity and mutuality, see Graumann (1995).

made up of an amorphous, partly unknown group, a potential audience (cf. 6.5.2), and occasionally, the addressee is the speaker himself, as in a soliloquy. Most typically, however, there is a direct primary addressee who is co-present in the context of the utterance event. In some multi-party situations, several individuals may sometimes take on or be assigned the position of direct addressees (as evidenced by, e.g., their providing direct feedback, listener support, to the speaker.)

In ch. 1.5, I proposed to regard the presence of an addressee as a criterion for defining the family of discourse types called 'dialogue'. Let us therefore first consider discourses with actually co-present addressees, leaving "remote audiences" for a later section. Such a listener's co-presence has immediate consequences for the activity in which the speaker is currently involved; I will analyze this role of the addressee as a fivefold one.

As a first point, we note that in conversation the addressee is very often the *prior speaker*, who provided important parts of the input to the speaker, as he was about to take over the floor. Most often, in the moment of initiating his contribution, the speaker has just tried to make sense of the other's contribution to discourse, and now he has to make his own utterance relevant to that contribution, i.e. respond to it, or else explain why he is not responding to it.

Thus, the listener has often been instrumental and (co-)responsible for the local context, in particular the (interactional) co-text, of the speaker's current utterance. More importantly though, the specific addressee is the *target of the speaker's recipient design* (or other-orientation).[7] That is, the listener is 'present in the speaker's mind', as he formulates his contributions to dialogue. Empirically, recipient design varies from addressing a particular person (personalizing) to orientation to a typified addressee, one who is a member of some (more or less specific) category.

The speaker must, at least to *some* extent, try to *accommodate to the addressee's presumed perspective;* a dialogue needs some degree of mutuality (Graumann 1995). Mead (1934) has described some elements of anticipation and perspective-taking in a non-verbal 'conversation of gestures', and a full-blown

---

7. Cf. also 'audience design' (Bell 1984). On the concept of 'recipient design', see Sacks et al. (1974). Note that recipient design is not just about the utterance being "directed outwards"; instead, it is oriented to a particular addressee or category of recipients. In a multi-party situation, one and the same speaker can design different parts of his utterance to different addressees, using a number of verbal and non-verbal means, e.g. body orientation and gaze. See esp. Goodwin (1981).

dialogue involves much more of mutual coordinations and anticipations (ch. 9.3). The other-orientation of the speaker's utterance is of course part and parcel of its dialogicality, the utterance being made somehow relevant to the other's prior contribution and at the same time anticipating what the other's next contribution might possibly be. Along these lines, Erickson (1986) talks about two notions of recipient design: retrospective and prospective aspects relating to, in our terms, response and initiative (ch. 9.6).

Thirdly, the addressee is normally quite active as a listener. She will act as a *feedback giver* and sometimes also as a virtual *co-author* (Duranti 1986). The targetted listener in a face-to-face situation, and certainly on telephone (Hopper 1992), gives, and is expected to give, a lot of listener support items ('continuers', 'backchannel items', etc., see ch. 9.5) during and immediately after the speaker's turn at talk. In many cases, addressees also step in as actual utterers, filling in missing words or, together with the speaker, collaboratively producing and completing utterances. Such phenomena (cf. ch. 5.4) have been described as coproduction of utterances, collaborative completion, duetting etc.

Fourthly, we have repeatedly pointed out that listeners are *active sense-makers*. Understanding an utterance involves 'responsive understanding' (Bakhtin); there can be no understanding unless the recipient actively tries to accommodate or assimilate the speaker's message to her own background knowledge, her own current discourse-in-context model (cf. ch. 8.2: IIa), and other relevant contextual factors.

Speaking with a recipient design, we noted, implies casting the other in the role of a certain type of 'implied responder'. And listeners, on their side, choose some kind of responsive attitude in their sense-making endeavours. Listeners in some situations are more actively geared, in their responsive understandings, towards actual responding than are listeners in other situations; unlike, say, members of a lecture audience or spectators at a theatre performance, addressees in a conversational interaction must be prepared to respond immediately. In other words, addressees must also assume the role of the *next speaker*. In other words, from the (prior) speaker's perspective, the addressee is cast as an 'implied responder', and from her own perspective, she is a possible 'next speaker'. In fact, there is a very strong 'power' (Linell 1990) in the response-initiative mechanism of dialogue to engage the addressee in actual responding and thus contributing to the continuation of the dialogue itself.

6.5.2   *Other listeners*

As, Goffman (1981), among others, has shown, there are many more listener roles than that of the direct addressee (cf. also Levinson 1988; Wadensjö 1998). · A theory of polyadic interaction has to recognize the various divergent communicative participant roles, or positions, of these recipients. Yet, there is a tendency (but not an absolute necessity) for each current speaker to select one listener at a time as his current primary addressee. Often, the addressivity (other-direction) of the speaker moves between the others present, as he produces his utterance(s) (Goodwin 1981). But the reciprocity of dialogue implies a tendency on the part of speaker B to *respond* to a *particular* other, namely the prior speaker A, and this, in turn, tends to make the latter (A) into the targetted addressee and a likely next speaker (ch. 6.5.1). This reciprocity may therefore lead to *dyadic* stretches of talk also in multi-party settings; multi-party discourse sometimes splits up into several, parallel or successive, two-party episodes (Parker 1984; Egbert 1997). (Naturally, parallel episodes can also involve several people.) The mutual nature of the face-to-face (rather than face-to-faces) encounter tends to marginalize other recipients to present, though ratified, "third persons".[8]

Having pointed out this 'dyadizing' tendency for speakers to single out one specific other as their main addressee, we must also admit that there is a danger in overstating this, leading to a possible *'dyadic bias'* in dialogue studies. Not only have researchers often been preoccupied with dialogues between two people, disregarding multi-party interaction (Aronsson 1991: 49). The dyadic bias also has a more esoteric aspect, namely that speaker and listener are often regarded only as individuals interacting "there-and-then" (in the specific interaction), as if they did not at the same time embody complex selves, representing different personal, professional and other socio-cultural identities, which can be expressed or addressed in divergent ways on different occasions.[9]

Truly dialogistic theory must therefore emphasize that the actual (and specific) primary addressee is not the only recipient. Audiences, whether actual or implied (virtual), present or absent (remote), must be regarded as important

---

8. This gives *some* justification to the (etymologically incorrect) understanding of 'dialogue' as "talk between two".

9. This aspect of the dyadic bias was pointed out to me by Lars Sigfred Evensen (personal communication, Sept. 1996).

objects of other-orientation. Speakers are "in dialogue" with different, though usually overlapping, sets of recipients and interlocutors, and with contexts associated with those (ch. 8). Writers, of course, often do not have a specific individual addressee in mind. But such differences should not be overstated; speakers too, who meet interlocutors in actual interaction, often have little knowledge of these partners' biographies and therefore have to address them partly on the basis of their assumed properties (based on presumed category memberships such as professional roles). In other words, conversational partners may be perceived as having multi-dimensional selves (just as speakers' own selves). Even dyads involve more than simply two interacting individuals. Dialogism must consider socioculturally defined roles, in addition to the narrowly situational dependencies.

Before dealing with the multivoicedness of speakers, however, let us remain for a moment with the analytically more straight-forward case of polyadic interactions, in which three or more persons are present and take part, or can potentially take part, in a multi-party discourse. In such situations, particular persons shift between various listener roles: direct addressee, indirect addressee, ratified listener, overhearer etc. (Goffman 1981: Goodwin 1981; Levinson 1988). Listeners are positioned and position themselves in different ways to particular utterances, or parts thereof. "Recipients are not simply listening to the talk but dealing with it in terms of how they are positioned by it" (Goodwin & Goodwin 1992: 181). Different ways of relating to utterances, on the part of listeners, may lead to different patterns of responding, e.g. as regards whether or not listeners choose to intervene and take turns. Shifting roles can also lead to parallel floors.[10]

In multi-party situations, speakers will design their utterances so as to both be directed towards different individual addressees, and be built to meet the expectations and needs (e.g. face needs) of other persons present. In the latter case, the speaker faces the task of having to build his utterances to fit different audiences at the same time; the case is known (in CA) as 'split audience'. The indirect addressees (and the bystanders) are co-present at least potentially as targets of other-orientation and as attending sense-makers. Accordingly, speakers may actually have to design their utterances so as to accommodate to the demands and interests of two (or more) addressees with divergent backgrounds, and this *split addressivity* may be made manifest in their actual utterances (and

---

10. See Parker (1984) on 'bifurcation' and Egbert (1997) on 'schisming'.

non-verbal conduct). For example, a participant in a televised talk show must address his interlocutors in the studio, but also the studio audience and, in particular, the spectators sitting in their homes. A teacher or an individual student · in class must take into consideration that his or her contributions to discourse are (over)heard by (the rest of) the class. A senior doctor who talks to a patient during the ward round knows that his utterances are attended to by the co-present junior doctors and nurses, and perhaps other patients lying in their beds in the same room, etc. To be sure, speakers can only partly be aware of the varying and sometimes conflicting demands and attitudes of different members of the audience, and of course, the possibilities of actually coping with all these demands simultaneously is limited.[11]

Particular positionings by the speaker presuppose or occasion particular positionings on the part of listeners. Different parts of a listener's identity may be focussed or activated in different parts of the discourse activities. Wadensjö (1998) analyzed these aspects of the dialogue interpreter's role in encounters between Swedish professionals and Russian lay persons; we find different listener roles geared to understanding without preparing an immediate personal response, others to understanding in order to be able to respond immediately in a turn of one's own, both these being opposed to the obligation of understanding the speaker's utterances in the very special way needed in order to provide a rendition in another language (as in the dialogue-interpreter's task). This involves different kinds of listenership, and a dynamics in negotiating speaker and listener positionings (Wadensjö, op.cit.). Partly in more general terms, Aronsson (1991) has discussed negotiations along scales of participant statuses from addressees over 'third persons' (ratified listeners) to 'non-persons'.

6.5.3 Principals and remote audiences

We have seen that dialogues have reflexive, response-initiative links at the activity level to prior and potentially following other discourses, i.e. actual or

---

11. Polyadic interactions in casual conversation have been analyzed by e.g. Goodwin (1981), Goodwin & Goodwin (1992), Egbert (1997), and others. Polyadic institutional discourse include e.g. doctor-child patient-parent interactions (Aronsson 1991) and court trials (defendant, prosecutor, prosecutor, defence lawyer, audience) (e.g. Aronsson et al. 1987), case conferences e.g. in social work (Sarangi 1998).

potential discourses outside of the present social encounter. This complicates the concepts of speaker and audience in additional respects.

Goffman (1981) has proposed the concept of 'principal' to denote a party, in whose name the author of an utterance speaks. The principal may be some other individual person, or, quite often in a modern diversified society, an organization, a company or a public authority, an institution, a profession or an interest group. This means that the individual speaker is not alone responsible for what he says; he appropriates words, concepts, statements, opinions etc. from the organization or profession, which 'speaks through' him. Speakers rent words and their meanings, or they are hired to author their utterances in the name of others. That is, speakers use words and meanings for purposes that are only in part their own. We recall Bakhtin's dictum "the word is half someone else's" (1981: 293-4).

The appropriation of the other's words occurs both in the concrete dialogue from utterance-to-utterance (as we saw in ch. 5.4), and within cultural traditions, in the continuity of praxis over long time stretches; communities and cultures "speak" through our discourses.[12] At the general level, this is necessarily true; we reconstruct our various cultural traditions — linguistic, ideological, conceptual — through our language use. However, in a given speaker's utterances, there are usually reflections and reconstructions of other, specific individuals' or groups' 'voices'. This applies to quotations (Tannen 1989; Clark & Gerrig 1990), as well as to less identifiable appropriations from other sources.[13] More generally, the identification of different identities in the same speaker parallels the acknowledgement of different 'personae' in the self (e.g. Taylor 1989). Most emphatically, perhaps, the issues of multivoicedness (or polyphony) have been explored by Bakhtin; in his view, individuals' utterances host many voices, several identities, some of which may be more personal, while many are 'social languages' (Wertsch 1990), associated with activity types, professions, roles and genres.

The other pole of the global dialogicality of discourses has to do with the fact that interactants may have to think of possible responses to the particular

---

12. As Wertsch (1991: 85) argues, these are the major sources for speakers, as they construct utterances. It occurs rather seldom that speakers borrow words from dictionaries. When we say that speakers retrieve words from mental 'dictionaries', this is first and foremost another perspective on their dependence on cultural traditions. From a dialogic point of view, however, it is important to point out that this process (of borrowing words from one's mental lexicon) is strongly intertwined with the local appropriation of words and concepts (from the other's or one's own previous utterances) on an utterance-to-utterance basis.

13. For aspects of voice theory, cf. Silverman & Torode (1980) and Wertsch (1991).

discourse event in forthcoming situations, some of them remote in time and/or involving other interlocutors. Especially, this holds for situations in which written reports (or audio or video recordings) are made in the situations (e.g. in the case of police interrogations, cf. ch. 12.6). However, it is true of discourse in many other situations as well, for example, as regards the stories of the adolescent Black girls in M.H.Goodwin's (1990) Maple Street, whose utterances may be gossiped about in subsequent situations.[14] The fact that speakers often have remote audiences to orient to, implies another complication of the issue of split addressivity.

6.6 Conclusion

Monologistic and dialogistic theories tend to look at the interrelations of speaking and listening in rather different ways. One point is that mainstream theories in linguistics and psycholinguistics tend to be predominantly biassed towards the speaker (Bell 1984); the listener's role tends to be belittled. Secondly, a sharp distinction is made between speakers and listeners, which does not seem to acknowledge the partly parallel tasks they have to cope with in interaction and sense-making. Thirdly, the roles of speaker and listener are each treated as fairly monolithic.

From a dialogistic point-of-view, matters look quite different. The activity of speaking is intertwined with those of listening and sense-making to a much larger extent than the transfer model of communication can do justice to. The speaker is continuously listener-oriented, monitoring his own (and the other's) communicative activities in accordance with his assumptions of a social world temporarily shared with the listener. The listener, in turn, is speaker-oriented, aiming at understanding what the speaker intends to make known (Rommetveit 1974: 112). There is a reciprocal setting and taking of perspectives (Graumann 1990, 1995).

---

14. For a penetrating analysis of gossip, see Bergmann (1987).

CHAPTER 7

Sense-making in discourse and the situated fixation of linguistic meanings

7.1 Linguistic meaning and situated interpretation

In the previous chapter it was argued that both speakers and listeners are active as sense-makers in dialogue. Accordingly, a dialogistic theory could not treat the speaker's meanings, and her efforts to make things known in communication, and the listener's understanding of those messages and efforts as if they were more or less entirely different tasks and achievements. As Lesser & Milroy (1993: ch.7) and others have pointed out, Searle's and Grice's theoretical endeavours can be seen as dealing with these tasks separately. In the next chapter (ch. 8), the intrinsic interdependencies of discourse, contexts and understandings will be explored up to a certain point. Some of the discussion of the role of contexts will be pre-empted in this chapter, where I will deal with the role of linguistic meaning in sense-making activities.

By *linguistic meaning* I mean both (what linguists explicate as) *lexical meanings*, i.e. semantic representations tied to lexical items (as entries in the mental lexicon), and *sentence meanings*, i.e. semantic representations pertaining to sentences (which are regarded as complex and syntactic, i.e. rule-derived, linguistic objects). It is also also customary in linguistics to distinguish between, on the one hand, this *sentence meaning*, which is some sort of abstract semantic representation pertaining to the complex linguistic expression, i.e. a sentence or the like, as a type, rather than as a situated token of that expression, and, on the other hand, the *situated interpretation(s)* (or situated meaning) pertaining to the use of a linguistic expression (perhaps of sentence form) in a given concrete situation. For the latter, there are many other terms, including in particular '*utterance meaning*'.[1] The positions characterized here as monologism vs. dialogism would assign rather different significances to these notions, or rather: to their counterparts in the various theories. I shall contrast these divergent positions in the following.

7.2 Meaning in fixed codes and fixed contexts, or accomplishments in situated activities

The monologistic point of departure is that each utterance is a linguistic entity, consisting of words (or morphemes etc) in a specific syntactic configuration. These linguistic properties, as a whole, provide the utterance with its linguistic identity and defines what it means at a 'linguistic' level. The semantic representation defines what is given by the language system as a 'linguistic' (or 'literal') meaning. (One could call this 'linguistic content', exploiting the connotation of 'content' as something "contained" within a form, i.e. here: the linguistic (expression) form.) In other words, this meaning or content is there "before" the expression type is used on a specific occasion, in a particular utterance event, with particular actors at a specific time and place etc. On this view, the linguistic meaning is a necessary precondition for the actors' sense-making; how could people understand each other if there were no common linguistic code?[2] The contexts, on the other hand, are thought of as being added as external circumstances and constraints, enabling the actors to derive particular situated interpretations of utterances, i.e. determining reference and particular, indirect and perhaps metaphorical, meanings of words used. In such cases, the literal meaning is not sufficient for anyone to understand the utterance in question. Yet, the contexts are often regarded as complicating "nuisance variables" (to adopt a characterization by Rogoff & Lave 1984), obfuscating the possibilities for people, especially perhaps analysts, to assign to utterances straightforward

---

1. E.g. Levinson (1983: 18ff.). Related, sometimes synonymous, terms are 'utterer's meaning' (Grice 1968), 'speaker('s)-meaning', 'occasional meaning', 'actor's meaning'.

2. As Taylor (1992) shows, most philosophers of language seem to have taken it as a pre-theoretical given that people ordinarily understand each other in communication. More specifically, they seem to make the tacit assumption that interlocutors ordinarily, but of course not always, understand utterances in the same way. A common "explanation" is found in the assumption of a fixed, context-free semantic representation, provided by the linguistic code. Such representations would be assumed to account for at least literal interpretations.

semantic ("literal") interpretations. Thus, two salient features of the monologistic theory of sense-making are the assumptions of a fixed common linguistic code and of contexts as external factors, in principle fixed in each specific case, influencing occasional interpretations made there. Another ingredient is the assumption of speaker intentions as determining utterance meaning.

Next, I shall adumbrate the dialogistic positions with respect to the assumptions of a fixed common code and of contexts as external constraints. Dialogism claims that the explanation of shared and mutual understanding must be grounded in analysis of the situated discursive and interpretive activities themselves, rather than simply by recourse to (the assumed existence of) a common code.[3] Dialogism would of course not abolish a notion of a common language, but it would insist that linguistic meanings are open potentials, rather than fixed coded meanings. In Rommetveit's (1984: 335) words, "vagueness, ambiguity and incompleteness — and hence also: versatility, flexibility, and negotiability — are inherent and essential characteristics of any natural language".

The meaning potentials in language are never sufficient for determining communicative meaning. Instead, intelligibility and intersubjectivity have to be accomplished, negotiated and completed by actors in the various communication situations. They are projects and products of discursive activities in contexts. Yet, we must not adopt an extreme position of 'radical interactionism'; although communicative meaning is always situated, it is *not totally constructed in situ*. It is possible to create situated understanding of, in and through discourse only because actors use linguistic meanings as resources for ('cues to') interpretations in contexts.

The concrete situation would normally crucially support parties' *establishing a common focus of attention on certain referents*. From there, they build shared understandings by *using discourse itself as a testing ground for trying out interpretations* (ch. 5.5). Words are used as clues to inferences about perspectives on referents (e.g. Gardiner 1932; Gumperz 1982, 1995). In addition, interlocutors implicitly rely upon implicit background assumptions which can be used as a common ground (Cicourel 1973: 34ff.; Clark & Marshall 1981; Clark 1996) and interlocutors regularly treat each other as cooperative and morally responsible agents, acting as if they understood each other. Thus, they develop routines of mutual trust that make shared practical understandings possible (Taylor 1992:

---

3. From the standpoint of dialogism, the search for unique, determinate, context-free, semantic representations (cf. fn. 1) is due to a pseudo-problem created by monologistic theory.

216ff.); to some extent, intersubjectivity must be taken for granted in order to be attained (Rommetveit 1974: 86; 1985: 189). And, "mutual understanding on the part of conversation partners is contingent upon reciprocally adjusted perspective setting and perspective taking. Reciprocal adjustment is achieved by an "attunement to the attunement of the other"[4] by which states of affairs are brought into joint focus of attention, made sense of, and talked about from a position temporarily adopted by both participants in the communication" (Rommetveit 1992: 23).

Naturally, totally shared understandings are an ideal rather than an empirical fact (cf. also Taylor 1992). What is communicatively relevant is an understanding "for all practical purposes" (Garfinkel 1967), rather than some fictive, fully determined or "complete" interpretation. In other words, interlocutors have rather different criteria of communicative adequacy than language theorists (cf. Taylor 1992: 215). One might say that interlocutors mutually sanction a level of considerable imprecision, incompleteness and indexicality;[5] they have access to situations for the purpose of reference and are not entirely dependent on verbal means for all aspects of sense-making. At the same time, the nature of dialogue allows conversationalists to explore their understandings in principle indefinitely.

The assumption of a fixed common code is motivated by the view that communication involves the listener in recovering an utterance interpretation that must be identical to the speaker's. The latter view of communication is unrealistic, and therefore the fixed code assumption seems to be unnecessary (Taylor 1992). However, this argument does not imply that there cannot be *any* kind of common code, or rather, common language. Dialogists cannot be absolved from the task of explicating what linguistic meanings are like. I will return to this problem presently (ch. 7.4).

Let us first formulate a dialogistic position with respect to contexts: Are contexts fixed external factors influencing occasional interpretations? No, dialogism amounts to proposing that the utterance and its contexts are mutually complementary and form an integrated whole; one part cannot be defined as prior to or independent of the other. There are intrinsic relations between

---

4. This formulation is due to Barwise & Perry (1983).

5. In addition, there are of course large empirical variations among activity types in kinds and degrees of vagueness. Sometimes, vagueness at particular points of discourse is specifically intended and designed by speakers. For a discussion of vagueness as an interactional resource in threatening phone calls, see Adelswärd & Linell (1994).

discourse, understanding and contexts, which mutually constitute, select and elaborate each other. There are always contextual dimensions, and these are essential preconditions for, or ingredients in, the situated understanding (or interpretation) of the utterance. These contexts do not only concern specific references in the concrete setting, but also abstract, and more global, conditions which have been described in terms of premisses of communication (Rommetveit), situation definitions, activity types (Wittgenstein, Levinson), and communicative genres (Bakhtin, Luckmann) (cf. ch. 12). Note that these conditions are not linked to linguistic expressions or singular utterances, but to the practices of communicating in specific ways (in activities with specific purposes); the utterance is embedded in an activity, it is *situated*. Schegloff et al. (1996: 40) claim that "[m]eaning lies not with the speaker nor the addressee nor the utterance alone as many philosophical arguments have considered, but rather with the interactional past, current, and projected next moment".

Utterances and their meanings (understandings, interpretations) are *essentially situated*, i.e. they are context-bound by their intrinsic nature and not just accidentally (extrinsically) so. The essential situatedness is a feature of action and meaning in general, not only of discourse (e.g. Suchman 1987, and references there). But again, "essential" situatedness does not mean total dependence on the concrete situation. Similarly, it is inappropriate to say that meanings and interpretations are "socially constructed in situ", period. We claim that all communicative meanings are accomplished, i.e. negotiated or confirmed, and completed (i.e. completed for current purposes) there-and-then, in situ, but we also claim that speakers come to the micro-situations, where actions and utterances are occasioned, with knowledge of topics and language, including (varying) access to meaning potentials of words and other expressions. Actual(ized) situated meanings cannot be made entirely independently of "predefined" meanings, i.e. parties' knowledge of what they assume to be collectively shared and conventionally endorsed meanings and meaning potentials (e.g. Rommetveit 1988: 37). In some activities, such predefined meanings account for a major part of the process of determining a situated interpretation, which means that actors in situ only make the last, but necessarily significant, accommodation, revision and completion (that is, again, the provisional completion for immediate and current purposes).

7.3 Situatedness: Contextualization, decontextualization and recontextualization

Let us return to monologism and have another look at how it copes with situatedness. Nobody would deny, I believe, the importance of situated interpretations in discourse. However, rather than saying that utterances *are* situated, it would, according to monologism, be more accurate to say that expressions, sentences etc., *become*, are made, situated by actors in particular settings. What actors do, it is argued, is to deploy linguistic items (words, sentences etc) with their pre-defined linguistic meanings and then derive situated interpretations by a process of *contextualization*. In other words, meanings, as given by the rules of the language system, are primary, they are given "first", and then we *use* them as a basis for specifying contextual (occasioned) interpretations. Language is conceptually and processually prior to 'language use', just as a computer programme must exist before it can be deployed by the user (cf. ch. 2.3).[6]

Monologism also prefers to distinguish between 'literal' or 'direct' vs. 'indirect' uses of linguistic expressions. For example, this idea underlies John Searle's (original) theory of direct vs. indirect speech acts. In *Speech Acts* (Searle 1969), the author argues for the "principle of expressibility", i.e. that it is, in principle (sic!), always possible to express explicitly all you mean to say (and only that).[7] To express oneself explicitly (at all points) is to organize one's utterances so that their linguistic meanings exactly ("literally") match one's intended meanings. This means that there would be cases of language use, in which contexts do not add anything to 'literal' meanings. Now, most utterances involve deictic (indexical) expressions, whose reference (by definition) cannot be established except in the particular situations where the utterance events take place. While monologists would of course concede to this, they implicitly treat this as an "innocent" (and presumably theoretically uninteresting) type of contextualization. Therefore, a more crucial point involves the above-mentioned activity-dependence of discourse (but also other aspects of context, cf. ch. 8).

Monologists would then argue that it is quite possible to understand sentences in a way that is independent of contexts. Thus, anyone can understand (at one level) what sentences like *It is raining.* or *The cat is on the mat.* mean,

---

6. For basically this account, see Clark & Clark (1977).

7. See Searle (1969: 88), and critique by Rommetveit (1983, 1988: 17ff).

without having in mind any particular reference situation. For example, we need not think of any specific cat, mat or surrounding situation, to understand what the latter sentence means 'linguistically', or, to put it somewhat differently, in what *general kind* of situation the sentence *could be* used meaningfully and truthfully. In other words, there seem to be cases, when we rely completely on the linguistically fixed (language-given) meanings, and thus need not bother about adding contextual considerations (introducing variables which are 'disturbing' from a linguistic point of view, cf. the "nuisance variables" of above). Johnson-Laird (1987) argues that the linguistic meaning is used as a 'default' meaning in situations, when no particular context is available.

The dialogistic stance involves a persistent claim that *all discourse is (essentially) situated*. Thus, we would refute the argument about default or context-free meanings. If people are able to discuss linguistic meanings of sentences (and words) and to orient to 'default meanings', then this occurs *as part of specific activities*, in which "normal" situated references are disattended. The exclusive relevance of linguistic meanings depends on specific "temporarily shared background assumptions" (Rommetveit 1988: 17). Parties must share certain knowledge of what sorts of things are going on in such activities. These activities may be linguistics lessons, seminars on logic, or, quite simply, discursive episodes in which the actors understand (implicitly) that they talk about and use language in specifically decontextualized ways. This is to say that *the decontextualizing practice is itself context-bound* and dependent on actors' implicit definition of the communication situation as one of treating language as an abstract structure. When taking part in such activities, actors know that the "game" involves the consideration of linguistic units and their semantic potentials in ways that must not refer to concrete settings and specific referents. In other words, cases where only linguistic meanings matter are quite rare, and far from being natural communicative events, and actors must presuppose and understand the particular premises of these exercises, something which is *not* included in the linguistic meanings of the expressions used. Moreover, we often cannot help imagining potential and fragmentary contexts even in such practices. People are thus implicitly asked to supply some sort of contexts, even when they are assumed to focus on 'default meanings'.

A dialogistic stance amounts to saying that meanings are never "not in a context". There are no completely context-free linguistic items and meanings that get 'contextualized' only when they are put to use in (new) specific communicative events. As I will argue in ch. 8.10, this is why 'recontextualization' is a more basic and more accurate notion than 'contextualization'.

7.4 The nature of lexical meanings: Stable features or dynamic potentials?

We are still left with the vexing question, what is the nature of linguistic meaning? Let us therefore bracket the problem of sentence meanings, and in general non-lexicalized complex expressions, since these are derived by rule (all linguists would argue this), and it is therefore possible to treat "the production of sentences" within a contextual theory of language use.[8] But we could not possibly deny that there "must be" some sort of lexical meanings, which actors use as resources in their linguistic practices and which must exist, in some form, "before" the specific communication situations. Therefore, it seems reasonable to focus the subsequent discussion on meanings of *lexical items*, since these seem particularly difficult to "explain away", even for a fairly radical dialogist. We might think of lexical items as belonging to some kind of (partly stable) 'stock of knowledge' (e.g. Luckmann 1992). We must then ask ourselves: How does this knowledge of language structure relate to the processes of linguistic practice and communicative interaction, and in what ways should we characterize lexical meanings at the abstract level?

I shall first say a few things about the latter question, although I suspect that nobody has a wholly satisfactory and conclusive answer to it. Traditionally, linguists have treated word meanings as *stable semantic properties* correlated with linguistic expressions. There has been a general preference for Aristotelian definitions in terms of necessary and sufficient conditions (or finite sets of stable semantic features); after all, this is the preferred format of dictionary definitions (and, in particular, definitions of scientific concepts), and thus seems to reflect the general "written language bias" in the language sciences. In recent decades, more divergent proposals have appeared, e.g. concepts based upon 'family resemblance' (Wittgenstein 1958) and 'prototypes' (Rosch 1977). Scholars seem increasingly prepared to admit many different kinds of conceptual-lexical structures.

---

8. It is interesting to note that Saussure (1916), generally regarded as a founding father of structural linguistics, thought that sentences could not be handled by a theory of language structure (*la langue*) but were better considered as utterances, structures produced in actual linguistic performance (*la parole*).

Whereas monologistic theories would tend to treat lexical meaning as fixed and given (in a metaphorical sense, at least) in the language system, dialogists would stress the dynamic and open properties of word meanings, and that actors can negotiate and redefine them in situ.[9] Words, and other linguistic components of utterances, are available as resources with *potentials* to be interpreted (in interaction with contexts) in certain preferred (or routinized) ways. The actual situated understandings of course emerge as results of communicative work "there-and-then", in the situations themselves (Marková 1992, with reference to Mukařovský's theory of meaning).[10] On this view, lexical knowledge, just as any other kind of knowledge, is ultimately relational, residing in relations between knower (who is a member of a culture) and known (cf. ch. 3.3.1). Lexical meanings should not be seen as objectified items, static (paralysed, as it were) and stored in books or processed by computers. (This view would be a significant example of 'the written language bias', ch. 2.5.) What is stored and processed are rather artifacts, used as resources by the knower in his attribution of meaning.

Despite the long scholarly traditions of lexical semantics, it would be premature to propose anything like a full dialogistic theory of word meaning. I shall therefore be content with enumerating some tentative points (cf. Linell 1992; Rommetveit 1992):

(1) a.   Lexical meanings are *semantic potentials*, which are partly open and not in all respects fixed prior to their possible applications.

     b.   Lexical meanings are *dynamic* and interact constantly with contexts; different activity types tend to invoke different parts of their semantic potentials. Contexts may reinforce some aspects of these potentials, while overruling others.

---

9. Most terms in semantics have been used in different ways. By "lexical meaning", we would here refer more to 'sense' (German: *Sinn,* Swedish: *betydelse*), rather than 'meaning' (German: *Bedeutung,* Swedish: *innebörd*), although it must be admitted that these terms are often used in partly unclear ways. Other terms are '(linguistic) signification' vs. '(communicative) significance'. Cf. Lyons (1977: 251, et passim).

10. The notion of 'semantic potential' has a long history, though Marková (1992) attributes it primarily to Humboldt. Other important figures in this tradition are the Prague structuralists Karcevskij and Mukařovský (see Marková, op. cit.: 52ff.). In recent years, it has been primarily associated with the work of Rommetveit (1974, 1988, 1990, 1992). Rommetveit (1974: 119) talks about lexical meaning as "meaning potential[s]" consisting of "set[s] of semantic potentialities".

c. Yet, lexical meanings are *relatively stable*; they are subject to historical change in the continuity of practice but far from freely changeable in singular and specific situations. Since words can be routinely used by speakers in new situations which are similar to situations experienced before, their lexical meanings may be apprehended as partly 'objectified'.

d. Lexical meanings are abstract and function as *constraints on cognitive processes* (or, in Givón's (1992) terms, 'mental processing instructions').

e. Lexical meanings are *rich in information*, rather than minimal sets of semantic features, and are often part of extensive semantic-associative networks; experiences of what words may mean are embedded in speakers' 'streams of life'.

f. Lexical meanings are often structured in terms of *core* vs. *peripheral* features; some parts of the semantic potential may be thought of as *implicative*; in addition to the relatively context-independent "core", they are, given certain contexts, liable to "connote" particular meanings which are defeasible in other contexts. The dynamic, and redefinable, tension between core and implicative features may facilitate semantic change over time.

g. Some uses, for example metaphorical and poetic applications, exploit what Rommetveit (1974: 126) calls the 'fringe potentialities' (otherwise perhaps marginal or not-attended-to parts of the semantic-associative networks); cf. Rommetveit's (op.cit.: 126–7) discussion of how the fringes of meaning of 'ship' and 'ocean' are exploited in utterances such as *My thoughts are ships on an ocean of curiosity*, and other instances of "creative transcendence of conventional language use".

h. Lexical meanings exhibit *variations in how they can be modelled*:
  * some might be described in terms of network of uses that are subject to 'family resemblance',
  * some might be organized around prototypical exemplars (with some sort of rules for how the words are extended to more marginal cases under specific contextual conditions), and

    *   still others are more susceptible to Aristotelian definitions (e.g. 'scientific' concepts which can be expressed in terms of necessary and sufficient conditions).[11]

  i.   Attempts to model lexical meanings (e.g. in dictionaries of some sort) involve *normative* elements, i.e. the user's or analyst's categorization is usually subject to some purpose of stipulation and regulation.

According to dialogistic theory (and especially point (1: i)), one should not treat dictionary meanings as given by the language system only. Rather, such meanings are a special kind of (man-made) abstract objects, which are the *products of specific types of sense-making practices*. In some social practices, i.e. language lessons, the construction and use of dictionary entries etc., we make such general and abstract ('linguistic') meanings communicatively relevant, and within these 'situated decontextualizing practices' (Linell 1992; cf. also Gustavsson 1988; Wertsch 1991) we have learnt to disregard otherwise quite pervasive elements of language understanding, such as specifying concrete referential meaning. Thus, the abstract outlook on language is itself embedded in, and mutually constitutive of, certain social practices (cf. ch. 14).

7.5 Fixed word meanings or temporary fixations

On the one hand, word meanings have been interactionally established over time, in the history of practices. On the other hand, these quasi-decontextualized meanings, as historical products, are constantly and potentially open to negotiation and temporary accommodation in specific utterance events. Sometimes, people indulge in arguments about how something which they attend to in the world should be described in words, and at other times, there is a negotiation of what a particular word or concept should mean as applied to a particular context (or set of contextual dimensions). For an example of the former, see A BAR OR A CLUB (ch. 12), for an example of the latter, see OPEN OR NOT OPEN (below, this section).

---

11. Allwood (1981) classifies theories of word meanings into three broad categories: "union of different cases", "essence", and "greatest common denominator", which, very roughly, correspond to the three types mentioned here. Cf. Linell (1992: 268–269).

If we think of the semantic potentials as parameters, the values of these parameters are finally set in actual communication. Even if words and expressions have 'potentials' to be situationally interpreted in various ways, there may sometimes be tendencies for certain fundamental ('default', primary) semantic responses to be activated. Yet, these 'activations' too are context-related, expressive and constitutive of contexts. The monologistic assumption of *fixed* word meanings reflects a need to have stable concepts in coping with the world. Dialogistic theory would prefer to assign priority to *fixations* of meaning; fixed meanings then become the orderly products of processes of situated and temporary fixations of meaning. Aristotelian definitions are among the most typical products of semantic fixation processes, and are referred to in specialized decontextualizing practices, whereas some of the other 'models' of lexical meaning, such as prototypes, family resemblance, semantic networks (core and periphery) etc., appear to be more closely at hand as resources directly applicable in mundane discourse.

The temporary fixation of word meaning has been discussed both in more theoretical arguments and in studies of authentic discourse. More general arguments have been offered by Rommetveit (1974, 1983, 1988, 1990, 1992), who has shown how the meanings of words like "to work", "to know (somebody)", "father", "democracy" etc. are dialogically constituted and negotiated in context. At the same time, Rommetveit's accounts demonstrate the impossibility of determining the meanings of utterances *in vacuo*, i.e. without considering their communicative contexts. Even Searle, originally a consistent monologist, admits the possibility that some word meanings are context-interactive (cf. his discussion of "to cut", 1992: 24–25). In many situations parties entertain different interests and therefore argue for different interpretations of crucial concepts. Hudelot (1993) describes this (in French) as the 'circulation' of word meanings in discourse.

Various studies of authentic discourse have shown how different aspects of word meanings get foregrounded and fixated under different contextual conditions. For example, in talks at social welfare offices, social workers and clients often negotiate meanings of significant terms; Linell & Fredin (1995) show how the meanings of crucial concepts like "co-habiting", "actively seeking jobs" etc. are subject to dispute, negotiation and sometimes joint agreement on what they should mean "there-and-then". Similarly, in a study of travel agency talk, Mazeland et al. (1995) show how customers and travel agency employees negotiate modifications in descriptive categories (such as what constitutes a "family" or what is the age limit of a "child"), in order to bridge the gap between customers' wishes and the agency's norms and available alternatives. There is an intrinsic, and highly significant, relations between category definitions and outcomes of the whole encounter, i.e. what allowances and subsistences can be offered by the social welfare office or what hotel accommodations become eligible at the travel agency. In another study of descriptive and defining practices, Mazeland (1994), using authentic data from work meetings of the personnel at a communal information centre, shows how the meaning of "open" (used about the centre, which is supposed to have certain "opening hours") is ambiguous: does it mean that the premises are physically open to customers (so that they can enter the building), or that the doors are open and the personnel there (but perhaps working with other tasks than receiving customers), or does it mean that the employees are available for services to the public?:

(2) OPEN OR NOT OPEN (Excerpt from Mazeland 1994. From a work meeting, where personnel at a municipal information centre discuss their policy with respect to customers who turn up at times outside of the centre's opening hours. The specific problem has arisen, because the centre has recently moved to a new building, which, for the next few months, is going to be open to the public for longer periods of the day than the opening hours of the centre. A is the head of the information centre, others are employees. Translation from Dutch. By courtesy of H. Mazeland.)

```
(..)
1.  A:    h we simply put somebody downstairs eh from eh 's half
          past eight a.m. at the desk (0.2) or in the depot.
          somebody who- (.) you know, in front of the [clientele
2.  D?:                                               [hh depot hehuh
3.  A:    well yes, there is that vista to the front of the hall
          (D?: yes) you know, you could say of someone who on the
          (the other-) who's asking questions to the desk (.) he
          will be- he's helped out. (.) you know somebody who who
          who is looking for something hh (0.3) he will get an
          answer (D?: hhuookhe heh) you AREN'T open officially. we
          will be open (from) the first of June hh
4.  E:    well. that makes no sense at all, you are open or you
          aren't open (0.3) you do (A: no) sit there or you don't
          (A: no) sit there
5.  A:    the problem is only- ((somebody coughs)) (that) the
          people who come who are standing at the desk and want to
          be helped out. hh do you help them out. or don't you help
          them out. (.) that's the problem until the first of June
6.  E:    no!
```

```
7.  C:     the management did take a decision about that. in
           principle they don't help out
           [so that one could say [normally it has to
8.  A:     [no in principle hh      [in principle we are closed
9.  C:     m-m (?: ehehh)
    (0.5)
10. E:     "yes madam in principle we are (A: yes) closed but I am
           willing to help you out this time" ((sarcastic tone))
11. A:     well
((A goes on to argue for a "practical solution", claiming that the
position of C and E amounts "somehow" to "an academic question"))
```

What A seems to be doing (in (2) and in the rest of the meeting) is to argue for a "practical" solution, in which he would rather not press the issue about the "openness"; instead, the issue for him concerns how to deal with customers who will turn up (2: 5). However, the others, particularly E, finds it important to make sure whether the centre is "open" or not, and what this would mean (2: 4). When forced in the dialogue to take a stand, A has to admit that the centre is "closed" (2: 3, 8), though only "in principle" (2: 8). E finds this compromise unacceptable, to judge from the sarcastic tone of the mock citation in 2: 10.

What is at issue in (2) is of course not abstract decontextualized word meanings. However, it is not just an episode-specific and temporary, situated interpretation of "open" (vs. "closed") which is determined here; the parties are also concerned with fixating the general meaning of the term as applied to their working conditions. This turned out to be a crucial practical (rather than just semantic) problem for the centre at the time Mazeland recorded his talks. Different parties turned out to have divergent interests; some would prefer to endorse official opening hours, while others were inclined to go for a "practical" solution to "help people out", if employees happened to be present behind the bar during non-opening hours.

Words can mean many different things — that is intrinsic to their semantic potentialities — but in actual communication more exact meanings and interpretations get negotiated and settled upon, and then exploited for specific purposes. The semantic fixation is dialogically constituted, temporary and, indeed, made for specific purposes. The example above shows this process at a local level, where it takes place in specific communicative episodes or particular speech events.

But there are also more long-term fixations, when word meanings get frozen and kept constant for the time being and for current purposes. For example, in a specific scientific study, terms are usually fixated and used in approximately the same sense across cases. Researchers create a context-specific monistic world in which expressions refer in unequivocal manners (cf. ch. 14). Sometimes, such semantic fixations are designed to last for a series of studies or for whole scholarly traditions. Dictionary meanings may be seen as results of attempts to fixate word meanings over a long time and across many situation types. In many administrative practices, including in particular jurisprudence, categories and their corresponding linguistic terms are the objects of far-reaching attempts to freeze meanings. The same is true of many political debates. Since different actors may often have different interests, it is no wonder that many bitter fights are fought over the meanings of words, and for the right to determine them. Ultimately, situated interpretations are dialogically constituted.

By way of summary. word meanings have been derived, by abstraction and decontextualization, collectively in cultural history, and are being recontextualized, renegotiated and perhaps redefined in ongoing practices. The fixed and stable meanings are not stable or quasi-stable by nature; they have their fixed meanings due to fixation processes (Rommetveit 1990, 1992). Meanings are not simply given, although they are frequently *taken as given* (Olson 1994), especially within certain activities and routines. Fish has put this as follows: "Meanings that seem perspicuous and literal are rendered so by forceful interpretive acts and not by properties of language." (1989: 9).

Wertsch (1991), developing a Bakhtinian approach to literal meaning, argues:

> "Literal meaning can certainly exist within this framework but not in some kind
> of a priori way. Instead, it is seen as a kind of meaning generated by a
> particular semiotic activity and a particular social language, namely the social
> language that concerns itself with the kinds of reflective activity found in
> modern, rational, literate discourse. The notion of literal meaning is thus part
> of a modern "linguistic ideology" (Silverstein 1987) that privileges a particular
> view of language and language activity." (op.cit.: 85).

In conclusion, we have seen how monologism, in its treatment of linguistic and situated meaning, gives priority to linguistic structure over praxis. It treats language use as a more or less unidirectional process of 'contextualization'. By contrast, dialogism views the relations between language, discourse and contexts as more complex: what is going on in actual discourse is not pure contextualization; rather, it involves de- and re-contextualizing practices (ch. 8).

Dialogism regards praxis as primary, and treats linguistic structures as interactionally generated, traded down, renegotiated and redefined. However, language is part of culture, into which we are constantly being socialized; it is "already there" when we, as actors, enter the continuity of praxis. And, of course, since language is there as a potent resource, it enables users to decontextualize. Decontextualized linguistic structures are themselves being managed in some interactional practices. Thus, we have pointed to particular activity types and communicative genres as premises and contexts for the abstraction of linguistic meanings, as well as for the language users' orientation (in their practices) to such abstract objects. I shall return to these issues in ch. 14, in an attempt partly to reconcile monologism with dialogism.

CHAPTER 8

Contexts in discourse and discourse in contexts

8.1 The incompleteness of language

Words and utterances do not express or contain the meanings actors want to convey in communication. Rather, words and their semantic potentials point to, allude to or admit of certain in situ interpretations. Hence, situated interpretations always go beyond the linguistic structure of discourse, the 'text' itself. This is what Merleau-Ponty called the essential incompleteness and allusiveness of language (Spurling 1977; cf. also Marková 1989). What we say is not said only in and through words but largely between, behind and beyond words. That is why a theory of discourse needs a theory of *contexts*. In this chapter I shall introduce some elements of a provisional version of such a theory.

Goodwin & Duranti, in their seminal paper (1992) which forms the introduction to their edited book *Rethinking Context*, discuss utterances and discourses in contexts as *focal events within fields of action*. Accordingly, an utterance or an action, taken as "a focal event", i.e. as a phenomenon focussed upon and to be described and explained, "cannot be properly understood, interpreted appropriately, or described in a relevant fashion, unless one looks beyond the event itself to other phenomena (for example cultural setting, speech situation, shared background assumptions) within which the event is embedded." (op.cit.: 3). Focal event and field of action are related very much as figure and ground, and are characterized as "two orders of phenomena that mutually inform each other" (ibid.: 4). I shall reformulate and develop some of the proposals of Goodwin & Duranti,[1] and also add a number of points.[2]

---

1. See also Auer (1992, 1995).

2. For another kind of 'contextualism' within so-called 'behaviour analysis', see Morris (1991).

8.2 Types of contextual resources

As we will see, the concept of 'context' is rather fuzzy, multi-faceted and hard-to-define, especially if taken in the singular, i.e. 'context' rather than 'contexts'. It might therefore be better to argue that a given piece of discourse is embedded within, or activates, a matrix of different kinds of contexts (or dimensions of context).

Nothing is a context of a piece of discourse in and by itself, as it were "objectively". Instead, we have *contextual resources*, potential contexts that can be made into actual, relevant contexts through the activities of the interlocutors in dialogue. For this reason, the following is a list not of contexts per se but of phenomena that can serve as contextual resources.

I. On the one hand, there are *immediate* contextual resources of basically two kinds:

I. (a) the *prior* (up to the simultaneously occurring) *discourse* in the encounter, i.e. what is often called *co-text*. Since we are concerned primarily with spoken interaction, this contextual resource comprises the whole interactional co(n)text covering the sequence of relevant actions prior to the utterance (or action) in focus; in some cases, this sequence may contain primarily, or even exclusively, non-verbal actions.[3]

The status of paralinguistic communication, i.e. 'body language' accompanying verbal utterances, is ambiguous. There are good reasons to view it as part of spoken discourse, yet it is often treated as 'para-textual', i.e. kind of co(n)textual, with regard to the 'text' of verbal discourse.

I. (b) the *surrounding concrete situation*, or concrete circumstantial setting, where 'concrete' means material or embodied, and spatially and temporally specific; in other words, the immediate perceptual environment (*"here-and-now"*) with its physical spaces, persons (and their physical positions, e.g. seating arrangements), objects, artifacts (including media such as books, papers, computers and other carriers of linguistic, and other, signals).[4] Of particular importance

---

3. If we were to analyze written texts, a host of different aspects of cotext, and other contexts, may become relevant. Genette (1991) distinguishes various forms of 'paratextuality'. (For a critical review, see MacLachlan & Reid 1994).

4. The reason why artefacts are relegated to this rather marginal position in this list is my bias towards treating mainly talk in face-to-face interaction. If and when information technologies, especially sophisticated computers and multi-media, are involved, they will naturally occupy a much more salient position among contextual conditions.

are such extra-discursive events which acquire a high degree of perceptual salience (Clark 1996: 81) and therefore are liable to be topicalized in discourse.[5]

II. On the other hand, we must deal with *mediate* (abstract) contextual resources of a number of partially overlapping kinds. These contextual dimensions are not directly and publicly manifest in the perceptually available situation and behaviours. Some are, however, more directly linked to the unfolding specific topics of the discourse:

II.   (a) what actors already assume, believe, know or understand about the things talked about in the discourse in question; this is often termed *'model'* (of discourse-in-context)[6] and is seen as something which gets continuously updated through discourse;

II.   (b) closely connected with the "discourse-in-context model" (IIa) is (what may the termed) the actors' model(s) of their *current and upcoming communicative projects*;[7] these are of course also successively updated through discourse.

Another two types are also rather closely related to the situation at hand:

II.   (c) *specific knowledge or assumptions about persons involved*; this (subjective or intersubjective) background knowledge is based upon actors' partly shared experiences and knowledge about each other's biographies. If, on the other hand, actors do not know each other, they probably treat each other according to (largely routine-like, taken-for-granted and hence culturally relevant assumptions

---

5. Cf., on this point, Bergmann's (1990) notion of 'local sensitivity' of conversation.

6. Such a 'model' is often described as a structured set of implied, presupposed and/or communicated propositions about the 'discourse-world'. The term 'model' has a clearly cognitivist ring (cf. Johnson-Laird, 1983), but similar concepts have been proposed by scholars of divergent persuasions. Accordingly, there are many terminological (and conceptual) proposals here; context spaces (Reichman, 1978), focus spaces (Grosz, 1977), situation models (van Dijk & Kintsch, 1983), discourse models (Kamp, 1984), discourse-world model (Beaugrande & Dressler, 1981: 194), discourse representation (Clark, 1996: 52), to mention just a few. I shall use the term discourse-in-context space (and sometimes topic space) for the presupposed and continuously updated 'model' of the discourse-in-context pertaining to a given topic (or topical episode, see ch. 10).

Note also that the discourse-world 'model' (IIa) and the above-mentioned 'concrete situation' (Ib) (and the apperception thereof) (cf. IIc, d) can be seen as reference situation vs. utterance situation, respectively. For example, in the case of a narrative they correspond to the story situation (world of the events narrated) vs. story-telling situation (cf. e.g. Tannen, 1989).

7. The relevance of the term/notion of 'communicative project' will be argued in ch. 11.

of) category memberships (e.g. as young or middle-aged, women or men, countrymen or foreigners, etc.).

II. (d) the *abstract situation definition*, or the *'frame'* defining the encounter as an instance of a certain activity type (Levinson 1979) or situated activity system (Goffman 1961) or communicative genre (ch. 12), e.g. a court trial, a family dinner-table conversation, a speech therapy session, a theatre performance etc.

The frame defines "what it is that's going on" in a situation, and it sets up an expectation structure among actors. Frames or framings evidently belong to the most central concepts in communication theory.[8]

Related to IId is IIe:

II. (e) the *specific organizational* context (and the actors' knowledge thereof); here belong sociopolitically determined working conditions, documents, regulations, hierarchies and divisions of labour among (professional) role incumbents, educational backgrounds surrounding the actors, especially those who act in their professional roles.[9]

However, IIe, in turn, is embedded within a broader cultural environment:

II. (f) the *sociohistorically constituted contexts of institutions and (sub)cultures* surrounding (in particular) IId and IIe.

Finally, at the most abstract end, we find the most general kinds of background knowledge:

II. (g) *knowledge of language, communicative routines and action types* (i.e. what actors have become acquainted with as a result of their acculturation within a linguistic and interpretive community)

II. (h) *general background knowledge*, i.e. fundamental or general assumptions about the world which may be said to belong to the culture's 'collective memory'

---

8. See esp. ch. 12 on activity types and communicative genres. Goffman (1974) offers a rich 'frame analysis' of human activities, highlighting the multiple ways of framing these activities, e.g. in serious and non-serious ways (cf. also Clark 1996, on 'layering' in discourse). Concepts similar to 'frame' have been used in many disciplines. For a useful overview, see MacLachlan & Reid (1994), who are inclined to prefer 'framings' to 'contexts' in general (see esp. pp. 5–11). Related but slightly different concepts are also 'script' and 'schema' (Bartlett 1961, talks about 'schema' as an 'organised setting', cf. Middleton & Crook 1996: 385).

9. The importance of organizational contexts is stressed by many researchers. For example, Cicourel (1981) warns us of the danger in making the analysis too fragmentary, by the analyst's leaving out of account the organizational premisses.

and therefore are usually taken as given by actors. What is sometimes called 'common sense' belongs to these culture-specific general assumptions about the world.

Many of these abstract contextual resources, especially IId–h, can be characterized as background knowledge, assumptions and expectancies. By invoking such sociocultural knowledge and routines, actors make sense in their communicative projects, and thus "social life achieves its recognizable, repeatable and recursive quality" (Boden 1994: 13). In this regard, it is important to stress the role of social institutions. This is perhaps particularly relevant in the analysis of (intra- and inter-)professional discourse and professional-lay interaction.[10]

8.3   Dimensions of contexts: cross-classifying contexts and contextual resources

The preceding cursory account of contextual resources needs some comments straight away. I shall bring up five points (and fill out the picture more in later paragraphs).

One point is that the hypercategory of 'immediate contextual resources' (Ia,b) might need a subclassification of *'local' vs. 'non-local'* ones. In both cases of pre-textual and concrete-situational resources, that which is closest in time (and space) is most 'immediate' and most likely to be used as contextual resources. If something happens in the situation (e.g. a person entering the room, a sudden bang), it acquires high perceptual salience and will therefore easily impinge on the conversationalists, causing them to topicalize it (Bergmann 1990: 'local sensitivity of conversation'). If an interlocutor has a choice between tying his utterance to the last things the prior speaker said, or to something said further back in the co-text, he will often go for the former. But, of course, people do go back to non-local (or global) topics too (ch. 10.6).

Secondly, one general comment concerns the fact that contexts are *semiotic phenomena*; they are meaningful in relation to discourse. They are not simply static, stable and tangible environments (but cf. ch. 8.4). This means that if we think of extra-discursive entities, such as bodies, objects, artefacts etc (cf. Ib), as

---

10. Although professional-lay interaction is one of my own primary interests, I will only in spots refer to it in this book, which is more concerned with basic theory. See, however, ch. 12 and references there.

contextual resources, these must be cognitively apprehended in order to function as contexts. In one sense, this moves features of the co-text and the concrete environment (Ia,b) closer to the abstract contextual resources (II), the latter sometimes being called 'cognitive environments'. Relevant co-text, for example, is not simply everything said just prior to a given utterance, but that part of prior discourse that is actively employed in the new act of sense-making. Accordingly, one can argue that terms like 'context' and 'frame' serve to reify dynamic processes. This is a reason for some researchers, e.g. MacLachlan & Reid (1994), to prefer terms like 'framing'. I shall, however, continue to use the term 'context(s)', even though I also, at the same time, would stress more dynamic terms such as *recontextualizing processes and practices* (ch. 8.10).

A third point is that our list above testifies to the fact that there cannot be one single context for each discourse or utterance. Rather, there is a *complex matrix of contexts*, assembled from an array of contextual resources. Alternatively, we could talk about a *context space*. Moreover, contexts and contextual resources are seldom completely shared by actors in a given situation. For example, the same activity can be framed or perspectivized (IId) differently by different actors. This is a fact I will return to several times (cf. e.g. chs. 8.9, 12.8).

Fourth, it is immediately evident that contexts and contextual resources vary and overlap considerably;[11] they may be situational or cultural, local or global, shared among interlocutors or not etc. A basic distinction is obviously that of Mukařovský (1977) between immediate situation and living cultural tradition (or Malinowski's, 1966, between context-of-situation and context-of-culture);[12] this is what I have termed *the double dialogicality of discourse* (ch. 3.5). Contexts anchor discursive events both in social and physical space at some point in time (the given situation token) and in cultural history. The latter socio-cultural context is of course almost endless, encompassing social routines, cultural knowledge, and, indeed, the language system itself (language as a stock of

---

11. I have chosen to use 'context(s)' as the more general term, preferring to use 'situation' (and the adjective 'situational') about the specific social and physical setting with its concrete (Ib) and abstract (IId) features. Contexts, then, also comprise knowledge of language, routines etc. belonging to sociocultural traditions that extend far beyond the specific situations with their time and space coordinates. Others may reverse the terminological conventions. It should also be pointed out that I use the adjectives 'contextual' (or 'contexted') and 'situated' (as opposed to 'situational') almost interchangeably.

12. Cf. Halliday (1990), Halliday & Hasan (1990), Vagle (1995).

knowledge). Any discourse or social action has its local and global historicity. Given the above-mentioned distinctions, however, socio-cultural contexts (or knowledge) comprise mainly IId-h.

One could collapse the various types of contextual resources into three major classes; *co-textual* (or discursive) *resources* (Ia), *situational resources* (Ib) and *background assumption resources* (II). In one form or another, something like this triplet tends to reappear quite often in the literature.[13] But things are seldom as simple as in hierarchically organized lists. Several of my listed categories in fact shade into each other. For example, if, as we noted a moment ago, by co-text we mean not only local features but also global ones (global features being those relevant for the entire interaction, or at least for large segments thereof), we approach the abstract contextual features, especially frames (IId) and "intertextual" relations. Prior discourse (Ia) and projected future discourse activities (IIb) cannot always be limited to discourse in the same encounter or conversation; interlocutors also take account of what (they think) has been said at earlier occasions and what may happen in upcoming encounters (as a possible outcome of what they say *now*).[14] At the same time, if by "background assumptions" we also mean "models" (in addition to "fundamental assumptions"), we come close to (what is successively constituted through) the

---

13. Givón (1989) presents three main divisions of context in his "ecology of contexts" (op.cit.: 73ff., 403): the *textual* shared-discourse context (cf. Ia), the *deictic* situation-shared context (cf. Ib), and the *generic* culturally-shared context (cf. II).

What I call immediate (I) and mediate (II) contexts correspond roughly to Schegloff's (1992) proximate and distal contexts, respectively.

Anward (1997: 131) too assumes roughly the same triplet of contextual resources when he argues that topics in talk activities may be about the "speech event" itself (i.e. the discourse, Ia), "the situation in which it [the speech event] is embedded" (cf. Ib), or "other situations", i.e. topics taken from various kinds of 'background knowledge' (in particular IIa,b; 'discourse models' according to fn. 6).

Obviously, there are many other ways to categorize dimensions of contexts. Goodwin & Duranti (1992: 6–8) adopt the following taxonomy from Ochs (1979):

(1) setting (social and spatial framework); (2) behavioural environment; (3) language as context (a) discourse (co-text), (b) language system; (4) extrasituational context and background knowledge.

I have left out the discourse-acccompanying paralinguistic (non-verbal) behaviours from my overview. If we consider paralanguage (which we, alas, most often do not do), it should be considered an integrated part of speakers' (and listeners') discourse (discursive behaviour), and thus, in my model of contexts, it would go with co-texts.

14. On this point, cf. chs. 11.10 and 6.5.3.

discourse itself (the co-text). The same holds true of communicative projects, which, in addition, may be global and also tied to situation definitions.

Finally, my account of types of contextual resources is, like most parts of this book, geared towards the analysis of direct *spoken* interaction between two or more people. This does not mean that the types of resources are immaterial to other kinds of communication, such as different 'literacy events' (Heath 1983), situations where texts are written or read. It is not true, for example, that written texts are autonomous, e.g. that they "contain" their meanings. A written text is not decontextualized *tout court*. But it seems safe to say that the relative importance of different contexts get shifted, as we move from spoken interactions to literary, scientific, administrative, and other texts; in general, immediate (situational) contexts get less important, and some sociocultural contexts will move more to the fore-front.

But there are considerable variations within both classes of spoken and written genres, and often the purposes of activities appear to be more consequential than the medium, speech or writing, itself. Any attempt at developing a general theory with a fixed hierarchy of contextual dimensions must therefore be called into question. In addition, it is of course important to recognize that the weighting and granularity assigned to different contextual dimensions will vary with analysts' foci and research interests. Despite this, the point just made about purposes means that if any, activity types and communicative genres (abstract situation definitions, IId) may be assigned a higher status, since they often circumscribe what aspects of other contextual dimensions are likely to become relevant (see ch. 12).

8.4 Two perspectives on contexts of discourse

Contexts are *intrinsically relational*; a context is always the context of something, i.e. in our case: of some particular utterance or discourse. However, these contexts have a characteristically *ambiguous status*, being both *outside of* and *integrated within* utterances and messages. Accordingly, there seems to be a tension between *two perspectives* in theoretical accounts of contexts. One is that of context as a more or less *stable outside environment*, the other is that of contexts as deeply *embedded within discursive activities* and as *emergent* with discourse itself. The former is, I believe, quite close to common-sense conceptions of environment, situation, and context, and it is connected with the 'conduit' model of communication (ch. 2.3). It is of course also typical of behaviourism in social psychology. Furthermore, linguistic semantics often entertains a Cartesian dichotomy between discourse (or text) and context, treating the latter as something which gets added to the former when its 'linguistic' meanings get 'contextualized' and, thus, interpreted in situ.

The other perspective treats contexts "as inherently locally produced, incrementally developed, and, by extension, as transformable at any moment" (Drew & Heritage 1992: 21). We are then talking about "a context of publicly displayed and continuously up-dated intersubjective understandings [which] is systematically sustained" (Heritage 1984a: 259). This view is adopted in most micro-analyses of authentic dialogue and discourse, e.g. within Conversation Analysis (e.g. Heritage, op.cit.; Drew & Heritage, op.cit.) or interactional sociolinguistics (Gumperz 1982). It stresses that contexts are never objective environments; contexts "only" comprise those contextual dimensions which stand out as salient or relevant to the actors. I will return to this principle of relevance below (ch. 8.5.2).

The above-mentioned ambivalence with respect to contexts is hard to avoid. One way partly to reconcile the two views on contexts as given (and presupposed) environments vs. emergent aspects of discourse would be to treat the former as contextual resources (cf. ch. 8.2) and the latter as resources *actually constructed and deployed as contexts* by interlocutors in dialogue. Some of the resources would then be relatively stable across situations and communicative activity types; this would hold especially for general background knowledge and (parts of) linguistic knowledge. A natural attitude to take, on the part of actors and analysts, is to treat them as stable until further notice ("for all practical purposes"). Yet one must note that while this is natural and necessary, it involves a simplification; these contexts are not always "there" as fixed ready-mades, since only parts of them are invoked and made relevant in actual talk-in-interaction. For other contextual dimensions (cf. (Ia, IIa, IIb) above) it is more immediately obvious that they must be regarded as locally produced and emergent over sequences.[15]

When we analytically distinguish discourse from contexts (an operation which is of course often well motivated), we get easily trapped in thinking of contexts as if they were there prior to discourse. The more dialogistic position

---

15. Correspondingly, Auer (1992) talks about (the fuzzy boundary between) contexts "brought along" and contexts "brought about".

must be to talk about the co-constitution of discourse and contexts; discourse-through-contexts and contexts-through-discourse. The ambivalence of contexts (external vs. emergent as integral parts) applies also to such other concepts as have been proposed as, or instead of, contexts. For example, many contextual dimensions have been treated, especially by philosophers and linguists, in terms of *presuppositions* (cf. Goffman 1983). A given utterance "presupposes" the existence of certain referents (cf. e.g. Ib) and the truth of various background assumptions (cf. IIc, d, e etc.); without them, the utterance, it is argued, could not be truthfully or felicitously issued. But presuppositions are not necessarily pre-supposed; they can be co-supposed: for example, the speaker (or his interlocutor) will discover that by uttering something specific he has co-communicated an implied (or 'presupposed') meaning he was not aware of, let alone had intended.

There are, then, several good explanations why theorists tend to vacillate between the two perspectives on contexts. My own text will draw upon notions from both perspectives, such as evoking and activating vs. (re)constructing contexts.[16]

8.5 Some additional properties of contexts

8.5.1 *Backgrounding*

Contexts are systematically, indeed by definition, *backgrounded* with regard to the focal event.[17] The utterance is action (and events) and (in principle) observable and attended to, and therefore focal. When a speaker refers to something in discourse, the referent is attended to and made into figure rather than ground. But the meaning of the utterance can only be accomplished by contextualizing it properly; when you try to understand something or make yourself understood, context is its 'silent partner' (Givón 1989: 8). As we noted above, contexts are

---

16. As yet further examples of ambivalences in the work of discourse analysts with regard to the nature of contexts, one may mention Erving Goffman, whose 'frame' concept (Goffman 1974) appears to take 'context' largely as a stable outside. In his last paper, Goffman (1983) seems to have retracted from this position, stressing instead the emergent nature of frames. John Gumperz, somewhat similarly, has repeatedly stressed the locally produced and emergent nature of contexts, and yet his notion of 'contextualization cue' (e.g. Gumperz 1982) suggests that when discourse is produced, it needs to be "contextualized", i.e. anchored in contexts outside of it.

17. Compare here the phenomenological notions of inner and outer horizons of experience corresponding roughly to background knowledge and parts of (the marginalized) situational (immediate) context, respectively (e.g. Graumann 1990).

both visible (the concrete, present, physical setting; co-texts) and invisible (e.g. background assumptions), and both are typically taken-for-granted ('presupposed', cf. above), silently supporting understanding and mutual understanding (Rommetveit 1990; Graumann 1995; Linell 1995). Utterances and contexts are also closely related to the concepts of 'explicit' and 'implicit', respectively.[18]

8.5.2   Relevance

As I have already pointed out, contexts are *not objective environments* (the way in which a behaviourist might describe 'situations').[19] As Culler (1988: ix) puts it, "context is not given but produced". The contexts "produced" are those aspects of physical, social and cognitive environments which are *assumed, perceived, believed or known to be relevant by actors* (and to be reconstructed as such by the analyst). These aspects are not relevant per se; they are *made* 'thematic' (thematized) and relevant ("made into relevant contexts") by actors. Gurwitsch (1964) proposed a distinction between a thematic field of relevant distinctions and a marginal field of merely present features.

The "principle of relevance" (Schegloff 1991, 1992; Wilson 1991) means that there is an intrinsic, and reflexive, relation between understanding an expression and finding its relevant context. On the one hand, you must know the relevant context in order to assign the (or a) situationally relevant interpretation to any given utterance, yet you have to know the utterance before you can (fully) determine its relevant context.[20] This is hopelessly and irredeemably circular for a determinist; to many, it seems methodologically untidy. What it means, however, is simply that discourse and context are understood in parallel (or in a spiralling way), as part and parcel of one and the same communicative activity, in communicative projects of making things attended to, known and understood through actions-in-contexts. Words reorient situations; by saying something, we

---

18. Harris (1981: 157) speaks about the 'cotemporality' between the implicit and the explicit.

19. One must abandon any "bucket" theories of context, according to which contexts are solid and stable "containers" for actors' utterances and interactions (Drew & Heritage 1992: 19).

20. This treatment of relevance is partly opposed to that of Sperber & Wilson (1986). These authors argue forcefully that an utterance can be understood, and understood as relevant, only in relation to a context. However, their urge is to specify contexts so that interpretations of utterances can be computed from prespecified knowledge of relevant contexts and the linguistic composition of the utterances.

transcend the situation from how it appeared just before; we modify our contextual matrices. (The dialogicality of single contributions to discourse will be further explored in ch. 9.2.) Relevant contexts provide structuring resources, opportunities and limitations, for transactions in discourse, but at the same time, they are structured in and through the discourse itself. Relevant contexts and relevant situated interpretations *mutually select, elaborate and constitute* each other.

The relevance condition holds for abstract as well as concrete contexts; they must all be invoked by participants and be consequential for the discursive actions, and the analyst should be able to demonstrate, in one way or another, their relevance as displayed in the data themselves (Schegloff 1991, 1992). It might be tempting to argue that at least concrete situations "are there" before the utterances and that interlocutors accommodate their utterances, "responding" to these situations. The settings would then also simply provide communicators with possible referents. At one level this may be true. And yet actors have to organize and reorganize their apperceptions of these contexts in the service of their discourse. In this way afffordances from the situation are transformed into what Goffman (1961: 26–34) terms "realized resources". The same argument holds for prior co-text (Korolija 1998a,b) and background knowledge. Contextual resources are not in themselves significant; "[t]hey can enter the dialogue and affect what is made known only through the participants, i.e. *qua* features of their temporarily and partially shared social world." (Rommetveit 1974: 51). In the course of their communicative activity, actors both "respond to" contexts and "renew" them; "renewing" involves initiating and activating new contextual aspects (cf. ch. 9.2); Thus, actors both accommodate to situations and assimilate contexts to their communicative projects. (For some examples, see below.)

By way of summary, then, relevant contexts are constructed for, in and through communicative projects. Contexts are themselves, to some extent, *communicative constructs.*[21]

8.5.3   *Partial sharedness*

Communication becomes possible by parties' *sharing* utterances and *contexts*. Shared and mutual understandings and inferences are possible only by assuming that shared contexts can be relied upon. In actual practice, however, contexts are

---

21. Others have preferred terms like cognitive constructs (cf. fn. 6) or semiotic constructs (Vagle 1995, following, among others, Halliday).

of course only partially shared (Rommetveit 1974, 1988, 1990). Partial contexts are either available to both parties (speaker and listener) in the moment of utterance, or they are *made available,* are being activated or evoked, or they become (re)constructable through the utterance itself. Parties may entertain partially different or competing contexts. Both discourse and contexts are resources for shared and mutual understanding, and both can therefore, usually in the dialogical interplay, also be sources of misunderstanding and miscommunication (Linell 1995).

8.5.4   *Dynamics of utterance, contexts and understanding*

All in all, there is a dynamic relationship between discourse and contexts, or, to use other terms, in *the triadic relation between utterance (discourse), understanding and contexts* (Fillmore 1985; cf. also Morris 1938).[22] The intrinsic relationships between these three poles can be expressed in the following way:

(a)   You understand an utterance by relating it to its contexts, i.e. by attributing meaning to it within a sufficiently coherent, though still perhaps fragmentary, network of knowledge; understanding is understanding-of-discourse-in-contexts.

(b)   You display (parts of) your understanding of the contexts (and prior utterances) by uttering something specific at a given moment in the interaction; utterances are expressions-of-understandings-in-contexts.

(c)   You construct or renew the contexts by producing and/or understanding the utterance; contexts are partly products and projects of sense-making activities, of producing-and-understanding-discourse-in-prior-contexts.

These ideas were formulated, with slightly different accents, by Rommetveit (1974) in terms of dialogical relationships between 'what is said' (utterance), 'what is tacitly and reciprocally presupposed in the situation' (contexts), and 'what is made known and reciprocally understood' (understandings). In similar veins, Dore & McDermott (1982: 396) point out that

---

22.   Utterance or discourse in this formula may be substituted by e.g. discourse contribution, speech event, discourse encounter (or a phase thereof), in short any stretch of discourse. 'Understanding' of course refers to the situated meaning or interpretation accomplished in an actual communication situation.

> "talk is not simply a set of propositions transmitted from encoder to decoder, in which context is occasionally useful as an added interpretive grid through which to pass strange utterances. Rather, people use talk reflexively to build the very contexts in terms of which they understand what they are doing and talking about with each other."

If something gets communicated through discursive actions, then aspects of the *contexts* of these actions get *co-communicated*. Fillmore (1985), following Ducrot (1972), talks about two messages being simultaneously communicated, one (textual) which is 'posed' and one (contextual) which is 'presupposed'. A special case is at hand when authors of novels or short stories play the game of taking the reader into *medias res* by talking about new referents in the very first sentences of the text as if these referents were already familiar (cf. the use of definite noun phrases). The existence of the referents in the story world are thereby at the same time presupposed and co-communicated.

Returning to the inherent ambiguity of contexts, we can also say that they are parts both of the messages (to be) communicated (communicative projects) and of the functional explanations of utterances. Explaining why the utterance U is said by A to B there-and-then (and in that particular way), we must posit bidirectional functional relationships; A says U *because of* the contexts present and *in order to* create contexted understandings (the backwards vs. forwards pointing aspects of the double meaning of 'why', cf. Foppa 1990). We have to assume both (a) that shared background explains how interlocutors can understand each other and why A says U (the retrospective aspect), and (b) that understanding-in-context is accomplished as intended or actual effects (changes brought about in the physical or social setting, e.g. if B performs an action, or in people's minds, i.e. in their knowledge states and 'models')) (the prospective aspect of 'why').

8.6 Recontextualizations at the micro-level; selective use of cotextual resources

All action and discourse is necessarily contextualized. However, since meanings are never completely devoid of contexts, and no thought or idea exists entirely out of context (we always get them from somewhere),[23] the notion of 'recontextualization' is actually a more fundamental notion than 'contextualization'.[24] The dynamic coupling, and the delicate intertwining, of discourses and contexts can be identified at several levels. Recontextualization is therefore a broad notion, and I shall return to this issue in ch. 8.10. In this paragraph, however, I shall concentrate on a few analyses of the relations between discourse contributions and their contexts, primarily their local contexts, within the flow of discourse on (more or less) an utterance-to-utterance basis.

Discursive actions are always contextualized for and by the actors. This is true in several senses. On the one hand, all discourse occurs at some place and time, and as part of some situated activity. On the other hand, communicating something new, making this known, understood and mutually understood, involves — one might say almost by definition — integrating it within some sufficiently coherent, and appropriately activated, body of knowledge (called by many names: discourse model, context space, cf. fn. 6). This might lead us to think that discourse involves simply contextualization of language. However, a closer analysis reveals a more intricate pattern; there are continuous vicissitudes of contextualizations, decontextualizations and recontextualizations.

Discourse involves building and using fragments of understanding and contexts. As interlocutors in dialogue, we are "struggling to establish temporary dyadic states of intersubjectivity in a contextually understood and only partially shared world" (Rommetveit 1988: 18). Hence, most situations may well be characterized by interlocutors' having partly discrepant understandings of the discourses and their relevant contexts. Yet, in many of these cases, we act as if contexts and understandings, for all practical purposes, can be taken for granted as intersubjectively valid.

In our flow of consciousness, streams of fragments, glimpses, impressions and associations get *cognitively organized locally*. We can think of this as the building of *episodes* in discourse. Actors construct a coherent text and an associated context space by starting from a fragment and building around and

---

23. As Fish (1980: 284) points out,: "A sentence is never not in a context. We are never not in a situation [...] A sentence that seems to need no interpretation is already the product of one [...]. " Cf. also Muhlhäusler & Harré's (1990) discussion of Katz' (1977) notion of 'null-context'. See also Searle (1979: 117), Bogen (1991: 48)

24. Contextualizing means, of course, "putting something in a context (or a matrix of contexts)", decontextualizing means "detaching something from its context(s)", recontextualizing (or transcontextualizing) "moving something from one context into another".

beyond this an *island of temporarily shared understanding* (ch. 10.9). In this
process, fragments of contexts are used as resources
   Let us now look at excerpt (1):

(1) THANKSGIVING (Tannen 1984: 91–2) (extract from a dinner party at
    Thanksgiving in Berkeley 1978: De=Deborah, 33; P=Peter, 35; C=Chad, 30;
    St=Steve, 33; Sa=Sally, Steve's former girlfriend, 29; the talk unfolds as
    parties are eating; in 1: 1, De introduces a new topic)

```
1.  De:   I wonder how our (0.5) [grandparents and pa]rents felt
          about Thanksgiving.
2.  P:                           [cranberry sauce. ]
3.  P:    cranberry sauce.
4.  De:   it wasn't their holiday.
5.  P:    it's a wonderful holiday.
      (1.5)
6.  P:    is that the cranberry sauce?
7.  De:   I wonder if they did it
8.  C:    =one holiday a year for stuf [for stuffing yourself?
9.  P:                                  [y'know what we should
          really have?
10. St:   could [we get this off the table?
11. De:         [(xxx xxx xxx)             y'know if they used to
          do it for [the kids, or whether they really] felt it.
12. P:              [I'd like if off the table.]
13. St:   it keeps coming back on the table. it must have a will of
          its own. [that's all I can say.
14. P:             [we should have more napkins.
15. St:   uh- well,
16. Sa:   Steve's parents (0.5) feel it. (0.5) they feel (0.5)
          really strongly
17. St:   =sure they do. yeah, it's a major uh --
      (1.0)
18. P:    it's always been my favourite holiday.
19. De:   well I wonder how
20. P:    =except maybe for (.) [Pesach
21. De:                         [well your paren- their parents
          were born in this country.
22. Sa:   yeah.
23. De:   but MY parents
24. P:    ((to C)): =>are you Jewish? you're not Jewish.<
```

As we can glean even from this simplified extract, there are multiple activities
going on in this dinner-table situation; parties have to attend to multiple demands
(cf. Goodwin & Goodwin 1992). The main topic in (1), on the traditions of
celebrating Thanksgiving, is broached by Deborah in 1: 1 and is then pursued
mainly but not exclusively by herself (e.g. 1: 4, 5, 7, 8, 11, 16, 17, 18, 21). Of

course, this topic is made relevant by the overall frame, the encounter being a Thanksgiving dinner. From this topic space, Peter, in 1: 24, seems to extract a couple of topical aspects, that of ethnic descent (cf. the word "parents" in the preceding turns) and Jewishness (cf. "Pesach" in 1: 20). In the meantime and partly in parallel discourses (Parker 1984), Peter and Steve have briefly referred to three objects in the concrete setting, i.e. the cranberry sauce (1: .2, 3, 6), the (shortage of) napkins (1: 9, 14), and the tape-recorder (which was placed on the dinner-table) (1: 10, 12, 13); of these, only the tape-recorder is briefly topicalized (on topics, see ch. 10), whereas the other two are simply referred to in the service of implicit requests. That aspects of the concrete settings may be used as resources in a conversation is well-known, and has been termed 'local sensitivity' by Bergmann (1990).

In an informal conversation, an interaction typically characterized by no overall agenda and hence no particular goals of achieving global coherence, topics are developed by local coherence from utterance to utterance. Sometimes, topics gradually shade into new topics, sometimes new topic spaces are built using only one or two brittle links, e.g. from the prior topic space(s) or from other contexts, in the latter case making topic spaces (topical episodes) more clearly bounded. Various aspects of the *contexts are used as resources* in these transitions or initiations; we could see this in (1) in the cases of (a) the general frame of the situation, as in 1: 1, and (b) features of the concrete setting, as in 1: 2, 1: 9, 1: 10 ('local sensitivity'), and (c) the co-text, i.e. the discourse of the prior topic (or topical aspect), as in 1: 24. Cases (a) and (b) show how aspects of extra-textual contexts serve as starting fragments, whereas in the last-mentioned case, pieces (fragments) of the discourse-in-context are extracted, decontextualized, from a preceding topic space, and the speaker (re)contextualizes them by starting to assemble a new context space around them. Incidentally, it might be argued by analysts who approach the discourse *ex-post-facto* that Jewishness is not a new topic in 1: 24, but that it was present as an underlying topical current in the whole extract cited in (1). Arguably, Deborah, in 1: 21, 23, implicates a difference between parents of different backgrounds, e.g. Jewish vs. non-Jewish. Even if this is so,[25] it does not change my basic argument that

---

25. Incidentally, Deborah Tannen, who was De=Deborah in this conversation, informs us (Tannen 1984: 92) that she was talking about all those parents and grandparents who were immigrants to the U.S., a tacit background assumption which was arguably not shared by the others who contributed to the topic in the episode cited.

there is a juncture (or, if you will, a partial disjuncture) between topics (or, if you prefer, topical aspects), a boundary between 'topical episodes' in the terminology of ch. 10, between 1: 23 and 1: 24; note also that Peter in 1: 24 addresses Chad, thus ignoring the previous speakers Deborah and Sarah. Transforming topical aspects from being only implicit or even hidden (though perhaps present in speakers' minds, something which we usually cannot know much about) to becoming explicit and mutually attended to is a major move in a conversation. However, what one can point to in (1) is that Peter seems to have prepared for 1: 24 (perhaps without being fully aware of it) in his previous contributions (note the trajectory from 1: 18 through 1: 20).

When topics are initiated, sustained and closed in discourse, there is a constant interplay between contextual resources and active construction and recontextualization. It is obvious that not all aspects of the concrete setting are deployed as resources; in (1), the cranberry sauce and the tape recorder are among the very few things selected for reference and (incipient) topicalization. But the same is true also of co-text. Whenever something is said (or done), it is added to the potential co-text, which can be understood as a pool of resources that can be used for building new utterances and new meanings by recontextualization. But only some of these resources are, through these new discursive actions, *made into relevant* (activated) *co-text*. For example, Sally in 1: 16 picks up the aspect of strong "feelings" about Thanksgiving from Deborah's 1: 11, thus ignoring other aspects of co-text, such as "if they used to do it for the kids" in 1: 11, or the talk about the tape-recorder and napkins in the interjacent lines 1: 12, 13, 14. Sally, thus, uses one fragment of prior co-text and recontextualizes it as part of an assertion about Steve's parents. Later, Deborah ignores much of the co-present interlocutors' feelings about Thanksgiving as expressed in prior co-text (cf. 1: 17, 18), and refocuses attention to possible differences between her own and others' parents. Other examples of the selective use of co-textual resources can be seen in (1), and indeed in any stretch of discourse. Relevant co-text is not just a static prior text; it is dynamically constituted by interlocutors' active deployment (Korolija 1998a).

8.7 Fragments of discourses and contexts

Discourse involves the handling of fragments: fragments of understanding and fragments of contexts. In addition, at least in multi-party conversations, one can point to the fragmentation in contributing to the same or different floors.[26] The property of being partially fragmentary pertains, I would argue, to any conversation or spoken encounter. In (1) we could follow the meandering topical trajectories through a few topic spaces (islands of understanding) and over some bridges or links connecting different islands. However, the fragmentary nature becomes more salient when one (or several) interlocutor(s) in the conversation have difficulties in expressing themselves and making themselves understood. The following extract involves both a 4–year old child and an aphasic woman:

(2) NOT RECALLING NAMES OF FLOWERS? (Tema K: H51: t15.24)
     (A=Anita, 4; T=Tora, aphasic, around 55; N=Nils, her husband, around 65; U=Ulla, their younger daughter, around 25; V=Vivan, their elder daughter and Anita's mother, around 30; B = researcher, who tape-recorded the interaction. Excerpt given in rough translation from Swedish.)
     (the whole sequence quoted lasts 2'41"; when we come in, talk among the adults has centred around an object available in the situation, a round, blue and pliable plastic disc, usable as some kind of pad, and Nils has read the label on it, saying that it was "made in England")

```
1.  A:    ((picking up the disc)) no, what can one do on this?
2.  N:    yep
3.  T:    ((looking at A)) ah it was ((yawning)) from Eng- land!
          from England ((laughs)), °it was°
4.  B:    °that's it°
          ((T starts humming "The Rain in Spain", 6 seconds))
5.  A:    ((simultaneously)) (xxx) ((inaudible))
6.  T:    what?
7.  A:    ((holding her closed hands over the disc, possibly seeing
          the shadows of her hands in the disc)) now I see my green
          han-
8.  N:    ((tittering)) °do you have° green-han-
9.  V:    do you have green
10. T:    what?
11. N:    do you have green-hands (xxx)
12. A:    what's that?
13. T:    ((unfocused forward gaze)) °h ha° there you see, that too
          that no c- can, nothing eh (2.0) no
14. A:    (xxx xxx)
```

---

26. To some extent, participants in (1) and (2) contribute to parallel floors, so that the discourses as wholes become fragmented from the point of view of participation framework as well. This aspect of fragmentation is evident for both analysts and actors (though not necessarily in exactly the same way).

```
15. T:    ((pointing with stretched left arm and finger high up))
          eh an'in up there
16. N:    in the hospital?
17. T:    ((pointing horizontally)) that I can't, you know (2.0)
          well, I see everything, right? ((moving hand back and
          fro)) but I can not, eh- say wh- this, eh
          whatchamacallit? ((groping gestures)) not eh (3.0) °mm°
18. A:    what are you gonna do?
19. T:    °eh°
20. B:    (xxx)
21. A:    ah
    (1.0)
22. N:    what did you say? (1.0) you can't say? what it's called?
23. T:    or- eh- no h- ((moves left hand and fingers in circles))
          the other you know it eh the lett- er or whatchamacallit
24. N:    °mm°
25. U:    (xxx)
26. N:    °letters°
27. T:    no more, that, what it called
28. N:    °figures°
29. A:    (xxx xxx)
30. T:    ((pointing far way, somewhat up)) that, here, that's ho-
          or --
          ((looking at N))
    (2.0)
31. V:    flowers?
32. T:    yeah eh ar-eh go ah eh
33. N:    plants? (0.5) °no°
34. T:    yes, what is it called, one wonders? hh ((hand towards
          mouth in adaptor-like gesture))
35. V:    you can't recall what the flowers are called, you mean?
          different flowers
36. T:    yeah, no (1.0) an' then (1.0) yeah, now I know, mm
          ((pointing far away, somewhat down)) I know what it's
          called today when he came, today yes ((sobbing sound,
          slurping))
37. N:    mhm
    (5.0)
38. T:    ((swallows)) an' sometimes they say no, that they can not
          make- (2.0) eh
    (2.0)
39. A:    I haven't seen that film
          ((B says something in the background))
40. T:    can only have (.) plack-an'-white there are also (2.0)
          some who have such th- kh things too!
41. N:    black-an'-white?
42. T:    b-b-ba-back, br- black-an'-white! that
43. V:    colours you mean?
44. T:    yes
45. N:    mm
46. V:    you can not recall which names the colours have, is that
          what you mean?
47. T:    m- mm (3.0) an' I can NOT I can't, there,
48. N:    tell what kind of colours they are?
```

```
49. T:    ((looking at N)) c-c-colour, go-
50. N:    ((nodding)) colours
51. T:    colours
52. V:    (xxx xxx)
53. T:    no, which colour I have (2.0) ((pointing far away))
          f'rexample
    (2.0)
54. V:    of different flowers?
55. T:    yes, that's it! (2.0) it's hard °with°
56. V:    aren't you gonna buy flowers, °by the way°
[...]
```

Basically, (2) consists of three episodes with associated topic spaces, the first one comprising 2: 1–4, the second one 2: 7–12 (or 2: 5–12), and the third one the whole stretch of 2: 13–17 and 2: 22–55. The latter one can perhaps be divided up into several episodes; it also surrounds some parallel discourses (with separate floors) (2: 18–21, 39). In 2: 56 a new topic is broached by Vivan, by stripping an element ("flowers") of its prior embedding discourse-in-context and recontextualizing it completely (note the use of °by the way°); in other words, "flowers" from the prior episode or topic space is used as a trigger for a new episode (which is not reproduced here).

An extradiscursive object, the blue plastic disc, serves as a trigger for at least the two episodes starting with 2: 1 and 2: 7 (or possibly the inaudible 2: 5). The reference to the plastic disc provides the link from the preceding discourse (where it had been talked about as "made in England", something repeated by Tora in 2: 3) to the episode 2: 1–4, as well as from this episode to that of 2: 7–12, although in the latter case the disc is not explicitly referred to (but it is (probably) there the little girl Anita sees her hands). One might either describe these episodes as triggered by the object (the plastic disc) in the situation, or one might prefer to say that the interlocutors seize the opportunity of constructing new episodes by topicalizing an aspect afforded by the situation.[27] This ambiguity again illustrates the equivocal status of contexts as both extrinsic and intrinsic to discourse (ch. 8.4).

The third episode, the long one, is quite enigmatic and dominated by the expression and understanding problems associated with Tora's utterances. It starts with Tora's initiative in 2: 13, where she apparently expresses her frustration at not being able to express what she means. This opens up quite a lengthy

---

27. The concept of 'affordance' is associated with Gibson (1966). In our context, it is important to stress that affordances are environmental opportunities which are themselves dialogically constituted.

negotiation on what exactly Tora is trying to talk about. This common project seems to have two foci, i.e., on the one hand, what Tora is referring to in the situation (flowers, plants, TV sets, colours?) and, on the other hand, what her expression problems are (cf. 2: 22, 35, 36, 46–48). Tora either does not quite know what she is trying to say, or she is unable to express it clearly enough for the others to build their islands of understanding in the current topic space. Tora also uses various gestures, mostly deictic (pointing) movements (illustrators; Ekman & Friesen 1969), as resources in the sense-making activity, but they are obviously not sufficient for the others to determine any clear reference.[28] In other words, Tora's talk seems to involve a good deal of 'local sensitivity'. Some of Tora's utterances seem to indicate reference to flowers (cf. 2: 31, 33, 35, 54), but for a while gestures and talk appear to be about TV sets (2: 36, 38, 40). Finally, the parties settle on (her difficulties in finding the names of) colours. Indeed, vague references to colours seem to have been present all the time, and this is what makes one suspect, at least in retrospect, that Tora's initiation in 2: 13, originally without apparent sequential relationship to the prior talk, was in fact elicited by association, recontextualized, from the preceding topic, where Anita and Nils talked about "green hands".

The extract (2), and most instances of aphasic communication, can be used to highlight the fragmentedness of speech. Recontextualization in general is a vulnerable process, and must be appropriately cued (cf. Gumperz 1982, on the notion of contextualization cues). In aphasic communication, the cues involved in de- and recontextualizing practices are often unclear, and therefore contextualization, the 'synchronization of consciousnesses' across topic shifts, and communication in general become troublesome. In (2), Tora's speech is in itself fragmented. The other parties to the conversation must work hard on interpreting this fragmentary discourse, and still they do not always succeed in building a mutually recognized island of understanding. Discourse, understandings and contexts remain fragmentary.

---

28. There are other significant gestures in (2). Note, for example, the circling hand movements in 2: 23, possibly illustrating a word-search, and the movement ending up in a self-adaptor (Ekman & Friesen 1969) in 2: 34, perhaps indicating bewilderment.

8.8 Local decontextualizations

Our examples also show that decontextualization is a central aspect of ongoing discourse. Interlocutors often leave one episode or discourse-in-context space by extracting, decontextualizing, a fragment and starting to build another epiosode or topic around it. This phenomenon is also illustrated in the building of embedded subsequences in e.g. repair sequences. Negotiating the referential or descriptive meaning of a term used in discourse is a common case of decontextualizing from the main line of discourse and recontextualizing the term.[29] I borrow the following examples:

(3) GORILLAS (Holt; SO88(II): 1: 3: 6; by courtesy of Paul Drew; H=Hal, L=Leslie)

```
1.  H:     (.) an' Leslie 'twas marv'lous (.) d'you know he had (.)
           forty nine g'rillas. .hh th-there. (b) (.) br[eeding in
           (xxx)
2.  L:                                                 [pf- f-
           forty nine wha: t?
3.  H:     g'rillas.
4.  L:     .hh oh ye: s?
```

(4) WHAT TIME IS IT? (from Schegloff et al. 1977; SPC: 10: 4: ST; D=Desk, O=Mr O, caller)

```
1.  D:     but it's et- on three uh'clock en she might just be free
           or between interviews.
    (1.0)
2.  O:     w-what time is it now sir?
3.  D:     three isn't it?
    (0.7)
4.  O:     (we:ll?) I thought it wz earlier d'n that.
    (0.3)
5.  D:     't's two uh'clock I'm sorry.
```

---

29. It is not just words which may be extracted from one topical episode and then used in another one. Goodwin & Goodwin (1992: 87, et passim) demonstrate how a speaker may "extract" a gesture, isolate it and then recontextualize it to generate topical talk around it. Similarly, speakers can recontextualize other features of a speaking performance, as is common in metacommunicative comments.

In (3), Hal is evidently in the midst of telling a story of some kind, when Leslie interrupts him in his construction of a discourse-in-context space, because she cannot identify a crucial element in Hal's utterance ("gorilla"). She extracts part of the prior co-text, backtracking to "forty nine" and then asking Hal to fill in the unclear element. (Alternatively, Leslie may have heard what Hal said in 3: 1, but is not sure whether she heard it correctly, and therefore asks for a repetition.) The repair sequence (3: 2–4) becomes a digression from the main line of discourse (Hal's story); something from the main context is recontextualized within a subordinate context space. The same phenomenon occurs in (4), although here it is the veridicality of a certain element, a time reference ("three o'clock"), in the context and co-text of the main line that is disputed (rather than unidentifiable), and therefore, this element is extracted (decontextualized) and recontextualized as the starting fragment of a subordinate episode dealing with what is the current time.

In the development of episodes in discourse (with their topic spaces), we usually take for granted the linguistic devices and resources deployed. But as we saw in examples (3,4), problematizations of these devices are sometimes occasioned, and these are handled through decontextualization-cum-recontextualization. Let me take another, different but still related, kind of example; so-called linguistic meanings, first and foremost lexical (dictionary) meanings, are usually regarded as decontextualized in themselves. This decontextualization, however, presupposes its own context, as we noted in ch. 7. To be sure, it can be found in the contexts of activities tied to the reading (writing, and using) of dictionaries, grammar books etc. But the embeddedness of the decontextualization can be seen most clearly in some contexts of spoken discourse. Extract (5) is from a grammar lesson (a Swedish teacher talking about a text with an 11–year-old Finnish girl studying Swedish as a second language; from Gustavsson 1988):

(5) A NASTY WORD (Tema K: E-LP1: 69–77)

```
69. T:   you know it says like this, the nastiest cat is called
         Måns, what does that mean?
70. P:   well he's the kind that can cheat
71. T:   mm but if one is nasty how is one then?
72. P:   he's the kind that doesn't like Pelle
73. T:   no but -- but if -- if someone is nasty, what's he like
         then?
     (4.0)
74. P:   don't know
```

```
75. T:     you don't know, let's look it up and see (P: mm) if we
           can find an explanation of it
      (13.0)
76. P:     °nasty° [(°xx°)
77. T:              [you can almost say someone is mean, one is evil
           (P: yes) if one is nasty, you can write that down, nasty
           is (.) the same as evil, you know what that is, don't
           you? (P: yes) one is evil to someone when one is mean to
           someone, and then one is nasty to that person
```

In this example (Gustavsson 1988: 75–6),[30] the pupil and her teacher have read
a passage from a well-known Swedish children's book. They seem to be talking
about the same thing, namely the meaning of the word 'nasty' (Sw. *elak*), which
has occurred in the text. Yet, it turns out that they are talking about it in two
rather different perspectives, if you will: in two different subjective contexts.
The girl tries to explain 'nasty' by specifying what it means in the text, that is,
in its natural situational co-textual setting where it was found. One of the cats,
Måns, was labelled 'nasty', since he cheated and was unfriendly (5: 72: "doesn't
like Pelle"). Yet the teacher frames her question "What does it mean?" in
another, and new, context, which was *not* given in the prior discourse but which
is frequently deployed in language lessons and, therefore, implicitly retrievable;
her contexts are the language lesson and its associated model of language as an
abstract system of words and lexical meanings. The teacher is looking for a
dictionary-type definition of 'nasty', for synonyms. In utterance 5: 77 she gives
two such substitutes, 'mean' (Sw. *dum*) and 'evil' (Sw. *stygg*). In the frame of
reading, it might seem entirely superfluous to give synonyms for a well-known
mundane word, whereas it might be relevant to talk about if and why that latter
word is meaningfully and justifiably used in the concrete instance. The latter,
evidently, was what the girl tried to do. The word-knowledge exercise within the
activity context of the language lesson, on the other hand, is a social practice, in
which concrete, situated references are immaterial; instead, words should be seen
in terms of the same abstract meanings across co-texts.

Gustavsson (1988) discussed examples like that of (5) in terms of "itemiza-
tion": taking an occurrence of a word from an ongoing discourse and discussing
it as a linguistic "item", and building a new topical episode, a discourse-in-
context space, around this item. The island thus constructed, he termed a
"linguistic enclosure". The problem with many such situated practices in teacher-

---

30. This example is also discussed in Linell (1992) and Gustavsson et al. (1993).

student discourse is that these enclosures are not quite tight; the student, and sometimes the teacher too, often fails to cut the topical links with the preceding discourse and thus tends to frame his or her contributions in a way that is more appropriate to the prior context space.

8.9 Perspectival conflicts and competing context spaces

Goffman (1974: 9) points out that there is a sense in which supporters of opposing teams at a football match do not experience and appreciate the same game. Indeed, having different roles in an encounter usually implies sustaining different perspectives; student and teacher do not experience the same tutorial class (MacLachlan & Reid 1994: 47). Other researchers (e.g. Goodwin & Goodwin 1992) have also demonstrated that you can have multiple contexts, e.g. several discourses and floors, occurring simultaneously in the same physical and social setting. What (5) is intended to show is the case of multiple interpretations (multiple realities; Schutz 1962: 207ff) and mixed contexts for the same stretch of discourse, in the same episode. There seem to be two *competing context spaces*, the message-oriented one and the item-oriented one (pertaining to the language exercise context), penetrating each other; as we observed before, the contexts seem to have fuzzy boundaries. What makes the type of language lesson exemplified in (5) problematic is that the specific metalanguage perspective easily clashes with a more mundane content-oriented perspective.[31]

Similar perspectival conflicts occur in other kinds of institutionalized discourse types (e.g. court trials as discussed by Gumperz 1995, or police interrogations, cf. Linell & Jönsson 1991). Participants seem to have different 'tacitly held contracts' (Rommetveit 1974) about what they are doing in the situation or what they are talking about. My last example is drawn from a speech therapy session:

(6)   A HOT DAY TODAY (From Hawkins 1989: 192–3; part of the excerpt is also discussed by Lesser & Milroy 1993: 139–140) (T = speech therapist, P = aphasic patient. The excerpt comes from a session in which T tries to test P's comprehension problems. P has just talked about a walk he had had with his wife in Edinburgh on the Sunday before. T then evidently poses a question (6: 1) to test P's general comprehension.)

---

31. For more examples of a similar kind, see Gustavsson (1988).

```
1.  T:    right. well, I'm going to ask you a couple of questions
          like we've done before. would you say it was a very hot
          day today?
2.  P:    er depends on where you're going, what time, from summer,
          they say in the middle of summer
3.  T:    today, is it very hot?
4.  P:    yes, I like it. sun can be very hot..er.. nice and
          breeze. it's lovely to lie back and enjoy it, you know.
5.  T:    is it raining today?
6.  P:    er ((cough)) it's quite ((cough)) pardon.. no it never
          put me off (T: uhuh) no I was quite happy (T: right) even
          if it was raining and then I'd see it would cloud away
          and would be blue (T: okay) and you're happy (T: yes) all
          over again, I always used to feel good about things
7.  T:    okay and the last one, is it Monday today?
8.  P:    Monday. that's the beginning (T: right) it is the
          beginning
9.  T:    is it Monday today
10. P:    it's a Monday
11. T:    is it Monday today
12. P:    oh this one you mean
13. T:    today
14. P:    oh now this is fourth fifth February. it's about the
          fourth fifth is it now
((thirteen more turns follow on the topic of days of the week))
```

In this example the therapist poses a number of yes/no questions, which are evidently motivated by a predefined agenda. (Incidentally, the *and*-prefacing of the question in 6: 7 is an indicator of this, cf. Heritage & Sorjonen 1994). The therapist seems to frame the activity as a test situation, and the patient's responses may be judged as inappropriate in that activity context. Furthermore, the responses may be taken as indicating some kind of comprehension problem on his part. However, as Lesser & Milroy (op.cit.) suggest, one should be cautious as to the exact nature of the problem. The test questioning frame is a highly artificial one, in which questions about rather obvious matters are asked in a fairly decontextualized manner; questions are handled as more or less autonomous units, and answers are not followed up (cf. e.g. the abrupt shift from the weather to weekdays in 6: 7). Furthermore, although the therapist appears to frame the test situation in 6: 1, the talk of the excerpt follows a stretch of discourse (not cited), in which the patient appears to talk quite extensively (though, probably due to his aphasia, somewhat vaguely) about a walk around Edinburgh on the previous Sunday. If, therefore, the therapist's questions are instead understood more in accordance with a mundane conversational frame, at least some of the patient's answers make more sense. For example, P's reflections on his feelings about sunshine and rain (6: 4,6) would make some sense in such a frame, and given this it is not entirely odd that the therapist's next question (6: 7) seems to give rise to some confusion on P's part. At the same time, P seems to take the questions as general ones, rather than respond to the specification "today" in the therapist's 6: 1,3,5,7, etc. In other words, the interlocutors arrive at different understandings (and, if you will, misunderstandings), since they use partly different, and conflicting, situation definitions as resources in the sense-making process.

8.10 Recontextualizations at a global level: Intertextuality and interdiscursivity

At the outset (ch. 8.2), I introduced a fairly comprehensive matrix of contextual resources. However, I have later dealt chiefly with local contexts (and associated frames), i.e. what Mukařovský (1977) terms 'immediate situation', not with the sociocultural, historically given contexts, i.e. Mukařovský's 'living tradition' (cf. Marková 1992: 49). In the course of going through different topics, I also introduced the notion of 'recontextualization', demonstrating how it can be applied locally, within episodes of single conversations. In this final paragraph, I shall broaden the scope beyond single discourses (or texts) and discuss recontextualizations across different texts and discourse types.

Communication situations do not occur in splendid isolation. On the contrary, they are connected in countless and subtle ways, across space and time, through artefacts (such as written texts or computer files) and human beings who wander between situations. This means that discourse and discursive content too will travel across situations. This ubiquitous phenomenon involves recontextualization.

Recontextualization may be defined as the dynamic transfer-and-transformation of something from one discourse/text-in-context (the context being in reality a matrix or field of contexts) to another. Recontextualization involves the extrication of some part or aspect from a text or discourse, or from a genre of texts or discourses, and the fitting of this part or aspect into another context (another text or discourse (or discourse genre) and its use and environment). In Goffman's (1974) terms, recontextualization usually amounts to reframing. Aspects of discourse which can be recontextualized include linguistic expressions, concepts and propositions, "facts", arguments and lines of argumentation, stories, assessments, values and ideologies, knowledge and theoretical constructs, ways of seeing things and acting towards them, ways of thinking and ways of saying things. When parts of texts or discourses are relocated through recontextualization, they are often subject to textual change, such as simplification, condensation, elaboration and refocusing (Bernstein 1990). Such changes of meaning often involve reversals of figure-ground relations.[32]

'Recontextualization' may seem to presuppose a more basic concept, namely 'contextualization' (a term used by e.g. Gumperz 1982; Auer 1995; Bernstein 1990, and others). Originally, the latter notion was based on the notion of context-free linguistic items (such as words and grammatical constructions, with their linguistically defined 'content'), which were thought to become "contextualized" when they appear in situated use and are assigned context-specific interpretations. But at the message level, i.e. when communication is taken to be primary rather than entirely parasitic on abstract language, recontextualization is in fact a more appropriate concept than contextualization; no linguistic message, no thought or intention, exists first without a context, and only then becomes "contextualized". For the human subject, there is always a contextual embedding of a discourse or text. Discourse and contexts are co-constituted and are brought into being as complementary aspects of the same sense-making process.

What I have just proposed also implies that recontextualization is never a pure transfer of a fixed meaning. It involves transformations of meanings and meaning potentials in ways that are usually quite complex and so far not very well understood. It is therefore important to consider recontextualizations themselves as sense-making practices; selected parts of discourses and their meanings in the prior, "quoted" discourse-in-context are used as resources in creating new meaning in the "quoting" text and its communicative contexts.

While 'recontextualization' is originally a text-based notion (e.g. as it is implied in the work of Bakhtin and Kristeva), it is of fundamental importance to all cognition and communication, including in particular talk-in-interaction (a contention which is, by the way, in the spirit of Bakhtin). Bernstein (1990: 59–61) used the term 'recontextualization' in the discussion of the reproduction of educational discourse. Here, the notion will be assigned a wider applicability

---

32. The concept of 'recontextualization', as intended here, does not imply that the objects involved exist for a time outside of contexts and are then put back into contexts again. The recontextualization process is always a transformation of both content and relevant contexts. The meaning of 're-' is here analogous to that of 're-' in e.g. "reform, revise, reproduce, rework, etc." rather than similar to the 're-' meaning "again", in e.g. "recopy, reprint, etc.". See Linell (1998).

and a more fundamental position in the theory of communication. Recontextualizations can occur at all levels of discourse:

(a) Some recontextualizations are *intratextual* (within the same text, conversation, or focused encounter). Some are, as we saw in ch. 8.6, very local; they concern relations between individual utterances and their responses in dialogue; here we find the incessant small shifts involving new aspects and parts of referential worlds and semantic fields, and the introductions of new formulations, new stresses and keyings. For example, a co-conversationalist may locally recontextualize aspects of somebody's prior contribution by providing a response or a follow-up question that implies a new perspective on the topic or a redefinition of the communicative project. Other intratextual recontextualizations occur at a 'middle-range' level; conversational episodes or textual paragraphs are usually not entirely unanchored in available contexts, and some involve the recontextualization of an element from a previous episode or context space to the new one (see ch. 10.7).

There are also recontextualizations *across* texts and discourses. Following (roughly) the terminology of Fairclough (1992), we can then distinguish between:

(b) *intertextual* phenomena, relating different *specific* texts, discourses and conversations, each anchored in its specific contexts, and

(c) *"interdiscursive"* phenomena, occurring at more abstract and global levels and concerning relations between discourse *types* (communicative activity types, genres etc.) rather than between specific text tokens.[33]

All these recontextualizations at different levels involve the recycling of givens as well as the reinterpreting of new meanings. Recontextualizations and the blending of perspectives can be studied in either (or both) of the following ways. We can analyze *intertextual chains*, i.e. pairs or series of communicative situations, or texts, in which (in some sense) the "same" content, e.g. the same "case", is treated. The other method amounts to looking at the product of various kinds of recontextualizations in the *"multi-voiced" mix within single texts*.

Recontextualizations may involve actual wordings, explicitly expressed

---

33. In proposing the term "interdiscursive", Fairclough seems to presuppose a more Foucauldian notion of "discourse". A "discourse" is then, roughly, all that has been said about some (widely defined) topic, in some particular culture-specific ways, e.g. within a specific genre, tradition, profession, time period, or the like.

meanings, or something only implicit or implied in the original text or genre. It may be fairly circumscribed and "concrete", or it may involve general attitudes, ways of thinking or arguing, ways of laying out or understanding patterns of discourse. There are actual ("direct") verbal quotes as well as general and rather vague influences. In no case are we faced with a true transfer of something; it is never the propagation of a fixed message across representational instances. Rather, it is a complex transformation, involving shifts of meaning, new perspectives, accentuation of some semantic aspects and the attenuation or total elimination of others. Even what is usually understood as "quoting" is a complex reconstruction process, which necessitates an analysis of both the quoted context and the quoting context.[34] For example, Günthner (1997), using data from everyday multi-party conversations among friends, notes that de- and recontextualizations in reconstructed (reported, quoted) utterances can be used to communicate the reporter's evaluative perspective or affective stance towards the reported utterances, their original contexts and the speakers "quoted". In bringing about such effects (in Bakhtinian terminology, reaccentuations), speakers make extensive use of prosody and paralanguage.

In general, formal aspects of linguistic expressions may be retained in the recontextualization processes, but this is seldom true of *all* aspects of oral quoting, except perhaps if a physical copy (technical recording) is being used. In addition, semantic aspects and communicative values are always (more or less) changed, due to the change of contexts. In addition, we should note that the idea of something (a piece of discourse) being transferred from one contextual matrix to another, i.e. recontextualized, is too simple also because most recontextualizations seem to involve the dragging along of some aspects of contexts from one situation of use to another. We are faced with the exploitations of relations between both texts/discourses ('intertextuality') and contexts ('intercontextuality').

In countless instances, in public debates as well as in everyday interactions, we observe encounters between representatives of different subcultures and interest groups within the late-modern, diversified society; lay people, scientists, politicians, bureaucrats, businessmen, media representatives etc, all with their different commitments, understandings and premisses for communication. Scholars are, amongst themselves, split into different disciplines and schools,

---

34. Cf. e.g. Tannen 1989; Clayman 1990; Clark & Gerrig 1990; see also the literature in linguistics on 'reported speech', e.g. Vološinov 1973; Coulmas 1986.

politicians into different parties and other more temporary constellations, etc. In such cases, views collide and coalesce. What is being exchanged is not only words and discourses, but the worlds that make discourse.

Intertextual and interdiscursive processes and practices cross professional boundaries in many ways. Professional-lay interaction often involves the clash between professional and lay perspectives. Interprofessional contacts, e.g. between technicians and sales personnel, between lawyers and physicians, or between social workers and the police, involve different kinds of professional knowledge and ideologies, different perspectives on, and different ideological and culture- and profession-specific approaches to the same or similar phenomena. When 'cases' travel within bureaucracies, often involving many kinds of experts, we can observe, in the chains of professional discourses and communicative activities, that labellings, problem definitions, biographical fragments of people are being recontextualized. A few glimpses of such phenomena will be given in ch. 12.

At a grand scale, whole bodies of knowledge may move into other sectors of society and then get transformed and reproduced in new ways. An interesting type of recontextualization involves the reinterpretation of scientific or scholarly theories into the lay world at large, e.g. common-sense reinterpretations of, say, Darwin, Einstein or Freud. The latter case was studied by Moscovici (1961) in a well-known monograph on social representations pertaining to how "psycho-analytic concepts were transformed as they passed from the technical language of psychoanalysts to become the common property of everyday reality" (Billig 1993: 44).

CHAPTER 9

Elementary contributions to discourse

9.1 Elementary building-blocks: Utterances, idea units and turns at talk

It may be disputed what kind of unit should be regarded as (the outer form of) the elementary constituent of dialogue. What are the basic "building-blocks" of discourse? There seem to be two major candidates, namely idea units (sometimes loosely called 'utterances') and turns at talk.

Basically, a *turn* is a continuous period when one speaker holds the floor, and the corresponding dialogue contribution is then those verbal and non-verbal actions taken by him during this period, designed to be part of the jointly attended discourse floor, and/or taken up as significant contributions to this floor. Sometimes, the verbal content of a such a contribution, a turn, is nil, but the absence of talk will then usually take on communicative significance (cf. ex. 4: 5 in ch. 5). There are cases, when the division into individual speaker turns becomes troublesome, and we might therefore want to talk about some turns as jointly constructed by several speakers (cf. SHAKING HANDS WITH RUBIN-STEIN in ch. 5). Some cultures and genres generously allow for parallel floors in the same gathering, so that several speakers may be said to take their turns simultaneously. However, such complications need not engage us for our present purposes.

One reason for regarding the conversational turn as the elementary dialogue contribution is that, apart from injecting content into the jointly produced discourse, it serves to regulate (and is regulated by) the current speaker's moment-to-moment discursive and social relations to her interlocutor(s) and her (their) contributions. Selecting this kind of unit and then arguing that it proves the dialogical principle may seem to be begging the question. Fortunately, the same kind of dialogicality, or double contextuality, is arguably present in other kinds of units. Therefore, the choice of elementary units will not have any impact on the argument concerning dialogicality.

The chief alternative candidate for the status of elementary discourse unit would be what some call *'utterance'*, others 'turn-constructional unit' (TCU; Sacks et al. 1974; Schegloff 1996), 'information unit' (Halliday 1967), 'idea unit '(Soskin & John 1963; Chafe 1980) etc., something which rather often corresponds roughly to a clause (simple sentence) and sometimes (the expression of) a proposition (Clark & Clark 1977). An 'utterance', says Levinson (1983: 18) is "the issuance of a sentence, a sentence-analogue or a sentence-fragment, in actual context". (I shall sometimes use the description 'sentence or sentence-equivalent'). Goffman (1983: 8) also uses the term 'sentential utterance' for this (he says) "elementary unit of talk", and goes on to say: "An encoding unit for thought seems to be involved, a message unit, the minimal package of propositional-like meaning." Similarly, Levelt (1989: 23ff.) argues for this kind of unit, which is also closely related to prosodically-based notions like 'phonemic clause' or 'tone group' (Halliday 1967) or 'intonation unit' (Chafe 1994) as units of speech processing. If they are indeed units of speech processing, they are probably also units of cognitive processing (hence terms like 'idea unit'). Some discourse analysts, e.g. Sinclair & Coulthard (1992), have argued that similar units also correspond to elementary (speech) acts or 'moves' in conversation. Several coding systems for dialogue, e.g. Stiles (1992), Goldberg (1983), Crow (1983), and others, use such units as the basis for their categorizations.

However, the term 'utterance' is quite vague and equivocal. Some use it, in contrast to the usage described above, for roughly any stretch of continuous talk by one person, regardless of length and structure, whether outside of turns (as listener support items, cf. ch. 9.4), or only part of a turn or in itself constituting a whole turn. In suitable contexts, I shall in fact use the term in this loose sense. Therefore, we would need another term for the unit described in the preceding paragraph. Though *'idea unit'* is perhaps not the most common term, I shall use it, when it becomes important to contrast this type of concept or unit with the turn.

Both idea units and turns can be understood in dialogical terms.[1] Which

---

1. The dialogical properties of idea units have been explored particularly by the FSP (Functional Sentence Perspective) school of text linguistics (e.g. Danes 1974). This school had its roots in Prague semiotics, and was therefore related to some of the most well-known 'dialogists', such as S. Karcevskij (cf. Marková 1992). Bakhtin himself seems to be open to several interpretations, when we try to determine the exact nature of the "utterance", which he took to be the elementary discourse unit. In Bakhtin (1984), his ground-breaking work on Dostojevsky's novels, he deals largely with monologues, and seems to have something like (what I now propose to call) idea unit in mind. However, in his essays on *Speech Genres* (Bakhtin 1986), he rather seems to have had turns at talk

kind of unit should be regarded as the elementary unit of discourse may depend on the purpose of analysis and the nature of one's empirical data. Several considerations may have to be taken into account. For example, the attractiveness of using the smaller chunks of idea units as analytical units in a dialogistic account will increase, as turns becomes longer, as in monological discourse. However, since I deal, in this book, mainly with spoken interactions, often with frequent speaker shifts (short turns), I shall regard conversational turns as the elementary contributions to discourse, and I shall call these simply *contributions to dialogue* (or discourse).

Such contributions, and their meanings and understandings, are *locally produced*. The same applies to idea units, which are arguably used as planning units by speakers, and they are often executed as prosodically coherent units, incrementally (ch. 5.6). The boundaries between such units ('transition relevance points', Sacks et al. 1974) seem to be decision points for speakers, who must make up their minds whether to relinquish the turn or to go on talking, and if so, on what topical aspect. Likewise, listeners use these boundaries as resolution and response points, where chunks so far received are interpreted (semantically resolved) and often on-line responded to, e.g. through backchannelling (cf. HALF A GLASS OF WINE in ch. 10.8). If listeners cannot make sense of what they have heard (or perhaps failed to hear), they can use these response points for initiating a repair sequence (Schegloff 1982: 88).

9.2 The response-initiative structure of contributions to dialogue

Having chosen conversational turns as contributions to dialogue, I shall now introduce some further examples. Needless to say, the examples introduced in the preceding chapters are of course sufficient for demonstrating the dialogical properties of such contributions, but in order to bring out some contrasts, I will start out here from two examples of talk sequences, one interactionally symmetrical and the other one asymmetrical:

---

in mind, although his own term remains the rather loose "utterance" (Ru. *vyskazanie*) (cf. Todorov 1984: 53).

(1) TERRIBLY DIVIDED (Tema K: E206: 122ff) (Excerpt from a Swedish social welfare office talk between a female social worker (=S), aged 37, and a female client (=C), aged 29. The main topic of the encounter is a dispute concerning the custody of C's children. The excerpt is taken some 120 turns into the talk. Rough translation from Swedish originals.)[2]

```
[...]
1.  S:   yes we never came to talk about that, if you should
         choose Fred or the children
2.  C:   =sure one chooses the children (S: mm) they are obvious..
         I I'm terribly divided 'cause I have feelings of guilt
         for these years --
3.  S:   I see
4.  C:   I can feel bad about it when I think of it, (S: yes) what
         I subjected them to and why I married after all, it has
         to do with feelings in the beginning (S: yes), then it is
         only some luggage so to speak
5.  S:   but Fred can be very charming, can't he ((laughs))
6.  C:   ((joins laughter)) he can be he can be charming
7.  S:   =he is impulsive, he is not [a rotten person all through
8.  C:                              [( xxx) no he is not but what
         is rotten about him is his abuse (S: mm) the mentality
         that goes with the abuse (S: mm) that's what's so
         difficult with him, he has many good sides too
9.  S:   =though the ability to come to grips with his abuse
10. C:   like they disappear, you know
11. S:   all the good sides
[...]
```

Although (1) is drawn from a professional-lay interaction, it is a fairly symmetrical interplay between two women, who discuss the merits and drawbacks of the former husband of one of them. The social worker initiates the topical episode (1: 1), but then the two both contribute, building upon each other's contributions without obliging the other to respond. There are several latchings without intervening pauses, and at least one case of overlapping talk (1: 7–8). S and C collaborate on producing some of the content (cf. ch. 5.4), such as the agreement that "he [Fred] has many good sides, but his [in]ability to come to grips with his abuse [makes] all the good sides disappear" (1: 8–11), somewhat like the parties to SHAKING HANDS (ch. 5: (2)) .

---

2. This excerpt and the following ones are taken from a corpus of social welfare office talk analyzed by Fredin (1993). See also Linell & Fredin (1995).

However, (1) is rather atypical of the main bulk of Swedish (and doubtless other kinds of) social welfare office talk. Hence, the more asymmetrical interaction of (2), from the same data corpus, is more typical:

(2) DO YOU LIVE BY YOURSELF? (Tema K: E105: 22ff.) (Social welfare office encounter between S, a female social worker aged 31, and C, a young women (22) with a baby, who seeks financial assistance)

```
[...]
1.   S:   okay, let's see here, but are you... now let's see here, do
          you live by yourself or are you cohabiting?
2.   C:   no I live by myself
3.   S:   you live by yourself
4.   C:   °yep°
5.   S:   mm an' you have you you live second-hand it says here too
          (C: mm), how for how long have you got that flat then?
6.   C:   six months
7.   S:   mm, from when
8.   C:   from the first
9.   S:   from the first of January?
10.  C:   mm
11.  S:   mm then it was eighty-two six months ahead, okay, this
          means then that your living situation -- that we know
          nothing (C: no) in six months
12.  C:   no
13.  S:   did you register at the local housing agency
14.  C:   yes but there is a mighty long queue there
15.  S:   yes there is but one has to register
16.  C:   yes but I HAVE registered there
17.  S:   you have?
18.  C:   °yes°
[...]
```

In this case, the social worker (S) is doing a lot of the talking. In particular, she introduces the topics and topical aspects to be dealt with through her questions, thereby obliging the client (C) to contribute. C does this rather minimally, with some exception for the short expansion in 2: 14. The first excerpt, (1), was a fairly symmetrical dialogue with two parties both carrying the discourse further by using each of their contributions for responding to the other's prior contribution and for introducing some new content for the other to respond to. Moreover, the forms of the contributions serve to invite, rather than oblige, the other to respond. By contrast, in (2), S has to work harder to get responses from C, using questions as 'soliciting' or 'obliging' initiatives. Moreover, by responding minimally, C contributes to the continuation and establishment of this asymmetrical

pattern. In some cases C's answers are treated as less than adequate and sufficient (2: 8, 16).

Despite the differences in various dimensions, some contributions (e.g. S's
questions in (2)) being more context-determining than others (in particular, in
comparison with C's answers in (2)), every contribution in (1) and (2) is taken
by the interlocutors both to be somehow relevantly related to the prior context
and to carry the dialogue further by supplying some new content. Even a
'minimal response',[3] i.e. a response that does no more than satisfying minimally
the demands of a prior contribution (which is often a question), introduces
something new. By being so limited, it can, however, be taken as an attempt to
initiate the closure of a local topical aspect (cf. ch. 9.6).

It is generally true that contributions to dialogue are related to their local
contexts, i.e. their preceding and following units, in a Janus-like manner. "What
is said is always in response (in some way or another) to what was said before
and in anticipation of what comes next" (Schiffrin 1994: 360); utterances are
both dependent on prior utterances and they create conditions for possible next
utterances. Heritage (1984a, 1987) refers to this as the 'double contextuality' of
dialogue contributions: they are, in his terms (1984a: 242), both *context-shaped*
and *context-renewing*. In partly different terms, the contributions may be said to
be both conditioned by contexts, and they condition contexts for the future
dialogue. Since most of this takes place on a moment-to-moment basis, a slightly
better wording might be that contributions to dialogue are both *occasioned* by
prior co-texts and surrounding situations and *occasioning* a new local context,
creating a 'field of relevance' (Goodwin & Goodwin 1992: 180) for next actions.
Such elementary contributions are the building-blocks for the production of orderliness and coherence in dialogue: they are 'linked actions', both *relevant to prior
co(n)text* and *providing opportunities for relevant continuations* (cf. ch. 5.7 on
dialogue as a series of opportunities, "micro-situations", for relevant continuations).[4]

The surrounding structure of co(n)texts in discourse is both 'enabling' and
'constraining' new contributions, as well as shaped (enabled and constrained) by
them (Watson 1992: 3). (A monologistic view of contexts would presumably

---

3. Note that I use this term in the sense described here, not in the sense of 'listener support item'
(ch. 9.6) as e.g. McLaughlin (1984: 102, 116) does. It must be admitted, however, that the boundary
line between minimal responses (in my sense) and listener support items is sometimes quite difficult
to draw.

4. Schiffrin (1987: 25) discusses similar properties as 'action structure'.

regard them as only constraining.) Contexts in discourse are dynamic; they are both "attended to" in discourse and "constituted as a dynamic phenomenon" through discourse (Goodwin & Goodwin 1992: 151).

The dialogicality of discourse and social interaction has been recognised by many scholars. For example, the philosopher Ernst Cassirer formulated a couple of 'laws' about the ways in which human situations are progressively clarified; the 'law of continuity' says that each outcome is a fulfillment of the preceding definition of the situation, while the 'law of new emphasis' states that each outcome develops the past definition of the situation (Garfinkel 1967: 115, Schilpp 1949).[5] There is an implicit contract (Rommetveit 1974) between speaker and listener to build utterances and their interpretations in such a way that the speaker, through each utterance, will offer something new, yet link it to what has already been given, and the addressee will interpret it precisely as both new and coherently linked, i.e. as relevant in context. (Accordingly, if the speaker deviates from this contract, he is supposed to signal this in discourse.)

The dialogicality of discourse contributions, their Janus-like nature, has also been analyzed in terms of *response-initiative structure* (Linell et al. 1988; Linell 1990; Linell & Marková 1993). Vološinov (1973: 86) says that the "*word is a two-sided act*. It is determined equally by *whose* word it is and *for whom* it is meant. (italics in original/PL)" That an utterance is largely defined with regard to the addressee ("whom it is meant for"), implies that it is both a response to the other and an initiative projecting a possible continuation by the other. The "now" of an utterance is located in the tensions between its origins and its possible consequences; all this determines what is at stake for the speaker. Similar ideas have been proposed in a 'three-step analysis' of dialogue contributions, in which a contribution is analyzed not only in terms of what it contributes and embodies "in itself" but also in terms of its 'relevant outsides', i.e. its relations to prior and next contributions (Marková 1990b). Schegloff (1996: 97) argues, very much in line with this, that any utterance in conversation goes through "three phases: as (incipient) next (in relation to the preceding utterance/PL), as current, and as prior (i.e. prior to the anticipated following utterance(s)/PL)".

What has just been said means, in my own terms, that each contribution is defined, in part, by its *response links*, i.e. its relations to the prior contribution(s)

---

5. Basically the same insight appears in the work of Schutz (1967). Cf. also Cicourel (1980).

in discourse, and its *initiative links*, i.e. its relations to the anticipated, and hence 'created', context for possible continuations in discourse. Through the latter aspect, the contribution itself creates elements of discourse *and contexts*, elements which will be 'prior context' for the next contribution and to which *that* contribution will be responsive. The responsive and initiatory aspects are thus intrinsically linked to each other. In Schutz' (1962) terms, the initiative aspect of a (prior) contribution is the 'because-motive' of the (following) response within the local sequence, and the response aspect of the next contribution is the 'in-order-to-motive' of the (prior) initiative.

9.3   Excursus: The elements of social action

At this point, it may be appropriate to shift the discussion back for a moment to a more basic level and relate the concepts of response and initiative to more fundamental elements of social action.[6]

Let us think of a person A ("the speaker") who wants to communicate something to another person B ("the addressee"). A must then do at least do the following:

(a)   call for B's attention, i.e. make B aware of the fact that A wants to communicate something,

(b)   refer to something (X) in the (concrete or abstract) contexts, i.e. pointing to X by some verbal and/or non-verbal means,

(c)   make something (Y) known, felt etc., i.e. tell something about the referents (X), request some action from B etc., which involves seeking to initiate a responsive reaction from B in the form of a cognitive process (comprehension), an emotional reaction, and/or a disposition (preparedness) to perform an action (a verbal utterance and/or a non-verbal action).

In doing this (a–c), A must (at least to some extent) *anticipate* B's *possible* reactions and responses, and continuously (to some extent) *monitor* B's *actual* reactions and responses.

---

6. Or 'sociation' (Couch 1986, alluding to the terminology of, among others, Georg Simmel). The Swedish sociologist Johan Asplund has developed a nuanced and partly original account of these elementary aspects of sociation in his theory of 'social responsivity' (e.g. Asplund 1987).

B, on her side, must:

(a) become attentive to the fact that A is (in the process of) communicating something,

(b) attend to the referents (in the concrete environment and/or some assumed background knowledge) that A points to,

(c) realise what A possibly intends to make known or felt, by trying to understand A's action or utterance and integrate its meaning with various kinds of background knowledge,

(d) prepare for a response to A's action or utterance, and often:

(e) in fact provide (at least part of) that response overtly, so that A can observe it.

And finally (although this point is not honoured by all analysts), A must:

(a) attend to B's reactions and overt response (action or utterance),

(b) realise what B's response means in relation to his own intentions, knowledge and feelings,

(c) provide some reaction, a response in his turn, to B's response.

This third step (a–c) is usually required for parties to complete a minimal communicative interaction (ch. 3.4.3). In fact, B's overt actions and utterances (B: (e) above) constitute the basis for new contributions to dialogue, i.e. B now becomes the speaker who must be understood by A. And then, A's response in the third step can be expanded to a full-blown contribution to dialogue, which in its turn calls for a response, etc. In other words, we have reciprocation of actions.

Reciprocation requires the coordination and synchronization of both parties' actions (and consciousnesses). Indeed, A's and B's actions are sometimes, in a sense, more of analytically distinct aspects of the interaction than sequentially separable units. That is, we are in fact faced with *joint activities* (Clark 1996) including:

(a) establishing mutual attention,

(b) establishing jointly attended referents,

(c) constructing (partly) shared understandings as a basis for distributing contributions to discourse.

Reciprocation is related to commonality (cf. Graumann 1995), and, as Rommetveit (1974: 37) points out,

"some commonality is being established by the very fact that two persons
engage in a dialogue. The I and you constitute in every single case a temporarily established *we* engaged in that particular act of communication as
opposed to *all others* (she, he, they) who are not so engaged. Whatever is
shared, presupposed, or assumed as already known — even if in principle
accessible to "the public" — is hence something shared, presupposed or
assumed by the speaker and the *us* within an intersubjectively defined *here-
and-now*." (italics in some cases eliminated from the original/PL)

At the risk of repeating myself, let me describe this in yet another, slightly
different way. Social activities involve and presuppose at least the following
elements. First, to engage in interaction, the individual must of course note the
presence and activities of others, and respond non-randomly to these others'
activities. This is the essence of the *responsive* aspect. The second element, the
initiatory aspect, has to do with anticipation; in order to organize one's actions
effectively in interaction, one must anticipate the other's responses to one's own
actions. Anticipating responses involves anticipating the other's interpretations of
one's own contributions. Hence, if looked at in genetic terms, this also generates
intentionality, the ability to take initiatives with an awareness of their possible
interpretations. It is the basis for becoming self-conscious, not only conscious. A
third basic feature of interaction, *reciprocation*, is contained in coordinating and
synchronizing this exchange of responses and initiatives. Thus, it is the "ability
of human beings to project futures and to detect the projected futures of others
that allow them to construct complex units of cooperative action" (Couch 1986: 127).

When reciprocation is at hand, mutual alignment and sequential organization
will be included. Note also that the temporal sequence with A's initiative
preceding B's response involves a basic asymmetry of interaction (cf. ch. 1.5).
But an interaction is not a simple sequence of initiatives, responses and reactions.
Rather, as I have already demonstrated, each action is both responsive and
initiatory, and this fact is at the same time the precondition and the result of
sustained reciprocated interaction.

An account of dialogue in terms of mutual attentiveness, responsiveness,
anticipation of other's (and self's) moves, shared focus and mutual communicative projects can be understood in evolutionary terms; for example, non-random
responding is more basic than anticipating the other's responses (e.g. Marková

1987).[7] But reciprocation and turn-taking are not simply the outcome of an organization in terms of responsive and initiatory moves; there is evidence that dialogical reciprocation is ontogenetically primary (Trevarthen 1992; Bråten 1992). The analysis in terms of 'elements of sociation' (Couch 1986) resonates with thoughts of, among others, Mead (e.g. three-step analysis, ch. 3.4.3) and Simmel (esp. when divergences between dyads, triads and larger groups are considered). The analysis claims that the elements described are basic to human sociation and interaction in general. I shall now return to their reflection in fully developed talk-in-interaction.

9.4 Varieties of contributions to dialogue

Dialogue contributions fall into different categories, depending on, among other things, the relative strength of the initiatory aspect with respect to the responsive aspect. Some contributions exhibit roughly a balance between responsive and initiatory aspects, as in the majority of turns in (1) and the social worker's turns in (2); these are locally tied initiatives, i.e. initiatives that are, in each case, relevant responses to the other's preceding turns. In other types of turns, either the initiatory aspect or the responsive aspect predominates. The latter is true of the above-mentioned (ch. 9.2) 'minimal responses'. The former is the case in (what might be called) a *'free'* (i.e. cotextually untied) *initiative*, as when an actor brings up a new topic that is entirely unconnected to the prior discourse. A case in point is 3: 6:

(3) NO MONEY (Tema K: E105: 53ff.) (From the same talk as (2), somewhat later in the interaction. S is currently inquiring about the circumstances of C and her baby daughter:)

```
[...]
1.  S:    how are you doing then? how's it working?
2.  C:    well it's working fine
3.  S:    eh she sleeps like she's supposed to
4.  C:    yes, she does
5.  S:    mm okay
      (4.0)
```

---

7. These correspond roughly, I think, to Couch's (1986) "elements of sociation" (though his specific terms are different), which he considers more basic than concepts like "self, other, role-taking, social object, initiating act, response, and alignment" (cf. Couch et al. 1986: xxiii).

```
6.  S:    and what you're seeking you come here because -- that is
          you have no money (xx)
7.  C:    I haven't
8.  S:    mm how much money have you got at present?
9.  C:    now you mean today or -- ?
10. S:    mm
11. C:    now I have almost nothing at all
12. S:    you haven't
[...]
```

The untied initiative (3: 6) proposes a new candidate topic. This is of course quite likely to be sustained as a topic (i.e. actually 'topicalized'), since it deals with the client's reason for coming. The episode-initiating turn (3: 6) occurs after a (potentially) topic-closing marker "mm okay" by S (3: 5) and a pause.[8] Moreover, 3: 6 is *and*-prefaced, which suggests that it is agenda-bound (Heritage & Sorjonen 1994). Furthermore, S uses a long introduction in it, with a double 'topicalizer' ("what you're seeking", "you come here because"), to mark the new initiative, which is then a strong move requiring the interlocutor, C, to redirect her attention to a new object.

Another important distinction would be that between 'soliciting' (or 'obliging') and 'non-soliciting' ('non-obliging') initiatives. *Soliciting initiatives* are basically questions and requests for immediate action,[9] i.e. initiatives that explicitly call for, and hence virtually oblige, a response on the part of the interlocutor. *Non-soliciting initiatives*, on the other hand, are typically comments, which are "given" by the speaker: they may (more or less strongly) invite but do not oblige a continuation by the other.[10] Empirical data unambiguously show that it is very hard for a conversational partner not to respond, when a soliciting initiative is addressed to her, whereas the options are a bit more open after non-

---

8. 'Topic bid' in the terminology of Maynard & Zimmerman (1984). See also Svennevig (1997).

9. A request for action can be aimed at some (discursive or other) measure to be taken by the addressee immediately, as a response to the request in the local context. It can, however, also concern actions to be taken some time in the future, usually outside of the present encounter. Such requests for distant action would not be considered soliciting initiatives.

10. The distinction between soliciting and non-soliciting initiatives is basically what Blank & Franklin (1980) term 'obliges' vs. 'comments'. Cf. also 'solicit' vs. 'give' in Wells et al. (1981: 74). It must be emphasized that the distinction between soliciting and non-soliciting initiatives is a fuzzy one, and the boundary can be drawn in different ways. The problems involved are discussed with respect to Initiative-Response Analysis (ch. 9.7) in Linell & Gustavsson (1987). If a coding system is to work, the distinction must ultimately be based on formal properties of turns (and overt aspects of the local sequential environment) of turns. For some relevant discussion of how to identify and code 'questions' (cf. soliciting initiatives) in authentic discourse, see also Heritage & Roth (1995).

soliciting initiatives. Basically, both interlocutors' contributions in (1) were largely non-soliciting initiatives, while S's contributions in (2), her questions, were soliciting initiatives.

However, when a speaker has made a contribution to an ongoing dialogue, her partner normally has several options with respect to possible continuations. This is true even after a soliciting initiative, as the partner may simply refuse to answer and stay silent (a reaction which, however, will ordinarily be treated by the interlocutor as a kind of response, cf. ch. 5.7). The *canonical* form of continuation is, however, a contribution that is *locally and focally linked to the other's prior contribution.* Here, 'local' means that the contribution is responsive to the immediately prior contribution (in the local co-text), rather than to something further back in the discourse, which would amount to responding 'non-locally'. 'Focal', on the other hand, means that the contribution ties up with the main content, or main topical aspect, of the other's prior contribution, rather than with either the form or some peripheral semantic aspect of that contribution, which would amount to responding 'non-focally' (for an example, see (4) below).[11] Non-focal responses may also evade a prior question or deflect the topic, but even as such they remain designed to somehow "respond" to the prior action.[12]

Another distinction among response ties is between ties to the other's prior contribution (i.e. the unmarked case) vs. to the speaker's own prior turn ('self-linking'). The contributions in (1), (2) and (3) were all local (except the untied initiative in 3: 6), focal and other-linked. To see examples of some of the other options, we have to introduce another excerpt:

(4) CAN'T LIVE IN THE STREET (Tema K: E106: 102ff.) (Excerpt from a social welfare office talk between a male client, C (aged 34), who has had drug problems and is now applying for economic assistance, and a female social worker, S (aged 33). The episode cited occurs well into the talk, and

---

11. The 'semantically peripheral' type comes close, *mutatis mutandis,* to McLaughlin's (1984: 278) definition of 'tangential talk' as "talk that is directed not to the underlying issue or point of some narrative or stretch of talk (in our IR analysis: prior contribution/ PL), but that appears to be locally relevant because it exploits a topical pathway from some minor element or character in the narrative."

12. Non-focal responses to questions are in Goffman's (1981: ch. 1) terminology 'responses' rather than 'replies'. Such actions are, in Boden's (1994: 123) wording, "presented as conversational objects which, while satisfying the [local/PL] constraints of conditional relevance and sequential implicativeness, [but they] do so by breaking frame".

the atmosphere has become fairly tense. In 4: 1, S is referring to the
demand on C to present a valid tenancy agreement.)

[...]
1. S: an' you know also that in order to get an allowance for
         rent you
2. C: mm but that I haven't got, that's what I've been saying
         all the time ((irritated tone)), I haven't got hold of
         it, you see
3. S: no but that's what you--
4. C: =what the fuck can I do, I have to have somewhere to
         stay, haven't I
5. S: mm but then you have to fix that if you're going to get
         an allowance from here to --
6. C: mm but now it is like this, I got two and one ((i.e. 2100
         kronor)) from the insurance last Friday an' then I've
         paid the rent and such out there
7. S: okay, then you have chosen to pay the rent and then --
8. C: yes, what the fuck can I do then, I can't for fuck's sake
         live in the street if I get a job, can I
         (3.0)
9. C: that you know yourself
         (3.0)
10. S: what is it I know myself, that -- ?
11. C: well, if you have nowhere to live how could you work
         then?
12. S: this is something I hear quite often, these circular
         arguments, as it were, then
13. C: this is not a circular argument
14. S: yes, I think it is
15. C: I don't, actually
[...]

There are several noteworthy ingredients in this stretch of talk. I can only
comment on a few of them. When C has claimed that he is unable to present a
valid tenancy agreement (4: 2), S seems to object to this, although her utterance
gets interrupted before very much has been said (4: 3). C gets irritated and
comes back immediately, continuing on his own points (4: 4); this turn can be
heard both as ignoring S's incipient counter-argument (4: 3) and as intercepting
it as soon as possible. Or, to put in slightly different words, even if 4: 4 can be
seen as a move to silence S for the moment (and thus in a sense a rapid response
to C's attempt in 4: 3), it is to be regarded primarily as a contribution tied to his
own prior contribution (4: 2), i.e. it is 'self-linked'. There follow a couple of
other-linked expanded responses leading up to C's 4: 8, which has features of a
rhetorical question. It does not lead to any overt verbal response on the part of
S. After a few seconds, C, in another self-linked contribution (4: 9), adds that S

knows the answer to 4: 8, thus confirming its character of a rhetorical question. After another fairly long pause, S finally provides a response, which, however, only amounts to a semantically rather empty, though interactionally potentially quite provocative, request for clarification (4: 10). C responds by something which again sounds like a rhetorical question (4: 11), and S counters with a move which is clearly a locally tied response (4: 12). However, it is not an attempt to respond to the main semantic content of 4: 11; rather, it is a meta-communicative remark on C's reasoning. It is therefore a rather clear case of what we may call a 'non-focal' response. This then gives rise to a short sequence, where the meta-communicative nature of C's reasoning has become the topic (4: 13–15). However, there is no further topical progression; the parties simply reassert (by minimal responses) their positions.

These are some examples of different types of 'linked actions' with their 'Janus-faced' (responsive-initiatory) make-up. It is of course possible to design one's dialogistic analysis in other ways. The general point is, however, as Bakhtin has argued, that all 'utterances' that are attended to and responded to in discourse, display the principle of dialogicality. Bakhtin (1986: 91) says, in a frequently cited passage, that "utterances are not indifferent to one another and are not self-sufficient; they are aware of and mutually reflect one another."[13] Each contribution to a dialogue is 'other-oriented', including an interpretation of prior contributions and at the same time being designed to call forth some kind of continuation, thus also involving a prospective "interpretation", or anticipation, of what is going to follow. At the same time, a certain contribution embodied in an utterance by a speaker A is a joint accomplishment in the sense that its action meaning gets developed and co-defined by the interlocutor B's uptake.[14]

---

13. While monologism may be said to see only initiatory aspects in utterances (e.g. Searle's philosophy), Bakhtin may perhaps be accused of slightly overrating the responsive aspects. Shotter (1993) follows Bakhtin rather closely, though his terms 'rhetorical-responsive version of social constructionism' may be said to include both responsive and initiatory ("rhetorical"?) properties. For some discussion of the quotation from Bakhtin (1986: 91), see e.g. Shotter (1993: 51ff.) and Wertsch (1991: 109–110).

14. For the analyst, this has interesting consequences. Rather than one-sidedly trying to imagine the speaker's intentions (as is often the case in monologism, e.g. ch. 6), the analyst must try to take the interlocutor's perspective. In judging what kind of contribution A has made in a dialogue, you are helped by B's manifest reaction. Thus, in analyzing A's contribution, you take B's perspective, and in analyzing B's contribution, you take A's. Cf. the principle of 'validation through next-turn' (Peräkylä 1997: 209).

9.5 Utterances that are not full-fledged contributions to dialogue

Dialogue contributions are *contributions to the joint discourse in which two (or more) interlocutors participate.* That means that genuine contributions are typically intended by speakers as contributing to the floor, but even more importantly, they are taken up and treated as such by the interlocutors (through responses which are also contributions and may in their turns give rise to further contributions). The definition just proposed implies that there are also utterances which do not end up as genuine, or acknowledged, dialogue contributions. (Conversely, the absence of an utterance may sometimes be treated as a significant action, i.e. a contribution, like, e.g., 5: 2 of ch. 5.). Amongst these items, we find, first and foremost, so-called listener support items, i.e. utterances in the form of response particles like "yeah, mm, mm-hm, no" etc, when these are not intended nor treated as attempts to gain the conversational floor. Such support items may have different functions, chief among them that of encouraging the speaker to continue (Schegloff 1982), but they do not, by definition, claim the floor and or bring the floor to the utterer.[15] They do not in and by themselves resolve topics, nor do they introduce new topical aspects (McLaughlin 1984: 116). If, however, such an utterance is indeed heard and taken up as a genuine dialogue contribution, i.e. accorded status in the text of joint discourse, it becomes, by definition, a (minimal) response.

Some other utterances fall outside of the jointly acknowledged discourse,[16]

---

15. Other terms for listener support items are 'continuers' (Schegloff 1982), 'encouragers' (Edelsky 1981), 'go-ahead signals', 'backchannel items' (Yngve 1970). Still others use the term 'minimal response' in this sense (McLaughlin 1984) (cf. fn. 3). Recent work (e.g. Sorjonen 1997; Gardner 1997) has pointed to many functions of such items, including giving signs of understanding and alignment, providing acknowledgements and (weak) assessments, indicating kinds of news receipt (cf. Heritage 1984b), signalling to the speaker to continue talking, etc. The overlap between such items and 'minimal responses' (to questions and requests) is considerable. 'Response particles' (which I take to be a form category, including items like "yes, no, mm, yeah, mm-hm, uh-uh" etc. in English, and similarly lots of items in other languages; cf. Sorjonen 1997, as regards Finnish) are used for all these purposes, although with a distribution of functions characteristic of each specific item.

In most of the transcripts of this book, listener support items are put within parentheses at approximately the positions in speakers' utterances where they occur. If an item of a similar type *could* be interpreted as a minimal (response) contribution, it is, however, shown in the transcript as a separate turn.

16. I do not here consider the possibility of parallel floors in multi-party settings. Cf. e.g. the notion of 'by-play' (M. H. Goodwin 1990).

in particular self-talk, utterances ('turn miscarriages') that are interrupted at an early stage, etc. Utterance 4: 3 above is an example of an attempt which, by C's treatment through 4: 4, gets effectively aborted. By interrupting, C ignores S's 4: 3, thereby treating it as a non-action, as something which is 'sequentially nonconsequential', i.e. without significance in the unfolding discourse.

9.6 Initiative and response as relational aspects of turns

What I have proposed to call 'initiative' and 'response' are *relational* properties of turns (or idea units), referring to the links from one turn, or unit, to the preceding turn(s) (or units) (responding aspect) and to the projected next turn (or unit) (initiative aspect). Basically, all units have this kind of Janus-like nature, with retroactive and proactive links. The single contribution to dialogue is essentially sequential; its "own" content is always understood in relation to its local (and other) contexts.[17]

To repeat then, this theory amounts to saying that, strictly speaking, every utterance is somehow a response to the micro-situation existing at the time of its incipience, and at the same time, every utterance has a context-renewing effect on the micro-world of the dialogical encounter, i.e. the micro-situation will always be, at least slightly, altered *after* the contribution has been made; what is required from new contributions, the relevance conditions, is changed all the time (ch. 5.7). However, as we have seen (ch. 9.4), the strength of the retroactive and proactive links may vary, which motivates the assumption of concepts like 'free initiative' and 'minimal response'.

In a *free initiative*, there are, by definition, no overt relations to the preceding discourse (co-text). Yet a free initiative can be regarded as a "Janus-faced" contribution too, although the proactive (initiatory) aspect is much stronger than the responsive one. Such contributions are of course often clearly responsive to the situation in which they occur. When a new 'episode' (for this notion, see ch. 10) is initiated, this is almost invariably done in a way that is situationally relevant. For example we saw, in ch. 8, how initiatives like 1: 2 and 1: 10 in

---

17. It may be argued that this formulation underestimates the importance of the internal content of the turn. But notice that the constituent idea units (turn-constructional units) of a long turn can each be analyzed analogically, i.e. as separate dialogical units with responsive and initiatory properties. After all, content and local contexts are co-constitutive.

THANKSGIVING introduced candidates for new topics, "cranberry sauce" and "the tape-recorder", respectively, which were obviously triggered by objects that were present in the situation, and thus available for the speakers to "respond" to. These examples demonstrate the 'local sensitivity' (Bergmann 1990) of talk to concrete situations. Similarly, one can regard 3: 6 (this chapter) to be an appropriate response to a micro-situation in which the prior topic has been potentially closed. In this case, however, the new topic is motivated by reference to shared background knowledge of which items belong to the agenda of the encounter at the social welfare office. By the introduction of the new topic through a 'free initiative' that is met with an adequate uptake in the dialogue, the topic of the previous episode becomes effectively closed, at least for the time being.

The bidirectional nature also applies to the opposite type of contribution, what we have termed the 'minimal response', i.e. a turn which seems to do no more than is called for by the prior speaker's preceding turn (which is often a question). We have seen several examples above, e.g. 2: 2, 4, 6, 8 etc. and 3: 2, 4, 5, 7, 11, 12. These can be heard as (just) responses, but they too involve changes of the current state of the micro-situation. Also when we look specifically at such limited utterance segments as response particles, such as "yes" and "no" (e.g. 2: 2, 14, 15, 16), when these start new expanded turns, they have both a reactive (responsive) side in acknowledging receipt and claiming understanding of the question and a proactive (initiatory) side in projecting the specific character of the forthcoming response, e.g. the speaker's agreement or disagreement with the prior speaker.

The definition of minimal responses says that they do not introduce a new topical aspect into the discourse; they merely contribute to resolving the topical aspect which was locally in focus in the preceding turn(s), i.e. the 'issue' of the prior (usually interrogative) utterance. For example, turns like the above-mentioned provide (candidates for) minimal responses to the local topics brought up in the previous speakers' turns. Note that such minimal contributions usually do not in themselves close the topical aspects that are locally in focus. And as I just alluded to, they also introduce some new content (but within strict limits of the current topic) into the discourse. Indeed, one could regard them as "minimal initiatives" as well.

In actual fact, listener support items too, which are interactionally and semantically even weaker than minimal responses, display dialogicality. They are clearly responding, albeit very weakly, to what the speaker says, and they contribute to taking discourse further by encouraging the speaker to continue.

However, sometimes when we are focussing on the contents, rather than the details of the interactional construction, of the unfolding discourse, we are entitled to bracket the contents (but not necessarily the interactional effects) of these encouragers.

Returning to the main point of this paragraph, the relational nature of the initiatory and responsive aspects, it is important to contrast the present theory with a theoretical conception which is terminologically similar, i.e. that of the so-called Birmingham school (Sinclair & Coulthard 1992; Coulthard 1992). The latter theory takes 'initiations' and 'responses' to be utterances or speech acts, and it describes them as constituents of larger units, so-called 'exchanges'. Accordingly, in an exchange of the type I-R-F, the three constituents are actual utterances by different speakers, the I(nitiation) by speaker A initiating a new exchange, the R(esponse) by speaker B responding to the initiation, and the F(eedback) by A reacting to the response, all the three being different constituents within one and the same larger discourse unit. This monologistic theory thus works with expressions, or speech acts,[18] produced by individual speakers, while our dialogistic theory uses abstract, inter-actional relations within a dialogically constituted discourse as the theoretical primes (Linell & Marková 1993). For the former theory, the basic unit type is an action that is *either* an initiation *or* a response (or a feedback move); units such as R/I (or F/I), i.e. both a response and an initiation within the same turn, are secondary combinations.[19] Within our dialogistic framework, the basic insight is that dialogue contributions have both responsive and initiatory inter-relational properties; this applies also to the minimal responses (response tokens) and the free initiatives, even if these two represent the polar cases.

---

18. For a critique of speech act theory, see ch. 11.2.

19. Somewhat more recent proposals within the Birmingham school (Coulthard 1981, Stubbs 1983, Coulthard 1992, Hoey 1991) include several complex categories, which acknowledge the presence of both response and initiation in the same turn, e.g. R/I (the unmarked type, both 'predicted' and 'predicting'), 'boundary initiation' and 'challenge=counter-initiation'. Given the theory of exchange structures, these additions deduct from the coherence of the model as a whole. In my view these patchings on the model reveal that monologistic theories of discourse face major theoretical difficulties. See also ch.11: fn.5.

9.7 Coding elementary contributions to dialogue

Dialogistic theory of discourse includes the assumption of the response-initiative structure of turns. On this conceptual basis, Linell et al. (1988) have developed a coding system, the so-called Initiative-Response (IR) Analysis, which is designed to categorize dialogue contributions into about twenty different categories, each consisting of a particular combination of a (type of) responsive link and a (type of) initiatory link. Each category in the coding system represents an operationalization of some particular response-initiative combination.[20] This model thus captures the relational (or dialogical) aspects of what happens between and across contributions. It is in these "transition spaces", where it is determined "when the action shall pass to another, to whom and for what" (Schegloff 1996: 97) that the interactional density is maximal.[21]

It is important to distinguish an empirical research *instrument*, such as a coding system (of which the IR model is an example), from a *theory* (such as a dialogistic theory of discourse). Designing and using a coding system necessarily involves bracketing some of the dialogicality and reflexivity involved in dialogue. For example, the operationalization of concepts, which is part of the development of coding categories, usually implies disregarding some of the actual complexities in the data. In the IR system, for example, one considers the response aspect of a 'free initiative' to be nil, and, similarly, with the initiative aspect of a 'minimal response'. More importantly, however, the very activity of coding is in several senses a monological one (ch. 14).

One may therefore dispute whether coding contributions in terms of predetermined categories and quantifying over coded contributions are practices that can be reconciled with a dialogistic approach. My claim is that coding and quantification can be used in discourse studies, and that there are good reasons for using such methods, provided that they are warranted by one's specific research purposes. I will not argue the case here, as the methodological considerations require

---

20. Space restrictions do not allow me to account for the IR coding scheme here. A full manual exists so far only in Swedish (Linell & Gustavsson 1987), but the main features should be clear from Linell et al. (1988) (cf. also Gustavsson 1988). The conceptual foundation of the system has been explored in Linell (1990) and Linell & Marková (1993). The system has been applied to a wide variety of dyadic interactions, e.g. language lessons (Gustavsson 1988), criminal court trials (Adelswärd et al. 1987), social welfare office talk (Fredin 1993), group discussions with mildly mentally retarded persons (Marková 1991), fictional drama dialogue (Rommetveit 1991b) etc.

21. At the same time, this means that an IR analysis performed at the turn level becomes less informative, if turns are very long.

too much space. However, Marková & Linell (1996) argue at some length that a coding system can be attuned to (some of) the dialogical properties of discourse, and the use of it is therefore not necessarily at odds with dialogism.

9.8 The dialogicality of larger units of discourse

To sum up, through their dialogue contributions "people establish environments for each other and for themselves, and (...) these environments constrain their next activities" (McDermott 1976: 20). Utterances are both informed by prior utterances, and consequential for next utterances. So far we have only explored this phenomenon in the local discursive context. However, analogical arguments apply to other levels.

One way to introduce this issue would be to build on considerations of the very elements of social action (although now in slightly different terms from those of ch. 9.3). To engage in social interaction, interactors must first attend to each other, and to each other's actions and behaviours (feelings and attitudes as displayed); one feature of this basic interaction is, very often, to establish mutual gaze for some moments (cf. an elementary greeting sequence). Secondly, interactors must establish a common focus in the world to be talked about; this, of course, could be something in the concrete setting, in the prior talk or in some absent discourse world building on prior (background) knowledge. These two aspects, *mutual attention* and *common focus* (cf. participation structure and topical content, ch. 10), are of course more or less tightly interwoven throughout the interaction. But this is not enough for creating a coherent interaction; actors must also tie their contributions together, thereby *sustaining and developing foci of attention and discourse topics over sequences of interaction.* Such more global units, episodes and topics, will be dealt with in the next chapter.

It is obvious, therefore, that the local structure on the turn-to-turn level has clear connections with larger units of discourse, such as the structure of topical episodes. For example, a free initiative can be seen as an attempt to bring up a new topic. Indeed, since initiatives, by definition, introduce something new into the discourse, each initiative can be taken to develop some topical aspect. A 'non-locally' linked contribution,[22] i.e. a turn which ties back to some other

---

22. This is another category in the IR system (ch. 9.7). A non-locally linked contribution has roperties both of coherence and non-coherence; it has ties with features of prior (but non-adjacent) co-text (as opposed to free initiatives) but does not involve responding to local (adjacent) turns (as opposed to local responses, cf. ch. 9.4).

turn occurring earlier or to a topic space that was actively explored some time back in the discourse, amounts to a renewal of a topic, a reopening of a topic space (Crow 1983: 144ff.). This opens up for a consideration of aspects of global coherence. It is therefore motivated to shift our analytic focus to the level of episodes in discourse and perform a dialogistic analysis there. This will be dealt with in the next chapter.

But dialogicality has other, more long-term dimensions too. In principle, every utterance could have a longer history within the discourse, an embeddedness in the situation, as well as a past within the history of prior discourses over a long time, an embeddedness in culture. Likewise, while every utterance projects possible continuations in the local context, i.e. expected or likely next-utterances, it may be consequential for larger, embedding activities, what we may call global contexts (cf. Goodwin & Goodwin 1992: 174). While the responsive-initiative links, as defined here, have to do with the moment-to-moment (utterance-to-utterance, contribution-to-contribution) unfoldings and modifications of local contexts, there are also links between 'what's going on' in a particular segment of dialogue, on the one hand, and what has happened in other past situations and what might happen in future situations.[23] We are then dealing with the dialogue at the level of 'speech event' (Hymes 1972). Bakhtin (1986) stresses that dialogicality applies to both levels of 'utterance' and 'speech event', which is to say that contexts get established and reestablished through discourse both locally and globally. (Indeed, one can discern intermediate levels ('meso-levels') too, such as that of 'episodes', cf. ch. 10.12). Note, however, that local and global aspects are thoroughly intertwined. For example, 'cues' (Gumperz 1982, 1995) to identification of global contexts are given (or given off) by speakers, and listeners, locally, in their unfolding discourse; speakers guide listeners to appropriate contextualization, to understanding of 'what's going on' (Goffman), facilitating conversational inferencing (Gumperz 1982, 1994), by cuing their discourse there-and-then (local cues to global contexts). Thus, "the actor's own actions are first order determinants of the sense that situations have, [i.e. situations] in which, literally speaking, actors *find* themselves" (Garfinkel 1967: 115). In ch. 12 I shall deal with dialogicality at the speech event level separately.

---

23. Compare what has been termed 'intertextuality' (Kristeva 1986), discussed in ch. 8.10.

CHAPTER 10

Episodes and topics

10.1 Topic progression in the flow of discourse

A dialogue (and also a monologue or a written text) is typically "about" something: it has some kind of "content", or "topics". Topicality can be given a preliminary definition as the property of 'aboutness' in discourse.

Topics in discourse have traditionally been treated either as semantic structures *in the text* (or discourse) itself, or as something *in the world* which the text is "about"; the text 'represents' aspects of the world. These are basically the options open to a monologistic theory. A dialogistic theory would not conceive of topics in terms of mapping the text onto (a representation of) a world, but rather as something characteristic of the *activities* of discourse-in-contexts, if you will, a semantic structure bridging discourse and contexts, and emerging with the unfolding verbal interaction, "as a developing and developed event over the course of action that produced it" (Garfinkel 1967: 40). Topics are being "constituted and transformed" as part of the discursive practices, "rather than existing independently and simply being referred to or talked about in a particular discourse" (Fairclough 1992: 41).[1] We can talk about the dynamic process of *topic progression*, rather than about static textual structures.

Topics are notoriously difficult to define in substantial terms, i.e. different discourse topics can seldom be adequately separated from each other by defining each topic "positively", i.e. "only" in terms of which set ('micro-world') of referents it is "about", or which sets of concepts or predicates it employs to describe whatever it is about. Instead, we have to study how the interactional flow is structured in terms of junctures (boundaries or boundary-like phenomena), as contrasted to more coherent or seamless stretches. Topics are, according

---

1. Fairclough (op.cit.) uses the term 'objects', rather than 'topics'.

to this view, characteristic of actors'*activities* of using *discourse and contexts* to
build islands of coherence and intersubjectivity in and through the interactions,
in the *acts* of referring, predicating, and connecting thoughts (idea units) with
one another in a discourse with a common floor, i.e. an interaction with a single
shared focus of attention. In talk, topics and tasks are closely related. Rather than
looking at the discourse as a text with fixed topics, we would therefore stress the
actors' efforts to create and sustain intersubjectivity by means of topical coherence and coordinated actions. "Topicality [...] is a matter not only of content,
but is partly constituted in the procedures conversationalists utilize to display
understanding and to achieve one turn's proper fit with prior turns." (Maynard
1980: 263) Thus, we can witness a shift of perspective from topics as exclusively
content-based to the organizations of sequences, the trains of interactional events
and actions (Schegloff 1990), and I shall use the notion of *episode*, rather than
topic per se, as the basic unit (ch. 10.3). Topical episodes are characterized not
only by what they are "about" (their "content"), but also by *how* participants
shape their discourse and organize their interaction. Topic structure and participation framework are closely related.[2]

Topicality and coherence are also closely connected concepts (Brown &
Yule 1983); they (partly) constitute each other. Topicality pertains to matters of
continued, sustained salience or importance, rather than to things subjected only
to peripheral or momentary attention (Givón 1995). Episodes, rather than single
utterances, support topics.[3] Cohesive devices, such as repetition of key words,
semantic associations, use of pronouns, ellipsis, and other anaphoric devices,
which tie utterances together, indicate that there is a topic space with a common
focus (Grosz 1977), and they help create this space in and through an episode in
discourse. A topic is both the project and product of coherence-building (cf. also
Goffman 1983).

However, the architecture of topicality and coherence is quite complex.
Topics are not the only resource speakers use to create coherence in discursive
episodes (ch. 10.5), and some episodes are poly- rather than monotopical
(ch. 10.4). Moreover, coherence and relevance can be both local and global.
There is usually coherence not only within (what we will call) topical episodes;
there are also links and bridges, semantic connections, between episodes

---

2. Cf. e.g. Goodwin & Goodwin (1990: 111) on topic-invoked participation frameworks.

3. Thus, the term 'topic' is used here as a 'discourse notion' rather than about a (functional) sentence
constituent (Keenan & Schieffelin 1976; Givón 1992).

(ch. 10.7). Thus, the dynamic flow of interaction creates patterns of coherence and fragmentation both within and between episodes. It is the connections across possible boundaries which sometimes make these boundaries hard to identify.

The term 'topic' derives etymologically from Gr. *topos* 'place'; when conversationalists "stay on" topic, they may be said to remain in the same place or (topic) space. However, our focus on episodes serves to stress that topics are in themselves dynamic; episodes are dynamic events, housing both action and topics.

10.2 The joint production of a topic

Talk-in-interaction is incrementally produced on a moment-to-moment basis: bits and pieces of discourse are selected and strung together in a process of local production, one 'idea unit' or turn-constructional unit makes another one possible and relevant, and once this new unit materializes, opportunities for further continuations, i.e. more idea units, are created, etc.

This principle of local production, i.e. that interaction is locally produced on a turn-to-turn basis, was demonstrated in ch. 9 with regard to elementary contributions to dialogue. There is a clear relation between, on the one hand, the initiative-response structure of these contributions and, on the other hand, topic structure. Thus, to take an initiative is to invite the listener to share a topic (or a topical aspect) and/or a perspective on that topic. But the producer of the initiatory contribution can only introduce a 'candidate' for a topic, because one single contribution can not build a topic. A sequence of contributions, bound together by response links, will be needed to establish and sustain a topic. In this way a topic becomes a joint accomplishment and a product of the dialogue dynamics of responses and initiatives (Linell 1990).[4]

The evolving discourse, locally produced, adds up to stretches of interaction. The flow of discourse is not unstructured at these more global levels; it is generally possible to analyze it in terms of *episodes*. An episode is a bounded sequence, a discourse event with a beginning and an end surrounding a spate of talk, which is usually focused on the treatment of some 'problem', 'issue' or 'topic'.

In ch. 8, some stretches of discourse were analyzed in terms of episodes and topic spaces, and some types of transitions between these fragments of discourse,

---

4. Cf. in this context the notion of 'communicative dynamism' of Prague school text linguistics (Firbas 1971).

the 'islands of shared understanding', were identified. In this chapter, I shall explore the notions of episode and topic somewhat further. By way of introduction, let me give another example:

(1) SKIING AND BALLOONING (Excerpt from a conversation between two students at the University of Wisconsin-Madison (1979), who volunteered to record a half-hour conversation to provide data for a project on everyday conversation. B, aged 27, and K, 21, were well acquainted, having worked together for a semester as members of a project group. They were asked to talk about anything they wished. The transcript was published in Craig & Tracy (1983) and subjected to analyses by many different contributors to that volume. The notation .. indicates a brief pause. I cite from line 105 in the original (turn organization has been slightly changed). Before this turn, B and K had talked about a friend and a stepbrother who had lived in Switzerland and done a lot of skiing there. In turn 1 (original: 105) K takes an initiative to redirect the conversation onto a (partially) new topic:)

```
1.  K:    do you ski?
2.  B:    no. I skied once, I tried to ski.. I went part away down
          the slope and sort of..tipped over [((laughs))
3.  K:                                         [((laughs)) .. that
          [was it. ((K coughs))
4.  B:    [everybody, ev::erybody in the whole (skis..) class had
          to.. first learn to fall down and then stand up again?
5.  K:    um hmm
6.  B:    everyone else including a nun wearing complete habit down
          to the ground
7.  K:    oh my [go::d
8.  B:          [was standing up. I was rolling around ((laughing)) in
          the snow, with my feet tangled, after twenty minutes of
          this the instructor finally gave up, and picked me up,
          but I never did learn to get up once I'd fallen down. I
          never learned to stop so I'd ski down the hill, I can do
          that,.. and I'd get to the bottom it would be time to
          stop or I'd come up to an obstacle that I couldn't get
          around, and the only thing to do would be to fall over.
9.  K:    =um hmm
10. B:    and then I'd have to wait there for ((laughing)) somebody
          to come and pick me out of the snow: : . hh and (K: oh
          no) I hated it, I got very cold and unhappy ((laughing))
          and quit.
11. K:    .hhh tha: t would be about my reaction too. [do you ever
12. B:                                                 [do you ski?
13. K:    cross country.
14. B:    um::.
```

15. K: but I don't.. I'on't think I could handle down hill.
           ((pause)) I've.. decided ((laughing)) I'm very
           uncoordinated and uh, ((pause)) jus- doesn't seem like
           fun. I'm not a speed enthusiast. the daring.. adventure
           type things don't.. get to me.. at all.
16. B: I don't mind speed on..on the flat but I'm.. terrified of
           heights. which makes me a [(((laughing)) bad candidate for
           skiing.
17. K: [(I love)
           I love the heights.
18. B: umm
19. K: (tha's)
20. B: umm.
      ((pause))
21. K: .hhh.. .hhh I'm gonna learn how to balloon or something
           like that so I can.. see the world.
22. B: that's always seemed like fun to me. I keep seeing ads in
           the paper for hot air ballooning now?
23. K: =you know there's a class?
24. B: nnn!
25. K: =in.. Madison? ((pause)) uhm, there's a ground school
           class? and then ((pause)) they.. also ((pause)) the air
           part of it but it gets really expensive. I was reading up
           on it one day.
      ((12 turns omitted, basically about ballooning))
26. K: ((first part of turn omitted)) so that's what I want to
           do on my honeymoon. go to California and.. and balloon.
           ((laughs))
27. B: ((laughs)) ((pause)) hmm::
28. K: but it would have to be someplace pretty.
      ((pause))
29. B: California would be interesting.
30. K: (I don't know)
31. B: if you missed you'd either hit the mountains or the
           ((laughing)) ocean ((laugh))
      ((pause))
32. K: hmm::.
33. B: have you picked out the long-suffering man who is going
           to put up with that kind of a honeymoon ye::t?
34. K: oh:. this is just a dream I mean. [(someone can plan this
           type of things)   .
35. B: [you've just designed
           this honeymoon ((laughing)) without having anyone in
           [mind ((laughs))
36. K: [.hhh I don't even want to get married, you know hhh
           ((pause)) .hhh I just thought that would alwa-.. that
           just always appealed to me. oh, I'd cuz I read it
           something.. in something that was.. in a McCalls or
           something one time that was.. (B: hm) y'know these are
           really neat things to do for honeymoons 'n.. or just (B:
           hhfff) for weekends that you want to go.. and have a good
           time.
37. B: maybe you get your parents to give it to you for a
           graduation present.

```
38. K:     no:,
39. B:     one balloon [lesson?
40. K:                 [that's not.. too practical.
41. B:     no::
      ((pause))
42. K:     nah, it's not worth it. I'm in to ((laughing))
           practical.. a lot of times
43. B:     umm. ((pause))
           have you heard anything about your internship. speaking
           of practical.
44. K:     =um:::. no I forgot to call about that.
45. B:     um hmm ((tone of mocking reprimand)) and that was very
           bad you'll have to call about that today.
((etc.))
```

It seems reasonable to analyze this stretch of talk into six consecutive topical episodes, each consisting of an 'island of shared understanding' which the conversationalists build together. (Of course, sharedness is always to some extent partial, as pointed out in ch. 8; here conversationalists do not always express a lot of it, e.g. when K talks about not getting married (1: 36) and B responds by linking back to earlier talk on ballooning (1: 37), which is followed of some uncertainty on the part of B whether K has understood her reference (1: 39).)

For convenience we might name the six episodes "B's skiing experience" (1: 1–11), "K's attitude to skiing" (1: 12–20), "ballooning" (1: 21–32), "honeymoons" (1: 33–36), "ballooning" (renewed) (1: 37–42), and "internship" (1: 43ff.). Note that it is not only the case that these episodes are, by and large, "about" different matters; episode structure is also signalled in and through the interactional patterns. Thus, in at least a couple of cases (1: 18–20, 1: 32), there are sequences involving pauses and weak affirmative utterances ("umm", "hmm."), which indicate that the prior topic is fading out ('topic attrition').[5]

Each of the episodes involves internal movements within a topic space (ch. 10.7), but there are also connections across episode boundaries. The actors manage to use various resources in prior episodes to carry their joint discourse over to the next. What is used for the transition across episode boundaries is not always the main issue of any of the episodes. For example, to get from "skiing" to "ballooning", B and K use the aspect of "loving or fearing heights" (1: 16–17). There is also one case in the present excerpt, in which virtually no semantic connection exists between two adjacent episodes, i.e. at the transition

---

5. For discussion of criteria for identifying episode boundaries, see Svennevig (1997: 187ff.) and Korolija (1998b: 42–44).

to "internship" (1: 43); here B "invents" a pro forma transition by using the notion of "being practical". Thus, the conversationalists take pains to make their discourse coherent in at least a perfunctory way. The phenomena of topic transitions were introduced already in ch. 8, and I shall return to these matters below (ch. 10.7).

10.3 Episodes: units of natural social interaction

'Episodes', then, would probably be the most neutral term for referring to relatively bounded sequences within the more comprehensive speech event or encounter as a whole. Episodes can be regarded as units of naturally unfolding social interaction (Korolija 1998b).[6] An episode is basically a train of discursive events, or a sequence of collective actions. Most, but not all, episodes are "about" something specific in the world; they are focused on, attend to and move within some kind of 'topic' (which has to be dynamically conceived, cf. below), and such episodes will be called *topical episodes* or, alternatively (depending on which aspects one wants to highlight), *topic spaces* or simply 'topical sequences'.

Talk-in-interaction cannot be exhaustively divided up into topical episodes. Since it takes, in general, two people to establish a topic in communication, there will be some utterances which fail to be included into topical episodes. These are primarily those utterances, in which the speaker tries to initiate a new topic but does not get his interlocutors' attention or is otherwise ignored; such utterances can be heard as 'topic candidates' that, for one reason or another, are never developed into topics. In other words, such utterances are not put on the jointly attended floor and are not responded to in a way that may be regarded as relevant to their content (the topic implicitly proposed), and the utterances remain

---

6. Extensionally, episodes would correspond more or less to what some analysts call 'transactions' (e.g. Sinclair & Coulthard 1992) or simply 'sequences' (CA). For yet other, related terms, see ch. 8, fn. 6. Cf. also Table 1 below.

An analysis of the stream of social behaviour in terms of 'episodes' was proposed already by Harré & Secord (1972), whose notion was later used by, e.g., Hare & Blumberg (1988). Other researchers use the term 'episode' in slightly different ways. van Dijk & Kintsch (1983) seem to be influenced by the theory of episodic memory. Chafe (1979) proposes units such as 'episode/paragraph' and larger 'memories/stories', where 'memory' and 'episode' are cognitive units, and 'story' and 'paragraph' the corresponding "verbalized" units of expression. For van Dijk (1982), too, episodes are semantic, rather than interactional, units. For an extensive account of episodes in talk, see Korolija (1998b).

isolated 'inserts' (in the terminology of Crow 1983: 148ff.), or even end up as 'aborted' contributions. In the following examples, the last part of M's 2: 2 is clearly outside of the topical episode to which the surrounding units belong:

(2) NO MORE MILK (From Crow 1983: 149)

```
1.  F.    it's up to you, whatever you feel comfortable with
2.  M:    well I don't feel comfortable with ((opens refrigerator))
          = oh      no more milk
3.  F:    then what're you gonna do it for?
```

As Crow points out, it is quite common that an insert accompanies some action that is going on concurrently with the conversation. Basically the same applied to Peter's utterances about the cranberry sauce and the napkins in THANKSGIV-ING (ch. 8: (1)); nobody responded to them and developed them into joint topics. And, in fact, these utterances were basically referring as part of (indirect-ly expressed) requests for action rather than putting the things meant into an argumentative context.

    In the remainder of this chapter, I shall first further explore the relations between episodes and topics. The term 'topical episode' may suggest a one-to-one correlation between topic and episode. However, there is no such absolute correlation. There are episodes with more than one topic, and episodes with no (focussed) topic at all. Second, I will discuss some cognitive and communicative functions of episodes, in particular that of developing an understanding of something that is shared among conversationalists, that of bringing the vague into something more precise and something consciously attended to, and that of resolving the tension between staying on topic and inaugurating new foci of attention into discourse. Finally, I shall consider the relation of episodes to other 'units' of talk-in-interaction.

10.4 Monotopical and polytopical episodes

Topical episodes are defined as more or less bounded sequences in interaction, dynamically focused on a coherent topic space. At the same time, topics are always in motion, in a constant flux. Sequences in talk develop gradually from one part of a topical (and contextual) space to another, or from one topical aspect to another. Sacks (1992) has pointed out that conversationalists often work hard to achieve *stepwise topical transitions*, in which one topic or topical aspect 'shades' into the other (Schegloff & Sacks 1973; Crow 1983: 142). If so, actors try to avoid clearly abrupt shifts with very sharply boundaried topic spaces. Therefore, when abrupt shifts ("especially if topics are introduced out of the blue", ch. 10.7) do occur, they are often signalled by discontinuity or boundary markers ("by the way, that reminds me of.., you know what?, before I forget,…"etc).[7] The above-mentioned "speaking of" in 1: 43 is another example.

Since topics are difficult to identify exclusively in terms of semantic substance, analysts are usually advised to use boundaries, i.e. junctures or partial ruptures, in the interactional and topical flow as the best method to determine episode structure and topic sequences.[8] However, even if we use boundaries as the criterion to identify topics (or topical episodes, topic sequences), then the sequences so identified will vary in character. We can imagine a continuum from those sequences, or episodes, which are topically fairly homogeneous, i.e. relatively 'monotopical' (or 'monothematic') (despite the movements within them), to those sequences, which are topically heterogeneous ('bi- or poly-topical', 'polythematic'), where talk at the beginning of the sequence is about something completely different from the talk at the end of the sequence, without there being any clear intervening boundaries; what we have is a "seamless web" of gliding, continuous transitions. The latter transitional phenomena are known as "topic glides",[9] and the resulting overall progression type has been termed 'topic shading' (Schegloff & Sacks 1973) or 'topic drift' (Hobbs 1990). READ-ING, EATING AND BEING BUSY (ch. 5) is a rather good example, though it contains at least one partial fracture (1: 20).

Another kind of polytopical episode is at hand if several topics, context spaces (Reichman 1978), are open at the same time and their respective constituent acts or utterances are intertwined through a stretch of discourse ('interlaced episodes').[10] This naturally results in a less neat episode structure.

---

7. Cf. also 'disjunct markers' (Jefferson 1978), 'explicit topic changes' (Planalp & Tracy 1980), and others.

8. It is a commonplace in recent literature on topicality that topics are hard to define and that *boundaries* be used for analytic purposes. See e.g. Brown & Yule (1983), Keenan & Schieffelin (1976), Crow (1983: 155), McLaughlin (1984), Adelswärd (1988), Schegloff (1990).

9. See Adelswärd (1988), and references there. Svennevig (1997) adopts the term 'coherent shifts'. On other types of topic shifts, see ch. 10.7.

10. This may occur in dyadic interactions too. It should not be confused with the case of parallel floors (discourses) in multi-party settings. Some researchers have argued that interlacing episodes are characteristic of some kinds of female conversational strategies.

If, on the other hand, conversationalists (or one of them) have specific goals for their interaction or specific topics on their agenda (in other words: specific, more or less pre-planned communicative projects), they may try to stay within homogeneous topic spaces, or if they discover that they have, in the course of the talk and interaction, slipped into something else, they may take measures to reinstall the topic assigned. This is especially common in institutional activity types.

10.5 Non-topical episodes

Topics, we have seen, are a resource for actors to build coherent episodes in discourse. But actors also have other kinds of resources at their disposal; frames of activity types and local sequential dependencies (Schegloff 1990) also serve to build episodes, and may sometimes make up for the absence of common sustained topics (see (3) MEMORY MASTERS below).

There are episodes or sequences that, in one way or another, are 'non-topical' or only 'semi-topical' ; these are moments and spates of talk when the interlocutors are not "doing topic talk" (Egbert 1997: 32), i.e. the interaction does not seem to "be about" anything "out there" in the world. Rather than being 'topical', many such episodes are geared towards regulating aspects of the interaction, and might be called relational, procedural or transactional.

Common examples of non-topical (procedural) episodes are sequences that are primarily designed to solve some interactional problem, such as opening or closing a conversation or encounter (Schegloff & Sacks 1973). Other procedural episodes focus on the management of the verbal activities themselves; points on an agenda, e.g. in a formal meeting, are sometimes managed as mini-episodes, during which issues are settled and decisions taken without very much talk "about" matters involved. Components in calls to an emergency center (Zimmerman 1992), e.g. achieving identification, aligning identities, requesting assistance, eliciting information, promising help, closing (op.cit.: 461) (all of which are local 'communicative projects', ch. 11), may be interactionally managed as procedural episodes or "agenda points". Some other episodes appear to be somewhat mixed, being partly topical and partly focussed on a procedural problem, i.e. more meta-oriented, such as so-called miscommunication events, especially the more bounded repair sequences (ch. 11.4).

More typical among non-topical episodes are perhaps sequences, in which talk is used to support or administer some non-verbal activity, such as passing around dishes with food, serving drinks etc. during coffee- or dinner-table talk. The above-mentioned utterances about the cranberry sauce and the napkins (THANKSGIVING) are relevant examples, although they never developed into proper episodes (which, incidentally, is quite typical). Yet another type of fairly non- (or semi-) topical episodes is talk between lovers in intimate situations, where the utterances are mainly mutual confirmations of love and affection.[11] Emotive rather than cognitive aspects of talk are significant here. Somewhat related are speech events in which the speaker is talking to a baby or a pet; such events are not primarily about anything in the world (except for the speaker's emotional relation to the recipient), nor is the recipient supposed to understand the words nor to respond as a competent conversationalist.

If the above-mentioned episodes are, in one sense or another, examples of not "doing topic talk", we find another type of episodes without any sustained topics in exclusively activity-sustained episodes, to which I will turn presently.

10.6 Local and global coherence

Coherence in episodes can be built either on local topical (and interactional) coherence or on global coherence (or, of course, on both).[12] Discourse evolves out of both "local contingencies and global responsibilities" (Boden 1994: 22).

There are several levels and types of global coherence, e.g. macro-topical and activity-sustained ones (Korolija 1998b). At least some kinds of global coherence may be thought of as a cumulative by-product of the actors' locally relevant contributions to their joint sense-making. It is partly the analyst who makes this coherence visible by selecting properties and discerning patterns in discourse, as part of his or her activity of constructing a descriptive model of discourse.[13]

Here I will concentrate on activity-sustained coherence. It is important to recognize that certain activities typically exhibit a lack of local topical coherence beyond adjacency pairs. In some cases of episodes with global coherence but little

---

11. For an example, see Channell (1997).

12. Many researchers have explored notions of local vs. global coherence, e.g. McLaughlin (1984: 36ff.), Craig & Tracy (1983), Hobbs & Agar (1985), Tracy (1984), Givón (1995: 362ff), Korolija (1998b).

13. For different versions of this point, cf. Hellman (1992) and Korolija (1998b).

local coherence beyond single question-answer pairs, the global coherence builds upon some macro-topical agenda, such as gathering personal data about a client in a professional-lay interaction. In such intermediate cases,[14] the framing activity type, along with the macro-topical agenda, works to hold together the episode.

In other cases, the activity frame seems to fulfill this function alone. This is the case in many types of quizzes and tests, where each question-answer exchange "is about" something particular, but there is no coherence between these adjacency pairs, i.e. the various questions posed are semantically entirely unrelated.

(3) MEMORY MASTERS (Excerpt from a Swedish TV "Memory Masters" show. Q = question-master (programme host), C = contestant. Rough translation from Swedish)

```
1.   Q:    what do you call an establishment for horse breeding?
2.   C:    stud-farm.
3.   Q:    correct. who won the world cup in down-hill skiing in
           1975?
4.   C:    Stenmark.
5.   Q:    wrong. how long did it take to build the castle of
           Versailles?
6.   C:    did you say Versailles?
7.   Q:    yes.
8.   C:    how exact does one have to be?
9.   Q:    you mustn't ask that.
10.  C:    thirty years.
11.  Q:    wrong, forty-seven years. what is a cineaste?
12.  C:    a connoisseur of films.
13.  Q:    correct. what was Caruso good at?
     ((etc.))
```

With the exception of embedded repair sequences (cf. 3: 6–9; note the restriction even on such sequences imposed by moves such as Q's 3: 9), there is no topical connection between successive questions, and their related answers, in this kind of activity. Yet, at one level, it is perceived as coherent and meaningful; both parties understand that they are engaged in an activity in which unrelated quiz questions are being asked, the point being that of testing B's ability to retrieve memory information very rapidly and thus to answer questions correctly on the spot. Something similar applies to many psychological tests (e.g. A HOT DAY TODAY in ch. 8). Hence, the

---

14. For an example, see PERSONAL DATA (ch. 12; ex. (6)).

activity-type context makes up for the absence of any co-textual coherence between question-answer pairs; the global coherence involved is chiefly activity-sustained.

We conclude therefore that though topic organization is common, it is not a universal property of discourse. The extent and the ways of organizing topical, procedural and other episodes in discourse are activity-specific (Korolija 1998b). In general, one might conjecture that the relative poverty or vagueness of one type of context or contextual resource will often be compensated for by other dimensions of contexts.

10.7 Topical trajectories and transitions between episodes

I have argued that topic spaces are dynamic, not static, in nature. This accords with phenomenological accounts of cognition and experience as mental processes of "locomotion within cognitive fields" (Graumann 1990: 110). Within an episode there is a "moving focus of attention" (Parker 1984). That is, interlocutors move through topic spaces or topic fields, rather than position themselves at one location in a ready-made structure. It is therefore often instructive to talk about *topical trajectories* through the collectively produced and sequentially organized discourse within a topic space. For example, in READING, EATING AND BEING BUSY (ch. 5: (1)) interlocutors moved along a trajectory from reading habits via sleeping habits to eating habits. In SKIING AND BALLOON-ING (this chapter: (1)) actors travelled through five or six different topic spaces.

Trajectories are first and foremost the movements being made while interlocutors build topic spaces, their islands of partially shared understandings. But, as was shown above, there are usually also *trajectories across boundaries* (topical junctures), and bridges between the islands. We are then concerned with 'topic shifts' (e.g. Crow 1983) or *transitions between topical episodes*. It is often instructive to study how new episodes are initiated, and how contexts of various kinds are used in this process. It turns out that new episodes and their topics are nearly always responsive to something in the contexts. In ch. 8 I analyzed such transitions in terms of (de- and) re-contextualizations, pointing out that the elements used to initiate new episodes can often be traced in one or several of the contexts relevant at the particular point in time. There appear to be some recurrent *episode initiation types*. Some of those discussed by Korolija & Linell (1996)[15] are:

(a) reopening an earlier topic, e.g. "ballooning" in 1: 37 (SKIING AND BAL-LOONING),

(b) recontextualizing an element from the preceding episode, e.g. "flowers" at the end of NOT RECALLING.. (ch.8: (2)), "heights" in initiating "ballooning" in 1: 21 (SKIING AND BALLOONING), "reading (in general)" taken from the episode on reading Goffman and used by Deborah for a new episode in READING, EATING AND BEING BUSY (ch. 5: 1: 1),

(c) initiating an analogous telling of some experience etc., as when B invites K to tell about her skiing experience in 1: 12 (SKIING AND BALLOONING),[16]

(d) introducing a topic candidate by referring to something in the concrete situation ('local sensitivity', ch. 8), e.g. the plastic disc in NOT RECALLING... and the tape-recorder in THANKSGIVING,

(e) topicalizing some predefined aspect of the abstract activity type, e.g. taking up an agenda-bound topic or subactivity (such as the reason for coming to the social welfare office, e.g. 3: 6 in NO MONEY (ch. 9)),

(f) broaching a topic which is unrelated to the prior co-text as well as to the concrete situation but which is somehow "near at hand" for the interlocutors, e.g. the speaker's or addressee's immediate plans or something from the common biography of (some of) the interactants,

(g) introducing a new topic totally "out of the blue"; in this case, usually based on (what appears to the other as) a mental leap on the part of the speaker, the accomplishment of intersubjective understanding may require some extra effort from the speaker (and her interlocutor);[17] cf. the speaker's use of the perfunctory tie of "being practical" in initiating "internship" in 1: 43 of SKIING AND BALLOONING.

---

15. See also Linell & Korolija (1997) and Korolija (1998b), who provide more examples of all types.

16. Cf. the frequent phenomenon of 'second stories' in conversation, see Pomerantz (1980).

17. When an actor initiates new topical episodes, as it seems, entirely "out of the blue" ((g) above), these topic initiations are presumably meaningful and motivated for the speaker, although they remain contextually unrelated for the analyst, and in many cases for the interlocutor too (hence the speaker may find it necessary to point out the abrupt topic shift).

Recall that this list is concerned with topic shifts enacted through the initiation of new episodes. Many of these shifts ((d–g) above) are sometimes termed 'abrupt' or even 'noncoherent' (e.g. Crow 1983: 146ff; Svennevig 1997: 187), in contrast to (i) such 'coherent' topic glides that occur episode-internally, as one topic (or topical aspect) is "touched off" from prior talk, thereby leading to a polytopical episode (ch. 10.4), and (ii) those shifts that are brought about by recontextualization and similar co-textually linked episode initiations ((a-c) above).[18,19] However, if we take coherence as a property of interaction-in-contexts rather than of verbal texts ('co-text'), we see that all the shifts (except possibly (g)) are in some way or another 'coherent' in relation to the whole set of situational and contextual resources available to the interlocutors.

A new episode is, by definition, initiated through a contribution which is not both locally and focally tied to the prior contribution (using the concepts introduced in ch. 9.4). One could say, however, with reference to the types of contextual resources introduced in ch. 8, that the new episodes, through their various retrospective links, are grounded in something given in the prior discourse (ch. 8: IA) in cases (a-c) above), in something given in the concrete situation (IB) in case (d), and in some abstract background knowledge (II) in cases (e-g). Accordingly, topics and episode transitions display a kind of bidirectional (response-initiative) structure too (cf. ch. 9.8); new episodes are, by definition, in some respects new (cf. initiatory, prospective aspects), but they are, as we have seen, also responsive to something which is contextually given.

Incidentally, the taxonomy just reviewed also suggests some ways in which topic progression might be activity-specific. Thus, it is an informed guess that type (d) is frequent in situations of 'open states of talk' (ch. 12.3), whereas (b-c) are generally thought to be frequently deployed by those who are skilled in "carrying on a conversation". Type (e) is surely quite characteristic of goal-directed institutional discourse types (ch. 12.6).

---

18. It must be admitted, of course, that there is a grey zone between episode-internal glides, on the one hand, and what I call 'recontextualizations' ((b) above) across boundaries, on the other (see Korolija 1998a).

19. Svennevig (op.cit.: 209) uses the terms 'non-focal' and 'non-local' coherence about these.

10.8 Topical development in monologue

We have just seen how topical episode sequences demonstrate the dialogical principle in operation again, i.e. the Janus-like responsive-initiatory nature of discourse units, which I discussed earlier with regard to elementary discourse contributions. Similar dialogical interdependencies and types of topical trajectories can be found within turns by one single speaker. The production of a (seemingly) monological turn takes place through the speaker's being "in dialogue" with his environment and contexts in several ways. As an example, consider (4):

(4) HALF A GLASS OF WINE (TemaK: B8: 1: 6) (From a booking interview at a maternal health care centre in Sweden, with a midwife (M) talking with an expectant first-time mother (W). The interview is the first encounter in a series for the two women, and takes place in early pregnancy. Here, W asks a question (4: 4) whether one may drink a glass of wine when one is pregnant, and M then indulges in a lengthy turn (4: 5) of reasoning. We will focus entirely on this turn. W's backchannel utterances are given within parentheses at approximately the positions in M's talk where they occur. Rough translation from Swedish. The inserted sign ¤ refers to a response point (see below), and the appended figure labels the idea unit following it)

```
1.  M:   alcohol, do you use (.) such like?
2.  W:   well, not now.
3.  M:   not now, no. (W: no) no:
4.  W:   I don't. but otherwise how is it, I have read (.) this
         thing with drinking a glass of wine (M: m-hm), is one
         allowed to do that or-- ?
5.  M:   ¤1 well it's up to you yourself so to speak. ¤2 we recom-
         mend that one abstains from alcohol completely when one
         is pregnant. (W: mm) ¤3 but then if one has half a glass
         of wine some time then that's not so dangerous. ¤4 one
         doesn't know where the limit is, you see (W: no) ¤5 so
         therefore one has sort of recommendations, ¤6 we go out
         and say that one should try and avoid alcohol (W: mm)
         entirely (W: mm) ¤7 but then it's Christmas time and hot
         mulled wine ((Sw. "glögg")), ¤8 and there is non-
         alcoholic mulled wine too, for that matter (W: mm. yes)
         ¤9 but it's, you know, up to you so to speak. ¤10 I keep
         saying that one is oneself big like this, right, and the
         baby is small like this, ¤11 but the baby gets just as
         much alcohol. (W: mhm) ¤12 so that if one thinks of that
         then then it will be more felt by the child, right (W:
         mm) by the alcohol. (W: mm) ¤13 there will be no alcohol
         effects from one's having half a glass of wine every
```

second month or something like that, right, there won't
be, of course (W: no) ¤14 but still one doesn't know in
the long range what influences there are, one doesn't
know that (W: no. no) ¤15 so therefore I keep saying that
one drives a car or is pregnant, *one doesn't drink* (M:
mm). ¤16 one will use that as a motto. (W: mm) ¤17 but if
now you have had a glass of wine before you got to know
that you were pregnant then you need not have a bad con-
science for that, you know (W: no) ((goes on))

There are a couple of comments that may be particularly relevant with respect to
(4: 5). When the speaker has completed, or is just about to complete, a turn-
constructional unit (TCU) or idea unit (ch. 9.1) (cf. the following ¤ signs), we
have a possible 'response point',[20] i.e. a point where some response from the
listener is relevant, and thus likely and expected. Indeed, the addressee (W)
frequently provides a listener support item ("mm", "yes", "no") precisely at such
points. Thus, the monological turn is actually laid out in collaboration with the
listener; the speaker calls for some response, when she has expressed an 'idea'
or an argument, and the listener, by providing this, confirms that she follows the
speaker's account and is prepared to receive more.

The speaker's discourse consists of idea units added to each other, partly
like contributions by different speakers in a dialogue. M's first unit (¤ 1, i.e. the
material before ¤2) may stand as a first response to W's preceding question.
However, M follows it up directly by providing an answer stating the position of
the preventive health care (¤2), probably something that W expected (and M
knew that W expected). However, ¤2 can also be regarded as a response by M
to her own first answer (i.e. ¤1). The same applies to ¤3; this is a statement that
somewhat modifies the impact of the rule just stated in ¤2. It is as if another
'voice' in the speaker's mind responds to what her first 'voice' had said; one can
easily imagine a situation, in which another speaker made the comment of ¤3. At
another level, although all the units are produced by one person (M), ¤1 and ¤3
can be said to voice a 'life-world' perspective and ¤2 the perspective of the institution, i.e. maternal health care. The midwife's self thus appears to be multi-voiced.

Similar comment — counter-comment structures appear in the subsequent
talk. For example, M comes to think of the approaching Christmas holidays and
the Swedish habit of drinking hot mulled wine (Sw. "glögg") (¤7), and this
generates another thought about the availability of non-alcoholic "glögg" (¤8). ¤7

---

20. Cf. the notion of 'transition relevance place' (Sacks et al. 1974).

and ¤8 end up as an aside, since M then returns to her previous claim; ¤9 reiterates the gist of the previous argument, and in particular of ¤1. So, different ideas are added up by the same speaker, but often in a fashion which is reminiscent of how different speakers contribute to a dialogue. Patterns of speakers' self-continuations in discourse mirror those of (interlocutors') possible (other-) continuations in dialogue.

This dialogistic argument, that monologue and thought are fundamentally dialogical, has been put forward by many, e.g. George Herbert Mead and Lev Vygotsky (cf. Leudar & Antaki 1988), as well as, of course, Bakhtin. The individual has internalized dialogical exchange patterns, using them to voice different aspects of his or her self. Accordingly, Marková (1990b) talks about 'semantic reversals' within turns and monologues (not only across turns); idea units will be responded to by new ideas, which will develop the argument or story in another direction. In this process, arguments give rise to counter-arguments which will in turn engender new counter-arguments; ideas get added as responses to ideas that emerged previously, thus making topics develop along trajectories.

10.9 Episodes as the locus for creating temporarily shared understanding

Topics in jointly attended discourse are the products of interactants' attempts at achieving intersubjectivity in understanding some particular things they find themselves talking about.

Discourse involves building and using fragments of understanding and contexts (ch. 8). As Ragnar Rommetveit has constantly reminded us, our realities are only partially shared and fragmentarily known. As interlocutors in dialogue, we are "struggling to establish temporary dyadic states of intersubjectivity in a contextually understood and only partially shared world" (Rommetveit 1988: 18). Under many circumstances, people undoubtedly have different knowledge of, perspectives on and opinions about the world and the specific situations they are in. Dialogue and discourse can then be used to develop a common view, a shared understanding for current purposes (and sometimes common understandings that last much longer). Even so, however, at least some situations are characterized by interlocutors having partly discrepant understandings also of the situated discourse, its various components (contributions) and relevant contexts.

As a further background for our reasoning on these points, we could bring in some insights from phenomenological psychology. In perception and cognition, we construct the world as apprehended by actively organizing it, selecting some features and disregarding others, segmenting the flow of impressions and events. "If we were not able to do such framing, we would be lost in a murk of chaotic experience and probably would not have survived as a species in any case", says Bruner (1990: 56). In order not to be lost in an otherwise bewildering environment, humans (and animals) organize the stream of fragments, glimpses, impressions and associations in some coherent manner, by means of linkages, memory traces, perceptual schemas etc. This is done in "dialogue with" interlocutors and ʋ ˌtexts. In our flow of consciousness, streams get *cognitively organized locally*, and so experience comes to us consciously apprehended and cognitively constituted (Schutz 1962, 1967). Focusing our attention on a few aspects, we bring order to a limited, situated and temporary, micro-world; we build 'islands of understanding'.

When we look at talk-in-interaction, we can study the processes of *collaboratively and (partially) intersubjectively constructed cognition*, what Schutz (1962, 1967) called the 'synchronization of two streams of consciousness'. We can think of the building of topical episodes and the construction of a coherent text and its associated context space as starting from a fragment and then building around and beyond this an *island of temporarily shared understanding*. How interlocutors use various kinds of contexts as resources to create coherence within topical episodes, and also to build bridges between episodes, was discussed in ch. 8.

In the flow of discourse and thought, people focus on limited chunks of information at each moment (Chafe 1979, 1994). In joint discourse, actors focus attention and interpretive efforts on a few aspects of the world. Constitutive of the activities involved is the handling of fragments: fragments of understanding and fragments of contexts. In addition, in at least multi-party conversations, one can point to the fragmentation resulting from actors' temporary forming of parallel activities and different floors;[21] to some extent, participants in THANKSGIVING (ch. 8: (1)) contributed to parallel floors, thus creating fragmentation from the point of view of participation framework too.

---

21. 'Schisming' in Egbert's (1997) terminology. See also Erickson (1982), Parker (1984).

The property of being partially fragmentary pertains, I would argue, to any conversation or spoken encounter. In THANKSGIVING and SKIING AND BALLOONING (1) we could follow the meandering topical trajectories through a few topic spaces ("islands of understanding") and across some bridges or links connecting the different islands. Naturally, the fragmentary nature of conversational interaction gets more salient in some settings than in others, e.g. when participants are present who are not fully conversationally competent; the interventions by an aphasic in NOT RECALLING NAMES OF FLOWERS (ch.8: (2)) may be a case in point.[22]

10.10 The gradual determination of indeterminate topics

In verbalizing a certain 'idea unit', e.g. within a lengthy turn or sequence of turns, the speaker — in dialogue with her interlocutor and with her contexts — makes some things explicit. At the same time, the utterance opens up for other things to be possibly said as continuations; these things are, e.g., implications, associations and interpretations related to what has been said so far, and they may often be said to be 'vaguely present' in the utterances produced hitherto. They afford interlocutors resources for interpreting what is being said and give them fuel for more talk. They offer a 'horizon' of what is not yet clearly visible (or hearable), but may emerge more explicitly in the immediate future. Indeed, the speaker (or her interlocutor) is rather likely to make some of these things actually verbalized in the next 'idea units' expressed, thus transforming them from vague possibilities into more distinct meanings. Once new ideas have been expressed in a new utterance, then this new unit, with its semantic potentials, opens up for new associations and implications as possible continuations. Each new unit is pregnant with opportunities for developing meaning; it represents a stage of "multiply determinable indeterminacy" (John Shotter, quoted by Rommetveit 1992: 36). However, only some potentials actually get realised; the things that, in the course of this continuous sense-making activity, are *not* 'brought into language' will remain 'lost opportunities' (Rommetveit 1988, 1991a).[23] In this way, topics are always "on their way", "departing for somewhere", continu

---

22. For an analysis of aphasic interaction from this point of view, cf. Linell & Korolija (1995).

23. Rommetveit (1988: 23) borrows this term from von Wright (1974: 34).

ously creating further stages of "becoming" (rather than states of "being").

The view of topic progression as continuous sense-making activities, where originally vague meanings, being potential, yet-to-be-exploited significances on the "fringes" of consciousness, are turned into something distinctly expressed, owes a lot to James's pragmatism and Schutz' phenomenology (cf. ch. 3.4.2), but of course very much also to Bakhtin's work (1986) (cf. also Rommetveit 1992; Foppa 1990).

10.11 Episodes and topics as emergent and dynamic events

Understanding involves fitting that which is to be understood into some kind of context, i.e. to make it cohere with something already known or understood. Similarly, the building of texts and topical episodes can be seen as building upon sense-making as coherence-building (Hopper 1983). For the actors, coherence may be regarded as "programmatically relevant" (Schegloff 1990: 73). However, one must not forget the other, complementary side of coherence-building, i.e. the demand to make dialogue *progress* by the introduction of *new* elements. Coherence and continuation (cf. also responsive vs. initiatory aspects) correspond to interlocutors' attempts at both maintaining and renewing topics (cf. also Bergmann 1990: 203). Another way of stating this amounts to saying that discourse should be seen as the result of a tension, or dialectics, between focusing and fragmentation, as these polar concepts pertain to attention, intention, action and understanding (cf. Parker 1984). Indeed, the selective attention and apprehension of the world is arguably a condition for survival (Bruner 1990); we cannot make more than a limited number of coherent links, or else we would either not make progress or we would end up in total confusion.

Topical episodes can, in general, be isolated as bounded sequences only in retrospect, when the discourse is over, properly recorded and in the process of getting analyzed. Some topical sequences are not pre-planned at all, only *ex post facto* can interlocutors (and all the more so, analysts) note that they have in fact been talking about some specific topic. Whilst a topic can often be seen as constituting a communicative project, it is not so often conceived as such in advance. (Generally, it is primarily in institutional settings that actors have (reasonably detailed) plans for topics. Even such projects are typically revised, "updated", through the communicative process itself. On communicative projects, see ch.11).

Some text-oriented linguists wish to analyze topical episodes as some kind of large, syntactically organized expression units (with associated meanings). But topical episodes are not built as comprehensive structures, as if resulting from ready-made representations in speakers' minds or heads; the sequences emerge as the interaction, and the discourse, gradually evolves. Topic development is a dynamic aspect integrated in action sequences and discursive events. The traditional isolation of topic structure has been due to the preoccupation with e.g. written prose, which is of course much less event- and action-oriented than talk-in-interaction.

Written texts often display a clear hierarchical structure with chapters, sections and paragraphs, which of course may invite an analysis in analogy with syntactic constituent structures. This is also what (at least the early) text-linguistic approaches have tried to ascribe to spoken discourse. However, Levy (1979) maintained, at quite an early stage, that the text-based approach is mistaken in suggesting that "discourse exhibits *the same kind of structure* as the structure of the sentence" (op.cit.: 206). Before Levy, Halliday & Hasan (1976) had claimed that

> "(a) text is a unit of language in use. It is not a grammatical unit, like a clause or a sentence; and it is not defined by its size. A text is sometimes envisaged to be some kind of super-sentence, a grammatical unit that is larger than a sentence but is related to a sentence in the same way that a sentence is related to a clause, a clause to a group and so on; by *constituency*, the composition of larger units out of smaller ones. But this is misleading. [...] A text does not *consist of sentences;* it is *realized by*, or encoded in, sentences. [...] It is a unit of a different kind." (p.1–2)

Levy proposes a "mind-based" rather than a "text-based" approach to texts,[24] viewing discourse "from the perspective of the producing and comprehending mind" (cf. also Chafe 1979; Givón 1989, 1995). A more dialogistic analysis would propose an interaction-based analysis, focussing on the interacting persons (with their minds).

From a dialogistic vantage point, the static, hierarchical analysis strikes us as highly implausible. It pictures discourse as if produced by one supercapable author, who had first planned it carefully and then laid it out in overt discourse. Indeed, this is what classical rhetorical theory has tried to teach speakers

---

24. Levy (1979: 184) criticizes, rightly I think, Halliday & Hasan (op.cit.) for being "text-based" too, despite some of their basic analyses.

(speakers then taken as those who make speeches rather than those who indulge in talk-in-interaction). This monologistic account is therefore clearly subject to a "written language bias" (ch. 2.5).

10.12 Units of talk-in-interaction

The discussion in the preceding paragraph raises the question: Can one be specific about what kinds of items are useful analytical units in the analysis of talk-in-interaction?

Table 1. *A partial hierarchy of units.*

	Units discussed in the literature and comparable in *some* respects: [25]
Elementary units (contributions):	
– idea units	turn-constructional units (TCU's), (speech) acts (DD)
– complex (multi-unit) utterances	
– turns	moves
(Potentially) full interactions:	
– local sequences (= sequences or interactions, each enacting a "local communicative project", for this notion: see ch. 11)	adjacency pairs, Clark & Schaefer's (1989) 'contributions to discourse', minimal three-part sequences, 'exchanges', 'sequences'(DD)
– (subepisodes)[26]	
– episodes (middle-sized, topic- or active-sustained episodes as defined in ch. 10)	'episodes' (DD)
– phases (major subactivities, esp. in goal-directed encounters, cf. ch. 12)	'talk activities'(DD)
– encounters (sometimes with one major core activity, often divided into phases and/or embedded in non-work-related talk, cf. ch. 12)	'speech events' and 'speech occasions'(DD)

25. "DD" refers to a hierarchy of units proposed by Dumesnil & Dorval (1989).

26. These are smaller topical units sometimes distinguishable within episodes.

Although the following chapters will have more to say on this issue, and despite the arguments of the preceding section, this might be the appropriate place to introduce what I consider a provisional proposal for a partial hierarchy of units (Table 1). I will do this in the form of a list that distinguishes between elementary contributions (cf. ch. 9), i.e. units which are not in themselves full interactions, and (potentially) full interactions.

Now to a number of caveats. In dialogism, actions and interactions are more basic than the resulting units of discourse. In addition, perhaps the most profound aspect of dialogism lies in the insistence that the actor, the progenitor of meaning, is (directly or indirectly) in constant interaction, "in dialogue" with, other actors and various kinds of situational and cultural contexts. Therefore, any stretch of discourse, created in actors' interaction with other actors, is embedded in a matrix of contexts. Moreover, it is not simply embedded or situated in contexts, but has a *reflexive* relationship to these contexts. Discourses and contexts mutually constitute and select each other, and hence they form a basic, indivisible whole. Of course, discourse units and contextual dimensions are analytically divisible, but it is not possible to think of them as independent objects that enter into unidirectional causal relationships.

Both elementary contributions and larger units, such as episodes, topics and whole activities, are reflexively related to their contexts, and to their pasts and futures. They are all characterized by sequential organization, joint (or social) construction, and act-activity interdependence. These points, which were proposed as elaborations of the Bakhtinian 'dialogical principle' (ch. 5.9), appear to be more basic than whatever units of analysis one may posit. While the principles are part of the general framework adopted, it remains to be an empirical task to explore what the dialogical units of analysis are (or should be). This explains why the list proposed must be regarded as a provisional one. In addition, a few extra comments are called for.

First, it is important to realise that *unit structure is activity-specific*; we cannot expect to find the same kinds of units in all sorts of discourse. Turns are not always very clearly delineated; some kinds of especially multi-party talk allow for a great deal of overlap, which may cast some doubt on the universal applicability of the notion. In any case, turns are most clearly delineated in, for example, (some kinds of) dyadic talk, in telephone conversations, and agenda-bound and chaired interactions. Furthermore, turns are of course more significant units in exchanges with frequent speaker shifts than in monological talk. Storytelling, for example, necessitates particularly long turns, even if some types of collaborative story-telling can be accomplished by duetting. Finally, talk cultures differ in their tolerance of overlapping and simultaneous talk; it has been argued that the rules of turn-taking that dominate many Western middle-class speech communities (Sacks et al. 1974) are not necessarily valid in cultures where simultaneous talk by several people is very common (Ochs 1976).

Episodes are not necessarily ubiquitous. They are typical of free informal talk. A rather different type of very clear episode structure occurs in agenda-bound, itemized interactions, e.g. formal meetings. Phases, and the distinction between core activities and other kinds of talk, are probably more pronounced in institutional encounters than in informal everyday settings.

Secondly, even if it is necessary, it is also somewhat dangerous to talk about "units", especially if this conjures up a grammatical analogy (ch. 10.11). In addition, it is misleading to think of local and global units only in terms of size, or in terms of constituent structures.[27] Elementary contributions and local sequences are "local", phases and whole encounters are "global", and episodes are in between. But the global structures are realized in and through local actions, and local moves may have global, i.e. more long-ranging, consequences. This point relates to the discussion of the act-activity interdependence (ch. 5.9.3).

The second point takes us to a third one. The units discussed above are, after all, more or less form-based, i.e. if they are valid units, they should be identifiable rather straight-forwardly in the flow of overt discourse. But there is another way of looking at discourse, more unequivocally in terms of actions and projects. This is what I am going to do in the next chapter.

---

27. Note therefore that the levels in the table are not related to one another like linguistic levels (phonology, morphology, syntax, semantics), nor are the units hierarchically structured like e.g. morpheme, word, phrase, clause, sentence, paragraph. This point has been made several times in the literature (see e.g. Schiffrin 1994: ch. 2).

CHAPTER 11

Communicative projects

11.1 Communicative actions as interactions

Communicative actions are collaborative accomplishments. When people "do things with words" (Austin 1962), they are dependent on one another, using utterances and understandings produced so far for the purpose of producing new utterances and understandings, thereby in turn making yet new actions and meanings relevant and possible. Actors operate within the interplay between different constituent acts and between discourse and contexts. The elementary unit of communication, whether we take this to be an idea unit or a turn at talk, is intrinsically sequentially positioned and related to its outsides, the prior units and the projected next ones (ch. 9). In other words, if we look at this kind of unit as an act, it is clearly an 'inter-act' (using a back formation from 'interaction', Linell & Marková 1993). The elementary contributions are of a social nature, either overtly jointly produced, or else at least 'virtually' social, since the other is the producer of prior and/or subsequent actions, and the speaker's own action is itself other-oriented (ch. 6.5). Yet, an elementary contribution is not in itself a communicative interaction. The instigator of a communicative action needs his interlocutor to 'complete' it (Leudar & Antaki 1988). Actors perform 'communicative projects' together. This holds most obviously for dialogue. Monologue, on the other hand, does not always, at least not on the face of it, involve interaction with others, but one may nevertheless talk about interaction between different roles or identities in the self, or interaction with a "virtual other".

In spite of all this, the most influential theory of linguistic action, of what people "do with words", to date is undoubtedly a monologistic one, namely speech act theory as developed by John Searle (1969, 1975, 1992). I shall therefore start by briefly characterizing this theory and point to its inadequacies.

11.2 Speech act theory: Monological acts by individual speakers

Speech act theory has its roots in philosophy and linguistics, not in the study of authentic discourse. At the most fundamental level, the philosophical assumptions of the theory are those of individualistic Cartesian philosophy. As we have seen (ch. 2), this individualistic or monologistic point of view portrays human agency, cognition and consciousness as (processes due to) faculties belonging solely to the individual rather than as actions and processes resulting from interdependencies between individual and environment.[1] It portrays the agent as an autonomous information-processing organism, not as a subject in continuous interaction with the physical and social environment.

With regard to linguistics, speech act theory was originally developed as an alternative, or rather a supplement, to traditional sentence-based semantics which was concerned with truth conditions and propositional content. As such a supplement, speech act theory claimed the universality of illocutionary content. However, it still shares a host of properties with its intellectual ancestors within linguistics. In general, most of these are part of the "written language bias in linguistics" (ch. 2.5).

For one thing, speech act theory continues to work with sentences (or sentence equivalents) as autonomous units. Autonomy means that whatever the relevant contextual conditions are considered to be, they are treated as extrinsic with regard to the speech act, as "outsides" (Bogen 1991). Secondly, classical speech act theory went on working with made-up examples in imaginary contexts (and of course written on paper) rather than with authentic connected spoken discourse. Thirdly, the theory still accepts the idea that the task of semantics or pragmatics is to map onto each possible expression (sentence) a unique semantic interpretation. (A weaker formulation is that this mapping should apply to each possible "reading" of the expression, which of course makes the argument vacuous.) Note that this view of linguistic semantics and pragmatics is characteristic of the work of both those who are concerned with sentences in abstracto and some of those who deal with situated utterances. In other words, it is

---

1. Searle seems to have modified his views on human intentionality in some respects over the years. He now seems to have left the position that intentions are (fully) behind or prior to action, and prefers to speak of intentionality *in* action (Searle 1991). Furthermore, in addition to individual intentionality, he has now more clearly emphasized the importance of shared or collective intentionality (Searle 1992: 22, 138).

common to, for example, Chomskyan generative grammar, Grice's (1975) theory of conversational implicature, Sperber & Wilson's (1986) theory of relevance, Labov & Fanshel's (1977: esp. ch. 3) model for analyzing real talk, and, of course, Searle's speech act theory. As Taylor (1992) argues, the assumption of unique and determinate semantic representations is an integrating part of a (largely implicit) theory of communication, according to which interlocutors must set up identical representations, or else they can not understand each other (see ch. 12.2).[2] Thus, while these theories naturally admit that many utterances are vague or ambiguous on the surface, they deny, in effect, that this also holds for a deeper level, where the effects of applying rules of implicature and interpretation should be abstracted from, bracketed or disregarded.

In their critical appraisal of speech act theory, Linell & Marková (1993) reviewed some of the relevant literature and pointed to some points, where the theory proves to be inadequate. For example, the theory does not cope satisfactorily with the *multifunctionality* of discourse contributions; most utterances fulfil several communicative functions, and some utterances are vague or ambiguous with respect to illocutionary function, and yet speech act theory assumes, in principle, that each utterance has one illuctionary point.[3] Classical speech act theory takes 'speech acts' like the following as examples; to assert, to ask a question, to order, to ask for (an object), to thank, to promise, to accuse, to name, to sentence (a person to imprisonment), etc. But there are countless other things that people "do with words" in discourse, such as: to respond (to someone's utterance or action), to initiate a repair, to confirm (what others have said), to make an assessment (or a second assessment), to establish agreement, to make a counter-argument, to be domineering, to (try to) be polite, to joke, to tease, to ridicule, to insult and to respond to such attempts etc., just to mention a small sample. Many of these acts are typically responsive in character, i.e. they presuppose certain prior acts, or they are parts of collaborative action sequences. Classical speech act theory characteristically treats all speech acts as active interventions on the part of the speaker, as (more or less pure) initiatives in the terminology of ch. 9, while virtually all responsive links in connected discourse are being neglected. Moreover, a closer look at the first-mentioned, "classical" speech act types reveals that they too are essentially dependent on, or part of,

---

2. Labov & Fanshel admit, however, that "the problem of "correct interpretation" can never be solved completely" (1977: 73).

3. For critique on this point, see also e.g. Levinson (1979), Streeck (1980), Duranti (1991).

local sequences and collaborative projects, a point I shall soon return to. In social life, we are not faced simply with the utterances and autonomous acts of, say, assertions, requests, promises, and expressions of condolence. Such communicative actions are always about something specific, are addressed to somebody specific, and are always part of interactions in particular situations. For example, an assertion is normally a response to a prior implicit (or explicit) query, and there is usually a point in asserting something particular.

Some of the inadequacies of speech act theory can be explicated as failures to cope with basic dialogical properties of discourse and its constituent elements. Thus, let us return to three points claimed to be basic tenets of dialogism in ch. 5.9:

The principle of *sequentiality* states that the meaning of any discourse contribution derives partly from its position in the sequence. Now, if every sentence-formed utterance is treated as an autonomous unit, this means that the meaning cannot be wholly accounted for. The solution of speech act theory has been to try to reduce actors' meanings to speaker intentions of individual utterances. A dialogistic theory must regard this move as misguided.

The principle of the *social nature and joint construction* of discourse and its contributions means that meaningful actions are collective accomplishments. It is true that idea units and sentence-sized utterances (the usual outer form of 'speech acts') are most often physically produced by single speakers, but their other-orientation makes them 'virtually' co-produced. They cannot be explicated solely in terms of individual speaker intentions. "Doing things with words" in dialogue involves taking on responsibilities for oneself and assigning responsibilities to others.

Finally, the principle of *activity-dependence*, or *activity-act co-constitution*, implies that individual utterances are dependent on the various over-arching communicative activities they are part of and partly constitute (Levinson 1979). The embedded constituent utterance and the embedding activity cannot be accounted for independently of each other. That elementary communicative acts and global activities co-constitute each other was of course envisaged already in Wittgenstein's (1958) concept of language game. According to speech act theory, however, it is the elementary speech acts that build up discourse; it is not the more global activities and language games that motivate speech acts (though Searle (1992) compromises this position somewhat).

11.3 Intentionality and responsibility

Linell & Marková (1993), and similarly Muhlhäusler & Harré (1990), have argued that the basic concern of speech act theory is the assignment of epistemic and practical responsibilities (although this is not stated in this way by the speech acts theorists themselves). Such phenomena, however, turn out to be collaborative accomplishments carried out over sequences of contributions. While speech act theory describes e.g. promises, questions, and assertions as acts embodied in singular utterances by individual speakers, these actions are better regarded as collective language games or, with a term I am about to suggest, communicative projects. Thus, for example, in a study of courtroom interaction and police interrogations, Linell et al. (1993) have analyzed the sociopragmatic variation in how defendants and suspects are made to state their position regarding guilt (or non-guilt) in petty offence cases (for some examples, see below, ch. 11.4). It is shown that the admission (or denial) of guilt is invariably a collaborative phenomenon, in which legal professionals' questions and up-takes are as important as the defendants' and suspects' contributions (usually answers to questions). Even if it is the defendant or suspect who has to take on legal responsibility by pleading guilty, one cannot describe the communicative expression of this as an individual speech act performed by this person in isolation; it crucially depends on the local discourse contexts, to which the judge (in court) or the police officer (in the police interrogation) contributes, and the whole "game" is better described as a collaborative project enacted over a sequence of turns at talk. Moreover, such a communicative project can, in *some* of the police interrogations, be quite implicit and embedded within more comprehensive projects, i.e. an explicit question is never formulated, nor does the suspect ever issue a statement pleading guilty or not guilty, but his or her position can be seen to transpire as an implicit conclusion from a lengthy interview in which the circumstances of the case are being explored by the two interactants. Such a perfectly natural way of solving the task of finding out a suspect's position on the issue of guilt would seem to be hard to reconcile with a theory of individual speech acts, but is quite compatible with a theory operating with a concept of 'language game' or 'communicative project'. Such a shift in theory from individual speech acts to collective 'communicative projects' involves a partial change of emphasis not only *from individuality to collectivity* but also *from intentionality* (behind actions) *to responsibility* (for possible consequences of actions).[4]

---

4. Duranti (1993a), using an argumentative route rather different from mine, arrives at a similar conclusion.

Space restrictions do not admit of a full assessment of Searlian speech act theory here. Yet, trying to summarize some of the arguments from the last two sections, I would claim that the theory has provided important insights but involves serious difficulties. Many of these have to do with its very distinctly monologistic perspective. The theory deals basically with the use of sentences, i.e. a certain kind of linguistic expression units, in (at best) rudimentary and imaginary contexts. These behavioural units are assigned meanings by recourse to individual speakers' intentions. But only a limited fraction of the situated meanings in actual communication and language use can be captured in this way. Action and utterance meanings are largely generated through sequential, interactional and genre-specific interdependencies. The inadequacies of speech act theory are clearly exposed, when the theory is actually applied to authentic discourse.[5]

11.4 From speech acts to local sequences, language games and communicative projects

It was argued in ch. 9 that every communicative action is collectively organized and accomplished; "it takes two to communicate and establish intersubjectivity". Logically, a communicative interaction involves several steps, minimally three (cf. ch. 3.4.3), though *empirically* we find, for various reasons, variations in how people "do things with words" together, e.g. as regards exactly what kinds of and how many elementary contributions are deployed. It seems universal that communicative actions involve co(n)texts and are sequentially organized. *People have to interact*, over sequences of elementary contributions, *to establish some-*

---

5. For critique of coding systems, designed for authentic discourse but based on speech act theory, see Linell & Marková (1993) and Marková & Linell (1996). Some theories of discourse structure rely heavily on speech act theory, e.g. the 'Birmingham school' (Sinclair & Coulthard 1992; Coulthard 1992; Edmondson 1981; Coulthard & Brazil 1992; for recent textbook accounts, see e.g. van Rees 1992; Stenström 1994). This kind of 'Discourse Analysis' ("DA", according to Levinson 1983) provides a certain, linguistic-structural perspective on discourse. It underestimates the semantic multifunctionality and indeterminacies in authentic discourse, and is largely incapable of capturing the emergent properties of utterances and their interpretations. It provides more of a retrospective text analysis than a dynamic process analysis, and shares with speech act analysis the difficulties to cope with contextual, sequential and social-interactional interdependencies. For an attempt (largely unsuccessful, in my view) to integrate parts of DA (and speech act analysis) with parts of Conversation Analysis, see van Rees (1992).

thing as a 'communicative fact', i.e. to have something said and mutually understood, or, in other words and in the terminology I propose for adoption, *to carry out a communicative project*. In these endeavours actors are partners in concerted activities (ch. 5.4).

Communicative projects can be, I will argue, small- or large-scale, i.e. local or more or less global. Let us first consider some local projects, i.e. such that are organized over a local, (more or less) bounded and often quite short sequence. In the preceding paragraph, I referred to the admission of guilt as a local communicative project carried out in certain judicial settings. Some examples of how this "game" is enacted in (Swedish) court trials are the following:[6]

(1) ADMISSION OF GUILT ((Tema K: A36, A5, A21: Excerpts from different trials, dealing with minor economic offences, in a Swedish District Court. J = judge, D = defendant. Rough translations from Swedish originals.))

(a)

```
1.    J: okay, is it correct, this,[7] John Eriksson?
2.    D: yes, I have admitted it, haven't I, so −
3.    J: you admit it.
```

(b)

```
1.    J: okay, does John Sigurdsson admit or deny all these
         deeds?[8]
2.    D: yes, I admit it.
3.    J: admits?
4.    D: yes.
```

---

6. For more examples showing the sociolinguistic variation in the admissions or denials, see Linell et al. (1993).

7. "this" refers to the prosecutor's charge which has been issued just before.

8. In somewhat formal situations, it is not unusual for Swedish, somewhat old-fashioned, professionals to use a person's name (here: John Sigurdsson) as a substitute for "you".

(c)

```
1.    J: okay, then I am going to ask you, John Gregersson,
      what is your stance with regard to this first act?
2.    D: it is true.
3.    J: you admit it?
4.    D: yes.
```

The admission appears to be a collective project for the parties involved, with a sequential organization, with different kinds of (complementary) contributions by the parties, and with a common goal. By participating in the language game, they all contribute in their different ways to the goal of completing a project dealing with the admission (or denial) of guilt on the part of the suspect. This is of course not to deny that participants may entertain divergent interests within this game, and they may also understand or frame the common project differently.

Clark and associates (Clark & Schaefer 1987, 1989) have argued that actors initiate and invite vs. respond to and complete sequences according to a recurrent pattern, which resembles what Sinclair & Coulthard (1992; Edmondson 1981; Coulthard 1992) term 'exchanges'.[9] In a generalized form, such a local sequence fits the following format:

(2)   Structure of (the interaction enacting) a local communicative project:

     (A: — prepare/ground

           ('pre'-initiative)) ⎫

                              ⎬ 'pre-sequence'

     (B: — respond to 'pre'-initiative) ⎭

     A: — initiate/present

     (A and/or B: — repair)

     B: — respond/accept

     (A and/or B: — challenge/negotiate)

     (A (and/or B): — check/recheck)

     (B: confirm)

     A: — confirm/give feedback

     (B: — confirm sharedness)

---

9. Clark and colleagues use the term 'contribution to discourse' for the whole sequence corresponding to the local project. Clark's notion initiate (invite) vs. respond to (complete) correspond to Edmondson's (1981) 'proffer' vs. 'satisfy', i.e. moves that form an 'exchange', the smallest unit of social interaction.

Here, the elements within brackets are optional; actors can add expansions before, within or after the core sequence (cf. Schegloff 1990). (Also, the third element (A: confirm) of the core sequence is sometimes omitted.) The optional preparatory sequence before the initiate/present contribution is a so-called 'pre'-sequence, often consisting of two paired contributions but sometimes of course further elaborated and extended (Sacks 1992; Levinson 1983). In the case of the admission-of-guilt project (examples (1)), the pre-sequence is usually not necessary, since the project is always initiated in a pre-defined slot in the trial. Yet, there are features of a 'pre'-like formulation in 1c: 1. The three-part format is fairly straightforward in (1a), whereas it is one notch more elaborated in (1c), with 1c: 1 as the initiation, 1c: 2 as the response, 1c: 3 as the checking, and 1c: 4 as the confirmation (in this case primarily accomplished by the defendant).

Clark & Schaefer (1989) argue that a 'contribution to discourse' (cf. fn. 9) includes a presentation phase (in which A is active) and an acceptance phase (in which B, or B and A, are active). That is, in their terms either respond/accept by B or this unit plus a confirmation or feedback (the latter by A, or by A and B together) belong to the latter phase and thus 'complete' the sequence (Clark: 'contribution').[10] Quite often, the initiate/present unit represents the "core act", indicating what kind of project (e.g. proposal, promise, admission, repair) the speaker is attempting; if this is the case, speech act theory would pick this unit as *the* act to carry the burden of the whole project. But there is not necessarily any substantial core act by the party who takes on or is assigned the main responsibility associated with the project. In the data corpus of the admission-of-guilt projects referred to above (Linell et al. 1993), the judge would always do the preparation and initiation of the sequence, and in some cases, the defendant, who does the "admission" with its social consequences, does little but respond minimally:

(3) ((Tema K: A12. Cf. (1a-c)).

```
1.     J: okay, John Rickardsson, is it correct what the
       prosecutor said here?
2.     D: yes.
3.     J: you admit it.
```

Note that it is the judge, not the defendant, who contributes the word "admit" here. The same was true of (1c).

---

10. In recent work, Clark (1996: 196) too has adopted the term 'local project'.

A local communicative project is typically sequentially organized, with the parties holding complementary roles, though the confirmation of shared understanding (the understanding for current practical purposes) and the closing are sometimes done through symmetrical contributions. The entire sequence represents a project with a clear direction, yet its situated materialization is typically interactionally negotiated and, as a result, may vary across instances.

While many local projects are intentionally introduced into the flow of discourse, some are simply occasioned by the incidents occurring. So, for example, when some interactional problem occurs, e.g. a misunderstanding, or a suspected misunderstanding, or a faulty expression, there arises locally a need to repair the situation. Such repairs are also local communicative projects, whose problems are typically solved over bounded sequences (much like (2)); the general structure of a 'local miscommunication event'[11] is roughly as follows:

(4) (–   precursors)
     –   core utterance (containing the major source, the 'repairable'))
     –   reaction (calling for a repair; 'repair initiation')
     –   attempted repair
     –   reaction to repair (sometimes expanded into a sequence)
     –   exit.

Here, the core utterance in the misunderstanding sequence is the one which contains the 'problem', or 'repairable'. However, if we focus on the repair project itself, it is rather the reaction, i.e. the utterance that reacts to something prior as being in need of repair, which is the initiating contribution. (How repairable, repair initiation, attempted repair, and reaction to repair are distributed on speakers A and B differs.)[12] What is termed 'precursors' in (4) is simply a local sequence containing sources or 'antecedents' for the 'repairable' that is later identified in the core utterance of the sequence. Thus, Linell (1995), among others, demonstrates that miscommunications in dialogue-interpreted discourse are often related to features occurring prior to the utterance identifiable as the "core"; such antecedents of problems can of course only be traced retrospectively, after the problem has been diagnosed.

---

11. Cf. Linell (1995). See also 'misapprehension sequence' (Jefferson 1972) and 'repair sequence' (Schegloff et al. 1977).

12. See Schegloff et al. (1977) on the categories of self- and other-initiation of repair, and self- and other-repairs.

In other cases, repairables are occasioned more locally, without any clear‎ precursors. For example, in the example cited as GORILLAS (3) in ch. 8.8, contribution 3: 1 is the core utterance, 3: 2 the reaction or repair initiation, 3: 3 the attempted repair, and 3: 4 the reaction to repair. As a further example, consider (5):

(5) WHAT? BEFORE WHAT? (From Crow 1983: 146. The excerpt starts with the conclusion of a conflict episode having to do with the possibility of M cheating on F (turn 1))

```
1.     M: I said I'd never do that. I'm saying though, I'm
       saying I've had all kinds o' opportunities 'n I've never
       done it, that's what I was saying. y'know.
2.     F: what were we talking about before this?
3.     M: what? before what?
4.     F: before this. I can't remember. oh! oh, oh, nothing.
       mm. I had the same boyfriend from the first grade (M: oh)
       to sixth grade
```

Seen in the terms just introduced, 5: 2 is the core utterance, and M contributes the reaction calling for a repair ("before what?") (5: 3). F then repeats what she said before ("before this") (5: 4), rather than provides an explanation. However, this small attempted repair project is occasioned by F's bringing up an issue which in itself can be regarded as an interactional problem (i.e. the interlocutors, in F's local formulation (5:2), have got off the track in their conversation), and in 5:2 he is calling for a repair of *that* problem. F solves the problem herself ("I had the same boyfriend", 5: 4); with regard to this, the sequence thus ends up as a self-initiated self-repair, although M's interstitial request for clarification may have had some impact on her performance. The most deeply embedded repair project is thus embedded within a somewhat larger one. Moreover, this larger project is arguably serving the purpose of trying to quit the prior topic; in 5: 2, F blatantly ignores what M has just said in 5: 1. Thus, this example also illustrates the nested structures and multi-functionality pertaining to many communicative projects, even those limited to quite short sequences. I will return to aspects of nesting presently.

11.5 The notion of a 'communicative project': A first approximation

Before proceeding to some additional examples, I need to backtrack a little and explicate some aspects of the notion of 'communicative project'. The concept and the term are due to Luckmann (1995), who in turn builds upon the notion of 'project in action' in Schutz's (1962: 67ff.) theory of action (cf. Luckmann 1992: 225). I have developed it here partly along my own lines.

In the flow of cognition and communication (cf. ch. 10.9), actors come to focus upon and indulge in communicative projects of many kinds and extensions. A communicative project aims at solving a communicative 'problem' of some kind; problems of establishing an interpretation or a shared understanding of something, of having something "done through language" (performing acts, cf. Wittgenstein 1953; Austin 1962), of creating a communicative fact (that something has been said, made known and possibly understood). A communicative problem can be understood as a coordination problem (Clark 1996); in and through dialogue, two, or more, people try to coordinate their mental and interpersonal activities. In this context, phrases like "(attempt) to solve a problem" is not meant to imply that conversationalists are constantly faced with difficulties and complications (even if, occasionally, they do have to work hard to bring about understanding). Rather, a 'problem' is simply a task to do or work out in transaction, and our general approach simply wants to stress that, in the conversational management of topics, understandings and misunderstandings etc, we deal with achievements, which result from the actors' (more or less) goal-directed work over time (Schegloff & Sacks 1973: 290). Even a most trivial establishment of a common reference is such an achievement. At the same time, in situations with e.g. language-impaired speakers, even this can involve great interactional and cognitive efforts (as was illustrated by NOT RECALLING NAMES OF FLOWERS?; (2) in ch. 8).[13]

The term 'project' can be used to refer to different aspects of a task, an action or an accomplishment: plan, process and/or product. Thus, a project is partly the action as planned or anticipated. A project is always to *some* extent intended or 'projected' before it is carried out. However, even if there is an anticipated direction and goal, projects are typically open and partly indeterminate, multiply determinable. The projection involves the opening of horizons for future actions and contributions. It embodies ideas guiding potential developments.

In other words, a project is not just a plan for or an anticipation of an activity. Above all, it is something *developed in the course of action*, something

---

13. See e.g. Linell (1991), Lesser & Milroy (1993), Colllins & Marková (1995), Goodwin (1995).

which is successively carried out and advanced step-by-step (incrementally; Clark 1996: 40), and eventually completed. It is also possible to talk about the projects when they have been brought to an end. This is what researchers do in analyzing data retrospectively, and conversationalists themselves often talk about what they have just done in discourse, although they usually do not use the technical term "project". Projects can be seen both as acting (the unfolding process) and as act (the action accomplished).

The openness and ambiguity (plan, process and/or product) of the term/concept 'project' serve to make this term attractive to dialogism. As we have seen, monologism tends to explicate discourse in terms of communicative 'plans' or 'intentions'. Plans, however, are made up *before* execution (even if they can of course be "revised"), they are assumed to be *determinate* (how else could you, according to monologism, "explain" what occurs in behaviour?), and, like intentions, they belong to *individual* minds. Thus, although 'plans' and 'intentions' normally refer to intended effects (to be achieved), they are assumed to be there before the communicative acts, and do not naturally refer to activities which have been completed. Partly the same argument goes for '(communicative) goal', which is another concept, or term, used about the intended effects of communicative actions.[14] On all these points, the connotations of 'project' seem more attuned to what goes on in dialogue.[15]

A human project in general can be either individual or collective. Most communicative projects start out from individual, albeit often rather vague, intentions (although there are, of course, cases of two or more individuals involved in jointly and consciously planned, or collusively planned, activities). In many cases, parties continue to entertain individual projects as parts of common, i.e. partly shared, activities. However, in another, and perhaps more significant, respect, a *communicative* project is necessarily *collective* (or at least 'social'); it cannot be performed and completed by only one person, but it always involves another (or others), i.e. it is *other-oriented* (and mutually other-oriented). To be sure, in some cases the project is initiated by one particular actor who may

---

14. The terms/concepts of 'plan' and 'goal' often co-occur in accounts of communicative behaviour and seem to be particularly popular in artificial intelligence (e.g. Levy 1979; Cohen & Perrault 1979).

15. '(Communicative) project' may also be seen as a substitute term for (communicative) 'action' or 'act'. Apart from the fact that the term 'act' is too easily associated with speech act theory (which we have partly discarded, ch. 9.2), I would wish, however, to exploit the slightly more precise semantic potential of the word 'project'. In this way, this concept will not eliminate the need to use terms like 'acts', 'actions', and 'activities' too.

sometimes also be the only one active in performing the overt actions connected to the project; yet, communication involves (per definition) (attempts at) achieving some kind of shared understanding, and a recipient must therefore take part to secure the felicitous completion of the project. At the very least, a 'virtual' other is involved.

A communicative project is defined primarily in terms of the problem or task that it is designed to solve and/or that it in actual fact solves (or seems to solve). There is often, in Clark's (1996: 33) terms, a 'dominant' goal. In other words, goals and purposes involved are important, perhaps *the* most important, features of communicative projects and activities. However, purposes are not simply residing in an abstract frame, but are oriented to by actors in interaction. Some purposes are shared among participants, whereas other activities are characterized by interlocutors' entertaining competing goals or talking at cross-purposes. We must therefore assume that some purposes and projects are collective and cooperative, whereas other goals and projects are more tied to role incumbents with different responsibilities and/or pursued by actors in competition. Yet, as was just pointed out, such individual projects cannot be carried out in isolation, i.e. without interaction.

We must therefore acknowledge a number of characteristics of human dialogue that modify the image of cooperative and symmetrical endeavours:

(a) many projects are characterized by *complementarity*, rather than symmetry, in participant roles;

(b) in many interactions, actors pursue *competing goals*, and may therefore be said to orient to individual projects, even if these need to be coordinated within an overarching collective project, such as having an argument;

(c) therefore, interactions house many different projects and purposes at different levels: projects are *nested* within other projects.

I shall deal with these issues in the following sections. There will also be a need for additional concepts, such as 'communicative strategy', which I propose to define roughly as a particular way of going about solving the problem defining a communicative project. I shall return to this aspect in ch. 11.9.

11.6 Communicative projects: Asymmetrical participation and collective accomplishment

Returning to the properties of natural dialogue, we note that many "problems" in discourse emerge on-line, *in situ*. Not all projects are pre-planned; actors can suddenly (or gradually) detect that something they have just said (or meant to say) can or must be reassessed, i.e. reorganized and refashioned into the initial fragments of a new communicative project that was so far not planned or not present in any actor's consciousness. Alternatively, something may happen in discourse or the surrounding situation which occasions interlocutors to carry out a project so-far unanticipated. For example, when the need for repair emerges in discourse, it usually happens in this last-mentioned way. A 'repairable' (the 'core utterance' of the miscommunication event, cf. (4) above) is identified on-line or retrospectively, usually either in the same turn ('self-initiated repair'; Schegloff et al. 1977) (in which case it may be almost immediate or on-line) or in the next turn ('other-initiated repair'). This then elicits a repair project, and so the rest of the repair sequence unfolds, until this local project is terminated, and the actors revert to their other projects, whether the same as the previous ones or newly invented ones.

Communicative projects are collectively accomplished, but often, indeed characteristically, with an *asymmetry of participation*. Therefore, actions also generate an asymmetric distribution of epistemic and practical responsibilities (Linell & Marková 1993). The examples brought up earlier showed these *complementary roles* (Rommetveit 1974) of interlocutors. Institutional discourses, with their prototypically differentiated roles of professional and client, generally strengthen the pattern of divided responsibilities (cf. ch. 12).

Perhaps, the division of labour and the co-construction of discourse are shown most dramatically in situations with a language- or speech-impaired person in conversation with an unimpaired speaker; this point was demonstrated by Goodwin (1995) in a study of an aphasic man, whose verbal repertoire was limited to the words "yes", "no" and "but" (plus a rich prosody) but who could communicate quite well in certain situations, with the help of supportive co-actors. The same point with an aphasic speaker, though one with considerably more language at his disposal, is shown in the following example:

(6)   THE TRIP TO SÄLEN ((Tema K: Hv16)) (An elderly male aphasic person,
      P, is talking with his female occupational therapist, O, about his leisure time
      interests. For a while the dialogue has slipped into the topic of a bad cold
      P recently had. When we come in, P broaches a new topic on his own
      initiative (6: 1). Among the persons mentioned, Catherine is P's daughter,
      Marie Christine his wife, and "the old man" his son-in-law. P's aphasia is
      of an anomic-semantic type; his speech is fairly fluent, but he has frequent
      word-finding problems. Rough translation from Swedish original.)

```
1.   P:   speaking of that then uh they've gone to-ah -- they were
          going to how-is-it-called s-. (2.0) hm (4.0) ((drumming
          with his fingertips on the table)) uh (0.5) well, I'll
          probably recall that too, it is out towards sä- ah (3.0)
          well-uh ((sighs)) erhm. ((sighs, drumming)) well --
2.   O:   who was going --
3.   P:   =ha they were going. Catherine was going there, yes (O:
          yes) and then she was uh (1.0), the children and the old
          man, or he (O: yes) the old man was going here, okay, and
          they went yesterday (O: yes), °by that°, and they were
          going to stay in somewhere in a ((shakes his head)) in
          such a small (0.5) cottage up there (O: I see) up towards
          eh--
4.   O:   up towards-- ?
5.   P:   =up towards on the world, wherever that is now
6.   O:   =I see, somewhere up in Norrland?
7.   P:   =yes, ah, yes some some, where is it sa- sän- sän- no,
          no, I don't remember
8.   O:   ss- (P: xxx) does it begin with <es->? sä-? is it Sälen?
9.   P:   =yes, eh it was something like that, yes, yes, sa-, maybe
          that's what it was called, °Sälen°, Sälen, yes, that's
          it, I think, okay, and they (O: I see) were going to have
          a keet- they were going to have such a bo- what's it
          called some… ((sighs)) eat, okay yes, they had such eh
          °cards°, no not cards, (2.0) uh (2.0) okay yes, they went
          somewhere by such °car° uh ah ((laughing in
          embarrassment, 2.0, drumming)) eating, no they don't eat,
          no, no, I am so stupid that it--
10.  O:   is it eh --
11.  P:   uh eat-, they uh ((6.0, drumming, sighs)) what are they
          going then?
12.  O:   what.. what were they going [to do
13.  P:                               [when they-- when they go by
          car, no, okay, first they go by car (O: yes) and then
          they had (0.5) uh, then they had ((4.0, drumming)) well.
14.  O:   go skiing?
15.  P:   =yes, yes of COURSE ((P looks at O, nods and smiles))
16.  O:   they were going SKIING!
17.  P:   =yes, okay, and there they were going to °be busy°
18.  O:   I see! the whole family then?
```

```
19. P:    yes, everybody, yes
20. O:    I see, and Catherine too then?
21. P:    yes, it was intended that I would go there actually, or
          Marie Christine too there, but then I was not so well
          with, uh, I got that one with--, you know, with the cough
          and so (O: I see), so I didn't bother, I let it go
22. O:    what, is it this week, now?
23. P:    yes, it was, it wa- it can, now now it turned so that it
          turned this time it went wrong all this just 'cause I was
          too early, here, so I don't know how it went you know,
          there was something wrong °there some way or another°,
          but they went in any case then (1.0) last week
24. O:    last week?
25. P:    yes, or yesterday, me see here, what is it now,
          yesterday, (3.0)
          °Sunday°, Sunday yes, that was yesterday okay
26. O:    yesterday °they went°
27. P:    yes, °I think it was° ((nodding))
28. O:    m-hm
```

This example also shows the nesting of projects within projects (ch. 11.8). The episode cited can be seen as part of an overall, much larger, communicative project, which is that of exploring the aphasic person's leisure-time interests and activities. Within this, P launches, partly as an aside, a more specific project, that of telling about his daughter's family travelling to Sälen, a well-known Swedish skiing resort. This is the sequence actually cited as excerpt (6). It starts out as P's individual project, but of course it is carried out in a dialogical manner. In fact, due to P's expressive difficulties, a lot of the communicative work is delegated to the occupational therapist. Like in many other communicative activities in which speech-impaired individuals take part, responsibility for achieving coherence and completing local (and global) projects falls more or less heavily on their interlocutors.

In the course of the episode (6) as a whole, a number of more local communicative projects are initiated and in many cases completed. These projects are focussed on establishing common references and on repairing unsuccessful attempts; O and P try to reassemble the story by installments, these local projects often being initiated by O's questions, about where they went (6: 4, 6, 8), what they were going to do (6: 12,14), who were going (6: 18,20), and when they went (6: 22,24,26). The establishment of a common referent in each case is confirmed by non-verbal means, especially by P's seeking gaze contact. When the major point of the story, that the family went on a skiing holiday, is achieved, he emphasizes this by nodding and, in addition, smiling (6: 15). O, on her side, also shows heightened involvement by intonational and other means (6: 16, 18). The two can thus be seen as *celebrating* their joint accomplishment, a feature which is quite common in communication, especially when parties have had initial difficulties in understanding each other (see e.g. Collins & Marková 1995). At the same time, the hierarchical structure of the story, e.g. that the point of skiing is the most important feature, is verbally and non-verbally marked in and through the actual behaviour.

Examples like (6) illustrate how communicative projects are social in nature; they are jointly managed, yet typically asymmetrical, in that parties have different and complementary roles within them.[16] In (6), it is P who has something to tell, but he cannot do it without the assistance of O. There is a *division of labour* in the communicative interaction. That the *communicative* work is distributed on the parties is fairly obvious, but one may argue that this also points to a kind of *distributed cognition*. That is, in many cases of coordinated activities (be they manual, communicative, and/or cognitive) in which different individuals perform different tasks, these tasks make no sense if taken individually but only if considered within their joint activity context. No individual performs the entire processing of any whole manual, communicative or cognitive system, and yet the manual work, the communicative exchange, or the cognitive accomplishments would not be possible without the constitutive individual contributions.[17]

11.7 Limits to sharedness: Misalignment of parties' projects, and coordination of competing goals

Communicative projects are *essentially* dialogical. Sometimes, single speakers do all the expressive work, but the projects are still 'virtually' dialogical, since monological utterances too are other-oriented and usually occur in an interactional context. However, most communicative projects are dialogical also in the

---

16. Some projects are (fairly) symmetrical, however. A mutual greeting project involves A's greeting B and then B's reciprocating this by a similar contribution. Yet, if A is the first to greet, she is taking the initiative, thus causing the project to become slightly asymmetrical.

17. Contrast this with the mainstream cognitivist assumption which conceives of cognition exclusively in terms of individuals' information processing (ch. 2.2). For references on 'distributed cognition', see ch. 2: n.5.

sense of being jointly produced; constitutive elements are produced by different actors, and the whole project is therefore collaboratively managed and completed.

I argued in ch. 11.6 that communicative projects are carried out in (at least perfunctory) cooperation, even if the participation is based on complementarity rather than symmetry. Communicative projects must be (partially) shared, at least in the sense that they involve both the speaker and her interlocutor(s); parties are mutually other-oriented. But few such projects are carried out by equals within homogeneous communities; sometimes, we find coalitions and oppositions between individuals and groups with divergent interests and preferences, exchanging "information, skills, services and scarce resources in complex relationships of power and position" (Boden 1994: 16). We may find misalignments between parties' different communicative projects in a given social encounter (e.g. CAN'T LIVE IN THE STREET in ch. 9), or misalignments between different versions of the "same" communicative project within a specific communicative activity (cf. A NASTY WORD and A HOT DAY TODAY in ch. 8).

In some clearly non-cooperative kinds of communicative activities, parties apparently have competing goals and use interactive means to outdo each other, to hurt, weaken, or defeat the other. Having an argument, engaging in a verbal duel, etc. are obvious examples. 'Moves' in malicious arguments are defined by a logic of responding to the interlocutor's blow by a counter-blow, rather than by trying to understand the other's contributions on her terms (Aronsson 1987). In such cases, we may talk about opposed individual projects: A wants to subdue B, and B tries to win over A. However, neither of these goals or projects can be carried out, unless A and B mutually accommodate their contributions. In order to accomplish a communicative project, people have to interact. They must coordinate their actions within their common activity (the row or the duel), or else there would be no communication, and hence no row or duel. (The alternative would be to break the interaction and walk out.) Hence, competitive goals (projects) too are coordinated within a common frame (project). (At a very general and abstract level, one can therefore even talk about a cooperative principle, cf. ch. 1.5.) In this respect. a competitive communicative encounter is like a tennis match, in which opponents do their best to outdo each other, while at the same time following the rules of the game; without the rule following, the game is gone, and with it the possibilities of winning the game.[18]

---

18. This analogy was suggested by Herb Clark (in a discussion at Bad Homburg, March 1991).

11.8 The nested nature of projects

Communicative projects in discourse are temporally (sequentially) organized, interlocking projects in action (cf. Schutz 1962); the performance of one project often provides the impetus and initiative for another one. Communicative projects also tend to be hierarchically organized, i.e. a large project often consists of smaller projects which in turn involve still smaller ones, etc. But the nestedness is not just a question of Chinese-box-like structures. It is also the case that one and the same activity can be part of many superordinate projects. Communicative projects share these properties with other human projects. Human conduct in general can be intended and/or interpreted as embodying many different projects. Recall, for example, Rommetveit's (1988) illustration with Mr. Smith who was doing many different things in and through the same physical activity of mowing his lawn (ch. 3.3.1). Similarly, what we say and do in discourse can be heard as belonging to several overarching projects. Some of these are short-term, being limited to a train of episodes in the concrete encounter, others are long-term, "aligned along individual-biographical systems of relevance or institutionally defined "careers", or cultural (e.g. religious) hierarchies of meaning" (Luckmann 1993: 11).

This means that we can have local as well as global communicative projects, and that projects can be nested within larger projects. In ch. 5.3, I discussed an example of a collaborative assessment sequence (THE ASPARA-GUS PIE) which, despite its seemingly trivial and sequentially quite limited nature, could be seen as a local communicative project embodying aspects of several larger projects.

One and the same actor can very well be faced with divergent goals, representing conflicting interests and commitments, a situation which either calls for a choice of one rather than the other project, or for a compromise solution of the communicative dilemma. Some communicative projects are complex in the sense that actors must find a suitable middle way between partially *conflicting demands*. For example, Adelswärd (1988), in her study of Swedish job interviews, found that successful job applicants had to find a compromise between presenting themselves as competent and suitable candidates and, at the same time, not boasting, i.e. not making the impression of being overly self-assured persons.

Most of the examples I have used deal with local communicative projects. However, the theory of communicative projects can be applied to other levels of discourse as well. For example, a whole social encounter, such as a doctor consultation or a police interrogation, may be regarded as enacting a global communicative project, such as diagnosing a patient's illness and proposing a cure, and (re)constructing a story and a written report of past events possibly involving the suspect's committing an offence (Linell & Jönsson 1991), respectively. These global activities (ch. 12) will of course encompass many smaller communicative projects, minimal, minor, local and middle-sized ones, some of which are overlapping or nested into others.[19] At the same time, they belong to much larger projects, such as the patient's persistent will to protect his health, or the suspect's desire to construct a positive self-presentation and to minimize sanctions from society. And the institutions of health care and judicial systems may be said to entertain long-term projects on an even grander scale.

11.9 Communicative strategies: Methods of accomplishing communicative projects

The term 'communicative strategy' has been used for referring to several kinds of discursive phenomena.[20] I propose to use it here in a specific sense, namely as referring to a specific (more or less intentional or at least recurrently used) way, or method, of going about solving (trying to solve) the problem or task defining a communicative project or communicative activity.[21] In some cases, specific strategies may pertain to, or be attributed to, single parties to communication, whereas in other cases they are clearly collective in nature. Different communicative strategies can also transform what may initially be taken as the same problem into different kinds of communicative projects, as with 'troubles-tellings' in phatic conversation vs. institutional advice giving (as discussed by Jefferson & Lee 1981). Communicative strategies also vary in scope, some being

---

19. As "middle-sized" projects one may consider, e.g., the activities of telling a story or a joke, treating a topic through an episode in discourse (ch. 10), or enacting a phase in an institutional discourse setting, e.g. the physical examination in the consultation, or the initial story-telling (often preceding a proper interviewing phase) in the police interrogation.

20. E.g. Levy (1979: 197).

21. Communicative activities may be regarded as global (collective) communicative projects (see ch. 12). One may note a rough similarity between, on the one hand, the notions of communicative activity, communicative project, and communicative strategy, and, on the other hand, Leontiev's concepts of activity, goal-directed action, and operation, within his general 'theory of activity' (1981).

tied to local projects, others to more global ones (e.g. entire activities, in the sense discussed in ch. 12).

Many local communicative strategies have been identified and described, although different terms, such as 'methods' or 'devices', have often been used. In fact, what I term (local) communicative strategies comes close to what ethno-methodologists claim are '(ethno-) methods' used by actors in talk-in-interaction. It is entirely beyond the scope of this book to do justice in any way to the immense literature building up in this field.[22] Just a few examples will be given here.

Clayman (1993) discusses how politicians and other public figures may deal with the communicative problem of answering questions at press conferences and news interviews in such a way as to avoid potentially pernicious implications without being (perceived as being) too evasive; they may then employ the strategy of 'reformulating the question'.

Drew (1998) points to 'defensive detailing', i.e. giving (too) many details or several complementary explanations, a strategy which many people indulge in when they feel that some behaviour or action of theirs may be taken up as untoward or reproachable and thus in need of some kind of extensive account. Similarly, in some situations when speakers have to convey bad news about events for which they may potentially be held partly responsible, they indulge in citing numerous unfortunate circumstances contributing to the outcome of events (Maynard, 1998).

Pomerantz (1980) describes how interlocutors use the strategy of telling about their own experience of something ('telling my side') as a "fishing device", not least if the projected topic is something which actually is about the interlocutor's life (of which the latter therefore has first-hand knowledge, while the speaker has only 'limited access', and at the same time, such a topic may threaten the interlocutor's face, if broached 'bald on record' (Brown & Levinson 1987)). However, beginning to 'tell one's own side' may be a way of rendering the "fishing" successful; it often triggers the delivery of a similar, or perhaps more authoritative, telling on the part of the other.

Maynard (1991), in a study of doctors telling diagnoses of children with certain illnesses to parents, points to a partly similar phenomenon as Pomerantz; he demonstrates the strategy of the 'perspective-display series', in which (in the

---

22. This constitutes the lion's share of the work done within Conversation Analysis today.

particular case mentioned) the doctor first asks the parents about *their* perspective on their child's difficulties, before he gives them *his own* professional version.

Reformulating the question, defensive detailing, citing unfortunate circumstances, telling one's own side as a fishing device, and asking for the other's perspective first, are different communicative strategies used in different kinds of projects. For an example of a whole set of strategies used in the same activity type or communicative project, we can turn to Silverman (1997), who analyzes at length the interactional difficulties in personalized advice-giving (his specific case is HIV counselling) by professionals. He shows how counsellors use various strategies for making the devices used ambiguous or less straightforward, hearable as anonymized information rather than formulated as plain personalized advice. These devices include, for example, 'advice-as-information sequences' ("information-about-the-kind-of-advice-we-give-in-this-clinic", op.cit.: 170), formulating hypothetical cases ("if so-and-so was the case, then..."), and using "oblique" references to both the counselling agent ("we" rather than "I") and recipients ("one", "some people").

Finally, let us look at one example in some more detail. Jönsson (1988), in her study of "mild" Swedish police interrogations, points out that when police officers suspect that their interviewees are not telling the truth, they do not say so bluntly, but rather employ a specific strategy of expressing doubt or mistrust by giving the interviewees several opportunities to change or supplement their stories. Excerpt (8) is a case in point:

(8) PASSING THE CASH-POINT (Tema K: P8) (From Jönsson 1988) (The suspect S is suspected of shop-lifting. He has just claimed that he never passed the cash-point before being caught. In 8: 1, the police officer P seems to express some doubts about this. Rough translation from the Swedish original.)

```
1.  P:   that's what happened, wasn't it?
2.  S:   I didn't pass the cash-point
3.  P:   you didn't
4.  S:   no
5.  P:   now the report says here that you did, but that must be
         wrong then?
         ((some turns omitted))
6.  P:   [...] but then you mean, I gather, that you didn't walk out
         ((i.e. without paying for the goods))
7.  S:   no, I never passed the cash-point
         [...]
8.  P:   now there is, you see, a witness here who says that you
         have passed the cash-point
```

The general pattern of the mistrust sequences described by Jönsson (1988) is that the suspect first gives some account which the police officer, on the basis of reports and other information available to him, has reasons to doubt (this part is not included in (8)). The police officer's position seems to involve both distrust of suspects as persons and mistrust of the "versions of reality" they advance. And still, rather than telling the suspect that he thinks he is lying, the police officer typically asks the suspect if he (S) has ("really") told everything relevant (8: 1) or if he (P) has understood everything correctly (8: 6). When S confirms this (8: 2, 7), P usually asks for a reconfirmation (8: 3), sometimes by asking S if he is "quite certain", or the like (thus often upgrading his request). Only thereafter does P object, revealing that he has contradictory information from other sources. In (8), he does this in two steps, first by just asking whether "the report" is "wrong" (8: 5), then by specifying what his contrary evidence consists of (8: 8). Since the topic in the police interrogation is the suspect's dealings, we have here a case that is reminiscent of Pomerantz's (op.cit.) 'limited access as a fishing device'. The overall strategy is recurrent in Jönsson's data; part of the explanation may be, as the author argues, that the police officer is anxious to keep up a good conversational climate, which may lure the suspect into talking, and therefore chooses not to use a very blunt and direct approach.[23] Moreover, the police officer's task is, strictly speaking, to get the suspect's version of the case, rather than argue that he may be lying (this should rather be argued by others, e.g. by the prosecution in court). Thus, the device of the mistrust sequence seems to be a strategy used to suggest, rather than explicitly claim, that the other is lying.

11.10   The past- and future-orientation of communicative projects

In the preceding paragraphs, I have dealt with the joint construction and the act-activity co-constitution with regard to communicative projects. The corresponding point about sequentiality was also implicit in the discussion. Thus, it is clear that

---

23. 'Limited access' is used by many professionals in discreetly addressing sensitive topics. See e.g. Bergmann (1992) on psychiatrists' discourse in intake interviews. There are numerous other examples of partly similar communicative strategies described in the literature. Many of them concern various tactics to broach sensitive topics or to convey dispreferred responses (e.g. Pomerantz 1984; Levinson 1983: 333ff.).

communicative projects are typically laid out as sequences; their internal organization is sequential. But if we look outside of these sequences that make up the overt manifestation of the projects, we will see that there are also links backwards and forwards from a project. If we look upon topical episodes as projects, they typically have local links backwards — they often emerge from prior talk — and when they are coming to a close, they tend to provide opportunities for interlocutors to move on to other topics, e.g. by recontextualizing some element from the project just terminated (chs. 8.6; 10.7).

As another type of example, consider story-telling in dialogue. Apart from being past-oriented in the sense that they (usually) are told about past events, they tend to be locally linked backwards by virtue of the fact that the opportunity to tell a certain story is usually negotiated and occasioned in the prior talk. At the same time, stories are proactive in the sense that they are told in order to score points with interactional consequences (Gülich & Quasthoff 1986).

Similarly, accounts are embedded in dialogue. They are usually produced because the speaker may feel a need, at a certain point in the interaction, to provide an explanation, an excuse, a justification, or the like. Once the account has been delivered and accepted, it can be exploited in the ensuing dialogue (Scott & Lyman 1968; Antaki 1988). Similar arguments hold for other kinds of local projects, such as complaints, accusations and blamings (Drew 1998), admissions (Linell et al. 1993), etc., not to speak of projects involving classical performatives such as sentencing, wedding, baptizing, promising etc. None of these projects occur in isolation, but they are always part of over-arching structures, i.e. larger projects.

We noted earlier that whole encounters can also be taken to be communicative projects. This holds especially for task-oriented (institutional) talks. They are characterized by past- and future-orientations that extend beyond the boundaries of the encounter. A doctor consultation or a police interrogation takes place for some particular reason, and the outcomes of such encounters (decisions, reports) are typically produced for future use. An encounter like a police interrogation is the locus for constructing a version of some (possibly unlawful) doings in the past, a version which is forwarded to other professionals (prosecutors, defence lawyers, probation officers, courts) and then used by them in future situations. A legal setting like the police interrogation involves the construction of social facts (Edwards & Potter 1992), pertaining to past events but presented in a version (documented in the police report) which has to be viable for future use.[24]

11.11 'Communicative project' as a discourse-analytic concept

As was indicated in the text above, 'communicative project' represents a kind of discourse-analytic concept akin to 'linguistic action' (especially as developed by Wittgenstein (1958) and, to some extent, Austin (1962), but different from Searle (1969, etc.)) and 'language game' (also Wittgenstein). It denotes a sequence enacting the performance of a communicative task, and evaluates the sequence in terms of its meaning accomplished in and through action and interaction. When actors or analysts perceive the flow of talk-in-interaction in terms of its communicative projects, they 'project' action meanings onto pieces of discourse (whether these pieces are already completed, still in progress or only anticipated). As we noted above, this can be done in many ways; just as it is impossible to tell how many actions or meanings there are in a given discourse, it is meaningless to try to count the number of communicative projects involved.

The notion of 'communicative project' is an analytical concept (in Schutzian terms: a 'second-order' concept), but it is directly or indirectly related to actors' own apperceptions of their own doings (cf. Luckmann 1993). Actors, in and by themselves, would normally not be capable of looking upon their own discourse in terms of these analytic concepts, but they should be able to recognize the accuracy of the analysis, once the meta-language has been explained to them (and provided that the analysis is accurate).

It might perhaps be argued that a bounded sequence embodying a local communicative project would represent the next constituent type above the 'elementary contribution' (ch. 9) in a hierarchy of discourse units such as that of Table 1 (ch. 10.12). However, such a constituent structure is hardly, by itself, an appropriate model for the flow of discourse. In particular, dialogue contributions (turns, or, for that matter, idea units, ch. 9.1) and communicative projects are not commensurable entities. The former, which are interactionally defined expression units with dialogical properties, are not complete communicative interactions. Communicative projects, on the other hand, are such entities by definition; they

---

24. Cf. Soeffner (forthc.) notion of "zukunftstauglich", "fit for future use". See also Cicourel (1968), Linell & Jönsson (1991), Jönsson et al. (1991).

are therefore units of meaning rather than of expression. This, of course, does not deny the fact that they are typically followed by more interaction (new projects, additional parts of overarching projects); in this sense they are interlocking, open and 'incomplete'. Elementary contributions to dialogue are the smallest units of communicative interaction, whilst communicative projects, even if we take only the local ones, may vary a great deal in extension and manner of articulation.[25]

In other words, the mini-theory of communicative projects treats the same phenomena as do mini-theories of contributions to discourse (ch. 9) and topical episodes (ch. 10), but it does so from another angle. Contributions, whether taken to be idea units or turns at talk, are elementary units which are not yet units of action and significance. Rather we may look at them as building blocks or procedural (action) constituents. Communicative projects, on the other hand, are by definition comprehensive units of meaningful action. Sometimes, of course, a discourse contribution and a communicative project can be extensionally identical, but they would still be different kinds of second-order constructs resulting from the analyst's applying different perspectives to the same data. (One may compare them, in this respect, to phoneme and word, or sentence and text, which can also very well be extensionally identical in specific instances.)

At the same time, however, communicative projects may be seen as bridging the gap between elementary contributions and local sequences, on the one hand, and the global, and more abstract notions of activity types and communicative genres. Whilst we may think of communicative projects of different sizes, in practice we may still primarily use the term about episode-sized sequences (at a 'meso'-level). If we use the term 'communicative strategy' about a culturally sedimented and routinized way of carrying out such a project

---

25. Communicative projects are constructs of a different kind than dialogue contributions. Many theories of discourse and conversation have proposed units consisting of two (or three) utterances (or turns) as the units ranked immediately above the utterance (turn). Thus, the Birmingham school (e.g. Coulthard 1992) has posited *exchanges* (two or three elementary units), and Conversation Analysis has put a lot of emphasis on *adjacency pairs* (the first pair part produced by A and the second pair part produced by B). I do not think that any of these constructs are basic and universal units of interaction. That is not deny that actors' adjacent turns often form pairs of the kinds described in CA. The notion of adjacency pair seems to be a rather monologistic one, assigning the initiative to the first speaker's first pair part and the response to the other speaker's following utterance. This gives the theory problems with the very common contribution type featuring both clearly responsive properties and clearly initiatory ones. The problems apply *a fortiori* to the exchange theory. As I argued in ch. 9, it is better to take initiative and response as abstract relational aspects of all turns.

(ch. 11.9), we approach the notion of 'communicative genre', as proposed by Luckmann (1985, 1989, 1992) and defined as a routinized (type of) solution to a recurrent communicative problem (see also Günthner & Knoblauch 1995). However, I shall prefer the more conventional usage of 'communicative genre' as referring to more comprehensive activity types accomplished in routinized manners in particular kinds of encounters (or texts). I turn to these matters in the next chapter.[26]

---

26. Luckmann (1985, 1989, 1992, 1995), who has proposed both notions of 'communicative genre' and 'communicative project' (though the former has been by far the most developed notion of the two), extends the notion of genre to cover various sorts of 'minor genres'.

CHAPTER 12

Situation definitions, activity types and communicative genres

12.1 Activity types as situation definitions

"Human beings routinely contact, interact with and leave each other's presence; in the process they initiate, construct and terminate various forms of social activity" (Couch 1986: 113). Such encounters very often involve discourse, and this discourse (including its paralinguistic accompaniment and relevant contexts) can be analyzed as consisting of comprehensive wholes which we may provisionally call *communicative activities*. They are joint activities, each with boundaries and an 'entry-body-exit' structure (Clark 1996: 36).

A communicative activity takes place in a 'focused interaction' when people "openly cooperate to sustain a single focus of attention, typically by taking turns at talking" (Goffman 1963: 24). It is roughly equivalent with what some research traditions call 'speech event' (Hymes 1972). Another related concept is 'situated activity system' (Goffman 1961: 96), and Forgas (1979) uses the term 'social episode' in approximately this sense. Sometimes, the whole of a communicative encounter is one comprehensive communicative activity, though in most cases the encounter consists of several activities in succession or (minimally) of a core activity (or several phases thereof), and the opening and closing phases. A *phase* is a bounded section of an encounter with an activity structure of its own, usually also with its own set of characteristic topics. A communicative activity is usually embodied in or realized through a more or less comprehensive sequence of talk (analyzable, at various ("lower") levels and from other viewpoints, in terms of its constituent discourse contributions, topical episodes etc; see ch. 10.12).

Communicative activities can be classified in terms of types, i.e. *activity types*. The activity type *defines the situation* for the actors; it tells them "what's going on" in the situation.[1] This of course does not exclude the fact that actors sometimes entertain more or less competing situation definitions of the interaction in which they are involved (ch. 8.9).

The concept of 'activity type' was introduced by Levinson (1979), who also pointed to the affinity of this concept to Wittgenstein's notion of 'language game': "I shall [...] call the whole, consisting of language and the actions into which it is woven, the "language-game" " (Wittgenstein 1958: 5). For Wittgenstein, one crucial point was that linguistic actions are, by their very nature, embedded in more comprehensive wholes. Accordingly, an important argument for the concept of activity type, or language game, is that elementary utterances, communicative acts, cannot be fully understood without reference to this overarching concept. "Activities provide context that guides the interpretation of events lodged within them" (Duranti & Goodwin 1992: 149). It is often claimed that, among all contextual resources there are (ch. 8.2), that of activity type, frame or genre overrides the others in importance.[2] At the same time, activities could not be brought into being without the acts that are constitutive of them.

Elementary contributions are usually indicative of the activity type to which they "belong". Consider, e.g., the following excerpt from Sacks' (1992) data from an emergency psychiatric hospital:

(1) LOSING INTERESTS (Extract from Sacks 1992: I: 53)

```
1.  A:   are you working?
2.  B:   no I'm not.
3.  A:   your husband supports you?
4.  B:   yes.
5.  A:   well, what do you do with yourself?
6.  B:   oh, I have a lot of interests. I work with theater. I do,
         oh, little community theater direction and things of this
         order.
7.  A:   do you find there are times when you lose interest in it?
8.  B:   yes. very d- I find there are times when I lose interest
         in everything and there have been times when I have
         stopped speaking for days.        .
9.  A:   I don't know anything about your sex life now, but are
         there times when you lose interest in sex?
10. B:   yes. completely so.
11. A:   right. sounds pretty clear cut as a depressive illness.
```

---

1. Terms like situation definition, frame, etc. were introduced in ch. 8.2 (cf. IId).

2. This is of course the main point of 'activity theory' (ch. 3.4.4). For a consistently activity-based theory of communication, see also Allwood (1976).

In this extract a number of questions are asked by a person A, and these questions are answered by another person B. Even if we had not got the information beforehand that the context is an emergency psychiatric hospital, we would probably have inferred that A must be somebody like a psychiatrist interviewing a candidate patient B. (If no sooner, this becomes pretty obvious in 1: 11.) It is possible that the same topics could have been brought up in a few everyday conversations too, e.g. between intimate friends, but they would hardly be treated in terms of this quite asymmetrical question-answer format, and from a friend one might have expected an expression of empathy rather than a delivery of a diagnosis (Jefferson & Lee 1981). The institutional activity administered by A is reminiscent of an abridged form of a medical-setting kind of agenda (asking about various symptoms and then delivering a diagnosis). The various questions and answers thus reflect the activity context involved (ch. 8.2: IId), which also provides a frame of interpretation. The situation is tacitly defined in a way that allows A to ask such a sensitive question as 1: 9 without too much fuss (but notice the preface "I don't know anything about...", which lacks a counterpart in the other questions). At the same time, the activity gets realized through these very questions (and answers). Acts and the overall activity are *interdependent*; they *co-constitute* each other (ch. 5.9.3).

As I pointed out above, the principle of act-activity co-constitution was envisaged in Wittgenstein's discussion of language games, and later forcefully demonstrated by Levinson (1979). For example, Levinson shows how a sequence embodying a communicative activity, such as the cross-examination in a criminal court trial in a rape case, cannot be reduced to the mere sum of its elementary contributions. I shall cite one of Levinson's excerpts:

(2)   SEVERAL MEN (Levinson 1979: 380; data originally from Toner 1977) (A = cross-examining attorney, W = young girl, allegedly victim of a rape, for which a defendant is being prosecuted)

```
1.   A:   [...] you have had sexual intercourse on a previous
          occasion haven't you?
2.   W:   yes.
3.   A:   on many previous occasions?
4.   W:   not many.
5.   A:   several?
6.   W:   yes.
7.   A:   with several men?
8.   W:   no.
9.   A:   just one.
10.  W:   two.
```

```
11. A:     two. and you are seventeen and a half?
12. W:     yes.
```

Here, the sequence of the defence attorney's questions in the cross-examination gets part of its significance from the fact that it is made in the service of some overall goal — we could say 'communicative project' (ch. 11) — which pertains to the whole sequence. Such a goal could be that of casting doubt on the rape victim's "innocence". To quote a whole paragraph from Levinson (op.cit.: 381):

> Here the girl's age is asked (cf. 2: 11/PL), even though the basic facts of the case, including this one, would be known to all parties. The point of the question is not to learn something from the answer, although it is in part to obtain the answer, to get the witness to state the answer. What can be the point of getting the witness to state what is already known to all present? It could be to obtain a confession, but in this case a statement of one's age is hardly a confession. We could spin the conundrum out, but the point, of course, is that the function of the question does not lie within utterance (2:)11 (or the answer in (2:)12), but in its *juxtaposition* with what has gone before. By careful juxtaposition (2:)11 does the job of suggesting that a girl of seventeen who has already slept with two men is not a woman of good repute. (italics in the original)

12.2 Communicative genres

Communicative activity types can be thought of as organized in terms of communicative genres. The concept of 'genre' is of course legion in such fields as folklore, literary studies, rhetoric and linguistics (e.g. Swales 1990), and in recent years it has gained popularity in the analysis of spoken interaction as well. For example, Bakhtin (1986) has described a notion of 'speech genre', and Luckmann (1985, 1989, 1992) has introduced an empirically based notion of 'communicative genre'.[3]

Swales (1990: 58, et passim) defines a genre as "a class of communicative events, the members of which share some set of communicative purposes." Genres are inherited, produced, recognized and named by the "parent discourse

---

3. A useful elaboration, largely building on Luckmann's theories, is provided by Günthner & Knoblauch (1995).

community". Swales further notes that "exemplars of a genre exhibit various patterns of similarity in terms of structure, style, content and intended audience", and that some exemplars will be viewed as more "prototypical" than others. Along similar lines, Luckmann (1992) defines 'communicative genre' roughly as a socially constructed (and thus historically specific), routinized solution to some kind of recurrent communicative problem in social life (op.cit.: 226, 228). That is, if members of a society or community often have to solve the same type of communicative problem (in Swales' terms; have similar communicative purposes), they develop routinized ways of carrying out the interaction. The individuals would not then have to select and construct their communicative acts ab novo, "spontaneously" in Luckmann's (1992: 224) words, but can rely partly on available communicative patterns, which have been to varying degrees pre-assembled by the discourse community, or culture at large, and can be used in tailoring the specific communicative project tokens. Communicative genres are thus originally interactionally developed, then historically sedimented, often institutionally congealed, and finally interactionally reconstructed in situ. They represent powerful communicative means in the construction and tradition of social reality and cultural knowledge.

'Communicative genre' and 'communicative activity type' are closely related terms.[4] However, although the issue is of course a matter of definition, I would prefer not to make them entirely interchangeable. Most but not all activity types have developed norms, routines and interactional patterns, so that we could talk about 'genres' being associated with the activities. However, there are activity types which are arguably not so culturally fixed. For example, a possible example might be communicative situations in which people, who are not intimates, are assigned the task of conversing with each other in order to produce a 'recorded conversation. This was what B and K had to do in the conversation from which SKIING AND BALLOONING (ch. 10: (1)) was taken. Naturally, the fact that the situation was arranged and the talk produced under such premisses is a significant factor which contributes to the definition of the activity type and must be given due attention by the analyst. However, despite the fact that Maynard & Zimmerman (1984) have identified some patterns of topical choice in such situations, it is doubtful if there are substantial norms for how subjects are to behave (apart from those which might be explicitly given by

---

4. Some, e.g. Günthner & Knoblauch (1995), takes 'communicative genre' to cover routinized ("pre-patterned") communicative projects of smaller sizes too.

the experimenter and which subjects may or may not orient to). One may therefore hesitate to call this a (full-blown) communicative genre; perhaps we could talk about a 'hybrid genre' (cf. below). There are probably numerous activity types that, in analogous ways, lack well-developed norms of interaction. New media often generate new forms of interaction. Radio and television programs have clustered into new hybrid genres. Other cases can be found in computer-network-based communication media, e.g. electronic mail dialogues or internet "chat" channels.[5]

There are many other discourses in which several activity types or communicative genres seem to get blended. Jefferson & Lee (1981) exemplifies this 'activity contamination' with a case in which the 'troubles-telling' of an informal phatic talk exchange is received not by empathetic affiliation (which would be genre-consistent, according to the authors) but e.g. by an analysis of the trouble (thus perhaps expressing a doubt that it *is* a problem) or by the immediate proposal of a remedy, which would otherwise be more typical of, or appropriate in, an institutional advice giving or a service encounter. I will return to mixed genres (ch. 12.3).

A communicative genre involves particular verbal (and non-verbal) means for solving the tasks or functions associated with the genre. Furthermore, genres regularly involve participants in characteristic social roles and participant frameworks, and they co-determine possible topics and turn-taking systems. Communicative genres themselves vary in the degrees to which they are routinized and institutionally congealed. Since the use of genres is normally linked to clearly defined types of social situations,[6] some of the most clear-cut genres are types of 'institutional discourse', i.e. cases of task-oriented discourse designed to deal with some specific activity, often involving professionals, or one professional and one or several lay persons. For example, court trials, police interrogations, school lessons, academic seminars, doctor-patient interactions, social worker-client interactions, job interviews, speech therapy sessions etc are

---

5. Cf. Severinson Eklundh (1986).

6. Genres may be said to tied to abstract situation definitions, as introduced in ch. 8 (IId). That is, once the activity is framed in a certain way, you can rely on the habits of an associated communicative genre. Conversely, if the habits of a certain genre can be identified, then the situation definition is also largely fixed.

institutional discourse activities, for which there exist communicative genres with socio-historically sedimented routines.[7]

12.3 Genres of 'ordinary conversation'

Ordinary or casual conversations, i.e. informal talk in various settings, also form communicative genres, although it is often less clear which these are. Yet, it is quite clear that there is not just one unmarked activity type of 'ordinary conversation', in spite of the fact that this is often used as something like an unquestioned category within e.g. Conversation Analysis (e.g. Atkinson & Heritage 1984). Depending on the cultural specifics, we might think of genres, or genre-like activity types, such as conversations at formal dinners (or, traditionally, in the drawing-rooms of "educated people"),[8] family dinner-table conversations, coffee-break talk at workplaces, short exchanges in a colleague's doorway, telephone conversations between acquaintances or between friends, talk penetrating intellectual problems (usually among e.g. friends or classmates), intimate talk between friends, sociable small talk between the newly acquainted in the doctor's waiting-room or in a train compartment, interstitial talk during manual work or when travelling (e.g. during car rides), love talk among lovers, fun-making talk among adolescents, disputes among children, etc. The fact that a piece of discourse takes place in a certain kind of social and physical environment does, of course, not by itself render it an instance of a specific corresponding communicative genre. The genre is rather something created in and through people's choice of communicative acts (ch. 5.9.3). Yet, everyday experience tells us that people often do enact specific communicative activities in different kinds of situations.[9]

When we deal with informal, casual or 'ordinary' conversation, we can think of many different conditions that characterize the various genres to different degrees and in different combinations. A basic distinction is the one

---

7. It is outside the scope of this book to further explore the specifics of such genres. Analyses of institutional, interprofessional and professional-lay interaction now abound in the literature (e.g. Boden & Zimmerman 1991; Drew & Heritage 1992; Maynard 1984; Boden 1994; Drew & Sorjonen 1997).

8. This perhaps comes closest to the connotations of the term 'conversation' in many languages.

9. Situations typically host particular sorts of social episodes in the sense of Forgas (1979).

alluded to in (a) below. In general, relevant distinctions and conditions include the following. Talk can be:

(a) *obligatory* (or not): i.e. parties are supposed to talk more or less continuously ("carry on conversation"), or they can but need not talk (Goffman 1983: 'open state of talk'). (This dimension will be further explored in ch. 12.5.)

(b) *casual* (or not): it emerges spontaneously when people happen to be mutually present, i.e. parties have not come to an appointment to carry out a specific activity;

(c) *non-task-oriented* (or more task-related): the talk exchange is not aimed at solving a particular task, or at discussing a specific issue or taking a decision on something (which is perhaps the major characteristic of institutional talk);

(d) *non-work-related* (or somehow work-related): it is not part of somebody's professional task;

(e) *opportunistic* (or not) with respect to topic development: there is no agenda of predetermined topics;

(f) *'organic'* (rather than regulated) with respect to turn-taking;

(g) *mundane* (or not): it belongs to everyday routines;

(h) *informal* (as opposite to ritualistic) with respect to form and sequencing of constituent actions;

(i) *face-preserving*; there is a preference for topics that are assumed to reduce tension and to alleviate social interaction, i.e. there is a dispreference for topics that may cause disagreement or conflict, or threaten the interlocutors' faces.

Some, but not all, "ordinary" everyday conversations are close to fulfilling all these (b-i) conditions (which are, incidentally, not mutually quite independent). (That is, the cases stated within the parentheses above are *not* typical of "conversation"). Nevertheless, many talk activities meet the characterizations only to some degree. For example, at workplaces or between colleagues, there occur many conversations that are not clearly part of a work task and in many ways casual and informal, but are nevertheless somehow work-related (Boden 1994).

In other words, many of the genres mentioned or alluded to in the last two paragraphs overlap with each other. There are many types of "impure" or *mixed genres*, in which one can trace features of several (perhaps partly conflicting) communicative projects and influences ('interdiscursive relations'; Fairclough 1992) from several other genres (e.g. Fairclough, op.cit.; Candlin & Maley 1997). For example, some institutional exchanges are often carried out under the guise of casual conversation (Fairclough 1992: 'conversationalization'). In some cases, such hybrid genres (Fairclough, op.cit.) may be thought of as communicative activity types being on their way of forming new and complex genres. This, for example, applies to many talk situations in radio and television, as well as to communication based on computer networks.

12.4 The global structure of activities: Core activities and phase structure

As was remarked above, communicative genres are often linked to types of social situations (cf. Luckmann 1992: 228). This means that they sometimes pertain to whole social encounters (e.g. a court trial, a doctor consultation etc). However, many social encounters contain characteristic phases, each of which may involve participants in a specific communicative genre or subgenre. First, institutional discourse types usually have a *core activity*, which is surrounded by opening and closing phases. The latter phases may involve some small talk and other features of informal conversation.[10] Secondly, the core activity, e.g. the doctor consultation proper or the police interrogation proper, usually has an *internal phase structure*. For example, (the core activity of) a doctor consultation often has a three-phase structure: history-taking, physical examination, and delivery of diagnosis and discussion of treatment, each of which is connected with characteristic communicative patterns. Police interrogations involve typical phases (Linell & Jönsson 1991), and the same applies, a fortiori, to court trials, which belong to the most institutionally congealed types (Aronsson et al. 1987).[11]

Informal conversations exhibit clear phase structures less often, although they too may involve more or less salient (sub)activities, such as joke telling,

---

10. Many institutional activity types allow for small talk also during core activities, perhaps as a means to create a more sociable atmosphere. This conversational feature thus invades institutional activity types, but to varying degrees, e.g. more in police interrogations (Linell & Jönsson 1991) than in criminal court trials (where small talk is virtually excluded), more in informal staff discussions than in formal board meetings.

11. Agar (1985) has proposed that 'diagnosis', 'directive' and 'report' are recurrent features of institutional talk, valid across different genres. Though these phenomena can be taken to form the basis for different phases, they are better construed as more abstract ingredients in activities.

gossip (Bergmann 1987), conversational argumentation (Knoblauch 1991), conversational teaching (Keppler & Luckmann 1991) or mutually malicious disputes (arguing)[12] (Aronsson 1987). These latter activities are naturally more loosely organized (and somewhat less clearly socially acknowledged), but they still exhibit characteristic and recurrent structural properties. Some of the genres form "families": e.g. didactic, reconstructive, or argumentative genres (Bergmann & Luckmann 1995).

12.5 Communication in relation to non-communicative activities

Activity types, and associated communicative genres, differ as to whether the communicative activity is the main (or perhaps only) activity in which participants are involved at the moment, or whether the communicative activity is either subordinated to some other, i.e. non-verbal, activity, or is simply accompanying but not an essential part of some other activity (e.g. small talk when carrying out some manual work, e.g. preparing food). Indeed, Clark (1996) proposes a 'discourse continuum' of joint activities ranging from those which are "mostly linguistic" to those which are "mostly nonlinguistic", a hierarchy of five levels:

"1. telephone conversations, newspaper items, radio reports, novels
2. face to face conversations, tabloid items, television reports, science texts
3. business transactions, plays, movies, coaching demonstrations, apprenticeship lessons, bridge games
4. basketball games, tennis matches, two people moving furniture, making love
5. playing a string quartet, waltzing, playing catch" (Clark 1996: 50)

---

12. A hostile argument exhibits rather specific topicality and coherence properties. As Aronsson (1987) has argued, part of the logic can be summarized in the following points:
(a) do not adopt the other's topic or perspective, since then you may end up in a disadvantageous position;
(b) show disparagement by not responding when asked or invited to do so;
(c) respond to emotional (rather than propositional) meaning: blows should be countered with counter-blows.

Most data analyzed in discourse analysis, and certainly in this book, belong to the first two levels, and so do examples (1) and (2) introduced in this chapter. These talk exchanges are subordinated to more long-term or global goals, such as diagnosing the state of a candidate patient (1) or assembling evidence in a court case (2), but it would not make sense to say that these talk exchanges are subordinated to, or accompanying, some other simultaneously occurring non-verbal activity.

The other types, e.g. Clark's levels 3 and 4, are, however, quite frequent in human social activities. Indeed, Wittgenstein's primary case of a "language game" concerned the use of language within a primary non-verbal activity, in which a "builder" is building a construction with "building-stones", which are either "blocks, pillars, slabs or beams". The builder's assistant "B has to pass the stones, and that in the order in which A", the builder, "needs them. For this purpose they use a language consisting of the words "block", "pillar", "slab", "beam". A calls them out; — B brings the stone which he has learnt to bring at such-and-such a call." (Wittgenstein 1958: 3) Though this example of a "primitive language" is a contrived one, there are clearly many approximations to this kind of instrumental language use in real life. Usually, language use that is instrumentally subordinated to or accompanying non-linguistic activities, involves a little more of interaction and linguistic structure than in Wittgenstein's example game, and in empirical reality the facts are usually not so clear-cut. However, to see the embeddedness of communicative activities in larger non-linguistic activities (or projects, cf. ch. 11), let us consider a few authentic examples.

(3) THAT'S PUSH (Excerpt from a communicative interaction of a young couple, J(ock) and R(oz), who are out rowing on a small lake. R is trying to cope with the beginner's difficulties in handling the oars. Extract from a longer episode. From Soskin & John 1963: 245–6.)

```
1.  J:   no...no...no! look, to turn --
2.  R:   you want to go this way?
3.  J:   look, to turn, put one up and one back, and pull.
4.  R:   oh, you mean do it like that?
5.  J:   yeah.
6.  R:   well, you can turn it --
7.  J:   yeah.
8.  R:   you mean like this?
9.  J:   all right, now reverse. you got them reversed?
10. R:   hmm?
11. J:   no, you're not reversing them.
12. R:   yes I am.
13. J:   now... now you are. okay, now push...push on both.
```

```
14. R:     which way? this way or that way?
15. J:     no, push.
16. R:     [that's push!
17. J:     [that's pull!
18. R:     that's pull!
19. J:     oh, THIS is push.
20. R:     what?
21. J:     you pull'em now. now push. the other way. put'em up.
           push. push out from'em.
           ((R follows J's directions))
22. R:     that's what I was doing before. like this. trying to go
           backwards.
```

One striking feature of this sequence is its high incidence of deictic expressions ("you", "like that", "this way", "the other way", "pull one up and one back", etc), which shows its high degree of dependence on the concrete circumstances as contexts for interpretation (Ib of ch. 8.2). (It would perhaps have been hard to tell at once what the utterances refer to, if we had not been informed about the nature of the context.) Clearly, the relative scarcity of descriptive linguistic terms indicates that we are faced with a communicative exchange which is subordinated to another concrete activity going on there-and-then. The sequence contains mostly instructions and responses to instructions (plus requests for clarification) related to a non-communicative activity, that of rowing. (It is only in 3: 22 that Roz contributes something like a comment.) On the other hand, the whole activity is a collaborative one, since Jock's instructions seem to have an impact on Roz's rowing, though it may be disputed if we are entitled to call it "helping Roz". We seem to be witnessing a simple kind of teamwork, in which Roz, for sure, does the physical part of rowing, but where the cognitive activities necessary are 'distributed' on the two actors (on 'distributed cognition', cf. ch. 11.6). The "distribution" of cognition becomes possible through the communicative activities which are (at least partly) integrated within the actors' other doings.

In the next excerpt, taken from a session of physical therapy, we can observe much of the same pattern, although there are a few more (meta-)comments on the activity:

(4) UP AND DOWN (Tema K: H48: t4: 24) (T(ora), an aphasic patient, is
     doing physical therapy with her physiotherapist I(ngeborg). T is lying on a
     bed with I standing at her side holding T's paralysed hand. T is supposed
     to stretch and bend her arm and fingers. The two maintain mutual gaze)

```
1.  I:     an' down to the mouth, an'then you can bend your fingers
2.  T:     mm
```

```
    (2.0)
 3. I:     yes
 4. T:     =so
 5. I:     an' up, upwards, upwards. there. ((patting T's arm))
    (2.0) ((T is humming))
 6. I:     an'try to STRETCH your fingers too, STRETCH them out ((I
           shows by stretching her own fingers))
 7. T:     mm oho
 8. I:     an'down to the mouth. mm
 9. T:     so
10. I:     yes. an'upwards
11. T:     to the hair
12. I:     good! an'up again, high up, high up, °high up°. an'to the
           mouth
13. T:     °to the mouth° ((smiling))
14. I:     yes. an' up
15. T:     °up up° now it doesn't work ((making faces))
16. I:     yes, stretch up
17. T:     str-
18. I:     stretch up
19. T:     °stretch up° yeah. it doesn't work
20. I:     now I think it's getting tired
    (3.0) ((T is panting))
21. I:     come on come on, up, yeah now it's getting hard, isn't it
22. T:     yeah:: (xx)
23. I:     does it hurt there?
24. T:     no
25. I:     it works harder when it's getting tired, 'cause you've
           done it now (T: yes) several times an'then — then it sort
           of gets too tired
```

In UP AND DOWN, the patient is involved in "active movements" (to use the physiotherapist's term). The activity as a whole involves the use of verbal instructions to guide the active movements by the patient. Apart from this 'work-related' (ch. 12.3) talk, there is not much conversation going on. No doubt, the physical strain on the patient also contributes to impeding her from indulging in other kinds of communicative activities. Likewise, the physiotherapist is also concentrated on guiding the patient's exercises, although characteristically, she throws in some comments and encouragements. When, however, the same patient is involved in "passive movements", i.e. when the physiotherapist is mechanically stretching and massaging the patient's muscles, the two regularly exchange other kinds of verbal utterances, which are then accompanying rather than supporting the non-verbal activity. This is illustrated in (5):

(5) I DID MYSELF (Tema K: H39: t12: 20) (T(ora), the aphasic patient, has
just finished some strength practices, and is lying on her back. N(omi), the
physiotherapist, is kneeling by her side, massaging Tora's hand. Nomi has
initiated a conversation by asking Tora if she has got a new splint for her
hand)

```
1.  T:     then, wh- when I ah when I.. had ..wh- when I had woken
           up then, so, so there was one like this ((pointing to her
           hand))
2.  N:     =oh yes.
3.  T:     an' then..I did myself eh eh ((points to hand))
4.  N:     good! training with your hand, then?
5.  T:     =yes, so.. that came in again here
6.  N:     oh, how marvelous (2.0) you feel a bit softer today, in
           fact
7.  T:     oh yes
8.  N:     it was a good splint she made. does it hurt?
9.  T:     no
10. N:     you don't make faces yet
  (8.0)
11. T:     imagine that s:::: it eh Yvette eh-ehrm my s: litt- eh l-
           si- his little sister, you know
12. N:     yes
13. T:     he is here again
  ((person-oriented dialogue carries on))
```

In this excerpt, the aphasic patient Tora contributes a number of initiatives (5: 1,
3, 5, 11) (although these are not always easy to decipher, cf. the same person's
contributions to NOT RECALLING NAMES OF FLOWERS? in ch. 8). Moreover, the talk appears to be accompanying, rather than instrumentally related to,
the physiotherapeutic training going on. Yet, some of the topics treated are
connected with the work carried out there-and-then. Thus, the physiotherapy,
together with other things in the situation or in the common biography of the
interlocutors, serve as topical resources, as discussed in ch. 10. The talk is
topically rather fragmented, interspersed with silences (e.g. 8 seconds following
5: 10), something which is also quite characteristic of the situation type.

Situations in which talk accompanies some other activity are of course quite
common. For example, when actors carry out some manual work, e.g. preparing
food or cleaning the house, they are in an 'open state of talk' (Goffman 1983),
characterized by "the right but not the obligation to utter words. In consequence,

there will be longish silences interspersed with short spurts of talk." (op.cit.: 43).[13] This applies, more or less, to (5) as well. Under such circumstances, talk is incidental, rather than essential, to the other activity (even if it may be socially desirable not to remain silent throughout).

12.6 Coherence, relevance and topic progression as activity-dependent

Various properties of the actual talk and interaction are reflexively related to the activity type. For example, the sheer amount of talk may vary significantly between activity types.[14] More interestingly, particular turn-taking patterns or sequence types, e.g. the complementary question-answer pattern typical of many institutional discourses, signal the associated situation definition. For example, several properties of the psychiatry excerpt in (1) are probably co-constitutive of the genre. The tyings involved in adolescents' discursive practices (cf. THE BIRTH CONTROL PILLS in ch. 5) are indicative of this particular genre, with its social roles and partly phatic character.

Discourse phenomena such as coherence, relevance and topic progression do not have universally valid manifestations. Rather, these aspects are also activity- and genre-specific; there are intrinsic relations (of co-constitution or reflexivity) between particular activity types and their properties. Some properties do of course generalize across a fairly wide range of activity types, though it is highly doubtful if there are empirically motivated "super-genres" such as institutional discourse vs. casual conversation. The examples below will differ somewhat as to how general or specific they are. The next one displays several features of what one might call "filling in personal data sheet", a (sub)activity type which occurs in many institutional encounters.

---

13. See also Schegloff & Sacks's (1973: 262) 'continuing state of incipient talk': "members of a household in their living room, employeees who share an office, passengers together in an automobile, etc." Such talk exchanges are often replete with instances of 'local sensitivity' (Bergmann 1990).

14. There is little data available on how genres differ in this respect. Soskin & John (1963) calculated some preliminary figures on a limited data set. In their corpus, four parties to breakfast and luncheon table conversations actually talked for 85–95 % of the time (i.e. 85–95 seconds out of 100 were filled with talk), whereas in the activity of "packing with wife", a situation with an 'open state of talk' (Goffman, see above), two parties talked 33 % of the time.

(6) PERSONAL DATA (Tema K: BU2: 2) (Extract from a booking interview between a qualified midwife/nurse (M) and a pregnant woman (W) who meet at a Swedish maternity clinic. W is a young woman (21) who is in the early stage (ninth week) of her first pregnancy. When we come in, M is just reaching for a blank to start filling it in. Rough translation from Swedish original.)

```
1.  M:     mm. you were born sixty-zero four-twenty-one ((reading a
           Swedish civic registration number: year-month-day))
2.  W:     yes.
3.  M:     three-two-eight-one? ((last digits of the registration
           number))
4.  W:     mm.
5.  M:     Karlsson Karin. do you have any other names than Karin?
6.  W:     yes, Tora, Ebba
   ((short pause, M takes notes))
7.  M:     mm, and you live at Stockholm Street ten? ((street
           numbers given after the street name in Swedish))
8.  W:     mm.
9.  M:     and that is one-one-one thirty-five ((postal code)) in
           Newtown?
10. W:     that's right.
11. M:     telephone home number is twenty-two twenty-two twenty-
           two?
12. W:     mm.
13. M:     mm. the child's father, what's his name then?
14. W:     Kurt Karlsson is his name.
15. M:     Kurt with K or C?
16. W:     with K.
17. M:     what is his surn-
18. W:     Karlsson K
19. M:     Karls- ((writing, seemingly hesitating))
20. W:     no K A R L S ((pronouncing the first letters of husband's
           surname))
21. M:     and when was he born?
22. W:     sixty six-zero two-thirteen
23. M:     mm
24. W:     the last ones I don't know ((referring to digits of
           registration number))
   ((etc.; M goes on to ask W questions about her work, her health
conditions etc))
```

Professional-lay communication often involves special formats which contribute to the constitution of the activity types. Some of the clearest cases of asymmetrical question-answer sequences can be found in sequences in which officials and professionals interview people about their personal data. Such activities abound in institutional contexts, very often being next to obligatory in a (usually introductory) data collecting phase (cf. Agar 1985), as in the midwife interviews from which (6) is drawn. Interviewer questions are usually pre-defined, in fact often formulated on printed forms which are to be filled in with interviewee answers, and there are often few explicit reactions from the interviewer to the answers provided by the interviewee. Few questions are occasioned as responsive links to previous interviewee turns. The latter's answers are quite simply registered.

"To seek a service" (e.g. from a doctor, a lawyer, a social worker) "is to expose oneself to questioning" (Goffman 1983: 41). Often the interviewee can limit his or her contributions to quite brief answers, especially if the question-answer sequence is part of filling in a data sheet, as in (6). That means that the whole frame is supported by artefacts, such as printed forms or computer sheets, which will have a further constraining effect on the interaction (Cedersund & Säljö 1993). Excerpt (6) displays two phases of the fill-in activity. First, M is just checking information which she evidently has before-hand (6: 1–12), where W gives no more than confirmatory minimal responses. From 6: 13 onwards, M asks W about data she has not had prior access to, and this obviously changes the interactional pattern somewhat.

In the data sheet fill-in activity, and in many other institutional question-answer phases, the client's sole responsibility is answering each local question in a relevant way. If the client provides some extra information which does not fit the frame, this is often ignored by the professional:

(7)   A LONG TIME SINCE I BUILT (Tema K: P8) (From the identification phase of a police interrogation, in which a police officer (P) is interviewing a suspect (S) on a charge of shop-lifting. See Linell & Jönsson 1991: 81)

```
[...]
1.  P:    profession, title, what do you usually call yourself?
2.  S:    well I ah (.) am listed as a brick-layer
3.  P:    I see.
4.  S:    it's a long time since I built, of course (P: yes) but --
5.  P:    now, let's see, what shall we write as address of
          residence right now?
6.  S:    well, you see, I am waiting for an apartment, you see
((a few turns omitted))
7.  P:    nine years of ah primary school, right?
8.  S:    no, I only went seven, my mum died in connection with
          that so I broke off
9.  P:    employment at the moment?
10. S:    well I had to get emergency public work now
11. P:    mm, but earlier employments, where have you been working
          lately if we go back a few years?
```

```
12. S:    well, I worked with my ah sister's former boyfriend, with
          sign-board work, Signs Limited (P: I see) you know such
          things that hang over shops
13. P:    how long did you have that job?
14. S:    well, I had it for a rather long time, you know, it was --
          it was seasonal work, you know (P: mm) so he worked down
          in Helsingborg this year when it was winter, half a year.
          (.) then ah I have (.) the last job I had now we can take
          (P: mm) it was at Lights Limited with the Ekbergs (P: I
          see), then I had both my hands in plaster, after an
          accident
15. P:    mm, we can leave that, I will just write what you have
          said.
16. S:    yes.
17. P:    ah healthy and fit for work we usually write, you know.
          you have no illnesses?
18. S:    no: , I hope not. (.) no, illnesses, I have had a cold
          since last autumn but ah ah (P: mm)
   ((pause))
19. S:    well, that counts as an illness, I guess
20. P:    well, this is, they're referring to more serious
          illnesses
   ((etc.))
```

Here, the suspect consistently tries to sneak in some extra information (bold-faced in (7)), thus providing some fragments of his biography. In general, some of this might serve his possible interest of supplying some mitigating life circumstances, when the background of an alleged criminal offence is going to be examined. The suspect tries to tell a story of his own. However, this evidently does not fit the frame of the questioning; as we can see, the bold-faced information is systematically ignored in the dialogue, through the police officer's failure to respond to it. Even more importantly, as Linell & Jönsson (op.cit.) show, the suspects' stories from their life-worlds do not find their way into the police reports; police reports only tell the legally relevant versions of the alleged offences.

Accordingly, another feature that makes institutional encounters such as those illustrated in (6) and (7) different from most casual conversations, is the coherence types. There is fairly little of explicit local coherence between answers and next questions, and instead the whole activity is held together by the overall goal of assembling personal data, a situation definition most often taken for granted by both parties. Many questions abruptly introduce new topics and topical aspects; thus, there are fewer topical glides than is usual in mundane discourse. The transitions between different items on the agenda at a formal meeting is a another clear case of this topical progression type. As a compensation for the lower incidence of local coherence links, there is a global coherence supported by some kind of institutionalized framing that defines the activity type as a global communicative project aiming at certain overall goals. Since the whole encounter is usually administered by the professional, he or she will also be responsible for its global coherence (Hobbs & Agar 1985).

Some activity types are designed to have neither global topical coherence nor local coherence (beyond question-anwer exchanges). Some examples are quizzes (ch. 10: (3) MEMORY MASTERS), language tests (ch. 8: (6): A HOT DAY TODAY), free association tests etc. The framing of the activity-type or genre itself can be said to provide the necessary coherence to such exchanges. But test "subjects" often do something more than simply adhering to such coherence patterns. In the language comprehension test exemplified (A HOT DAY TODAY), the relevant thing for the speech therapist was to test whether the aphasic patient was able to understand simple questions and to give standard decontextualized answers. For the patient, on the other hand, the questions might have been understood partly in another frame, in which the therapist's different questions were taken as initiating some everyday conversational comments on various topics. Although such tests are part of scientific decontextualizing practices, they are socially located (Middleton & Crook 1996: 388) and are interpreted (consciously or unconsciously) by test "subjects". The same applies to free association tests, sometimes used in psychology. "Subjects" frame them in different ways, e.g. as exercises in giving poetic (or otherwise witty) associations, or as tasks in which one is supposed to provide elements of standard dictionary definitions of the stimulus words.[15]

The asking of unrelated questions in these various test frames are somewhat extreme examples of activity-sustained coherence as a substitute for topical coherence. But the general point is that the topic progression type is co-constitutive of the institutionalized communicative genre.

By way of summary, then, communicative genres are characterized not only by specific purposes (problems to which they represent routinized solutions), by particular social and interactional roles for participants, by characteristic topics and special vocabularies (and other linguistic features), but they are co-constituted also by particular patterns of turn-taking, topic progression and internal coherence, as well as by particular relevance criteria.

---

15. For discussion of differerent response patterns in free association tests, see e.g. Rommetveit & Blakar (1979).

12.7 The creative accomplishment of routines within genres

I proposed earlier, following Luckmann's definition, that communicative genres involve 'routinized' ways of coping with communicative tasks. This does not mean, however, that actors simply follow predefined patterns and rules. (Such might be the case with formal rituals, e.g. religious ceremonies. Even there, some features are subject to individual variation in actual performance.) But most genres involve actors in creatively reconstructing the activities. Specific communicative projects, such as the admission of guilt in court trials (ch. 11.3), or whole speech events, such as calls to emergency dispatch centers (Zimmerman 1992), are carried out in creative ways, actors being responsive to various factors in the specific cases. Schegloff (1986) has argued more generally, but also with specific reference to openings in telephone calls, that acting in accordance with routines must be regarded as 'achievements' by the actors there-and-then in the specific cases. Zimmerman (op.cit.) says, with regard to emergency center calls, that "the accomplished shape of a given call is not a mechanical reproduction of some ideal-typical structure; nor is it a consequence of following (however imperfectly) a script or a protocol." (p. 460). Furthermore, the routinized components of calls "do not function as a template but are rather resources that may be modified, augmented, used repetitively or not at all because the contingencies to which these components are responsive are altered, unusual, recurrent, or absent." (ibid.: 461).

12.8 The partial sharedness of activities and genres

Activity types are particularly well suited for raising the issue of sharedness in discourse, and therefore I shall use this opportunity to make some remarks on this topic. One should note, however, that the arguments can be applied to other communicative projects at other levels as well.

At a basic *conceptual* level, discourse is shared among participants. It is dialogical in nature. Luckmann (1992: 223) refers to "the principle of the reciprocity of perspectives" as a "basic principle of human social life" (cf. also Graumann 1990, 1995). In dialogue and communication, there must be some basic co-operation to ensure the co-ordination, or mutual other-orientedness, necessary for any communicative exchange. But beyond this, there are large *empirical* differences amongst communicative encounters and activities, as regards the degrees of symmetry or mutuality intended or actually achieved; there are many kinds of asymmetries and partial mutualities (Linell & Luckmann 1991; Graumann 1995). If two or more persons are involved in the accomplishment of a certain task or project, in instantiating an activity type, this does not necessarily mean, of course, that they are both (or all) equally committed to the task, equally familiar with the rules and expectations connected with the genre in question, or that they share the same interests and understandings.

It is important to recall first of all, that the basic co-ordination of communicative actions and interactions does not preclude the existence of divergent or competing interests and concerns on the part of the individual participants. A competitive exchange, such as a negotiation or an argument, presupposes mutual other-orientation and obeyance of some basic communicative principles; without this the communication would cease altogether. This issue was discussed in ch. 11.7 (recall Clark's tennis analogy).

We can thus say that there are communicative genres and activity types that are characterized by a *systematic dividedness of interests* within a game in which both actors orient to each other's actions; actions are still mutually co-ordinated. For example, many police interrogations and court trials are typical examples (see below). But apart from this, there are many other kinds of asymmetries in the various communicative genres (Linell & Luckmann 1991). There may be *asymmetries of participation*, e.g. complementary patterns of questions and answers (the latter being largely governed by the former), even if both parties are oriented to one common overall goal; in fact, this is quite typical of professional-lay discourse.

In a diversified society, people can not be equally competent in taking part in all types of communicative genres. There are vast *asymmetries in participants' familiarity* with, and knowledge of, particular genres. In general, professionals are more familiar with routines and relevances of the various communicative (and other) activities than are their lay interlocutors. Due to the asymmetries of participation, professionals also have greater possibilities to set the agendas of encounters and to determine the perspectives on things talked about (Linell & Luckmann 1991; Drew & Heritage 1992). Clients and other lay persons often have to try to adopt the perspectives set by the other. Yet, being unfamiliar with some of the relevances of the professionally defined activity type, they cannot help applying more of an everyday life perspective on matters of substance. (Sometimes, they may consciously intend to avoid the professional perspective, and/or the professionals themselves may strive for adopting, at least temporarily, the client's perspective.) The discrepant perspectives of doctors and patients have been analyzed by e.g. Mishler (1984) in terms of the "voices" of "medicine and everyday life world", respectively. In a similar vein, Linell & Jönsson (1991) (cf. A LONG TIME SINCE I BUILT, (7) above) analyzed the sometimes discrepant relevances of police officers and suspects in police interrogations, which are interviews designed to investigate cases of (in our data corpus) theft and shop-lifting. For example, police officers sometimes asked simple questions like "Why did you do this?", referring to a case of shop-lifting, and this was taken up by some suspects as meaning roughly "What made you end up as a shop-lifter?", and hence the question was responded to by an account of their conduct in terms of more or less far-reaching everyday-life circumstances (like recent illnesses and depressions, difficult economic conditions, an unhappy childhood etc). The police officer, on his part, intended, in each case, his questions as asking for technical aspects of the allegedly criminal act and for the subjective intent on the part of the suspect in the moments of the shop-lifting event itself.

How an individual utterance (e.g. "Why did you do this?" from above) is understood is dependent on how the overall activity is implicitly defined, and sometimes parties to an interaction may have discrepant views on this. In such situations, where interlocutors entertain divergent interests, the actors may also talk about the "same thing" but in different perspectives, express themselves in different words, thereby trying to construct contrasting and competing versions of the "same" events in the world. Many court trials provide prototypical examples. One recurrent type is the rape trial, in which the focal events are discursively constructed by the prosecution as criminal acts of rape and by the defense (possibly) as consensual sex. Consider, for example, the following extract from the cross-examination of a witness, the alleged victim of a rape:

(8) A BAR OR A CLUB (Excerpts from a trial for rape, recorded in a municipal criminal court trial in Eastern United States. The alleged rape victim, W (=witness), is being cross-examined by the defence attorney. (A). W has conceded that she had known the defendant for "two or three years" before the alleged rape. In the excerpt, A asks questions about the night before the alleged rape, when W met the defendant (not by arrangement) in a place which A describes as a "bar" and W as a "club". The example is discussed at length in Drew 1992: 478ff, 489, and also in Gumperz 1995: 106f).

```
1.  A:    an' you went to a:uh (0.9) ah you went to a ba::r? in
          Newtown (0.6) is that correct?
```

```
(1.0)
2.  W:      it's a clu:b.
3.  A:      it's where uh (.) uh girls and fellas meet isn't it?
(0.9)
4.  W:      people go:there.
((several turns omitted))
5.  A:      an' during that eve:ning (0.6) uh: didn't Mistuh Anderson
            come over tuh sit with you
(0.8)
6.  W:      sat at our table.
((several turns omitted))
7.  A:      well yuh had some uh (p) (.) uh fairly lengthy
            conversations with thu defendant uh: did'n you?
(0.7)
8.  A:      on that evening uv February fourteenth?
(1.0)
9.  W:      we: ll we were all talkin.
(0.8)
10. A:      well you kne:w at that ti: me. that the defendant was.
            in:terested (.) in you (.) did'n you?
(1.3)
11. W:      he: asked me how I'(d) bin: en (1.1) j- just stuff like
            that
```

As usual, the defence attorney (here: A) seeks to produce a version of the events prior to the rape, which is potentially damaging to the victim's (here W) case. Here, A seeks to suggest that W had in fact been quite friendly, even intimate, in her interaction with the defendant. W uses other words to produce a more "innocent" version. Compare A's "bar" "where girls and fellas meet" (8: 1,3) with W's "club" where "people go" (8: 2,4), and A's suggestion that the defendant "came over to sit with" W and had "fairly lengthy conversations with" her (8: 5,7) with W's competing formulations that he "sat at our table" and "we were all talkin" (8: 6,9), and similarly A's "you knew that the defendant was interested in you" (8: 10) with W's "he asked how I'd bin" (8: 11). The opposed parties within this adversarial trial genre use different descriptive practices, always in contrast to the other's choice of words, thereby trying to produce different interpretations and inferences (Drew 1992; Gumperz 1995).

Returning to the issue of sharedness, we can say that communicative activities are characterized by a tension between, on the one hand, trying to create a shared discourse and, on the other hand, trying to get one's own perspective to colour the joint discourse. All human communication and cognition is perspectivized, i.e. all subject matters are seen and understood from some point-of-view, and in every moment of a dialogue, each actor sees the current topic in some particular perspective, in accordance with some 'model' (ch. 8.2: IId) (however "partial" or "shallow" this may be), and uses the communication either to attune this perspective to the other's or trying to have his or her own perspective accepted more or less at the expense of the other's. Thus, even if a communicative activity can be classified as an exemplar of a genre, and hence be seen as firmly anchored within a discourse community, and even if the participants are fully familiar with the genre, it does not follow that their discursive projects are shared in all respects.

12.9 Classifying communicative activities in families

Communicative activities and genres can naturally be classified along many dimensions.[16] I have repeatedly emphasized tensions in actual dialogues between cooperation and competition, between attunement to the other and pursuit of one's own interests, and between symmetry and asymmetry. There are cases of shared projects, as well as competing individual projects within the same frame (ch. 11.7). Some activities are characterized by relative symmetry (participants contribute approximately the same amount of talk and the same type of moves (types of dialogue contributions), etc.), whereas other activities are more based on an asymmetrical division of communicative labour.

Table 2. Cooperation/competition vs. symmetry/asymmetry

Point of collective activity:	Pattern of participation:	
	Relative symmetry	Relative asymmetry
Cooperation	Symmetrical, consensual equitable interaction, e.g. some informal conversations	Asymmetrical division of labour (complementarity) in the pursuit of common goals, e.g. many professional- lay interactions
Competition	Symmetrical, competitive interactions, e.g. full- blown arguments, quarrels, verbal duels	Asymmetrical interactions, with subordinate party exhibiting passive resistance, e.g. trials and interrogations with resistant or reticent interviewee

16. For a taxonomy of communicative genres in other terms, see Bergmann & Luckmann (1993, 1995). See also Swales (1990).

These dimensions suggest a crude taxonomy of communicative activities, and discourse types, according to Table 2. Using suitable operationalizations of various properties of dialogue, it is possible to provide an empirical underpinning of such a taxonomy in partly quantitative terms. For example, initiative-response (IR) analysis (ch. 9.7) could be one method among others for doing this (Linell 1990).

PART III

Monologism and dialogism reconciled?

CHAPTER 13

Dialogism: opportunities and limitations

In the preceding chapters I have illustrated various dialogical principles as applied to talk-in-interaction. I have also tried to identify some recurrent themes in the philosophy of human action and communication that are central to dialogism. In this chapter I will indicate how dialogism can be extended to analyze other kinds of communication and cognition.

Another aim of this chapter is partly opposite to the first one; I shall recommend some caution in treating dialogism, and social constructionism, as an omnipotent framework. A dialogistic approach is not suitable for everything. It is therefore an important task to come to grips with what its opportunities and limitations are or should be. Accordingly, I will, in the present chapter, raise a few other points which recur in the theories of human action and interaction. Some of these points have been extensively discussed in the philosophy of the social sciences, and I shall be content with articulating a reasonable dialogistic position on the issues involved. In doing so, I shall therefore sketch, however briefly, (what I take to be) a more sophisticated and moderate dialogism, as distinct from a more naive and simplistic stance according to which all mono-logistic theories are simply misguided. Later, in Chapter 14, I shall attempt to secure a place for monologism in the explanation of some human practices.

13.1 Dialogical principles and the theory of discourse structure

Central to dialogism is the assumption that a number of basic entities are interrelated in terms of intrinsic, conceptual interdependencies; one concept cannot be defined independent of, or thought of as prior to, the other. There are reflexive relations between dialogue contributions or activities and their contexts, between expression and meaning, between selves and others, between minds and social environments, between individuals and communities, between language structure and discursive reconstruction, between stability and change in human experiences. The essence of interaction, and hence the starting point for its analysis, lies in the interaction itself. We do not have individuals *and* society, but interactions of individuals *in* social and cultural contexts; the whole complex forms a system in Bateson's (1973) sense.

In dialogism, actions and interactions are more basic than the resulting discursive units. In addition, perhaps the most profound aspect of dialogism lies in the insistence that the actor, the progenitor of meaning, is (directly or indirectly) in constant interaction, "in dialogue" with, other actors (interactants) and various kinds of situational and cultural contexts. Therefore, any stretch of discourse, created in actors' interaction with other actors, is embedded in a matrix of contexts. However, it is not simply embedded or situated in contexts, but has a *reflexive* relationship to the contexts. Discourses and contexts mutually constitute and select each other, and hence they form a basic, indivisible whole. Of course, discourse units and contextual dimensions are analytically separable, but it is not possible to think of them as independent objects that enter into simple unidirectional causal relationships.

The list of "units" suggested in ch. 10.12 is no doubt only a fairly provisional one, and it is in no way intended to be exhaustive. Indeed, given the dynamics of dialogue and the multifarious genres of discourse, it is reasonable to assume that actors construct different kinds of relevant (first-order) units in different contexts. The theory (with its second-order units) must of course do justice to this. Nevertheless, I suspect that (something like) the above-mentioned concepts cannot be entirely dispensed with in an explanatory theory of human discourse and interaction. It must be stressed, however, that a lot of work remains to be done before such a comprehensive theory can be fully articulated.[1]

---

1. Linguists often criticize Conversation Analysis, and sometimes the field of language use studies in general, for the absence of a theoretical framework (e.g. van Rees 1992). I would partly concede to some of the points raised in this debate. At the same time, it seems mandatory to stress that it is neither feasible nor desirable to attempt to make a formal model of the kind that linguists have proposed as theories of linguistic structure or grammatical competence. Mainstream theoretical linguistics is stuck with the insistence that a real 'theory' must allow for the formulation of (formalized) models of hypothetical constructs from which patterns of 'surface' phenomena can be derived. If we look around for various philosophies of human science, this requirement is seldom upheld when we are dealing with human action and human culture. While there is of course nothing intrinsically wrong with formalization, it has been combined, within mainstream linguistics, with a particular and fairly weak notion of 'explanation'. One would normally require from explanans phenomena that they are somehow understood on independent grounds and thus could provide some

13.2 Dialogue theory and empirical methods

Dialogism is more a matter of 'theory' (a theoretical framework, a general epistemology) than a set of specific empirical methods.[2] When it comes to method, many dialogists would undoubtedly argue that the nature of dialogue necessitates qualitative methods that attempt to account for the multifaceted, dynamic and reflexive properties of specific discourses and their contexts. A cornerstone in the methodological arsenal is sequential analysis, which amounts to saying that no utterance should be analyzed in isolation from the contexts and the sequence in which it is positioned.

Quantification, however, is highly desirable too, especially if comparative studies across individuals, groups and situations are to be performed. Quantification presupposes some kind of coding of units of discourse. Coding practices always involve decontextualizing and abstracting from, and hence disregarding, many properties of the dynamic flow of interaction. It is therefore a conceptually tricky business to code and count "units" in discourse and interaction. Accordingly, Conversation Analysis (e.g. Atkinson & Heritage 1984) has traditionally been programmatically against quantification.[3] And, as should be obvious by now, the discussions in this book share many assumptions with CA and other interactionist approaches. Yet, Marková & Linell (1996) argue that it is possible, within certain limits, to conceive of empirical methods of coding and quantification which are derived from, or at least consonant with, a dialogistic theory.

It would require too much space to explore and explain what opportunities there are within a dialogistic theory for empirical methods of coding-and-quantifying.[4] It was proposed in ch. 13.1 that actions and interactions are more basic than discursive units. Therefore, if one still opts for methods that identify and code units, these units should capture aspects of actors' interactions in their joint discourse, rather than individuals' acts considered as autonomous entities

---

understanding of the explananda, but the theoretical entities of grammatical models (abstract categories, nodes, parameters, principles) are typically uninterpreted abstract concepts with no other motivation than their position in an integrated structural model. The model imposes an abstract structure upon data, but it does not provide any causal or functional explanations. The use of such 'models' amounts to abstract description, rather than explanation. Cf. e.g. Öhman (1988).

2. And yet, as the preceding section (incl. fn.1) points out, one may dispute that there is a 'theory'.

3. But cf. Schegloff (1993), Heritage & Roth (1995), Heritage (1995: 402ff).

4. For further discussion, see Marková & Linell (1996).

(Marková & Linell 1996). The analyst's second-order constructs should reflect the interlocutors' first-order constructs as they emerge with the unfolding dynamic discourse. The so-called 'initiative-response' (IR) analysis, which was briefly mentioned in ch. 9.7, and 'topical episode analysis' (TEA), as described by Korolija & Linell (1996), are attempts of this kind. They adopt the strategy of coding units in their local contexts (on a turn-to-turn or episode-to-episode basis, respectively) and in terms of the interactional and locally occasioned, retroactive vs. proactive, relations of these units. The next step is to aggregate over sequences of such units, yielding various numerical measures of participation, dominance, coherence and use of contextual resources in interaction. Whilst remaining partly decontextualizing (as any coding system must be), these kinds of coding systems would satisfy some requirements of dialogism (Marková & Linell 1996; Heritage & Roth 1995).

Most coding systems work with some kind of elementary units (e.g. turns in IR analysis), coding each unit as it emerges in the local context, but some systems work with larger stretches of discourse. For example, TEA (mentioned above) uses a partly 'retrospective' (more text-analytic) strategy, first identifying larger units, i.e. episodes etc., which can only be done once these sequences have been completed, and then coding these in relevant dimensions. Similarly, one may, for example, categorize repair sequences into different types (a possibility referred to in Schegloff 1993). Yet another possibility, also consonant with a dialogistic framework, combines features of the retrospective approach with attempts to capture local, emergent discursive actions; TEA, which involves coding of episode transitions as a crucial moment, would be a case in point.

13.3 Extending dialogue theory: A general epistemology for communication and cognition

Dialogism assumes social communication to precede individual (verbal) thought, and dialogue to be more basic than monologue. (Monologism proposes more or less the opposite on both points.) "Humans do not converse because they have inner thoughts to express, but they have thoughts because they are able to converse", says Billig (1987: 111). That dialogism is a plausible framework from a genetic point-of-view has been argued not only in a long tradition in the philosophy of the human sciences (e.g. Marková 1990a). It is also fairly widespread among e.g. developmental psychologists of a neo-Vygotskyan persuasion (e.g. Rogoff 1990), but variants of it have also been proposed by biologists like Maturana & Varela (1980), computer systems theorists like Winograd & Flores (1986), and specialists in infant communication (Trevarthen 1992; Bråten 1992).

13.3.1 *Monological speech and thought*

The primary case for dialogism is naturally dialogue, defined as talk-in-interaction. But dialogism makes more universal claims: it is supposed to be a theoretical framework valid for monological speech and thought as well. In Hermans & Kempen's (1993) terms, everybody has a "dialogical self". Thinking is largely arguing with other dimensions of one's self (cf. Billig 1987). The thinker is, according to the dialogistic theory, not a Cartesian ego, but a profoundly social being:

> "[T]hinking is not an activity separating one [person] from another but is the continuation in another place of a public communion with dialogical others. Just as external *dialogue* is reason arguing with itself in public performance, internal *dialogue* is reason arguing with itself in anticipation or in memory of public performance."(Tyler 1990: 299).

Vygotskyan and neo-Vygotskyan theories argue strongly for the irreducible social component of cognitive abilities:

> "We come to be able to plan, direct, control, and to organize our own 'higher mental functions or processes' as we come to incorporate within ourselves the forms of talk that others use in controlling, directing, and organizing our behaviour for us. [...] [W]e come to 'instruct' ourselves as others instruct us." (Shotter 1993: 41).

The speaker "talks with an active expectation of a response" (Shotter, ibid: 52), i.e. he adopts an other-orientation (ch. 6.5). Also in soliloquy or thinking, the active subject develops her topics and arguments with some sensitivity to how a potential responder, a "virtual addressee", may react, perhaps with a counter-argument. There is a "hidden dialogicality" (Bakhtin 1984: 197). Monological speech is thus intrapersonally dialogical, though interpersonally it exhibits only limited dialogicality (which makes monological discourse authoritative; Wertsch 1991: 78–9).

In a monological stretch of discourse, in inner speech or in thought in general, the individual has internalized the different 'voices' and made them into different aspects of his self, whether these aspects are more globally stable or only locally constituted. This was demonstrated in HALF A GLASS OF WINE in ch. 10.9. In monologue, idea units expand into new such units, much like contributions to dialogue develop in a pattern of responses and initiatives. And, "in connection with inner speech, processes such as the formulation of an argument in order to circumvent counterarguments anticipated from other voices", or viewpoints, are legion (Wertsch 1991: 53). Mukařovský (1977), who adduces 'the interpenetration of two contextures' (cf. ch. 8 on contexts) as a defining property of dialogue, argues that such an interpenetration can occur within the same individual "becoming the vehicle for two well-differentiated subjects of an utterance" (Mecke 1990: 199).

13.3.2 Dialogism and written texts

Written texts, being permanent records, encourage the view that the meanings of texts "are there" "in the texts themselves". But meanings are of course assignments and accomplishments by human beings, writers and readers. The production of meaning takes place in interactions, on the one hand in the writer's struggle with thoughts and words in conceiving and formulating the text, and in her interplay with the text so-far produced, and, on the other hand, in the reader's efforts in assigning meaning to the text and in using the text as a vehicle, as a means for activating semantic potentials of words and text chunks, in the service of creating an understanding which somehow fits the contexts given and the purposes which are relevant for him.

Understanding always involves putting discourse into contexts (ch. 8), and this holds for written texts as well. Readers select relevant features of existing contexts and activate or create relevant background contexts as a support for interpreting the text (e.g. Sanford & Garrod 1981); understanding involves the building of a discourse 'model'.[5] The written discourse helps the reader in this activity by indirectly (in and through the reader's interpretive activities) pointing to interpretations. However, the text does not "contain" these interpretations. Language itself is "essentially incomplete and allusive" (Merleau-Ponty), or as Garfinkel (1967) says, in a study of psychiatric records, "occasional and elliptical":

---

5. Cf. concepts referred to in ch. 8, fn. 6.

"[A] prominent and consistent feature is the occasional and elliptical character of its remarks and information." "In their occasionality, folder documents are very much like utterances in a conversation with an unknown audience which, because it already knows what might be talked about, is capable of reading hints." (op.cit.: 200–1)

While psychiatric files are a particular communicative genre, with its specific background presuppositions, the point about "incompleteness and allusiveness" holds true in general.

Written texts are of course always somehow 'other-oriented'; they presuppose something about an "implied reader" (to use a concept from literary theory).[6] Yet, it becomes something of a moot point if written texts are also interpreted dialogically, in a way which is analogous to that of spoken utterances. There are, among dialogists, different views on the relation between the interpretation of spoken dialogues and that of written texts (Crowell 1990), and some would say that arguing that the reader is in dialogue with his texts amounts to speaking metaphorically (Crapanzano 1990: 276). Crapanzano points out that the interpreter of a text has "a burden that the conversationalist does not: to give expression to his "conversational partner's" — the text's — meaning" (ibid.: 275). However, the conversationalist must also, to some extent, be attuned to the other's perspective, so the difference is hardly absolute. On the other hand, the interaction with written texts, and other permanent records, introduces other conditions, constraints and opportunities, into the dialogical process, and therefore, the differences between talk-in-interaction and the reading of texts, and amongst different genres within each of these categories, must be carefully explored, theoretically as well as empirically.[7]

The text on the printed page or the computer screen is an artifact of major importance, because it keeps symbols, "expressions", fixed (at least for some time) and it will therefore to some extent govern and constrain, perhaps somehow "fixate", the user's range of interpretation. On the other hand, an individual reading a text several times may also have ample opportunities to develop varied and critical interpretations. All the same, it is fairly clear that writing, in general, introduces more of a decontextualizing attitude into cultural practices, and hence it tends to bolster monologism (see ch. 14). The permanence of expression has

---

6. Cf. Iser (1974).

7. The piont that texts are quite different from interactions is forcefully argued by Ricoeur (1986).

often led people to believe that the text also carries with it a determinate, objective and fixated (hence permanent) meaning or interpretation.[8]

13.4 Dialogism as opposed to radical social constructionism

13.4.1 *Subjects and agency*

Within dialogism, there is a great deal of emphasis on abstract aspects of contexts, i.e. premisses for communication, frames of understanding, situation definitions, routines, and traditions. Communicative practices are often described as being routinized in terms of activity types and communicative genres. It has also been claimed that through the individual speaker we hear different interests, traditions, 'voices' talking; for example, in the specific court trials, social worker-client interactions, doctor consultations etc., 'voices' of traditions and professions are echoed and 'ventriloquated' (Bakhtin, cf. esp. Wertsch 1991). This raises doubts about the role of the subject, the human agent, within dialogism.

It is, in this context, essential to recall that the self is both agent and reflexive being (Marková 1992: 59), i.e. that contexts are "only" there as resources, enabling (as well as constraining) the agent's actions. Dialogism cannot be reduced to a Parsonian theory of actors as being determined entirely by forces deriving from social structures, roles and positions.[9] We must somehow explain human *agency*, the ability to think and act freely (under the given circumstances). Therefore, dialogism must not be understood as a position which dissolves or deconstructs the self to the point where subjective agency is reduced away.[10] The subject can not be seen only as a nexus of social relations, a mindless puppet at the mercy of socially established forces.

---

8. This is, according to some monologistic theories, what is actually "there in the text", as opposed to what different readers, with their limited background knowledge, memory limitations and various mental distractions, are able to attribute to the text.

9. For a forceful argument to this effect, see Heritage (1984a), who contrasts the positions of Parsons and Garfinkel.

10. The latter is a possible interpretation of extreme discourse-based versions of social constructivism. See e.g. Stetsenko & Arievitch (1997), who refer to the work of K. Gergen, Harré, and others.

Instead, the subject is also the origo of choice, volition and agency, of "forces that "energize" the individuals to interact with one another" (Turner 1991: 588). More specifically, two aspects of human agency deserve to be stressed, both distinguishing humans from computers. One is the ability to instigate events or initiate actions (or inhibit impulses for action) in ways that can be described as due to "choice" or "free will". Another characteristic is the ability to assign meaning to situations, events, behaviours and actions.[11] The subject is the centre of intended discursive (and cognitive) action, and the source of the innovative content of utterances (regarding not only the initiatory aspects, but also the responsive ones, which involve creative interpretive work too, cf. ch. 9). Ethnomethodology assigns a central role in interaction to actors' own knowledge and understanding (Heritage 1984a). The same position is characteristic of social constructionism, much less so of social realism and radical interactionism (ch. 4).

13.4.2 The material basis as constraints on discursive construction

Dialogism, at least in some variants, comes close to social constructionism, a succinct formulation of which would be that human experience, cognition, emotions, and other mental or sociocultural phenomena are discursively constructed, or communicatively constituted. To put it briefly, we experience the world in particular ways, under specific perspectives, because we talk, and hence think, about it in certain ways in discourse and interaction.

However, there are different views on how exactly social constructionism should be understood (e.g. Holstein & Miller 1993). One position, hardly defensible in a radical version, is that everything gets discursively constructed in situ, through talk and other kinds of symbolic interaction (cf. ch. 4.2 on micro-reductionism). Another alternative, considerably more popular and favoured in this work, adds socio-cultural traditions as contexts in which actual discourse is embedded. These socio-cultural structures that talk relies upon are *also* discursive in origin, apart from their being continuously reconstructed, confirmed or

---

11. The first ability seems to be shared, to some extent, with some animals, whereas the second one appears to be more or less restricted to humans. On the other hand, sense-making must largely be accounted for in socio-cultural and social-interactional terms. Perhaps, the ability to initiate action is the basic property located, or embodied, in individuals (even if that, too, is socio-culturally penetrated).

negotiated in novel situated discourse. In this way, we attribute a 'double dialogicality' to action and communication (ch. 3).

Are then perceptions, conceptual systems, modes of thought, and norms of behaviour and interaction totally dependent on (present and prior) discourse only? The answer must be no: social, cultural and mental phenomena are also dependent on material constraints, i.e. conditions of a non-discursive nature. Some such basic boundary conditions are physical or physiological in nature, while other constraints can be described as macro-economic. Even if we are concerned with discourse and the making of meaning in the human sciences, a dialogistic stance need not, and must not, be combined with a denial of the existence of physical realities. Even if these realities "out there" are constructed and apprehended by human minds in partly socioculturally determined ways, the constructions are nevertheless (in many cases) *constructions of something* ("out there").

Discourse provides only part, though sometimes a large part, of the story of human life. There are physical and social practices that are *non-discursive* in nature, even though they are reflexively conditioned by surrounding discursive practices, i.e. how we talk and think about them; among countless examples are mowing a lawn, driving a car, making love and playing football.[12] There are also practices, and related norms and knowledge structures, that are indeed communicative and *discursive* in nature, but even these are ultimately constrained by physical and physiological processes; examples are talk and thought about the physical environment or about the above-mentioned practices.[13]

Spoken discourse is a particularly complex form of human behaviour. On the one hand, at the expression level, talk is embodied spoken behaviour, dependent on neurophysiological and phonetic constraints but of course deeply culturally penetrated, i.e. structured lexically, grammatically, phonologically, prosodically, and paralinguistically according to conventions of specific languages. On the other hand, at the content level, action and meaning in discourse are socially constituted, even if our perceptions and conceptions are not independent of the material world. In other words, what we can think and do is embodied, rather than entirely spiritual. As perceivers, thinkers and speakers we are dependent on physiologically given functions (something which we get painfully

---

12. Cf. also ch. 12.4. Such activities can of course take on secondary communicative meanings, when they are carried out in special ways, on particular occasions, in the service of communicating specific messages. Cf. on Mr. Smith mowing his lawn, ch. 3.4.1.

13. For a more radical, relativist and discursive-constructionist stance, see e.g. Potter (1996).

aware of, when somebody, e.g., loses his eyes or hands, or has a stroke causing aphasia). Thus, spoken language, the basic medium of talk-in-interaction, as well as e.g. sign language, is *embodied*. But language, in modern literate societies, involves to a large extent *artifacts*, i.e. objects with physical properties and constraints: writing and written texts, pictures, new technological media etc., which enhance and transform our discourses and cognitive processes in many far-reaching respects (Olson 1994).

If we claim that action and discourse are constrained by material conditions, we are not arguing for a causal theory from material conditions to discourse. Rather, we claim that in discourse we orient to, among other things, apperceptions of the material world, and that these apperceptions are significantly constrained by our senses' capacities of providing patterned stimuli from the physical world itself. Social construction and reconstruction do not take place in vacuo, but are (inter)dependent with/on affordances from the material environment, and with/on the socio-economic conditions and the socio-cultural traditions within which they are embedded.

In spite of this, some social constructionists argue as if our understanding of the world, indeed the world itself, as it appears to us, were entirely built upon discursive construction. Take, for example, social problems, a field of primary importance for social constructionism (e.g. Spector & Kitsuse 1977); social problems are not simply objective conditions, but depend on interpretive practices through which people argue or claim that things can be seen as, e.g., 'crime', 'poverty', 'homelessness' and 'prostitution'. Such things become socially real, 'real in their consequences' to paraphrase the so-called 'Thomas theorem',[14] in and through their being communicatively constructed. But can the above-mentioned 'problems' really be understood as products of only claims-making and constitutive definitional practices, as a 'strict' constructionist position would entail (Holstein & Miller 1993)? A weaker form of constructionism ('contextual constructionism'; Best 1993) admits that social problems are to a considerable extent framed by ways of talking about them in special ways, but it is opposed to a 'strict' constructionism, which shuns all assumptions about the physical and socio-economic world. Material conditions are phenomena in the world that strongly influence how we construct and talk about e.g. crime and poverty. To take some other examples, handicaps and disabilities of various

---

14. After the American sociologist W.I. Thomas (1928: 522): 'if men define situations as real, they are real in their consequences'.

kinds, e.g. aphasia and dyslexia, are largely socially constructed, and our conceptions of, say, illnesses such as AIDS is thoroughly dependent on the ways we talk, and think, about them. But it would be misleading, indeed cynical, to forget that disabilities and illnesses have a substantial material and physiological basis in organic problems or dysfunctions, and to claim that the existence of the physiology of the lesion or illness is irrelevant to or outside the theory as a whole. Furthermore, as Best (1993) points out, a strict social constructionism could not argue for a difference between the social constructions of, the claims made about, say, AIDS, for which there is overwhelming medical evidence, and satanism (with blood cult, ritual murders etc.), for which little or no "objective" evidence has hitherto been found (in the modern Western societies where it allegedly is prevalent). For these and other reasons, we would argue for *contextual*, rather than 'strict', social constructionist theories of all the various phenomena that constructionists have analyzed, such as emotions, taboos, mental (and other) illnesses, personalities, careers, autobiographies, history, gender phenomena, or 'social problems' (e.g. Sarbin & Kitsuse 1994; Holstein & Miller 1993).

To summarize, material reality is "out there", even if our apprehensions of it are created and transformed through practices of cognition and discursive construction ("rhetoric"; Potter 1996; Edwards 1997). Potter (op.cit.) points out that discourse can be used to manufacture "out-there-ness". This means, among other things, that a linguistic description can be designed so as to depict things as if they were objective "facts" "out there" even in cases where they are clearly not. But it does not follow from this, I argue, that the discourse analyst must always be agnostic, indifferent or ironical about external reality, let alone deny its existence. We should adopt a form of social constructionism that is capable of navigating skilfully between the Scylla of naive objectivism and the Charybdis of extreme relativism.

The theory of discourse in the world of contexts must assign a proper place to the material circumstances which afford the senses and the mind with substantial experience. Fairclough (1992), arguing in this vein, insists that discursive practices

> "are constrained by the fact that they inevitably take place within a constituted, material reality, with preconstituted 'objects' and preconstituted social subjects. The constitutive processes of discourse ought therefore to be seen in terms of a dialectic, in which the impact of discursive practice depends upon how it interacts with the preconstituted reality" (p. 60).

"[S]trict constructionism push[es] the analyst into a contextless region where claims-making can only be examined in the abstract" (Best 1993: 143). Such a contextless theory is not compatible with dialogism.

13.5 Dialogism as a context-specific framework

Dialogism, as a way of viewing discourse, is of course "a culturally and historically specific ideology of language" in itself (Crapanzano 1990: 272). It must be
taken as reflexively related to its contexts.[15] It serves purposes that are partly
different from those which govern the development of monologistic theories.
However, this is not to reduce dialogism to one out of several equally viable
epistemologies; there are good reasons to adopt dialogism as the overarching
framework for understanding human communication and cognition. On the other
hand, we must not be blind to the differences between the objects and aims of
different scholarly and other practices. There is clearly a need to find a princi-
pled stance on the issue of how (or whether) one can reconcile the more natural-
science oriented approaches to human behaviour and information processing with
the dialogistic approaches of the social sciences and the humanities.

I think it would be a misconstrual of the dialogistic epistemology to propose
that all aspects of linguistic behaviour can be described in terms directly or
indirectly derived from a theory of social interaction. Some factors clearly derive
from the capabilities of individuals and individuals' organisms, e.g. neurophysio-
logically based, processing constraints. Also the planning involved at some levels
of the utterance production process (Levelt 1989) would be dependent on the
individual organism and/or biologically constrained in a substantial sense.
However, again, we would contend that the human being, with his or her
biological endowments and individual processing constraints, puts these resources
to use within cognitive projects which are ultimately socially and dialogically
based.

13.6 The limits of dialogism

Dialogism, at least as I would understand it, is neither a radical interactionism,
nor a 'strict' social constructionism, nor does it deny the existence of a material

---

15. That the activity of analyzing discourse is itself reflexively related to its subject matter and its
contexts is a point which often seems to be bracketed within e.g. Conversation Analysis (cf. Wilson
1991). In other branches of ethnomethodology the "double reflexivity" (the reflexivity of the data in
(e.g.) discourse analysis, and the reflexivity of the analyzing practices) is taken up as a major issue
(e.g. Woolgar 1988). See also ch. 14 below.

reality. As I argued in ch. 4.3, the dialogistic (or contextual) variant of dialogism takes a middle way, stressing the necessary interplay between cultural knowledge and routines, on the one hand, and situated interpretations, on the other hand, in the continuity of social, cultural, and linguistic practices. In this chapter, I have, furthermore, argued for a role, within the overall theory of human action and communication, for subjective agency, as well as for material constraints.

It would also be foolish to argue simplistically that the world of human experience is characterized by a maximal degree of dialogicality and contextualization. That would, in my view, be a naive dialogistic stance. Instead of plainly claiming that everything is thoroughly contextualized, it would amount to a more sophisticated dialogistic stance to maintain that many human practices are strongly decontextualizing and aim at creating "monologistic" positions. On the other hand, such decontextualizing practices are themselves context-bound. This point will be further substantiated in the last chapter of this book.

CHAPTER 14

Reconstructing monologism as a special case

14.1 Monologism and dialogism as perspectivized frameworks

Any description of reality is subject to perspectives, and these perspectives reflect understandings and pre-understandings, interests and commitments on the part of the individuals and communities who promote them. Monologism and dialogism, taken as general epistemologies or analytical frameworks, are no exceptions; each of them involves certain characteristic perspectives.

Monologism assumes as primary entities social "realities", such as power structures, cultural roles, and language, and individual, cognitive "realities", such as processing constraints and individual intentions, and seeks to explain interactions, and other "dialogical" phenomena, as secondary and epiphenomenal, or at least as in principle derivable. Dialogism, by contrast, would construe practices and interactions as primary entities, and seeks to explicate how language, traditions, routines, roles, knowledge, theories etc. are embodied as aspects pertaining to the continuity of praxis, and how it is from there that they can be and indeed have been abstracted. Communicative intentions, too, must, according to dialogism, be understood largely as emergent with interactions, and as part of collaborative projects (some of which are instigated by individuals). Truth, knowledge and discourses are socioculturally determined, and ultimately activity-specific, i.e. 'disciplinary' in a Foucauldian sense.

As we have seen, monologism in general attempts to provide generalizations about language and linguistic actions by postulating all the various linguistic units and rules. These are seen as entities in principle autonomous from particular contexts. Similarly, social structures and cultural systems are construed as existing prior to, or independently of, social and cultural practices. Monologism is largely a decontextualizing paradigm. Dialogism, by contrast, is built upon the intrinsic and inalienable relations between discursive practices and their contexts. In this final chapter, I shall argue that it is possible, and indeed necessary, to oscillate between decontextualizing and (re)contextualizing perspectives, viewing them as alternative frameworks to be used for different purposes under different circumstances. At the same time, however, I shall stick to the proposal that we should regard dialogism as the most basic and comprehensive theory of cognition, communication and language, and the monologistic practices will be reconstructed as context-specific decontextualizing variants.

14.2 In support of monologistic practices

If one tries to argue strongly for the validity of dialogism, as I have done in this book, it can be seen as something of a distressing fact that monologism remains so dominant in most language sciences. Why is it that monologism is such an attractive, and partly successful, paradigm for the language sciences?[1] The answer seems to be that there are very strong forces backing it. The account can refer to decontextualizing needs and tendencies at several levels.

At the most general level, monologism builds upon the development of a very general, biologically induced tendency, namely the need for cross-situationally valid categorization in cognition. In order to cope with recurrent problems in the world, human beings need to develop stable perceptual, cognitive and linguistic categories and concepts. On the other hand, the application of categories to new situations involves dynamic accommodations and assimilations. Thus, there is a universal tension between stability and change, or between decontextualization and (re)contextualization, in our interactions with the world, and these two poles have been given quite different priorities in monologism and in dialogism.

However, the observation that cognition and communication involve categorization does not take us to a full-fledged monologism. This, I would argue, involves additional fixations of linguistic categories. This grand-scale 'fixation of perspectives' (Rommetveit 1990, 1992) has been supported by several historical conditions, of which I would like to single out two major forces, the impact of literacy and the need, or predilection, within some activity types for decontextualizing practices. These two are of course deeply intertwined, but I will separate them for analytical purposes.

---

1. Cf. Still & Costall (1991: 55) who put the same question with regard to cognitivism.

Attitudes to language, mind and communication have been built up and supported systematically by our literate traditions in societies. Artifacts like scripts — writing on paper — and later computers create firm and permanent structures. This applies to the 'software' (symbolic representations) as well as the 'hardware', i.e. the infrastructure of paper, computer discs etc. By carrying more or less stable representations of language, writing supports the conception of language as based upon invariant and discrete units and structures. Writing, especially in print, fixates linguistic signs on record, it freezes aspects of expression and makes them stable across physical copyings. This idea of stability and invariance can then easily spread to our conception of linguistic meaning. Accordingly, the permanence of written texts objectified language and also made language more into an object of reflection. Literate cultures, in professional and scholarly contexts as well as in society at large, developed their ideas about language to a very large extent on the basis of written language. This need not be a necessary and universal consequence of literate culture, but it is undeniably characteristic of our culture-specific literacy practices in the Western civilization (cf. Wertsch 1991: 85).

Once our conception of language was firmly settled, influenced as it was by the practices of using, reflecting upon and analyzing written language, it was also used in the analysis of spoken language. I have referred to this extensive impact of the study of written language as 'the written language bias' in the language sciences (ch. 2.5). We recall that the traditional monologistic view of language has been brought along *also* when linguists and psychologists have started to study *spoken language and interaction*. A good illustration is the fate of speech act theory (ch. 11.2). Monologism has carried along an enormous traditional backing, when it came to be used in the study of dialogue and discourse.

The historical reliance on monologism in the language sciences, and in society's attitudes to language, is only part of the story, however. Monologistic perspectives have a much larger place in our society, as the basis for many kinds of abstracting and decontextualizing practices. What we do in these (relatively) monologistic activities is that we create a space, or an enclosure (Gustavsson 1988), for fixating a frame, i.e. defining a context or situation, in which some specific premises are (assumed to be) valid. Within such frames, when perspectives have been fixated, they are often taken as given, stable and, quite simply, self-evident (Rommetveit 1990: 92, "fixation of perspectives"). Certain assumptions, theories and ideologies are assigned monological authority. By the disciplined use of language, we seek to establish and constitute, i.e. fixate, specific correspondence relations between observations of the world and their linguistic re-presentations.

Such projects involve decontextualization in several ways. Or rather, it would be more accurate to say that we are faced with recontextualizations (ch. 8.10), which involve a considerable amount of certain systematic and disciplined types of decontextualizations. First, such projects presuppose fixed contexts, which will only under exceptional circumstances be problematized; in other words, the context is taken as given in such a way that we forget about its status as a contingent and silent presupposition. Secondly, because the contingencies of contexts are forgotten, we will treat that which is within the frame, enclosure or context as context-free or context-less; things stand out as decontextualized. Yet, such decontextualizing activities are of course themselves context-bound, tied to the specific frames that we have posited but backgrounded to the point of oblivion. Contexts are taken for granted, but the embedded activities are orderly social activities that are determined by, and themselves determining to some extent, particular theoretical assumptions and practical purposes, endorsed in precisely these (usually professional) contexts. In other words, they are *at the same time "monological" and "dialogically constituted"*. Linell (1992) identifies a number of such *situated decontextualizing practices*, all involving the use of language, and Wertsch (1991: 39) points to the same kinds of practices as specific 'discourse modes' or 'speech genres' (and one might of course also regard them as 'language games' or 'communicative genres', cf. ch. 12).

Since I have, in this book, refrained from going into institutional discourse in detail, we have not encountered many instances of manifestly decontextualizing practices. However, some glimpses can be found in the police officer's concentration on legally relevant facts and his concomitant disregard of the suspect's life-world perspective in A LONG TIME SINCE I BUILT (ch. 12), or the speech therapist's framing of a conversation with an aphasic as a test situation rather than as a talk about current everyday realities in A HOT DAT TODAY (ch. 8). Some more radical examples of situated decontextualizing practices are the application of law and administrative rules within bureaucracies, discussing language in e.g. language lessons (Gustavsson 1988) or defining lexical meanings for dictionaries and the like, doing logic exercises, coding discourse in terms of predefined category systems (Marková & Linell 1996), and, in connection with this, the use of measurement (Lynch 1991), and countless other varieties of doing science, particularly perhaps in the natural sciences (cf. discussion in Rommetveit 1992).[2] It is a significant fact that most of them are quite substantially and concretely dependent on the use of writing and written texts. These largely monological practices have of course a proper place in many activities which are useful and necessary in a highly diversified society.

If our surrounding world ("Umwelt") is always in motion, we define it, fixate it, for descriptive, explanatory and pedagogical purposes in science. In doing so, scientific disciplines build upon (the belief in) relatively unified traditions of writing and using systematic texts, relying on a certain body of fixated, i.e. already determined, meanings: "a body of special, interpretative resources into which the properly trained professional reader has been 'educated' in making sense of such texts" (Shotter 1993: 25). For specific, i.e. situated, scientific purposes, theorists try "to represent the open, vague, and temporally changing nature of the world as closed, well-defined and orderly" (ibid.: 25).

14.3 From decontextualizing practices to decontextualized theories

It is an important point that theories and ideologies are associated with, and ultimately built upon, *practices* of some kind. Practices are, by definition, context-bound and activity-specific; one always does something at a particular point in time, in a particular place and for a particular purpose. Often, as in the case of sciences, the practices involved are professional, institutionalized and "disciplined", i.e. constitutive of disciplines (Taylor 1992: 10).

In the case of monologism, the practices involved are, as we have seen, decontextualizing and "reality-fixating" (Rommetveit 1992). However, partly for this reason, monologism tends to conceal its historicity and activity-specificity by treating theories, cultural artifacts or linguistic systems as objective entities, existing before whatever practices they may be used for (ch. 4.1). That is why it may be particularly illuminating for us, when we deal with such theories and ideologies, to focus on the fact that they are founded on practices, which are subject to certain perspectives that have been adopted by practitioners for certain purposes. For once one has become socialized into thinking within a certain

---

2. For an ethnomethodologist, the practices of doing science, e.g. laboratory work or coding data, will, by virtue of their being orderly situated (communicative and cognitive) activities, be interesting as objects of study (e.g. Lynch 1991, 1993; Latour 1987; Woolgar 1988). Such practices can be looked upon as particular kinds of situated decontextualizing practices.

perspective, thus also having adopted a particular kind of theory or ideology, it may be difficult to realise that the theory is *not* self-evident or objective, i.e. to realise that it is in fact dependent on human concerns, interests and commitments. This is particularly true if the theories are part of mainstream scientific traditions.

However, before turning to some examples of typically monological theories belonging to mainstream traditions within the language sciences, let us recall that it is hardly possible to be systematic *anywhere* in research without being to some extent monological. Thus, researchers who adopt a dialogistic 'process' perspective on discourse and dialogue, will be partly monological in their own activities of carrying out systematic analyses. In other words, aspects of 'products' (not only processes and practices, cf. ch. 1.1) will be included. This is obvious when it comes to 'global' units, such as 'episodes' (ch. 10); these units can be identified only when they have actually been produced. But also when we wish to describe local processes in talk (along CA lines), we work with the manifest products of the actors' local decision-making and distributed cognition.

The decontextualizing ('monological') ingredient in research is most conspicuously present if generalizability is part of the objectives (which it is, in some form or another, for most researchers). Thus, the researcher fixates a perspective on data and tries consistently to hold on to the same organizing principles. Coding interaction in terms of particular kinds of units is a case in point. But in general, analysts always make some contribution to the way facts are described (*facta* means things *made*) and to which properties and patterns in the data are selected and made salient. The analyst's activity is not merely a simple reconstruction, i.e. a copy, of the actor's constructions. At some points, this (re)constructive activity on the part of analysts becomes particularly conspicuous, although not all analysts seem to be aware of it. For example, one could make a case for the contention that some aspects of global coherence are largely the analyst's constructs (ch. 10.11). (This of course in no way implies that these constructs are not based on properties afforded by data.) Similarly, large parts of the grammarian's theoretical constructs may be derivative of the analyst's model rather than being simply inherent in the linguistic system per se.[3] At the same time, it is hard to see how we could do away entirely with such (partly) monological theories. Indeed, we need to integrate parts of them in our models of

---

3. That the grammar is partly the emergent product of the grammarians' analytical activities has been forcefully argued by e.g. Hopper (1988).

discourse and interaction. And this is so for at least two basic reasons: there are recurrent structures in linguistic practices, and we need to be systematic and consistent in science and research.

Let me now turn to some cases where, I think, we can see clear distinctions between mainstream monological theories and distinct dialogical alternatives. As usual, I stick to examples from the language sciences.

Consider, for example, the case of *dialogue interpreting*, i.e. the polyadic interaction in which an interpreter transmits messages between two primary parties, usually a professional (e.g. a police officer, a physician, a nurse) and an immigrant or foreigner (appearing as a suspect, an applicant for residence permit, a patient etc.), who meet in a face-to-face encounter but can only speak mutually unintelligible languages. We are faced here with a peculiar polyadic interaction, in which the interpreter has the task of translating originals from one language to the other and thus to render these original messages comprehensible for the other party. Traditionally, studies of interpreting have been based on translation theory, in which the basic questions often revolve around the adequacy of translations. This amounts to a monologistic view; the interpreter is viewed as an "information processing device", whose accuracy of transmission is evaluated and who, in events of miscommunication, tends to be blamed for "faulty translations". There are strong professional traditions and interests backing such an approach;[4] interpreters are obliged (by ethical rules) to translate as accurately as possible, they are trained to concentrate on translation, and they are therefore naturally interested in perspectivizing the research so as to focus on this aspect.

However, a dialogue interpreter has a much more complicated interactional role, which cannot be characterized only as that of a "translator"; she is also necessarily a coordinator of the interaction, being the only one who understands everything that is said in the situation and hence also the only one who can effectively monitor and guide major aspects of the interaction. A dialogistic analysis (Wadensjö 1998) would of course not deny that translation is an essential part of the interpreter's activity, but it would avoid disregarding other aspects of the interaction between the people present. The whole encounter is a

---

4. There are also research traditions. Translation theory is to an overwhelming extent concerned with written texts, and as far as oral interpreting has been researched, most attention has been paid to conference interpreting, in which the interpreter is usually isolated in a booth, unable to interact with primary parties. She has to translate originals unidirectionally from one language to the other, rather than bidirectionally as in the case of dialogue interpreting.

complex one, in which misunderstandings typically are, to some extent, collaboratively developed (Wadensjö, op.cit.; Linell 1995). The choice of a dialogistic
analytic framework implies that the interpreter's role is taken at face value,
rather than being described as one which (ideally) involves only translation (thus
following the normative expectations of many of those involved). It then
becomes an empirical question to explore how interpreters cope with the task of
rendering originals accurately and faithfully under various situational constraints
(Wadensjö, op.cit.).

The study of dialogue interpreting just referred to raises the issue of how to
look at misunderstandings and *miscommunication* in communication. With an
individualistic framework, "errors" and "failures" of communication are traced
to individuals who are supposed to perform inaccurately now and then, i.e. when
something goes wrong in their information processing. A dialogistic analysis will
often make it clear that miscommunication events are deeply social in nature;
discrepant understandings develop from different pre-understandings and from
subtle interplays between these and the contributions to dialogue by different
individuals. Also, the traditional (i.e. monologistic) view is that miscommunication always amounts to failed or inadequate communication. Thus, it implicitly
builds upon the normative ideal of a totally shared understanding resulting from
identical semantic representations. Actually, this is only one interpretation of the
phenomenon of communication, and arguably often a less fruitful one (Taylor
1992). A dialogistic theory would not make such a sharp distinction between
communication and miscommunication; it would treat nonsharedness of understanding as a natural condition of communication, and as something which is
used as a resource for carrying the dialogue further, e.g. through repair and
negotiation, in order to develop, elaborate and improve individual and shared
understandings (Linell 1995).

As our next example, let us take theories of *learning*. Here we are concerned with theories and ideologies that have served educational systems for a
very long time, and accordingly, there are strong professional and sociopolitical
interests involved (teachers, school administrators, researchers in education etc.).
If I am allowed to simplify matters a little, the traditional institutionalized view
on learning implies that it consists in (the more or less successful) retention of
information provided as input to the learners. The typical test involves opportunities for the learner to display his or her knowledge of and ability to apply the
subject matter once received as input. The degree of retention is measured by the
output. Traditionally, in schools and other educational institutions, both inputs

and outputs are communicated verbally. Thus, the learner is again, usually implicitly, viewed as an individual processing information in a chain of communication transfers (ch. 2.1; Säljö 1991, 1992). A dialogistic view would of course not deny that the internalization of input is part of learning, but it would normally pay more attention to the interplay between more factors in the various situations in which the learner is involved. Learning would be seen more in terms of a process of interaction with the environment, as increasing abilities to cope with new kinds of situations and problems (e.g. Rogoff 1990).

Traditional schooling perspectives, building upon a Cartesian dichotomy of knowledge and learning, tend to see the former as unproblematic and the latter as *the* problem, at least for educational institutions. Dialogists can of course not treat learning as unproblematic either, but they wish to regard it as a natural component of many discursive practices, not just of teaching contexts. Moreover, what dialogism will do in addition is to problematize the nature of knowledge (cf. Lave 1993).

Perspectives on *language* as such are of course the most central example to be brought up in this context. The analytic approach of linguistics, that of viewing language as a supra-individual stable system of signs (expressions with associated meanings), as objective structures uncontaminated by various 'performance' variables, may to some extent be a necessary one for the discipline of linguistics. It tries to focus on linguistic dimensions, which are supposedly cross-situationally valid. However, it is important to realise that this approach was for a long time motivated by specific concerns and supported by strong professional and political interests, ranging from the drive to standardize national languages (and perhaps endorse social stratification) to the practical needs to provide grammars of foreign languages or workable dictionary definitions of words. As I have remarked several times, the historicity of this specific monologistic stance is seldom admitted by present-day linguists, who usually claim they deal with the objective nature of language *tout court*. Regardless of this, it would be useful sometimes to shift to an alternative framework, in which language is seen in a fundamentally different perspective: as mediational means and flexible resources with dynamic potentials to be used for communicative purposes in various kinds of contexts. The particularly poor analysis of 'performance' within theoretical linguistics lumps together such profoundly different factors as, on the one hand, the sensitivity of linguistic choice to differences in communicative projects (eminently significant for the understanding of language) and, on the other hand, individual speaker properties, such as personality traits, memory limitations and distractions etc (which may be important too, but in different contexts, and less so in linguistics).[5]

Examples of monologistic theories of language and communication could easily be multiplied. We can summarize our argument as follows. These theories are not objective accounts of a linguistic reality existing independently of actors' and researchers' perspectives. Rather, they are crucially related to historical conditions, to people's various decontextualizing practices involving language. Such practices are useful, sometimes necessary, for specific purposes. For example, in order to explore some aspects, say properties pertaining to language structure, it may be desirable to control, keep constant or temporally disregard contextual parameters. But this is basically a methodological trick; it is not that the world out there is static, but in order to explore it, we may have to 'fixate' it.

14.4 Conclusion

In conclusion, then, we argue that dialogism may subsume, rather than exclude the possibility to explain, work undertaken within monologist models. There is no inherent contradiction in claiming that partly monological activities recur in our dialogically constituted world. Moreover, dialogical interactions can never have "only" context-specific features; there are always tensions between stability and change, between decontextualizing and contextualizing forces. At the same time, what we have called "monological activities" can never be entirely "monological"; they are also bound to specific contexts, purposes, interests, concerns and commitments. As 'situated decontextualizing practices', they are themselves situated.

Therefore, monologism is an analytic framework which can be deconstructed and reconstructed as embedded with a more general epistemology of dialogism. It is dependent on specific contextual conditions for its application. Generally, it is supported by literate strategies in a large number of advanced practices in modern society. Researchers often make phenomena look more 'monological' than they actually are (or would look like from the dialogistic vantage point). Such decontextualizing and 'monologizing' activities are neces-

---

5. Cf. the classical formulation by Chomsky (1965: 3), quoted above in ch. 4, fn.6.

sary as scientific or administrative approaches to the world. But they remain bound to their own contextual conditions, and their fruitfulness can not cast doubt on dialogism as the superordinate epistemology.

It has been said that "[o]ne needs to choose one's paradigm rather than work out a compromise" (Farr 1996: 73). I have chosen dialogism, but have I also compromised it? I hope not. But I have argued for a particular version and vision of it.

References

Adelswärd, Viveka. 1988. *Styles of Success*. (Linköping Studies in Arts and Science, 23). Linköping: Department of Theme Research.

Adelswärd, Viveka, Karin Aronsson, Linda Jönsson and Per Linell. 1987. The unequal distribution of interactional space: Dominance and control in courtroom interaction. *Text* 7: 313–346.

Adelswärd, Viveka and Per Linell. 1994. Vagueness as an interactional resource: The genre of threatening phone calls. In Walter Sprondel (ed.), *Die Objektivität der Ordnungen und ihre kommunikative Konstruktion*. Frankfurt: Suhrkamp, 261–288.

Agar, Michael. 1985. Institutional discourse. *Text* 5: 147–168.

Allport, Floyd. 1924. *Social Psychology*. Boston: Houghton-Mifflin.

Allwood, Jens. 1976. *Linguistic Communication as Action and Cooperation*. (Gothenburg Monographs in Linguistics, 2). Göteborg: Department of Linguistics.

Allwood, Jens. 1981. On the distinction between semantics and pragmatics. In Wolfgang Klein and Willem Levelt (eds), *Crossing the Boundaries in Linguistics*. Dordrecht: Reidel, 177–189.

Allwood, Jens. 1985. On relevance in spoken interaction. In Sven Bäckman and Göran Kjellmer (eds), *Papers on Language and Literature. Presented to Alvar Ellegård and Erik Frykman*. (Göteborg: Gothenburg Studies in English, 60), 18–35.

Antaki, Charles. (ed.) 1988. *Analysing Everyday Explanation: A casebook of methods*. London: Sage.

Anward, Jan. 1997. Parameters of institutional discourse. In Gunnarsson et al. (1997), 127–150.

Aronsson, Karin. 1987. Verbal disputes and topic analysis: A methodological commentary on a drama case study. In Florence van Zuuren, Frederick Wertz and Bertha Mook (eds), *Advances in Qualitative Psychology*. Lisse:

Swets & Zeitlinger 193–205.

Aronsson, Karin. 1991. Facework and control in multi-party contexts: a paediatric case study. In Marková and Foppa (1991), 49–74.

Aronsson, Karin, Linda Jönsson and Per Linell. 1987. The courtroom hearing as a middle ground: Speech accommodation by lawyers and defendants. *Journal of Language and Social Psychology* 6: 99–115.

Asplund, Johan. 1987. *Det sociala livets elementära former* ("The Elementary Forms of Social Life"). Göteborg: Bokförlaget Korpen.

Atkinson, Maxwell and John Heritage. (eds) 1984. *Structures of Social Action.* Cambridge: Cambridge University Press.

Auer, Peter. 1992. Introduction: John Gumperz' approach to contextualization. In Auer and Di Luzio (1992), 1–37.

Auer, Peter. 1995. Context and contextualization. In Jef Verschueren, Jan-Ola Östman and Jan Blommaert (eds), *Handbook of Pragmatics 1995.* Amsterdam: John Benjamins.

Auer, Peter and Aldo di Luzio. (eds) 1992. *The Contextualization of Language.* Amsterdam: John Benjamins.

Austin, John. 1962. *How to Do Things With Words.* London: Oxford University Press.

Bakhtin, Mikhail. 1981. *The Dialogic Imagination: Four Essays.* Translated by Carol Emerson and Michael Holquist, edited by Michael Holquist. Austin: Texas University Press.

Bakhtin, Mikhail. 1984. *Problems of Dostoevsky's Poetics.* Translated and edited by Carol Emerson. Minneapolis: University of Minnesota Press.

Bakhtin, Mikhail. 1986. *Speech Genres and Other Late Essays.* Transl. by V. McGee, edited by Carol Emerson and Michael Holquist. Austin, Texas: University of Texas Press.

Bartlett, Frederick. 1961. [1932] *Remembering. A study in experimental and social psychology.* Cambridge: Cambridge University Press.

Barwise, John and John Perry. 1983. *Situations and Attitudes.* Cambridge, MA: The M.I.T. Press.

Bateson, Gregory. 1973. *Steps to an Ecology of Mind.* Suffolk: Palladin.

Bavelas, Janet B. and Nicole Chovil. 1994. Redefining language: An integrated message model of language in face-to-face dialogue. Ms. University of Victoria: Department of Psychology.

Beaugrande, Robert de and Wolfgang U. Dressler. 1981. *Introduction to Text Linguistics.* London: Longman.

Bell, Alan. 1984. Language style as audience design. *Language in Society* 13: 145–204.

Berger, Peter and Thomas Luckmann. 1967. *The Social Construction of Reality*. Harmondsworth: Penguin.

Bergmann, Jörg. 1987. *Klatsch: Zur Sozialform der diskreten Indiskretion*. Berlin: de Gruyter. English translation by John Bednarz, Jr: *Discreet indiscretions: The social organization of gossip* [1993] . New York: Aldine de Gruyter.

Bergmann, Jörg. 1990. On the local sensitivity of conversation. In Marková and Foppa (1990), 201–226.

Bergmann, Jörg. 1992. Veiled morality: notes on discretion in psychiatry. In Drew and Heritage (1992), 137–162.

Bergmann, Jörg. 1998. Introduction: Morality in discourse. *Research on Language and Social Interaction* 31:3–4.

Bergmann, Jörg and Thomas Luckmann. 1993. Formen der kommunikativen Konstruktion von Moral: Gattungsfamilien der moralischen Kommunikation in informellen, institutionellen und massenmedialen Kontexten. (Moral-Projekt: Arbeitspapier, 1). University of Konstanz.

Bergmann, Jörg and Thomas Luckmann. 1995. Reconstructive genres of everyday communication. In Quasthoff (1995), 289–304.

Bernstein, Basil. 1990. *Class, Codes, and Control. Vol. 4: The structuring of pedagogic discourse*. London: Rouledge.

Best, Joel. 1993. But seriously folks: the limitations of the strict constructionist interpretation of social problems. In Holstein and Miller (1993), 129–147.

Billig, Michael. 1987. *Arguing and Thinking: A rhetorical approach to social psychology*. Oxford: Blackwell.

Billig, Michael. 1993. Studying the thinking society: social representations, rhetoric and attitudes. In Glynis Breakwell and David Canter (eds), *Empirical Approaches to Social Representations*. Oxford: Clarendon Press, 39–62.

Bilmes, Jack. 1985. Why that now? Two kinds of conversational meaning. *Discourse Processes* 8: 319–355.

Bilmes, Jack. 1988. Category and rule in Conversation Analysis. *Papers in Pragmatics* 2: 25–59.

Blank, Marion and Eleanor Franklin. 1980. Dialogue with preschoolers: A cognitively based system of assessment. *Applied Psycholinguistics* 1: 127–150.

Bloomfield, Leonard. 1933. *Language*. London: Allen & Unwin.

Blum-Kulka, Shoshana and Elda Weizman. 1988. The inevitability of misunderstandings: discourse ambiguities. *Text* 8: 219–241.

Boden, Deirdre. 1994. *The Business of Talk: Organization in Action.* Cambridge: Polity Press.

Boden, Deirdre and Don Zimmerman. (eds) 1991. *Talk and Social Structure: Studies in Ethnomethodology and Conversation Analysis.* Cambridge: Polity Press.

Bogen, David. 1991. Linguistic forms and social obligations: A critique of the doctrine of literal expression in Searle. *Journal for the Theory of Social Behaviour* 21: 31–62.

Bourdieu, Pierre. 1977. *Outline of a Theory of Practice.* Cambridge: Cambridge University Press.

Bourdieu, Pierre. 1989. Social space and symbolic power. *Sociological Theory* 7: 14–25.

Brown, Gilian and George Yule. 1983. *Discourse Analysis.* Cambridge: Cambridge University Press.

Brown, Penelope and Stephen Levinson. 1987. *Politeness: Some universals in language usage.* Cambridge: Cambridge University Press.

Bråten, Stein. 1992. The virtual other in infants' minds and social feelings. In Heen Wold (1992), 77–97.

Bråten, Stein. Fc. Dialogues and Feelings in Infants and Adults. Ms. Oslo: Department of Sociology.

Bruner, Jerome. 1990. *Acts of Meaning.* Cambridge, MA: Harvard University Press.

Buber, Martin. 1958. *Ich und Du.* Heidelberg: Lambert Schneider Verlag.

Burke, Peter. 1993. *The Art of Conversation.* Ithaca, N.Y.: Cornell University Press.

Button, Graham. (ed.) 1991. *Ethnomethodology and the Human Sciences.* Cambridge: Cambridge University Press.

Candlin, Christopher and Yon Maley. 1997. Intertextuality and interdiscursivity in the discourse of alternative dispute resolution. In Gunnarsson et al. (1997), 201–222.

Cedersund, Elisabet and Roger Säljö. 1993. Bureaucratic discourse, conversational space and the concept of voice. *Semiotica* 97: 79–101.

Chafe, Wallace. 1979. The flow of thought and the flow of language. In Givón (1979a), 159–181.

Chafe, Wallace. 1980. The deployment of consciousness in the production of a narrative. In Wallace Chafe (ed.), *The Pear Stories: Cognitive, cultural, and linguistic aspects of narrative production.* Norwood, N.J.: Ablex, 9–50.

Chafe, Wallace. 1994. *Discourse, Consciousness and Time*. Chicago: The University of Chicago Press.

Channell, Joanna. 1997. 'I just called to say I love you' : Love and desire on the telephone. In Keith Harvey and Celia Shalom (eds), *Language and Desire: Encoding sex, romance and intimacy*. London: Routledge, 143–169.

Chomsky, Noam. 1965. *Aspects of the Theory of Syntax*. Cambridge, MA: The M.I.T. Press.

Chomsky, Noam. 1986. *Knowledge of Language: Its Nature, Origin and Use*. New York: Praeger.

Cicourel, Aaron. 1968. *The Social Organization of Juvenile Justice*. New York: John Wiley.

Cicourel, Aaron. 1973. *Cognitive Sociology*. London: Cox and Wyman.

Cicourel, Aaron. 1980. Three models of discourse analysis: The role of social structure. *Discourse Processes* 3: 101–132.

Cicourel, Aaron. 1981. Notes on the integration of micro- and macro-levels of analysis. In Knorr-Cetina and Cicourel (1981), 51–80.

Clark, Andy. 1997. *Being There: Putting brain, body, and world together again*. Cambridge, MA; The M.I.T. Press.

Clark, Herbert H. 1996. *Using Language*. Cambridge: Cambridge University Press.

Clark, Herbert H. and Eve Clark. 1977. *Psychology and Language: An introduction to psycholinguistics*. New York: Harcourt Brace.

Clark, Herbert H. and Richard Gerrig. 1990. Quotations as demonstrations. *Language* 66, 764–805.

Clark, Herbert H. and Catherine Marshall. 1981. Definite reference and mutual knowledge. In Aravind Joshi, Bonnie Webber and Ivan Sag (eds), *Elements of Discourse Understanding*. Cambridge: Cambridge University Press, 10–63.

Clark, Herbert H. and Edward Schaefer. 1987. Collaborating on contributions to conversations. *Language and Cognitive Processes* 2, 19–41.

Clark, Herbert H. and Edward Schaefer. 1989. Contributing to discourse. *Cognitive Science* 13, 259–294.

Clark, Herbert H. and Deanna Wilkes-Gibbs. 1986. Referring as a collaborative process. *Cognition* 22: 1–39.

Clark, Katerina and Michael Holquist. 1984. *Mikhail Bakhtin*. Cambridge, MA: Harvard University Press.

Clayman, Steven. 1990. From talk to text: newspaper accounts of reporter-source interaction. *Media, Culture and Society* 12: 79–103.

Clayman, Steven. 1993. Reformulating the question: A device for answering/not answering questions in news interviews and press conferences. *Text* 13: 159–188.

Cohen, Philip and Raymond Perrault. 1979. A plan-based theory of speech acts. *Cognitive Science* 3, 213–230.

Cole, Michael and Yrjö Engeström. 1993. A cultural-historical approach to distributed cognition. In Gavriel Salomon (ed), *Distributed Cognitions: Psychological and educational considerations*. Cambridge: Cambridge University Press. 1–46.

Collins, Randall. 1981. Micro-translation as a theory-building strategy. In Knorr-Cetina and Cicourel (1981), 80–108.

Collins, Sarah and Ivana Marková. 1995. Complementarity in a dialogue involving impaired speech. In Marková et al. (1995), 238–263.

Cook, Vivian and Mark Newson. 1996. *Chomsky's Universal Grammar: An Introduction*. 2nd ed. Oxford: Blackwell.

Cooper, William. 1980. Syntactic-to-phonetic coding. In Brian Butterworth (ed.), *Language Production, vol. 1: Speech and Talk*. London: Academic Press, 297–333.

Corsaro, William. 1982. Something old and something new: the importance of prior ethnography in the collection and analysis of audiovisual data. *Sociological Methods and Research* 11: 145–166.

Costall, Alan. 1991. 'Graceful degradation': Cognitivism and the metaphors of the computer. In Still and Costall (1991): 151–169.

Couch, Carl. 1986. Elementary forms of social activity. In Couch et al. (1986), 113–129.

Couch, Carl, Stanley Saxton and Michael Katovich. (eds) 1986. *Studies in Social Interaction: The Iowa School*. Parts A and B. Greenwich, Conn.: JAI Press.

Coulmas, Florian. (ed.) 1986. *Direct and Indirect Speech*. Berlin: Mouton de Gruyter.

Coulthard, Malcolm. (ed.) 1992. *Advances in Spoken Discourse Analysis*. London: Routledge.

Coulthard, Malcolm and David Brazil. 1992. Exchange structure. In Coulthard (1992): 50–78.

Couper-Kuhlen, Elizabeth and Margret Selting. (eds) 1996. *Prosody in Conversation: Interactional Studies*. Cambridge: Cambridge University Press.

Craig, Robert and Karen Tracy. (eds) 1983. *Conversational Coherence: Form, Structure, and Strategy*. Beverly Hills: Sage.

Crapanzano, Vincent. 1990. On dialogue. In Maranhão (1990), 269–291.

Crow, Bryan. 1983. Topic shifts in couples' conversation. In Craig and Tracy (1983): 116–135.

Crowell, Steven. 1990. Dialogue and text: re-marking the difference. In Maranhão (1990), 338–360.

Cuff, E.C. 1993. *Problems of Versions in Everyday Situations*. (Studies in Ethnomethodology and Conversation Analysis, 2.) Lanham, MA: University Press of America.

Culler, Jonathan. 1988. *Framing the Sign: Criticism and Its Institutions*. Oxford: Blackwell.

Daneš, František. 1974, Functional sentence perspective and the organization of the text. In František Daneš (ed.), *Papers on Functional Sentence Perspective*. Prague: Academia.

Denes, Peter and Elliot Pinson. 1963. *The Speech Chain: The physics and biology of spoken language*. Baltimore: Bell Telephone Laboratories.

Denzin, Norman. 1992. *Symbolic Interactionism and Cultural Studies: The politics of interpretation*. Oxford: Blackwell.

Dik, Simon. 1978. *Functional Grammar*. Amsterdam: North-Holland.

Dore, John and Ray McDermott. 1982. Linguistic indeterminacy and social context in utterance interpretation. *Language* 58, 374–398.

Dorval, Bruce (ed.) 1990. *Conversational Organization and its Development*. Norwood, N.J.; Ablex.

Drew, Paul. 1992. Contested evidence in courtroom cross-examination: the case of a trial for rape. In Drew and Heritage (1992), 470–520.

Drew, Paul. 1998. Complaints about transgressions and misconduct. *Research on Language and Social Interaction* 31:3–4.

Drew, Paul and John Heritage. (eds) 1992. *Talk at Work*. Cambridge: Cambridge University Press.

Drew, Paul and Marja-Leena Sorjonen. 1997. Institutional dialogue. In van Dijk (1997), 92–118.

Ducrot, Oswald. 1972. *Dire et ne pas dire*. Paris: Hermann.

Dufva, Hannele. 1992. *Slipshod Utterances: A study of mislanguage*. (Diss.) (Studia Philologica Jyväskyläensia, 26). Jyväskylä: University of Jyväskylä.

Dumesnil, James and Bruce Dorval. 1989. The development of talk-activity frames that foster perspective-focused talk among peers. *Discourse Processes* 12: 193–225.

Duranti, Alessandro. 1986. The audience as co-author: An introduction. *Text* 6: 239–247.

Duranti, Alessandro. 1991. Four properties of speech-in-interaction and the notion of translocutionary act. In Jef Verschueren (ed.), *Pragmatics at Issue.* Selected papers of the International Pragmatics Conference, Antwerp, August 17–22, 1987. Amsterdam: John Benjamins, 133–150.

Duranti, Alessandro. 1993a. Truth and intentionality: an ethnographic critique. *Cultural Anthropology* 8: 214–245.

Duranti, Alessandro. 1993b. Intentions, self, and responsibility. An essay in Samoan ethnopragmatics. In Jane Hill and Judith Irvine (eds), *Responsibility and Evidence in Oral Discourse.* Cambridge: Cambridge University Press, 24–47.

Duranti, Alessandro and Charles Goodwin. (eds) 1992. *Rethinking Context: Language as an interactive phenomenon.* Cambridge: Cambridge University Press.

Dwyer, Kevin. 1982. Moroccan Dialogues: Anthropology in Question. Baltimore: John Hopkins University Press.

Edelsky, Carol. 1981. Who's got the floor? *Language in Society* 10: 383–421.

Edmondson, Willis. 1981. *Spoken Discourse: A model for analysis.* London: Longman.

Edwards, Derek. 1997. *Discourse and Cognition.* London: Sage.

Edwards, Derek and Jonathan Potter. 1992. *Discursive Psychology.* London: Sage.

Edwards, Derek, Jonathan Potter and David Middleton. 1992. Towards a discursive psychology of remembering. *The Psychologist*, Oct. 1992: 441–446.

Egbert, Maria. 1997. Schisming: The collaborative transformation from a single conversation to multiple conversations. *Research on Language and Social Interaction* 30: 1–51.

Ekman, Paul and Wallace V. Friesen. 1969. Categories, origins, usage, and coding: the basis for five categories of non-verbal behavior. *Semiotica* 1: 49–98.

Engeström, Yrjö. 1987. *Learning by Expanding: An activity-theoretical approach to developmental research.* Helsinki: Orienta-Konsultit.

Engeström, Yrjö. 1996. The tensions of judging: Handling cases of driving under the influence of alcohol in Finland and California. In Engeström and Middleton (1996), 199–232.

Engeström. Yrjö and David Middleton. (eds) 1996a. *Cognition and Communication at Work*. Cambridge: Cambridge University Press.

Engeström, Yrjö and David Middleton. 1996b. Introduction: Studying work as mindful practice. In Engeström and Middleton (1996a), 1–14.

Erickson, Frederick. 1982. Money tree, lasagna bush, salt and pepper: Social construction of topical cohesion in a conversation among Italian-Americans. In Tannen (1982), 43–70.

Erickson, Frederick. 1986. Listening and speaking. In Deborah Tannen and Jay Atlatis (eds), *Georgetown University Round Table in Languages and Linguistics 1985*. Washington, D.C.: Georgetown University Press.

Fairclough, Norman. 1992. *Discourse and Social Change*. Cambridge: Polity Press.

Fairclough, Norman. 1995. *Critical Discourse Analysis: the critical study of language*. London: Longman.

Falk, Jane. 1980. The conversational duet. In *Proceedings of the 6th Annual Meeting of the Berkeley Linguistics Society* 6, 507–514.

Farr, Robert. 1987. Self/other relations and the social nature of reality. In Carl F. Graumann and Serge Moscovici (eds), *Changing Conceptions of Conspiracy*. New York etc: Springer-Verlag, 203–217.

Farr, Robert. 1990. The social psychology of the prefix 'inter': A prologue to the study of dialogue. In Marková and Foppa (1990), 25–44.

Farr, Robert. 1991. Bodies and voices in dialogue. In Marková and Foppa (1991), 241–258.

Farr, Robert. 1996. *The Roots of Modern Social Psychology 1872–1954*. Oxford: Blackwell.

Farr, Robert and Serge Moscovici. (eds) 1984a. *Social Representations*. Cambridge: Cambridge University Press.

Farr, Robert and Serge Moscovici. 1984b. On the nature and role of representations in self's understanding of others and of self. In Mark Cook (ed.) *Issues in Person Perception*. London: Methuen, 1–27.

Farr, Robert and Ragnar Rommetveit. 1995. The communicative act: an epilogue to mutualities in dialogue. In Marková et al. (1995), 264–274.

Ferrara, Alessandro. 1990. A critique of Habermas's Diskursethik. In Maranhão (1990), 303–337.

Figueroa, Esther. 1994. *Sociolinguistic Metatheory.* Oxford: Pergamon.

Fillmore, Charles. 1985. Frames and the semantics of understanding. *Quaderni di Semantica* 6: 222–254.

Firbas, Jan 1971. On the concept of communicative dynamism in the theory of functional sentence perspective. *Sbornik Praci Filosoficke Fakulty Brnenske University* A 19: 135–144.

Firth, Alan. (ed.) 1995. *The Discourse of Negotiation.* Oxford: Pergamon.

Fish, Stanley. 1980. *Is There a Text in This Class? The Authority of Interpretive Communities.* Cambridge, MA: Harvard University Press.

Fish, Stanley. 1989. *Doing What Comes Naturally. Change, Rhetoric and the Practice of Theory in Literary and Legal Studies.* Durham: Duke University Press.

Fodor, Jerry. 1976 [1975]. *The Language of Thought.* Hassocks: Harvester Press.

Foppa, Klaus. 1990. Topic progression and intention. In Marková and Foppa (1990), 178–200.

Foppa, Klaus. 1995. On mutual understanding and agreement in dialogues. In Marková et al. (1995), 149–175.

Forgas, Joseph. 1979. *Social Episodes: the study of interaction routines.* London: Academic Press.

Fornäs, Johan. 1995. *Cultural Theory and Late Modernity.* London: Sage.

Fredin, Erik. 1993. *Dialogen i socialt arbete.* ("Dialogue in Social Work"). (Diss.) (Studies in Communication = SIC, 36). Linköping: Department of Communication Studies.

Gadamer, Hans Georg. 1975. *Truth and Method.* Translation of "Wahrheit und Methode" by G. Barden and J. Cumming. New York: Seabury Press.

Gardiner, Alan. 1932. *The Theory of Speech and Language.* Oxford: Clarendon Press.

Gardner, Rod. 1997. The Conversation Object Mm: A weak and variable acknowledging token. *Research on Language and Social Interaction* 30: 131–156.

Garfinkel, Harold. 1967. *Studies in Ethnomethodology.* (Prentice-Hall). New edition 1984 (1992). Cambridge: Polity Press.

Gee, James. 1991. A linguistic approach to narrative. *Journal of Narrative and Life History* 1: 15–39.

Genette, Gérard. 1991. Introduction to the paratext. *New Literary History* 22: 261–272.

Gernsbacher, Morton and T. Givón. (eds) 1995. *Coherence in Spontaneous Text.* Amsterdam: John Benjamins.

Gibson, James J. 1966. *The Senses Considered as Perceptual Systems.* Boston: Houghton Mifflin.

Giddens, Anthony. 1984. *The Constitution of Society.* Cambridge: Polity Press.

Giddens, Anthony. 1991. *Modernity and Self-Identity.* Cambridge: Polity Press.

Giles, Howard, Nik Coupland and Justine Coupland. 1992. Accommodation theory: Communication, context, and consequence. In Howard Giles, Justine Coupland and Nik Coupland (eds), *Contexts of Accommodation.* Cambridge: Cambridge University Press, 1–68.

Givón, T. (ed.) 1979a. *Syntax and Semantics, vol. 12: Discourse and Syntax.* New York: Academic Press.

Givón, T. 1979b. From discourse to syntax: Grammar as a processing strategy. In Givón (1979a), 81–112.

Givón, T. 1989. *Mind, Code and Context.* Hillsdale, N.J.: Erlbaum.

Givón, T. 1992. The grammar of referential coherence as mental processing instructions. *Linguistics* 30: 5–55.

Givón, T. 1995. *Functionalism and Grammar.* Amsterdam: John Benjamins.

Goffman, Erving. 1959. *The Presentation of Self in Everyday Life.* New York: Doubleday Anchor.

Goffman, Erving. 1961. *Encounters: Two studies in the sociology of interaction.* Indianapolis: Bobbs-Merrill.

Goffman, Erving. 1963. *Behavior in Public Places.* New York: The Free Press.

Goffman, Erving. 1974. *Frame Analysis.* Cambridge, MA: Harvard University Press.

Goffman, Erving. 1981. *Forms of Talk.* Philadelphia: University of Pennsylvania Press.

Goffman, Erving. 1983. Felicity's Condition. *American Journal of Sociology* 89: 1–53.

Goldberg, Julia. 1983. A move toward describing conversational coherence. In Craig and Tracy (1983), 25–45.

Goodman, Nelson. 1978. *Ways of World-Making.* Hassocks: Harvester Press.

Goodwin, Charles. 1981. *Conversational Organization: Interactions between speakers and hearers.* New York: Academic Press.

Goodwin, Charles. 1995. Co-constructing meaning in conversations with an aphasic man. *Research on Language and Social Interaction* 28: 233–260.

Goodwin, Charles and Alessandro Duranti. 1992. Rethinking context: an introduction. In Duranti and Goodwin (1992), 1–42.

Goodwin, Charles and Marjorie Harness Goodwin. 1990. Interstitial argument. In Allen Grimshaw (ed.), *Conflict Talk*. Cambridge: Cambridge University Press, 85–117.

Goodwin, Charles and Marjorie Harness Goodwin. 1992. Assessments and the construction of context. In Duranti and Goodwin (1992), 147–189.

Goodwin, Charles and John Heritage. 1990. Conversation analysis. *Annual Review of Anthropology* 19: 283–307.

Goodwin, Marjorie Harness. 1990. *He-said-she-said: Talk as social organization among Black children*. Bloomington and Indianapolis: Indiana University Press.

Graumann, Carl F. 1986. Language — the interface between individual and social. *Newsletter of the Social Psychology Section of the British Psychological Society* 15: 5–19.

Graumann, Carl F. 1988. From knowledge to cognition. In Daniel Bar-Tal and Arie Kruglanski (eds), *The Social Psychology of Knowledge*. Cambridge: Cambridge University Press, 15–29.

Graumann, Carl F. 1990. Perspectival structure and dynamics in dialogues. In Marková and Foppa (1990), 105–126.

Graumann, Carl F. 1995. Commonality, mutuality, reciprocity: A conceptual introduction. In Marková et al. (1995), 1–24.

Graumann, Carl F. and Margaret Wintermantel. 1984. Sprachverstehen als Situationsverstehen. In Johannes Engelkamp (ed.), *Psychologische Aspekte des Verstehens*. Berlin: Springer-Verlag, 205–229.

Grice, Paul. 1968. Utterer's meaning, sentence-meaning and word-meaning. *Foundations of Language* 4: 1–18.

Grice, Paul. 1975. Logic and conversation. In Peter Cole and Jerry Morgan (eds), *Syntax and Semantics, vol. 3: Speech Acts*. London: Academic Press, 41–58.

Grosz, Barbara. 1977. The Representation and Use of Focus in Dialogue Understanding. Technical Note 151, Stanford Research Institute.

Gülich, Elisabeth and Uta Quasthoff. 1986. Story-telling in conversation. Cognitive and interactive aspects. *Poetics* 15: 217–241.

Gumperz, John. 1982. *Discourse Strategies*. Cambridge: Cambridge University Press.

Gumperz, John. 1995. Mutual inferencing in conversation. In Marková et al. (1995), 101–123.

Gunnarsson, Britt-Louise, Per Linell and Bengt Nordberg. (eds) 1997. *The Construction of Professional Discourse*. London: Longman

Günthner, Suzanne. 1997. The contextualization of affect in reported dialogues. In Susanne Niemeier and René Dirven (eds),*The Language of Emotions* Amsterdam: John Benjamins, 247–275.

Günthner, Suzanne and Hubert Knoblauch. 1995. Culturally patterned speaking practices — the analysis of communicative genres. *Pragmatics* 5: 1–32.

Gurwitsch, Aron. 1964. *The Field of Consciousness*. Pittsburgh: Duquesne University Press.

Gustavsson, Lennart. 1988. *Language Taught and Language Used*. (Diss.) (Linköping Studies in Arts and Science, 18). Linköping: Department of Theme Research.

Gustavsson, Lennart, Per Linell and Roger Säljö. 1993. Discourse in language and discourse on language. *International Journal of Educational Research* 19: 265–276.

Haavisto, Vaula, 1998. Changing Court Practices: The transformation of discourse and legal culture in a Finnish district court. Ms. Helsinki: Department of Education.

Habermas, Jürgen. 1981. *Theorie des kommunikativen Handelns*. 2 vols. Frankfurt: Suhrkamp.

Halliday, Michael. 1967. Notes on transitivity and theme in English: II. *Journal of Linguistics* 3: 199–244.

Halliday, Michael. 1990 [1978]. *Language as Social Semiotic*. London: Edward Arnold.

Halliday, Michael and Ruqaiya Hasan. 1976. *Cohesion in English*. New York: Longman.

Hanks, William. 1996. *Language and Communicative Practices*. Boulder, CO: Westview Press.

Hare, Paul and Herbert Blumberg. 1988. Dramaturgical Analysis of Social Interaction. New York: Praeger.

Harré, Rom and Grant Gillett. 1994. *The Discursive Mind*. Thousand Oaks, CA: Sage.

Harré, Rom and Paul Secord. 1972. *The Explanation of Social Behaviour*. Oxford: Blackwell.

Harris, Roy. 1980. *The Language Makers*. London: Duckworth.

Harris, Roy. 1981. *The Language Myth*. London: Duckworth.

Harris, Roy. 1995. *Signs of Writing*. London: Routledge.

Harris, Roy. 1996. *Signs, Language and Communication: Integrational and segregational approaches*. London: Routledge.

Hawkins, Peter. 1989. Discourse aphasia. In Pamela Grunwell and A. James (eds), *The Functional Evaluation of Language Disorders*. London: Croom Helm, 183–199.

Heath, Christian. 1986. *Body Movement and Speech in Medical Interaction*. Cambridge: Cambridge University Press.

Heath, Christian. 1992. Gesture's discreet tasks: Multiple relevances in visual conduct and in the contextualization of language. In Auer and di Luzio (1992), 101–127.

Heath, Christian and Paul Luff. 1992. Collaboration and control: Crisis management and multimedia technology in London Underground line control rooms. *Computer Supported Cooperative Work* 1: 69–94.

Heath, Shirley Brice. 1983. *Ways with Words: Language, life and work in communities and classrooms*. Cambridge: Cambridge University Press.

Heen Wold, Astri. (ed.) 1992. *The Dialogical Alternative: Towards a theory of language and mind*. Oslo: Scandinavian University Press.

Heidegger, Martin. 1975 [1933]. *Early Greek Thinking*. New York: Harper & Row.

Hellman, Christina. 1992. *Implicitness in Discourse*. (Diss.) Stockholm: Department of Linguistics.

Heritage, John. 1984a. *Garfinkel and Ethnomethodology*. Oxford: Polity Press.

Heritage, John. 1984b. A change-of-state token and aspects of its sequential placement. In Atkinson and Drew (1984), 299–345.

Heritage, John. 1987. Ethnomethodology. In Anthony Giddens and Jonathan Turner (eds), *Social Theory Today*. Cambridge: Polity Press, 224–272.

Heritage, John. 1995. Conversation Analysis: Methodological Aspects. In Quasthoff (1995), 391–418.

Heritage, John and Andrew Roth. 1995. Grammar and institution: questions and questioning in the broadcast news interview. *Research on Language and Social Interaction* 28: 1–60.

Heritage, John and Marja-Leena Sorjonen. 1994. Constituting and maintaining activities across sequences: and-prefacing as a feature of question-design. *Language in Society* 23: 1–29.

Hermans, Hubert and Harry Kempen. 1993. *The Dialogical Self*. London: Academic Press.

Hobbs, Jerry. 1990. Topic drift. In Dorval (1990), 3–22.

Hobbs, Jerry and Michael Agar. 1985. The coherence of incoherent discourse. *Journal of Language and Social Psychology* 4: 213–232.

Hobbs, Jerry and David Evans. 1980. Conversation as planned behavior. *Cognitive Science* 4: 349–377.

Hoey, Michael. 1991. Some properties of spoken discourses. In Roger Bowers and Christopher Brumfit (eds), *Applied Linguistics and English Language Teaching*. (Developments in English Language Teaching, 99). London: Modern English, 65–84.

Holquist, Michael. 1990. *Dialogism: Bakhtin and His World*. London: Routledge.

Holstein, James and Gale Miller. (eds) 1993. *Reconsidering Social Constructionism: Debates in Social Problems Theory*. New York: Aldine de Gruyter.

Hopper, Paul. 1988. Emergent grammar and the a priori grammar postulate. In Deborah Tannen (ed.), *Linguistics in Context: Connecting observation and understanding*. Norwood, N.J.: Ablex, 117–134.

Hopper, Robert. 1983. Interpretation as coherence production. In Craig and Tracy (1983), 81–98.

Hopper, Robert. 1992. *Telephone Conversation*. Bloomington, Indiana: Indiana University Press.

Hudelot, Christian. 1993. *La circulation interactive du sens dans le dialogue*. Paris: LEAPLE, C.R.N.S. Paris V.

Husserl, Edmund. 1973. *Experience and Judgment*. Evanston, Ill.: Northwestern University Press.

Hutchby, Ian and Robin Wooffitt. 1998. *Conversation Analysis*. Cambridge: Polity Press.

Hutchins, Edwin. 1991. The technology of team navigation. In Jolene Galegher, Robert Kraut and Carmen Egido (eds), *Intellectual Teamwork. Social and Technological Foundations of Cooperative Work*. Hillsdale, N.J.: Erlbaum, 191–220.

Hutchins, Edwin and Tove Klausen. 1996. Distributed cognition in an airline cockpit. In Engeström and Middleton (1996a), 15–34.

Hymes, Dell. 1972. Models of the interaction of language and social life. In John Gumperz and Dell Hymes (eds), *Directions in Sociolinguistics*. New York: Holt, 35–71.

Hymes, Dell. 1974. Why linguistics needs the sociologist. In Dell Hymes, *Foundations in Sociolinguistics: an Ethnographic Approach*. Philadelphia: University of Pennsylvania Press.

Hymes, Dell. 1986. Discourse: scope without depth. *International Journal of the Sociology of Language* 57: 49–89.

Iser, Wolfgang. 1974. *The Implied Reader: Patterns of Communication in Prose Fiction from Bunyan to Beckett.* Translation of "Der implizite Leser" [1972]. Baltimore: John Hopkins University Press.

Jacoby, Sally and Elinor Ochs. 1995. Co-construction: An introduction. *Research on Language and Social Interaction* 28: 171–183.

James, William. 1996 [1909]. *A Pluralistic Universe.* Introduction by H.S. Levinson. Lincoln and London: University of Nebraska Press.

Jefferson, Gail. 1972. Side sequences. In David Sudnow (ed.), *Studies in Social Interaction.* New York: The Free Press, 294–338.

Jefferson, Gail. 1978. Sequential aspects of story telling in conversation. In Jim Schenkein (ed.), *Studies in the Organization of Conversational Interaction.* New York: Academic Press, 219–248.

Jefferson, Gail. 1990. List-construction as a task and resource. In George Psathas (ed), *Interaction Competence.* (Studies in Ethnomethodology and Conversation Analysis, no. 1). Lanham, Maryland: University Press of America, 63–92.

Jefferson, Gail and John Lee. 1981. The rejection of advice: managing the problematic convergence of a "troubles teller" and a "service encounter". *Journal of Pragmatics* 5: 399–422.

Johnson-Laird, Philip. 1983. *Mental Models.* Cambridge: Cambridge University Press.

Johnson-Laird, Philip. 1987. The mental representation of the meaning of words. *Cognition* 25: 189–211.

Jönsson, Linda. 1988. *Polisförhöret som kommunikationssituation.* ("The police interrogation as a communicative situation") (Studies in Communication = SIC, 25.) Linköping: Department of Communication Studies.

Jönsson, Linda, Per Linell and Roger Säljö. 1991. Formulating the past: On remembering in the police interrogation. *Multidisciplinary Newsletter for Activity Theory* 9/10: 5–11.

Kamp, Hans. 1984. A theory of truth and semantic representation. In Jeroen Groenendijk, Theo Janssen and Martin Stokhof (eds), *Formal Methods in the Study of Language.* Dordrecht: Foris, 1–41.

Katz, Jerrold. 1964. Mentalism in linguistics. *Language* 40: 124–137.

Katz, Jerrold. 1977. *Propositional Structure and Illocutionary Acts.* New York: Crowell.

Keenan (Ochs), Elinor and Bambi Schieffelin. 1976. Topic as a discourse notion. In Charles Li (ed.), *Subject and Topic*. New York: Academic Press, 335–384.

Kendon, Adam. 1990. *Conducting Interaction: Patterns of behavior in focused encounters*. Cambridge: Cambridge University Press.

Keppler, Angela and Thomas Luckmann. 1991. 'Teaching': conversational transmission of knowledge. In Marková and Foppa (1991), 143–165.

Knoblauch, Hubert. 1991. The taming of foes: the avoidance of asymmetry in informal discussions. In Marková and Foppa (1991), 166–194.

Knorr-Cetina, Karin and Aaron Cicourel. (eds) 1981. *Advances in Social Theory and Methodology: Toward an integration of micro- and macro-sociologies*. London: Routledge & Kegan Paul.

Kögler, Hans Herbert. 1996. *The Power of Dialogue: Critical Hermeneutics after Gadamer and Foucault*. Translation by Paul Hendrickson of "Die Macht des Dialogs" [1992]. Cambridge, MA: The M.I.T. Press.

Korolija, Natascha. 1998a. Recycling cotext: The impact of prior conversation on the emergence of episodes in a multiparty radio talk show. *Discourse Processes* 25: 99–125.

Korolija, Natascha. 1998b. *Episodes in Talk: Constructing coherence in multiparty conversation*. (Diss.) (Linköpings Studies in Arts and Science, 171). Linköping: Department of Theme Research.

Korolija, Natascha and Per Linell. 1996. Episodes: Coding and analyzing coherence in multiparty conversation. *Linguistics* 34: 799–831.

Krippendorff, Klaus. 1993. The past of communication's hoped-for future. *Journal of Communication* 43: 3: 34–44.

Kristeva, Julia. 1986. The bounded text. In Robert Davis (ed.) *Contemporary Literary Criticism: Modernism through poststructuralism*. New York: Longman, 448–466.

Labov, William and David Fanshel. 1977. *Therapetic Discourse*. New York: Academic Press.

Latour, Bruno. 1987. *Science in Action*. Cambridge, MA: Harvard University Press.

Lave, Jean. 1988. *Cognition in Practice: Mind, mathematics and culture in everyday life*. Cambridge: Cambridge University Press.

Lave, Jean. 1993. The practice of learning. In Seth Chaiklin and Jean Lave (eds), *Understanding Practice: Perspectives on activity and context*. Cambridge: Cambridge University Press, 3–32.

Lazarus, Moritz. 1879. Über Gespräche. In M. Lazarus, *Ideale Fragen*. Berlin: Wintersche Verlagshandlung, 233–265. Also in Claudia Schmölders (ed.), *Die Kunst des Gesprächs*. München: dtv-Bibliothek, 264–286.

Leech, Geoffrey. 1983. *Principles of Pragmatics*. London: Longman.

Leontiev, Aleksei N. 1981. The problem of activity in psychology. In James Wertsch (ed.), *The Concept of Activity in Soviet Psychology*. Armonk, N.Y.: M.E. Sharpe.

Lerner, Gene. 1989. Notes on overlap management in conversation: The case of delayed completion. *Western Journal of Speech Communication* 53: 167–177.

Lesser, Ruth and Lesley Milroy. 1993. *Linguistics and Aphasia: Psycholinguistic and pragmatic aspects of intervention*. London: Longman.

Leudar, Ivan and Charles Antaki. 1988. Completion and dynamics in explanation seeking. In Antaki (1988), 145–155.

Levelt, Willem. 1989. *Speaking*. Cambridge, MA: Bradford.

Levinson, Stephen. 1979. Activity types and language. *Linguistics* 17: 365–399. (Reprinted in Drew and Heritage (1992), 66–100.)

Levinson, Stephen. 1983. *Pragmatics*. Cambridge: Cambridge University Press.

Levinson, Stephen. 1988. Putting linguistics on a proper footing: Explorations in Goffman's concepts of participation. In Paul Drew and Anthony Wootton (eds), *Erving Goffman: Exploring the Interaction Order*. Cambridge: Polity Press, 161–227.

Levy, David. 1979. Communicative goals and strategies: Between discourse and syntax. In Givón (1979a), 183–210.

Liberg, Caroline. 1990. *Learning to Read and Write*. (RUUL, 20) (Diss.) Uppsala: Department of Linguistics.

Linell, Per. 1979. On the similarity between Skinner and Chomsky. In Thomas Perry (ed.), *Evidence and Argumentation in Linguistics*. Berlin: de Gruyter, 190–199.

Linell, Per. 1982. *The Written Language Bias in Linguistics*. (Studies in Communication = SIC, 2). Linköping: Department of Communication Studies.

Linell, Per. 1988. The impact of literacy on the conception of language: The case of linguistics. In Säljö (1988), 41–58.

Linell, Per. 1990. The power of dialogue dynamics. In Marková and Foppa (1990), 147–177.

Linell, Per. 1991. Dialogism and the orderliness of conversational disorders. In Jane Brodin and Eva Björck-Åkesson (eds), *Methodological Issues in Research in Augmentative and Alternative Communication*. Stockholm: The Swedish Handicap Institute, 9–21.

Linell, Per. 1992. The embeddedness of decontextualization in the contexts of social practices. In Heen Wold (1992), 253–271.

Linell, Per. 1995. Troubles with mutualities: Towards a dialogical theory of miscommunication and misunderstanding. In Marková et al. (1995), 176–213.

Linell, Per. 1997. Dynamics of discourse vs. stability of structure: Sociolinguistics and the legacy from linguistics. Paper read at the Roundtable on Sociolinguistics and Social Theory, Gregynog Hall, Newton, Mid Wales, 7–9 July 1997.

Linell, Per. 1998. Discourse across boundaries: On recontextualizations and the blending of voices in professional discourse. *Text* 18:143–157.

Linell, Per, Lotta Alemyr and Linda Jönsson. 1993. Admission of guilt as a communicative project in judicial settings. *Journal of Pragmatics* 19: 153–176.

Linell, Per and Erik Fredin. 1995. Negotiating terms in social welfare office talk. In Firth (1995), 299–318.

Linell, Per and Lennart Gustavsson. 1987. *Initiativ och respons: Om dialogens dynamik, dominans och koherens.* ("Initiative and Response: On the dynamics, dominance and coherence of dialogue") (Studies in Communication = SIC, 15). Linköping: Department of Communication Studies.

Linell, Per, Lennart Gustavsson and Päivi Juvonen. 1988. Interactional dominance in dyadic communication: A presentation of initiative-response analysis. *Linguistics* 26: 415–442.

Linell, Per and Linda Jönsson. 1991. Suspect stories: perspective-setting in an asymmetrical situation. In Marková and Foppa (1991), 75–100.

Linell, Per and Natascha Korolija. 1995. On the division of communicative labour within episodes in aphasic discourse. *International Journal of Psycholinguistics* 11: 143–165.

Linell, Per and Natascha Korolija. 1997. Coherence in multi-party conversation: Episodes and contexts in interaction. In T. Givón (ed.), *Conversation: Cognitive, Communicative and Social Perspectives.* Amsterdam: John Benjamins, 167–205.

Linell, Per and Thomas Luckmann. 1991. Asymmetries in dialogue: Some conceptual preliminaries. In Marková and Foppa (1991), 1–20.

Linell, Per and Ivana Marková. 1993. Acts in discourse: From monological speech acts to dialogical inter-acts. *Journal for the Theory of Social Behaviour* 23: 173–195.

Linell, Per and Ragnar Rommetveit. 1998. The many forms and facets of morality in dialogue. *Research on Language and Social Interaction* 31:3–4.

Litt, Theodor. 1924. *Individuum und Gesellschaft*. Leipzig: Barth.

Local, John and John Kelly. 1986. Projection and 'silences': Notes on phonetic and conversational structure. *Human Studies* 9: 185–204.

Lotman, Jurij. 1990. *Universes of the Mind: A semiotic theory of culture*. Bloomington: Indiana University Press.

Luckmann, Thomas. 1985. The analysis of communicative genres. In B.F. Nel, R. Singh and V.M. Venter (eds), *Focus on Quality*. Durban: Institute for Social and Economic Research, University of Durban-Westville, 48–61.

Luckmann, Thomas. 1989. Prolegomena to a social theory of communicative genres. *Slovene Studies* 1–2: 159–167.

Luckmann, Thomas. 1990. Social communication, dialogue and conversation. In Marková and Foppa (1990), 45–61.

Luckmann, Thomas. 1992. On the communicative adjustment of perspectives, dialogue and communicative genres. In Heen Wold (1992), 219–234.

Luckmann, Thomas. 1993. Remarks on the description and interpretation of dialogue. Second draft of a paper read at Bad Homburg, Nov. 1993. University of Konstanz: Department of Sociology.

Luckmann, Thomas. 1995. Interaction planning and intersubjective adjustment of perspectives by communicative genres. In Ester Goody (ed.), *Social Intelligence and Interaction*. Cambridge: Cambridge University Presss, 175–186.

Lynch, Michael. 1991. Method: measurement — ordinary and scientific measurement as ethnomethodological phenomena. In Button (1991), 77–108.

Lynch. Michael. 1993. *Scientific Practice and Ordinary Action: Ethnomethodology and Social Studies of Science*. Cambridge: Cambridge University Press.

Lyons, John. 1977. *Semantics*. Vol. 1. Cambridge: Cambridge University Press.

MacLachlan, Gale and Ian Reid. 1994. *Framing and Interpretation*. Carlton, Victoria: Melbourne University Press.

Malinowski, Bronislaw. 1972 [1923]. The problem of meaning in primitive languages. In C. K. Ogden and I. A. Richards, *The Meaning of Meaning*. 10. ed. London: Routledge & Kegan Paul.

Maranhão, Tullio. (ed.) 1990. *The Interpretation of Dialogue*. Chicago: The University of Chicago Press.

Marková, Ivana. 1982. *Paradigms, Thought and Language*. Chichester: Wiley.

Marková, Ivana. 1987. *Human Awareness: Its social development*. London: Hutchison.

Marková, Ivana. 1989. Incompleteness of speech and coping with emotions in therapist-patient dialogues. In Adrienne Bennett and Kevin McConkey (eds), *Cognition in Individual and Social Contexts*. Amsterdam: Elsevier, 203–213.

Marková, Ivana. 1990a. Introduction. In Marková and Foppa (1990), 1–22.

Marková, Ivana. 1990b. A three-step process as a unit of analysis in dialogue. In Marková and Foppa (1990), 129–146.

Marková, Ivana. 1991. Asymmetries in group conversations between a tutor and people with learning difficulties. In Marková and Foppa (1991), 221–240.

Marková, Ivana. 1992. On structure and dialogicity in Prague semiotics. In Heen Wold (1992), 45–63.

Marková, Ivana. 1994. Sociogenesis of language: Perspectives on dialogism and on activity theory. In Willibrord de Graaf and Robert Maier (eds), *Sociogenesis Reexamined*. New York: Springer, 27–46.

Marková, Ivana. 1995. Language and the epistemology of dialogism. Ms.

Marková, Ivana. 1997. On two concepts of interaction. In Michèle Grossen and Bernard Py (eds), *Pratiques sociales et médiations symboliques*. Bern etc: Peter Lang, 23–44.

Marková, Ivana and Klaus Foppa. (eds) 1990. *The Dynamics of Dialogue*. New York: Harvester Wheatsheaf.

Marková, Ivana and Klaus Foppa. (eds) 1991. *Asymmetries in Dialogue*. Hemel Hempstead: Harvester Wheatsheaf.

Marková, Ivana, Carl F. Graumann and Klaus Foppa. (eds) 1995. *Mutualities in Dialogue*. Cambridge: Cambridge University Press.

Marková, Ivana and Per Linell. 1996. Coding elementary contributions to discourse: Individual acts vs. dialogical interactions. *Journal for the Theory of Social Behaviour* 26: 353–373.

Maturana, Humberto and Francisco Varela. 1980. *Autopoiesis and Cognition: The realization of the living*. Dordrecht: Reidel.

Maynard, Douglas. 1980. Placement of topic changes in conversation. *Semiotica* 30: 263–290.

Maynard, Douglas. 1984. *Inside Plea Bargaining: The Language of Negotiation*. New York: Plenum Press.

Maynard, Douglas. 1991. The perspective-display series and the delivery and receipt of diagnostic news. In Boden and Zimmerman (1991), 164–192.

Maynard, Douglas. 1998. Praising vs. blaming the messenger: Moral issues in deliveries of good and bad news. *Research on Language and Social Interaction* 31:3–4.

Maynard, Douglas and Don Zimmerman. 1984. Topical talk, ritual and social organization of relationships. *Social Psychology Quarterly* 47: 301–316.

Mazeland, Harrie. 1994. Deskriptieve praktijken: Pragmatische analyse van categoriseringen. In F. Maes et al. (eds), *Perspektieven in taalbeheersings-onderzoek*. Dordrecht: ICG Publications, 267–279.

Mazeland, Harrie, Marjan Huisman and Marca Schasfoort. 1995. Negotiating categories in travel agency calls. In Firth (1995), 271–297.

McDermott, Ray. 1976. Kids Make Sense: An ethnographic account of the interactional management of success and failure in one first grade classroom. (Unpubl. diss.) Stanford University.

McLaughlin, Margaret. 1984. *Conversation: How Talk is Organized*. London: Sage.

Mead, George Herbert. 1934. *Mind, Self, and Society*. Chicago: Chicago University Press.

Mead, George Herbert. 1973. *Philosophy of the Act*. Chicago: Chicago University Press.

Mecke, Jochen. 1990. Dialogue in narration (the Narrative Principle). In Maranhão (1990), 195–215.

Merleau-Ponty, Maurice. 1962. *Phenomenology of Perception*. Translated by Colin Smith. London: Routledge & Kegan Paul.

Middleton, David and Charles Crook. 1996. Bartlett and socially ordered consciousness: A discursive perspective. Comments on Rosa (1996). *Culture & Psychology* 2: 379–396.

Middleton, David and Derek Edwards. (eds) 1990. *Collective Remembering*. London: Sage.

Miller, Gale and James Holstein. 1993. Reconsidering social constructionism: introduction. In Holstein and Miller (1993), 5–23.

Mishler, Elliot. 1984. *The Discourse of Medicine: Dialectics of medical interviews*. Norwood, N.J.: Ablex.

Moerman, Michael. 1988. *Talking Culture: Ethnography and Conversation Analysis*. Philadelphia: University of Pennsylvania Press.

Morris, Charles. 1938. *Foundations of the Theory of Signs*. Chicago: The University of Chicago Press.

Morris, Edward. 1991. The contextualization that is behaviour analysis: An alternative to cognitive psychology. In Still and Costall (1991), 123–149.

Moscovici, Serge. 1961. *La psychoanalyse: son image et son public.* Paris: Presses Universitaires.

Moscovici, Serge. 1984. The phenomenon of social representations. In Farr and Moscovici (1984a), 3–69.

Moscovici, Serge. 1988. Notes towards a description of Social Representations. *European Journal of Social Psychology* 18: 211–250.

Muhlhäusler, Peter and Rom Harré. 1990. *Pronouns and People: The linguistic construction of social and personal identity.* Oxford: Blackwell.

Mukařovský, Jan. 1977. Two studies of dialogue. In John Burbank and Peter Steiner (eds), *The Word and Verbal Art.* New Haven and London: Yale University Press.

Nystrand, Martin. 1992. Social interactionism versus social constructionism: Bakhtin, Rommetveit, and the Semiotics of Written Text. In Heen Wold (1992), 157–173.

Ochs Keenan, Elinor. 1976. The universality of conversational postulates. *Language in Society* 5: 67–80.

Ochs, Elinor. 1979. Planned and unplanned discourse. In Givón (1979a), 51–80.

Ochs, Elinor, Emanuel A. Schegloff and Sandra Thompson. (eds) 1996. *Interaction and Grammar.* Cambridge: Cambridge University Press.

Ochs, Elinor and Carolyn Taylor. 1992. Family narrative as political activity. *Discourse and Society* 3: 301–340.

Öhman, Sven. 1988. Empiricism and universal grammar in Chomsky's work. In Larry Hyman and Charles Li (eds), *Language, Speech and Mind.* Studies in Honor of Victoria Fromkin. New York: Routledge, 254–268.

Olson, David. 1994. *The World on Paper: The conceptual and cognitive implications of writing and reading.* Cambridge: Cambridge University Press.

Papoušek, Mechthild. 1995. Origins of reciprocity and mutuality in prelinguistic parent-infant 'dialogues'. In Marková et al. (1995), 58–81.

Parker, Richard. 1984. Conversational grouping and fragmentation: A preliminary investigation. *Semiotica* 50: 43–68.

Pateman, Trevor. 1987. *Language in Mind and Language in Society.* Oxford: Clarendon.

Pearce, Lynne. 1994. *Reading Dialogics.* London etc: Edward Arnold.

Peräkylä, Anssi. 1997. Reliability and validity in research based on tapes and transcripts. In David Silverman (ed.), *Qualitative Research: Theory, method and practice*. London: Sage, 201–220.

Pfloog, Detlev. 1995. Mutuality and dialogue in nonhuman primate communication. In Marková et al. (1995), 27–57.

Planalp, Sally and Karen Tracy. 1980. Not to change the topic but...: A cognitive approach to the management of conversation. In Dan Nimmo (ed.), *Communication Yearbook, 4*. New Brunswick, N.J.: Transaction.

Pomerantz, Anita. 1980. Telling my side: "limited access" as a "fishing" device. *Sociological Inquiry* 50: 186–198.

Pomerantz, Anita. 1984. Agreeing and disagreeing with assessments: some features of preferred/dispreferred turn shapes. In Atkinson and Heritage (1984), 57–101.

Pomerantz, Anita and B.J. Fehr. 1997. Conversation Analysis: An approach to the study of social action as sense making practices. In van Dijk (1997), 64–91.

Potter, Jonathan. 1996. *Representing Reality: Discourse, Rhetoric and Social Construction*. London: Sage.

Potter, Jonathan and Ian Litton. 1985. Some problems underlying the theory of social representations. *British Journal of Social Psychology* 24: 81–90.

Pylyshyn, Zenon. 1989. Computing in cognitive science. In Michael Posner (ed.), *Foundations of Cognitive Science*. Cambridge, MA: The M.I.T.Press, 49–91.

Quasthoff, Uta (ed.) 1995. *Aspects of Oral Communication*. Berlin: de Gruyter.

Reddy, Michael. 1979. The conduit metaphor — a case of frame conflict in our language about language. In Anthony Ortony (ed.), *Metaphor and Thought*. Cambridge: Cambridge University Press, 284–324.

Reichman, Rachel. 1978. Conversational coherency. *Cognitive Science* 3: 283–327.

Resnick, Lauren. 1991. Shared cognition: thinking as social practice. In Lauren Resnick, John Levine and Stephanie Teasley (eds), *Perspectives on Socially Shared Cognition*. Washington, D.C.: American Psychological Association, 1–22.

Resnick, Lauren, Roger Säljö, Clotilde Pontecorvo and Barbara Burge. (eds) 1997. *Discourse, Tools, and Reasoning: Essays on Situated Cognition*. Berlin: Springer.

Ricoeur, Paul. 1986. *Du texte à l'action. Essais d'herméneutique, II*. Paris: Seuil.

Rogoff, Barbara. 1990. *Apprenticeship in Thinking.* New York: Oxford University Press.

Rogoff, Barbara and Jean Lave. 1984. *Everyday Cognition: Its Development in Social Context.* Cambridge, MA: Harvard University Press.

Rommetveit, Ragnar. 1974. *On Message Structure.* London: Wiley.

Rommetveit, Ragnar. 1980. On meanings of acts and what is meant and made known by what is said in a pluralistic social world. In Michael Brenner (ed.), *The Structure of Action.* Oxford: Blackwell, 108–149.

Rommetveit, Ragnar. 1983. In search of a truly interdisciplinary semantics: A sermon on hopes of salvation from hereditary sins. *Journal of Semantics* 2: 1–28.

Rommetveit, Ragnar. 1984. The role of language in the creation and transmission of social representations. In Farr and Moscovici (1984a), 331–359.

Rommetveit, Ragnar. 1985. Language acquisition as increasing linguistic structuring of experience and symbolic behavior control. In James Wertsch (ed.), *Culture, Communication and Cognition: Vygotskyan Perspectives.* Cambridge: Cambridge University Press, 183–204.

Rommetveit, Ragnar. 1988. On literacy and the myth of literal meaning. In Säljö (ed.), 13–40.

Rommetveit, Ragnar. 1990. On axiomatic features of a dialogical approach to language and mind. In Marková and Foppa (1990), 83–104.

Rommetveit, Ragnar. 1991a. On epistemic responsibility in human communication. In Helge Rönning and Knut Lundby (eds), *Media and Communication. Readings in Methodology, History and Culture.* Oslo: Norwegian University Press, 13–27.

Rommetveit, Ragnar. 1991b. Dominance and asymmetries in A Doll's House. In Marková and Foppa (1991), 195–220.

Rommetveit, Ragnar. 1992. Outlines of a dialogically based social-cognitive approach to human cognition and communication. In Heen Wold (1992), 19–44.

Rommetveit, Ragnar and Rolv Blakar. (eds) 1979. *Studies of Language, Thought and Verbal Communication.* London: Academic Press.

Rosch, Eleanor. 1977. Human categorization. In N. Warren (ed.), *Advances in Cross-Cultural Psychology.* Vol 1. London: Academic Press.

Sacks, Harvey. 1992. *Lectures on Conversation. Vols. I-II.* Edited by Gail Jefferson. Cambridge: Blackwell.

Sacks, Harvey, Emanuel A. Schegloff and Gail Jefferson. 1974. A simplest systematics for the organization of turn-taking in conversation. *Language* 50: 696–735.

Säljö, Roger. (ed.) 1988. *The Written World*. Berlin: deGruyter.

Säljö, Roger. 1991. Piagetian controversies, cognitive competence, and assumptions about human communication. *Educational Psychology Review* 3: 117–126.

Säljö, Roger. 1992. Human growth and the complex society: Notes on the monocultural bias of theories of learning. *Cultural Dynamics* 5: 43–56.

Sanford, Anthony and Simon Garrod. 1981. *Understanding Written Language*. Wiley: Chichester.

Sarangi, Srikant. 1998. Interprofessional case construction in social work: the evidential status of information and its reportability. *Text* 18: 241–270.

Sarangi, Srikant and Stef Slembrouck. 1996. Archetypes of discourse: Conversation and the public sphere. Paper presented at the International Pragmatics Conference, Mexico City, July 1996.

Sarbin, Theodore and John Kitsuse. (eds) 1994. *Constructing the Social*. London: Sage.

Saussure, Ferdinand de 1964. [1916]. *Cours de linguistique générale*. Publié par Charles Bally et Albert Sechehaye. Paris: Payot.

Schank, Roger and Robert Abelson. 1977. *Scripts, Plans, Goals and Understanding*. Hillsdale, N.J.: Erlbaum.

Schegloff, Emanuel A. 1982. Discourse as an interactional achievement. In Tannen (1982), 73–93.

Schegloff, Emanuel A. 1984. On some questions and ambiguities in conversation. In Atkinson and Drew (1984), 28–52.

Schegloff, Emanuel A. 1986. The routine as achievement. *Human Studies* 9: 111–152.

Schegloff, Emanuel A. 1990. On the organization of sequences as a source of "coherence" in talk-in-interaction. In Dorval (1990), 51–77.

Schegloff, Emanuel A. 1991. Reflections on talk and social structure. In Boden and Zimmerman (1991), 44–70.

Schegloff, Emanuel A. 1992. In another context. In Duranti and Goodwin (1992), 191–227.

Schegloff, Emanuel A. 1993. Reflections on quantification in the study of conversation. *Research on Language and Social Interaction* 26: 99–128.

Schegloff, Emanuel A. 1996. Turn organization: One intersection of grammar and interaction. In Ochs et al. (1996), 52–133.

Schegloff, Emanuel A., Gail Jefferson and Harvey Sacks. 1977. The preference for self-correction in the organization of repair in conversation. *Language* 53: 361–382.

Schegloff, Emanuel A., Elinor Ochs and Sandra Thompson. 1996. Introduction. In Ochs et al. (1996), 1–51.

Schegloff, Emanuel A. and Harvey Sacks. 1973. Opening up closings. *Semiotica* 8: 289–327.

Schiffrin, Deborah. 1987. *Discourse Markers.* Cambridge: Cambridge University Press.

Schiffrin, Deborah. 1994. *Approaches to Discourse.* Cambridge: Blackwell.

Schilpp, Paul. (ed.) 1949. *The Philosophy of Ernst Cassirer.* Evanston, Ill.; The Library of Living Philosophers, Inc.

Schutz, Alfred. 1962. *Collected Papers, Vol. 1: The Problem of Social Reality.* The Hague: Nijhoff.

Schutz, Alfred. 1967. *The Phenomenology of the Social World.* Translated by George Walsh and Frederick Lehnert. Evanston, Ill.: Northwestern University Press.

Scollon, Ron and Suzanne Scollon. 1995. Somatic communication: How useful is 'orality' for the characterization of speech events and cultures? In Quasthoff (1995), 19–29.

Scott, Marvin and Stanford Lyman. 1968. Accounts. *American Sociological Review* 33, 46–62.

Searle, John. 1969. *Speech Acts.* Cambridge: Cambridge University Press.

Searle, John. 1975. A classification of illocutionary acts. *Language in Society* 5, 1–23.

Searle, John. 1979. *Expression and Meaning.* Cambridge: Cambridge University Press.

Searle, John. 1991. 'Meaning, intentionality and speech acts' and 'The background of intentionality and action'. In Ernest Lepore and Robert van Gulick. (eds), *John Searle and His Critics.* London: Blackwell, 81–102, 289–300.

Searle, John. 1992. 'Conversation' and 'Conversation reconsidered'. In John Searle et al., *(On) Searle on Conversation.* Papers compiled and introduced by Herman Parret and Jef Verschueren. Amsterdam: John Benjamins, 7–29, 137–147.

Severinson Eklundh, Kerstin. 1986. *Dialogue Processes in Computer-Mediated Communication*. (Diss.) (Linköping Studies in Arts and Science, 6). Linköping: Department of Theme Research.

Shannon, Claude and Warren Weaver. 1949. *The Mathematical Theory of Communication*. Urbana, Ill.: University of Illinois Press.

Shepherd, Gregory. 1993. Building a discipline of communication. *Journal of Communication*, 43: 3: 83–91.

Shotter, John 1990. The social construction of remembering and forgetting. In Middleton and Edwards (1990), 120–138.

Shotter, John. 1991. The rhetorical-responsive nature of mind: A social constructionist account. In Still and Costall (1991), 55–79.

Shotter, John. 1993. *Conversational Realities: Constructing life through language*. London: Sage.

Silverman, David. 1997. *Discourses of Counselling: HIV Counselling as Social Interaction*. London: Sage.

Silverman, David and Brian Torode. 1980. *The Material Word*. London: Routledge and Kegan Paul.

Silverstein, Michael. 1987. Cognitive implications of a referential hierarchy. In Maya Hickmann (ed.), *Social and Functional Approaches to Language and Thought*. Orlando: Academic Press, 125–164.

Sinclair, John and Malcolm Coulthard. 1992. Towards an analysis of discourse. In Coulthard (1992), 1–34. (Originally published in 1975.)

Skinner, Burrhus F. 1974. *About Behaviorism*. New York: Knopf.

Soeffner, Hans-Georg. Forthc. 'Truth' and decision-making: Discovering the truth by police and judicial methods. Ms. University of Konstanz: Department of Sociology.

Sorjonen, Marja-Leena. 1997. *Recipient Activities: Particles nii(n) and joo as Responses in Finnish Conversation*. (Diss.) University of California, Los Angeles.

Soskin, William and Vera John. 1963. The study of spontaneous talk. In Roger Barker (ed.), *The Stream of Behavior*. New York: Appleton-Century Crofts, 228–287.

Spector, Malcolm and John Kitsuse. 1977. *Constructing Social Problems*. Hawthorne, NY: Aldine de Gruyter.

Sperber, Dan and Deirdre Wilson. 1986. *Relevance*. London: Blackwell.

Spurling, Laurie. 1977. *Phenomenology and the Social World*. London: Routledge & Kegan Paul.

Steinglass, Matt. 1998. International man of mystery: The battle over Mikhail Bakhtin. *Lingua Franca*, April 1998: 33–41.

Stetsenko, Anna and Igor Arievitch. 1997. Constructing and deconstructing the self: Comparing post-vygotskians and discourse-based versions of social constructivism. *Mind, Culture, and Activity* 4: 159–172.

Stenström, Anna-Brita. 1994. *An Introduction to Spoken Interaction*. London: Longman.

Stiles, William. 1992. *Describing Talk: A taxonomy of Verbal Response Modes*. Newbury Park: Sage.

Still, Arthur. 1991. Mechanism and romanticism: A selective history. In Still and Costall (1991), 7–26.

Still, Arthur and Alan Costall. (eds) 1991. *Against Cognitivism*. Hemel Hempstead: Harvester Wheatsheaf.

Streeck, Jürgen. 1980. Speech acts in interaction: A critique of Searle. *Discourse Processes* 3: 133–154.

Stubbs, Michael. 1983. *Discourse Analysis*. Oxford: Blackwell.

Suchman, Lucy. 1987. *Plans and Situated Actions*. Cambridge: Cambridge University Press.

Svennevig, Jan. 1997. *Getting Acquainted in Conversation: A study of initial interactions*. (Diss.) University of Oslo: Department of Scandinavian Studies.

Swales, John. 1990. *Genre Analysis: English in academic and research settings*. Cambridge: Cambridge University Press.

Swearingen, Jan. 1990. Dialogue and dialectic: The logic of conversation and the interpretation of logic. In Maranhão (1990), 47–71.

Tannen, Deborah. (ed.) 1982. *Analyzing Discourse: Text and Talk*. (Georgetown University Round Table on Language and Linguistics, 1981). Washington, D.C.: Georgetown University Press.

Tannen, Deborah. 1984. *Conversational Style*. Norwood, N.J.; Ablex.

Tannen, Deborah. 1989. *Talking Voices*. Cambridge: Cambridge University Press.

Taylor, Charles. 1989. *Sources of the Self: The making of modern identity*. Cambridge, MA: Harvard University Press.

Taylor, Talbot. 1992. *Mutual Misunderstanding: Scepticism and the theorizing of language and interpretation*. London: Routledge.

Tedlock, D. 1979. The analogical tradition and the emergence of a dialogical anthropology. *Journal of Anthropological Research* 35: 387–400.

Thomas, Jenny. 1995. *Meaning in Interaction: An introduction to pragmatics.* London: Longman.

Thomas, W.I. 1928. Situational analysis: the behaviour pattern and the situation. In M. Janowitz (ed.), *W.I. Thomas on Social Organisation and Social Personality.* Chicago: University of Chicago Press.

Todorov, Tzvetan. 1984. *Mikhail Bakhtin: The Dialogical Principle.* Translated by Wlad Godzich. Manchester: Manchester University Press.

Toner, Barbara. 1977. *The Facts of Rape.* London: Arrow.

Tracy, Karen. 1984. Staying on topic: An explication of conversational relevance. *Discourse Processes* 7: 447–464.

Trevarthen, Colin. 1992. An infant's motives for speaking and thinking in the culture. In Heen Wold (1992), 99–137.

Turner, Jonathan. 1991. *The Structure of Sociological Theory.* (5 ed.) Belmont, CA: Wadsworth.

Tyler, Stephen. 1990. Ode to dialog on the occasion of the un-for-seen. In Maranhão (1990), 292–300.

Vagle, Wenche. 1995. The context of radio talk in sociosemiotic perspective. Paper presented at 12. Nordic Conference on Mass Communication Research. Helsingør, August, 1995.

van Dijk, Teun. 1982. Episodes as units of discourse analysis. In Tannen (1982), 177–195.

van Dijk, Teun. (ed.) 1997. *Discourse as Social Interaction.* (Discourse studies: A Multidisciplinary Introduction, vol. 2). London: Sage.

van Dijk, Teun and Walter Kintsch. 1983. *Strategies of Discourse Comprehension.* New York: Academic Press.

van Rees, Agnes. 1992. *The Use of Language in Conversation.* An Introduction to Research in Conversation. Amsterdam: SICSAT (International Society for the Study of Argumentation).

Vološinov, Valentin N. 1973. *Marxism and the Philosophy of Language.* Translated by Ladislav Matejka and I. R. Titunik. New York: Seminar Press.

von Wright, Georg Henrik. 1974. *Causality and Determinism.* New York: Columbia University Press.

Vygotsky, Lev. 1986. *Thought and Language.* Translation revised by A. Kozulin. Cambridge, MA: The M.I.T. Press.

Wadensjö, Cecilia. 1998. *Interpreting as Interaction.* London: Longman.

Wagner, Wolfgang. 1996. Queries about social representations and construction. *Journal for the Theory of Social Behaviour* 26: 95–120.

Watson, Rod. 1992. The understanding of language use in everyday life. In Graham Watson and Robert Seiler (eds), *Text in Context: Contributions to Ethnomethodology*. Newbury Park: Sage, 1–19.

Watson, Rod and Wes Sharrock. 1991. Something on accounts. *The D.A.R.G. Newsletter* 7: 2: 3–11.

Weber, Max. 1978 [1922].. The nature of social activity. Translation of "Wirtschaft und Gesellschaft, Vol 1" (Tübingen, 1911). In Max Weber, *Selections in Translation*. Edited by W.G. Runciman. Cambridge: Cambridge University Press, 7–32.

Wells, Gordon, Margaret Maclure and Martin Montgomery. 1981. Some strategies for sustaining conversation. In Paul Werth (ed.), *Conversation and Discourse: Structure and interpretation*. New York: St. Martin's, 73–85.

Wertsch, James. 1985. *Vygotsky and the Social Formation of Mind*. Cambridge: Harvard University Press.

Wertsch, James. 1990. Dialogue and dialogism in a socio-cultural approach to mind. In Marková and Foppa (1990), 62–82.

Wertsch, James. 1991. *Voices of the Mind*. New York: Harvester Wheatsheaf.

Wertsch, James. 1995. The need for action in sociocultural research. In James Wertsch, Pablo del Rio and Amelia Alvarez (eds), *Sociocultural Studies of Mind*. Cambridge: Cambridge University Press, 56–74.

Wertsch, James. 1997. *Mind as Action*. New York: Oxford University Press.

Wertsch, James and William Penuel. 1996. The individual-society antinomy revisited: Productive tensions in theories of human development, communication, and education. In David Olson and Nancy Torrance (eds), *The Handbook of Education and Human Development: New Models of Learning, Teaching and Schooling*. Oxford: Blackwell, 415–433.

Wilkes-Gibbs, Deanna. 1986. *Collaborative Processes of Language Use in Conversation*. (Ph.D. Diss.) Palo Alto, CA: Stanford University.

Wilkes-Gibbs, Deanna. 1995. Coherence in collaboration: Some examples from conversation. In Gernsbacher and Givón (1995), 239–267.

Wilson, John. 1989. *On the Boundaries of Conversation*. Oxford: Pergamon Press.

Wilson, Thomas. 1991. Social structure and the sequential organization of interaction. In Boden and Zimmerman (1991), 22–43.

Winograd, Terry and Fernando Flores. 1986. *Understanding Computers and Cognition: A new foundation for design*. Norwood: Ablex.

Wittgenstein, Ludwig. 1958. *Philosophical Investigations*. Translated by G.E.M. Anscombe of *Philosophische Untersuchungen* [1953]. 2nd ed.. Oxford: Blackwell.

Woolgar, Steve. 1988. (ed.) *Knowledge and Reflexivity*. London: Sage.

Wynn, E. 1980. What discourse features aren't needed in on-line dialogue. *Proceedings of the 18th Annual Meeting of the Association for Computational Linguistics and Parasession on Topics in Interactive Discourse*. Philadelphia, 87–90.

Yngve, Victor. 1970. On getting a word in edgewise. *Papers from the Sixth Regional Meeting, Chicago Linguistic Society*. 567–578.

Zimmerman, Don. 1992. The interactional organization of calls for emergency assistance. In Drew and Heritage (1992), 418–469.

Zimmerman, Don and Deirdre Boden. 1991. Structure-in-Action: An Introduction. In Boden and Zimmerman (1991), 3–21.

Zlatev, Jordan. 1997. *Situated Embodiment: Studies in the emergence of spatial meaning*. (Diss.) Stockholm: Department of Linguistics.

Appendix: Transcription conventions

.

The excerpts from authentic discourse used in this book have been drawn from many different sources. All excerpts are verbatim records of the spoken discourse (with the obvious reservation that data from other languages than English, in most cases from Swedish, are given in (pretty close) translations). All names of persons, places etc. appearing in the Swedish recordings have been altered in the transcripts used here.

Various transcription conventions were used in the originals, and some attempts have been made to adapt them to a common standard. Yet, this has not proved possible in all cases; excerpts vary in the degree of detailing. For example, focal stress has been marked only in a few cases.

In general, the format used in the excerpts may be characterized as a simplified kind of transcript, which includes only a selection of details. Whilst accuracy of transcription is important in empirical studies of dialogue and discourse, the excerpts presented here are designed to illustrate general principles, rather than to serve as working transcripts.

The following conventions have been used, when possible:

Underlining of (the orthographic counterpart of) the syllable nucleus (e.g. read, novel) denotes that the word is stressed with a syntactically focal accent

UPPERCASE (often with underlining of syllable nucleus) indicates words which are spoken in a louder volume and/or with emphatic stress

[(left bracket) on two adjacent lines, the one placed right above the other, marks the approximate beginnings of simultaneous (overlapping) talk by two speakers

[in the very beginnings of two adjacent lines indicates that two speakers start speaking at the same time

(xxx) denotes talk (words) which the transcriber has not been able to decipher

i.e. words within single parentheses indicate transcriptionist's doubt that the transcript is correct

] on two adjacent lines indicates end-points of overlapping talk (marked out in the excerpts only in a few exceptional cases)

= (equal sign) at the beginning of a turn indicates that this turn is latched on the previous one, without any interjacent pause whatsoever

... denotes a pause of moderate length (usually less than a second)

(2.0) marks a timed pause of (here:) about 2 seconds

(.) denotes a micro-pause, usually less than a quarter of a second

((pause)) denotes an untimed pause

- (single dash sign) in the middle of a word denotes that the speaker interrupts himself

-- (double dash signs) at the end of an utterance indicates that the speaker leaves his utterance incomplete, often with an intonation which invites the addressee to complete the utterance

° ° (degree signs) denotes speech in a low volume ('sotto voce')

* * (asterisks) indicates laughter in the speaker's voice while pronouncing the words enclosed

> < (arrows) denotes speech (between the arrows) which is spoken at a faster rate than the surrounding talk

< > denotes speech (between the arrows) which is spoken at a slower rate than the surrounding talk

[...] indicates that some talk has been left out from the excerpt

(P: yes) (as an example) marks the occurrence of a listener support item, i.e. something (here: yes) said by a person (P) who does not hold the floor and whose utterance is not perceived as claiming and/or acquiring the floor; the utterance is put approximately at the place in another speaker's (the current floor-holder's) talk where it occurs

((material within double parentheses)) marks comments on how something is said or on what happens in the context

Index

In the series IMPACT: STUDIES IN LANGUAGE AND SOCIETY the following titles have been published thus far or are scheduled for publication:

1. PÜTZ, Martin (ed.): *Language Choices. Conditions, constraints, and consequences.* 1997.
2. KIBBEE, Douglas A. (ed.): *Language Legislation and Linguistic Rights. Selected Proceedings of the Language Legislation and Linguistic Rights Conference, the University of Illinois at Urbana-Champaign, March, 1996.* 1998.
3. LINELL, Per: *Approaching Dialogue. Talk, interaction and contexts in dialogical perspectives.* 1998.
4. OWENS, Jonathan: *Neighborhood and Ancestry. Variation in the spoken Arabic of Maiduguri, Nigeria.* 1998.
5. ANDREWS, David R.: *Sociocultural Perspectives on Language Change in Diaspora. Soviet immigrants in the United States.* n.y.p.